Ōoku

✿ THE INNER CHAMBERS

by **Fumi Yoshinaga**

VOL. **2**

Ōoku

THE INNER CHAMBERS

by Fumi Yoshinaga

vol. 2

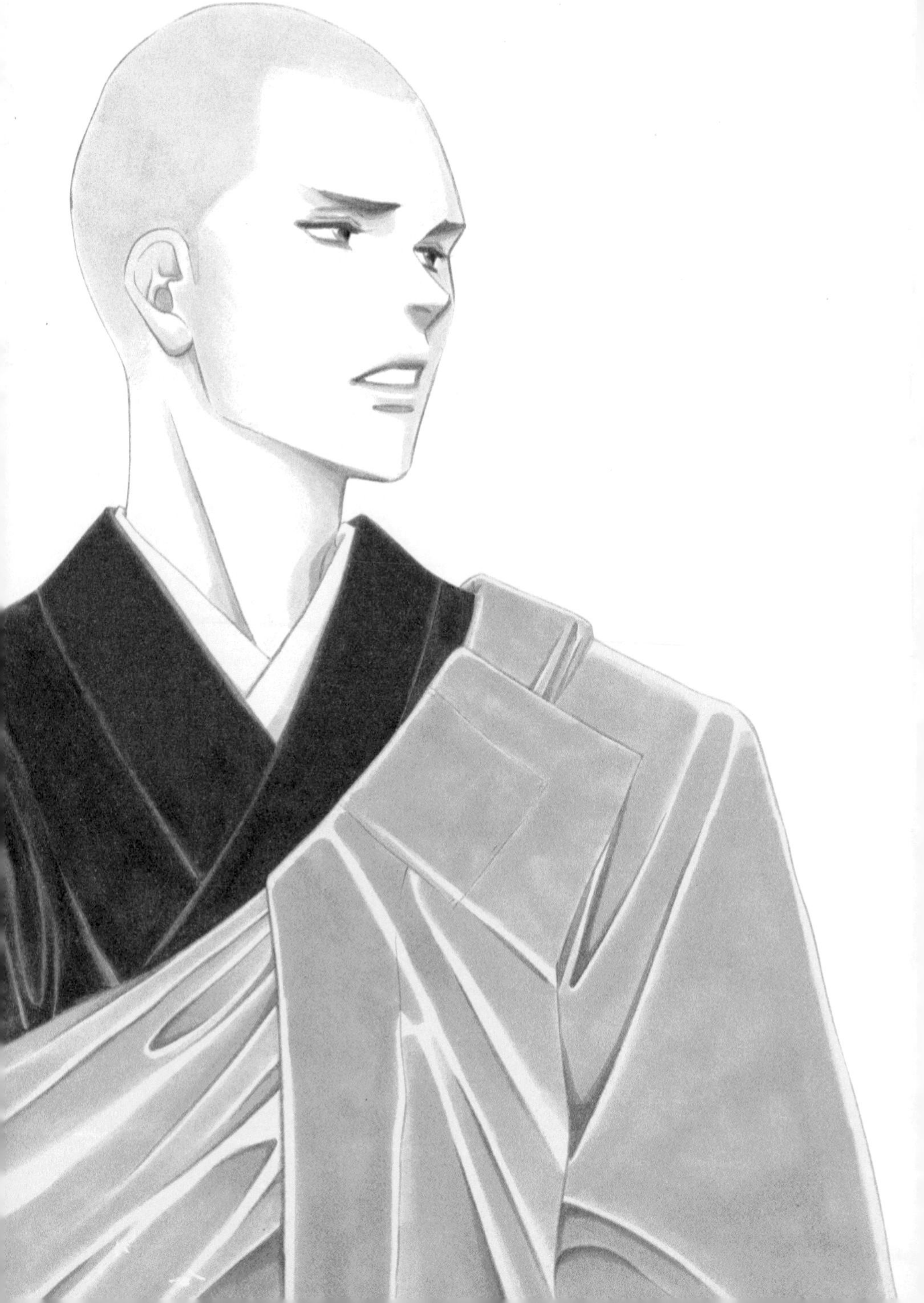

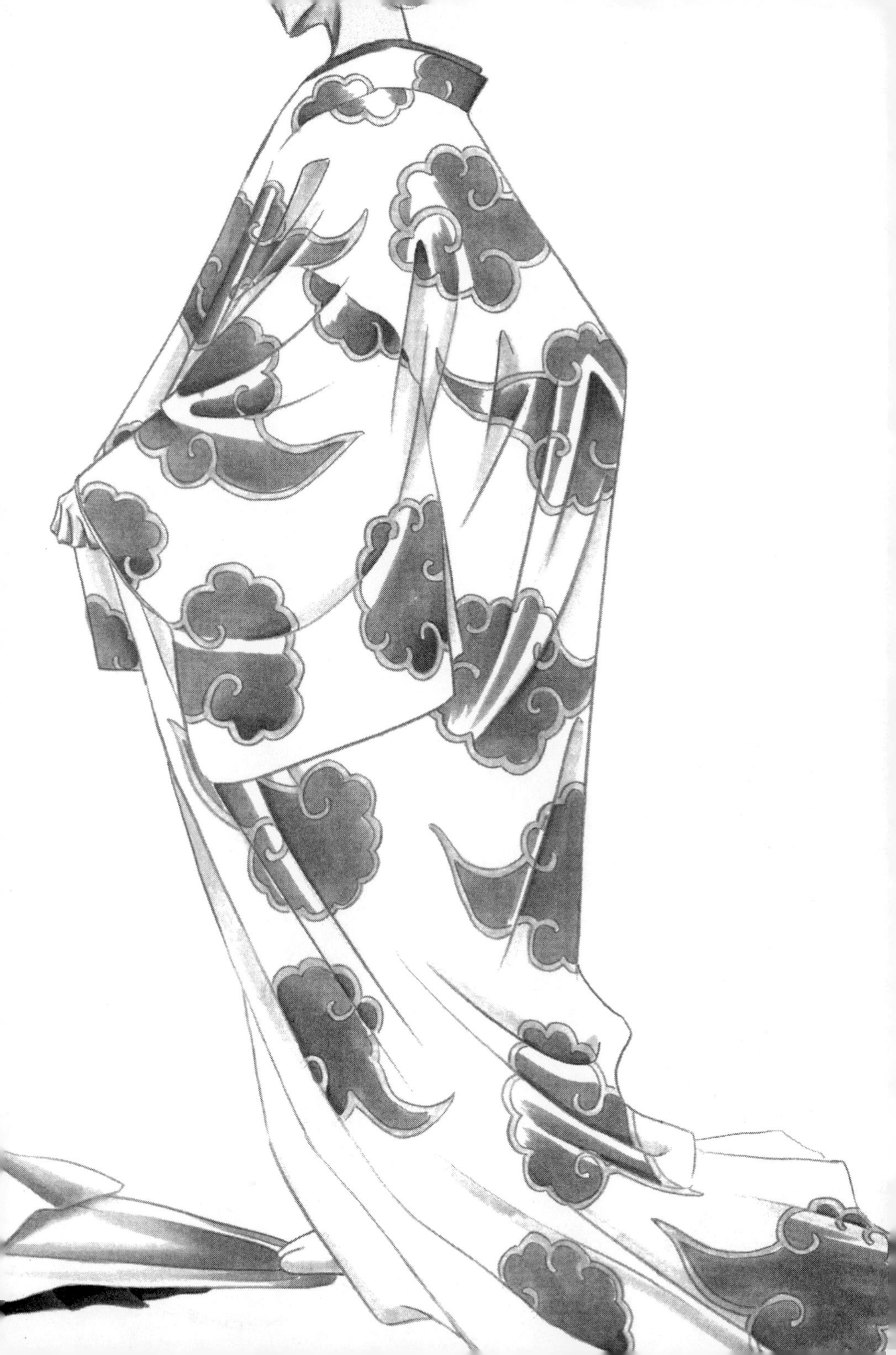

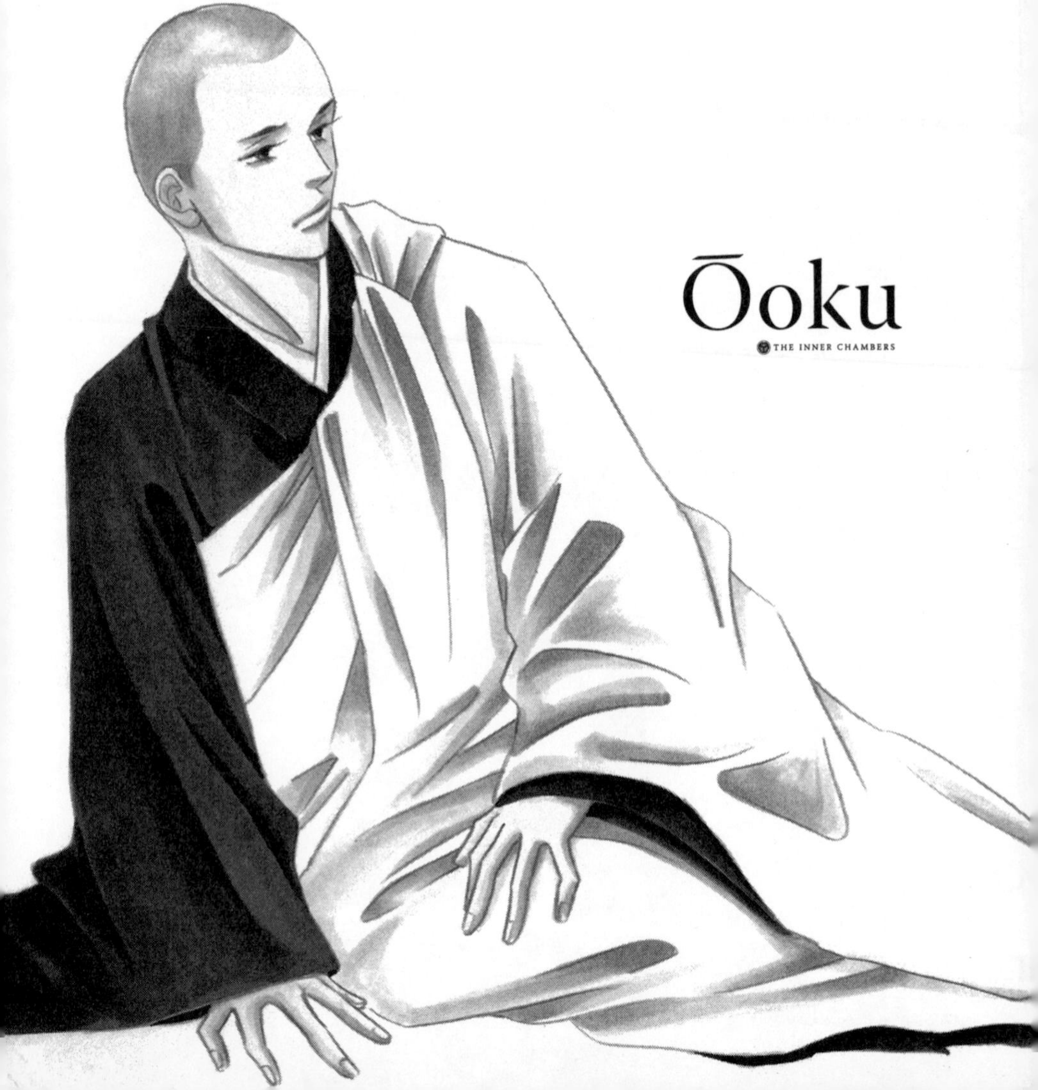

Ōoku

THE INNER CHAMBERS

TABLE *of* CONTENTS

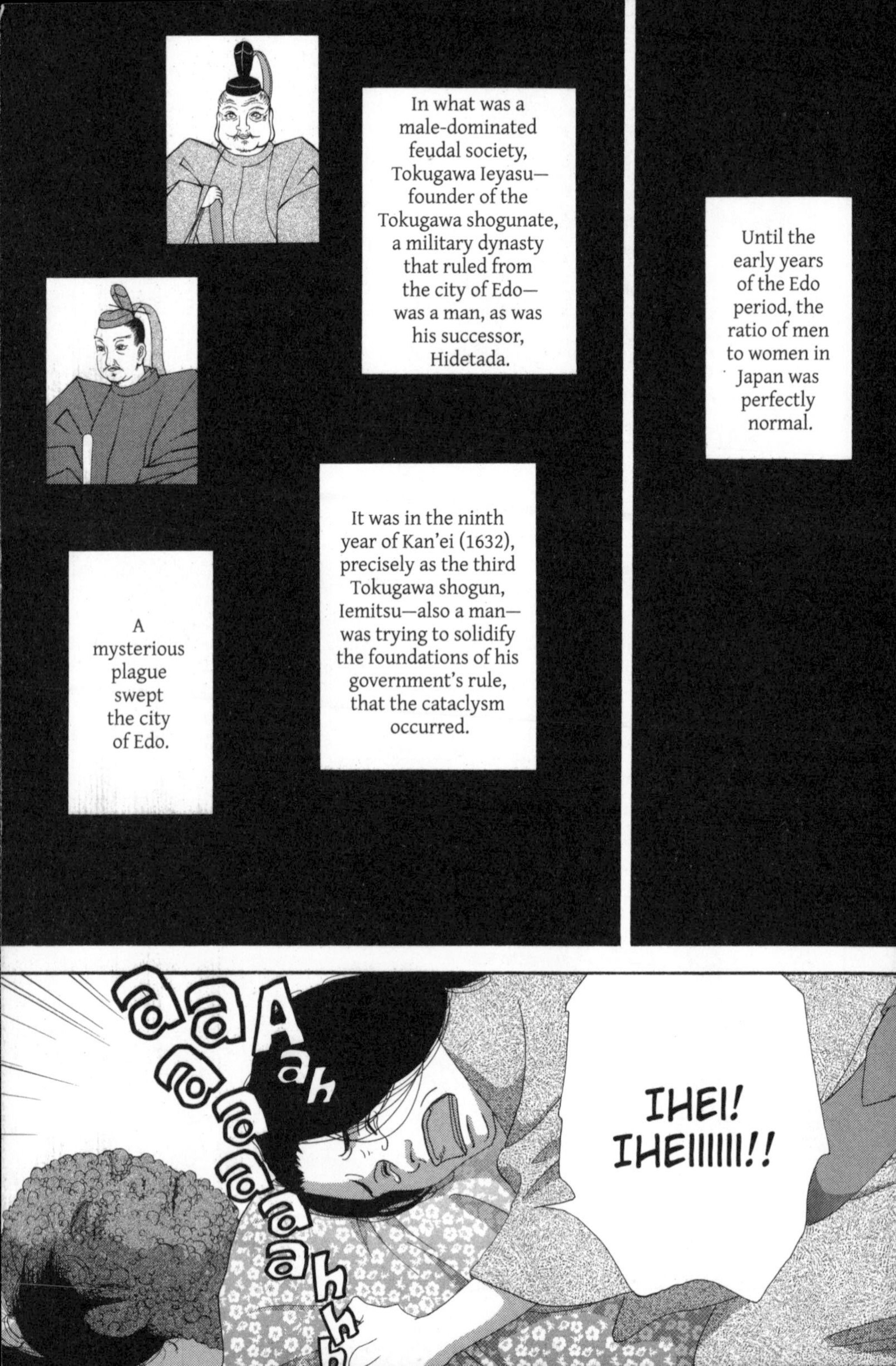
Until the early years of the Edo period, the ratio of men to women in Japan was perfectly normal.
In what was a male-dominated feudal society, Tokugawa Ieyasu—founder of the Tokugawa shogunate, a military dynasty that ruled from the city of Edo—was a man, as was his successor, Hidetada.
It was in the ninth year of Kan'ei (1632), precisely as the third Tokugawa shogun, Iemitsu—also a man—was trying to solidify the foundations of his government's rule, that the cataclysm occurred.
A mysterious plague swept the city of Edo.
IHEI! IHEIIIIIII!!
AAAaaaaaaaaaahhh

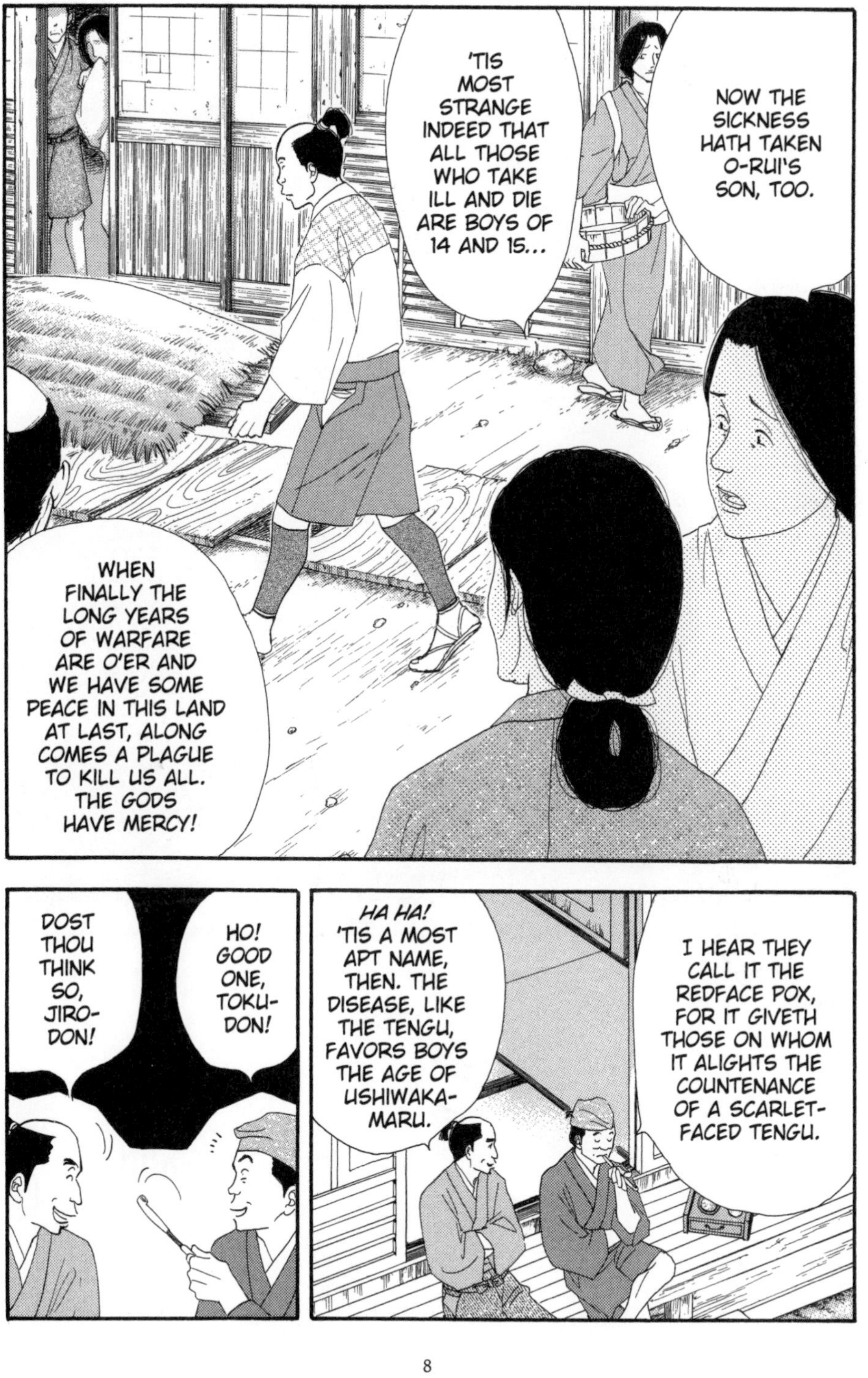
NOW THE SICKNESS HATH TAKEN O-RUI'S SON, TOO.
'TIS MOST STRANGE INDEED THAT ALL THOSE WHO TAKE ILL AND DIE ARE BOYS OF 14 AND 15...
WHEN FINALLY THE LONG YEARS OF WARFARE ARE O'ER AND WE HAVE SOME PEACE IN THIS LAND AT LAST, ALONG COMES A PLAGUE TO KILL US ALL. THE GODS HAVE MERCY!
I HEAR THEY CALL IT THE REDFACE POX, FOR IT GIVETH THOSE ON WHOM IT ALIGHTS THE COUNTENANCE OF A SCARLET-FACED TENGU.
HA HA! 'TIS A MOST APT NAME, THEN. THE DISEASE, LIKE THE TENGU, FAVORS BOYS THE AGE OF USHIWAKA-MARU.
HO! GOOD ONE, TOKU-DON!
DOST THOU THINK SO, JIRO-DON!

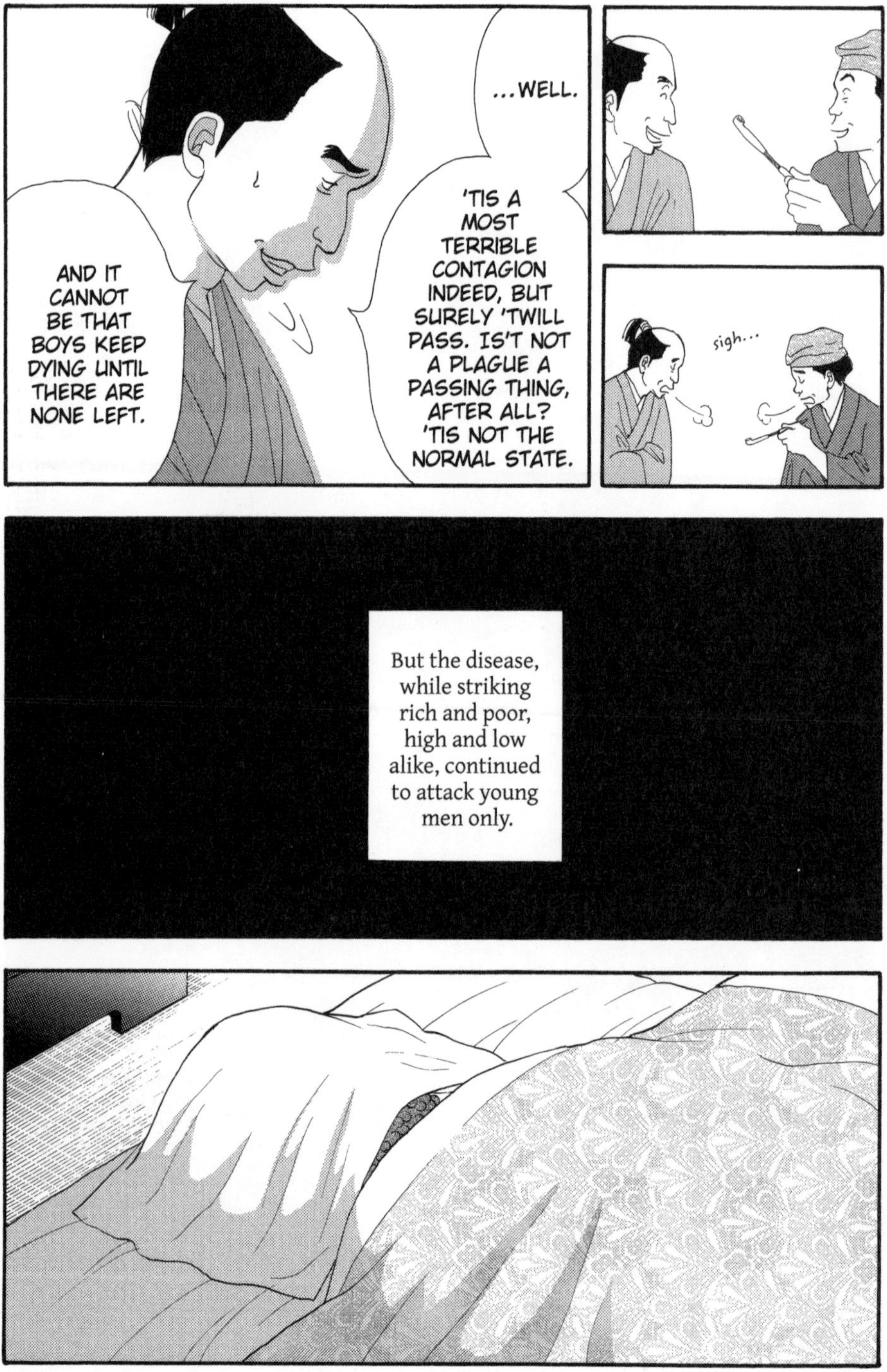
sigh...
...WELL.
'TIS A MOST TERRIBLE CONTAGION INDEED, BUT SURELY 'TWILL PASS. IS'T NOT A PLAGUE A PASSING THING, AFTER ALL? 'TIS NOT THE NORMAL STATE.
AND IT CANNOT BE THAT BOYS KEEP DYING UNTIL THERE ARE NONE LEFT.
But the disease, while striking rich and poor, high and low alike, continued to attack young men only.

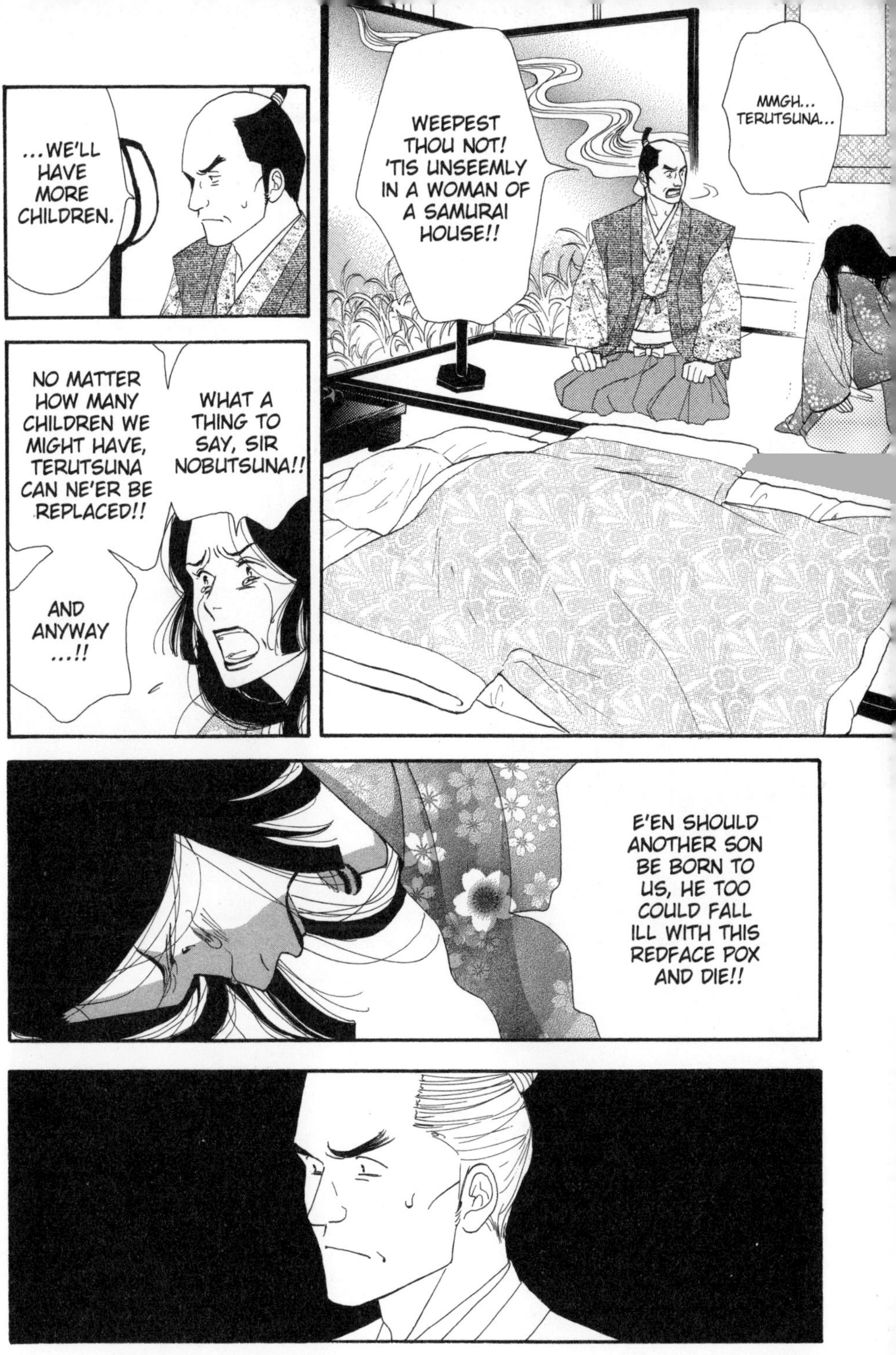
MMGH... TERUTSUNA...
WEEPEST THOU NOT! 'TIS UNSEEMLY IN A WOMAN OF A SAMURAI HOUSE!!
...WE'LL HAVE MORE CHILDREN.
WHAT A THING TO SAY, SIR NOBUTSUNA!!
NO MATTER HOW MANY CHILDREN WE MIGHT HAVE, TERUTSUNA CAN NE'ER BE REPLACED!!
AND ANYWAY ...!!
E'EN SHOULD ANOTHER SON BE BORN TO US, HE TOO COULD FALL ILL WITH THIS REDFACE POX AND DIE!!

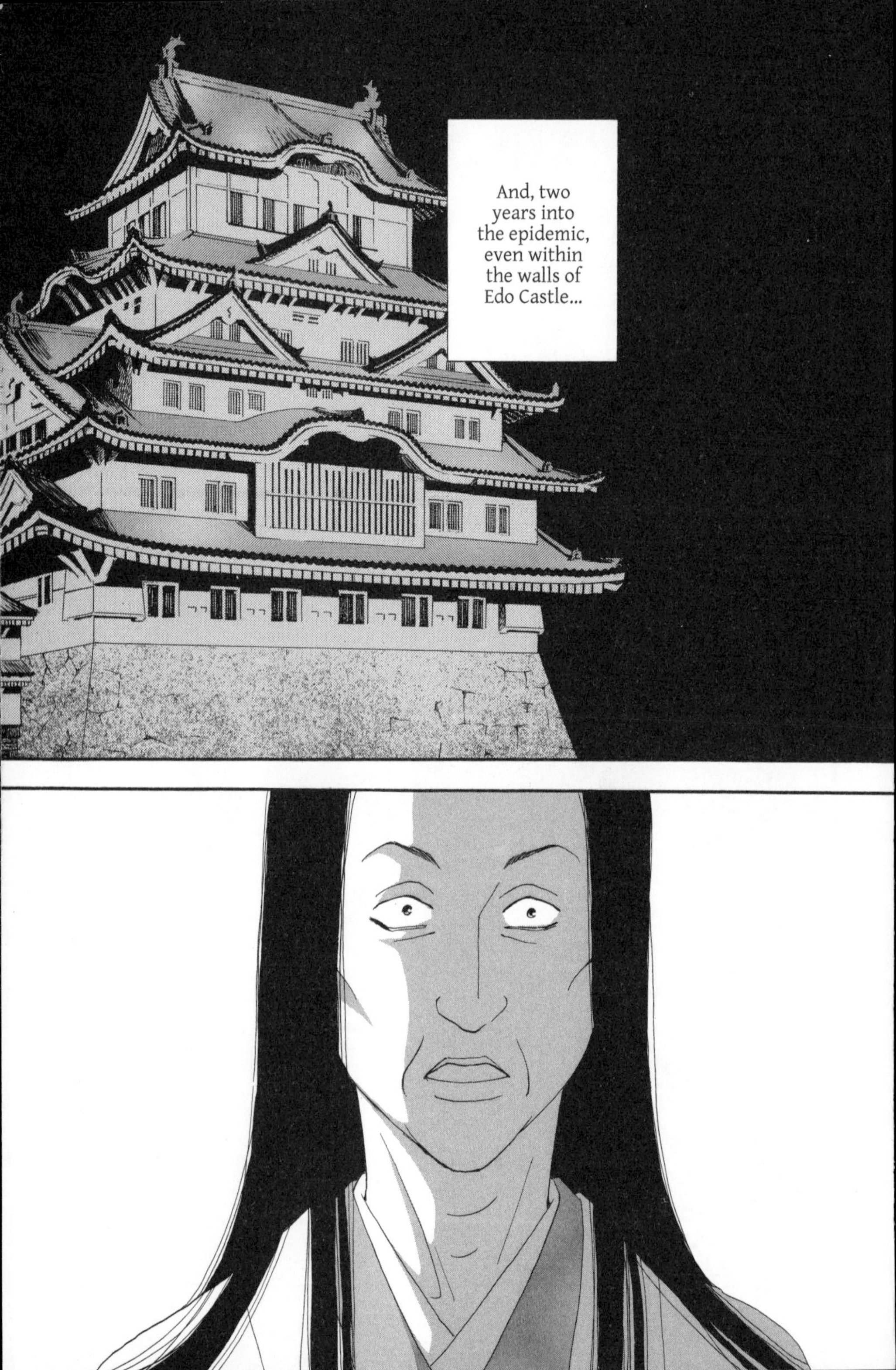
And, two years into the epidemic, even within the walls of Edo Castle...

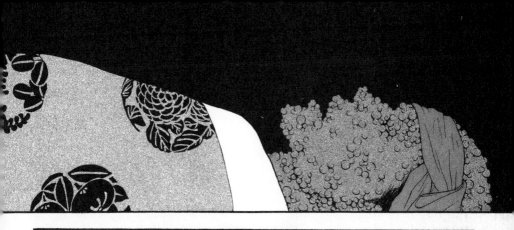

OH...!! LADY KASUGA! HIS HIGHNESS IS...!!

HIS HIGH-NESS...

...OUR LIEGE, LORD IEMITSU, HATH BREATHED HIS LAST...!!

THWOK

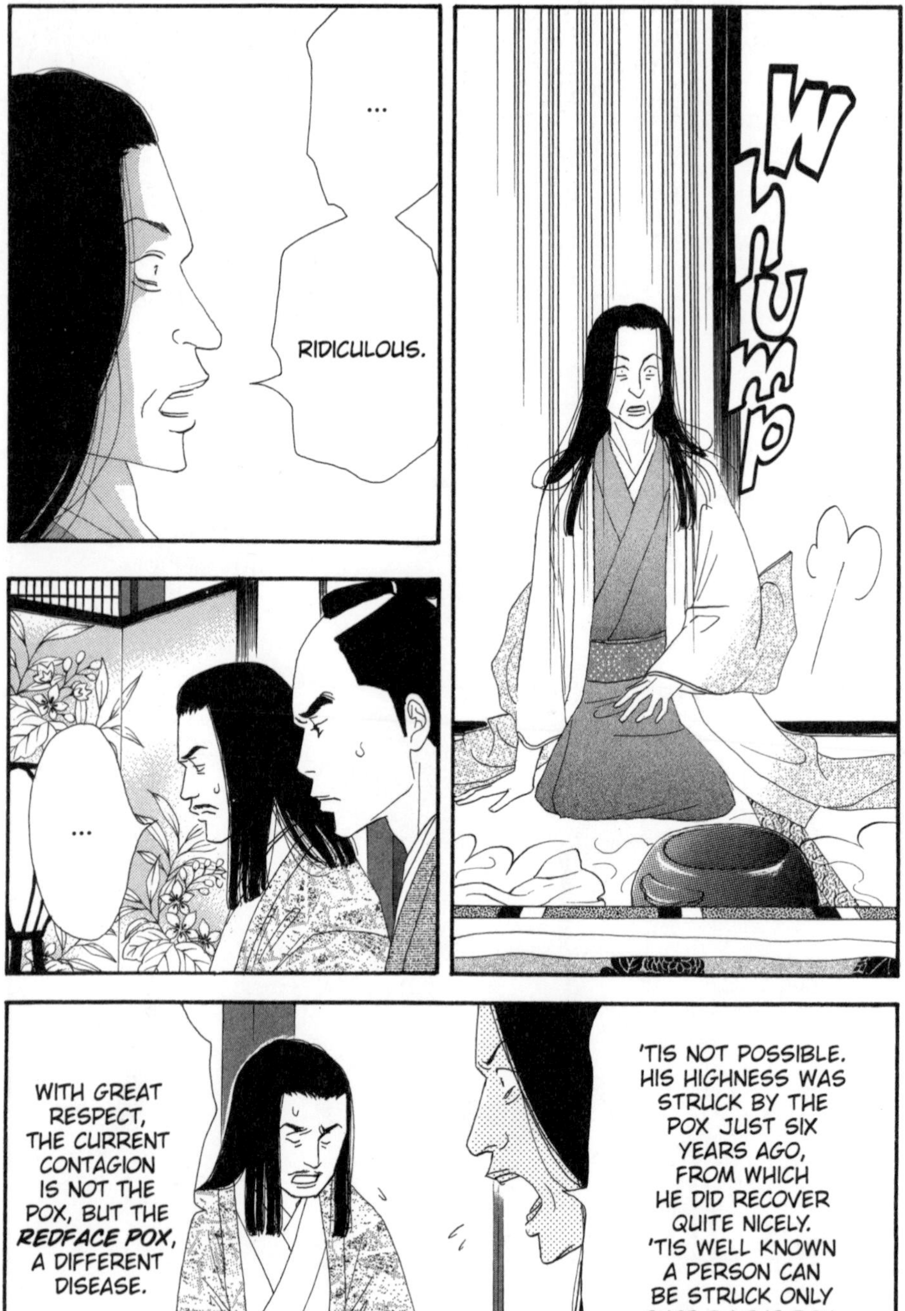
WHUMP
...
RIDICULOUS.
...
'TIS NOT POSSIBLE. HIS HIGHNESS WAS STRUCK BY THE POX JUST SIX YEARS AGO, FROM WHICH HE DID RECOVER QUITE NICELY. 'TIS WELL KNOWN A PERSON CAN BE STRUCK ONLY ONCE BY THE POX, NEVER MORE!
WITH GREAT RESPECT, THE CURRENT CONTAGION IS NOT THE POX, BUT THE REDFACE POX, A DIFFERENT DISEASE.

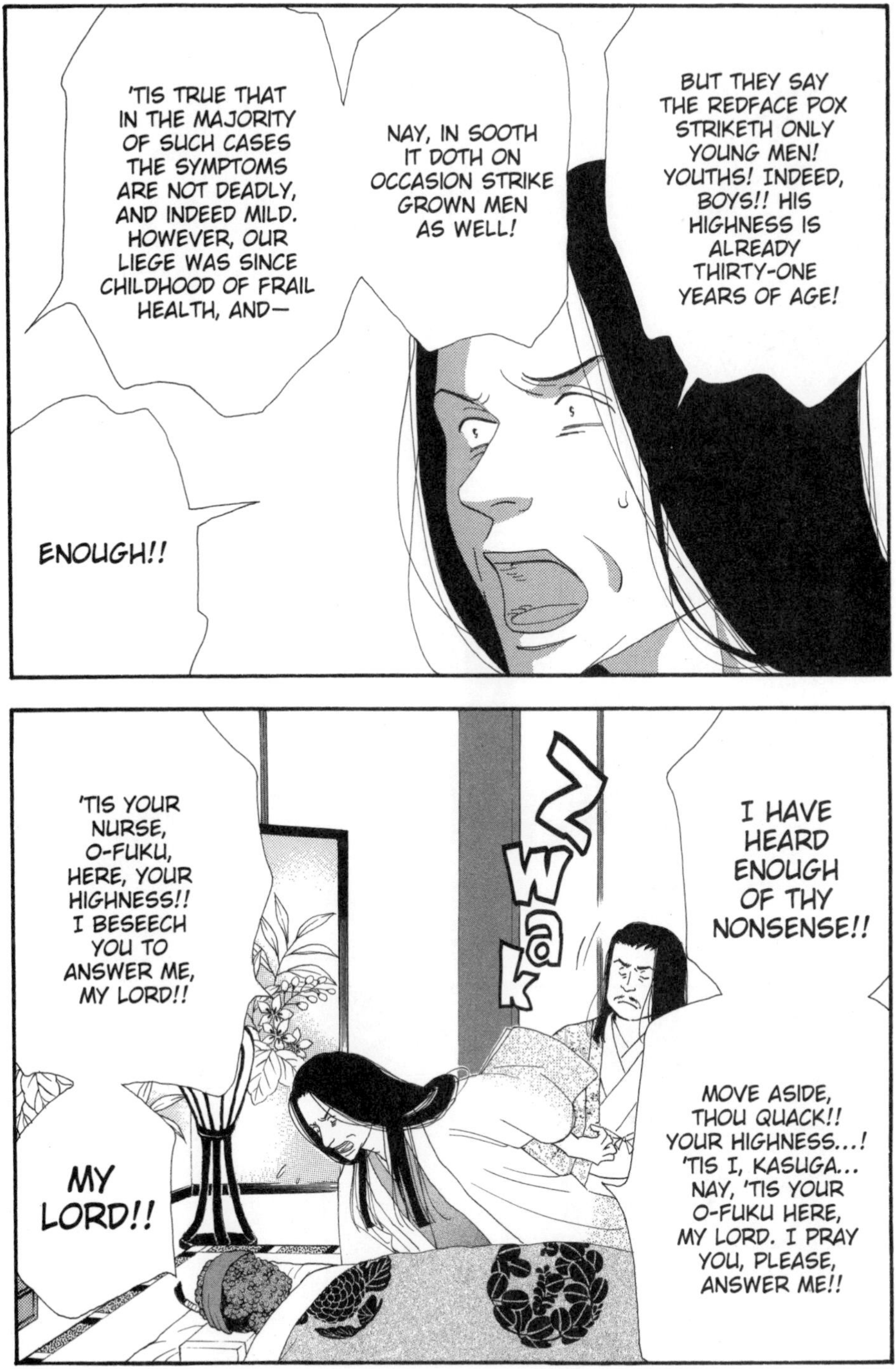
BUT THEY SAY THE REDFACE POX STRIKETH ONLY YOUNG MEN! YOUTHS! INDEED, BOYS!! HIS HIGHNESS IS ALREADY THIRTY-ONE YEARS OF AGE!
NAY, IN SOOTH IT DOTH ON OCCASION STRIKE GROWN MEN AS WELL!
'TIS TRUE THAT IN THE MAJORITY OF SUCH CASES THE SYMPTOMS ARE NOT DEADLY, AND INDEED MILD. HOWEVER, OUR LIEGE WAS SINCE CHILDHOOD OF FRAIL HEALTH, AND—
ENOUGH!!
I HAVE HEARD ENOUGH OF THY NONSENSE!!
ZWAK
'TIS YOUR NURSE, O-FUKU, HERE, YOUR HIGHNESS!! I BESEECH YOU TO ANSWER ME, MY LORD!!
MOVE ASIDE, THOU QUACK!! YOUR HIGHNESS...! 'TIS I, KASUGA... NAY, 'TIS YOUR O-FUKU HERE, MY LORD. I PRAY YOU, PLEASE, ANSWER ME!!
MY LORD!!

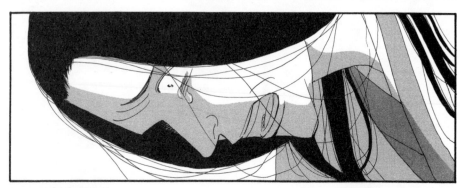

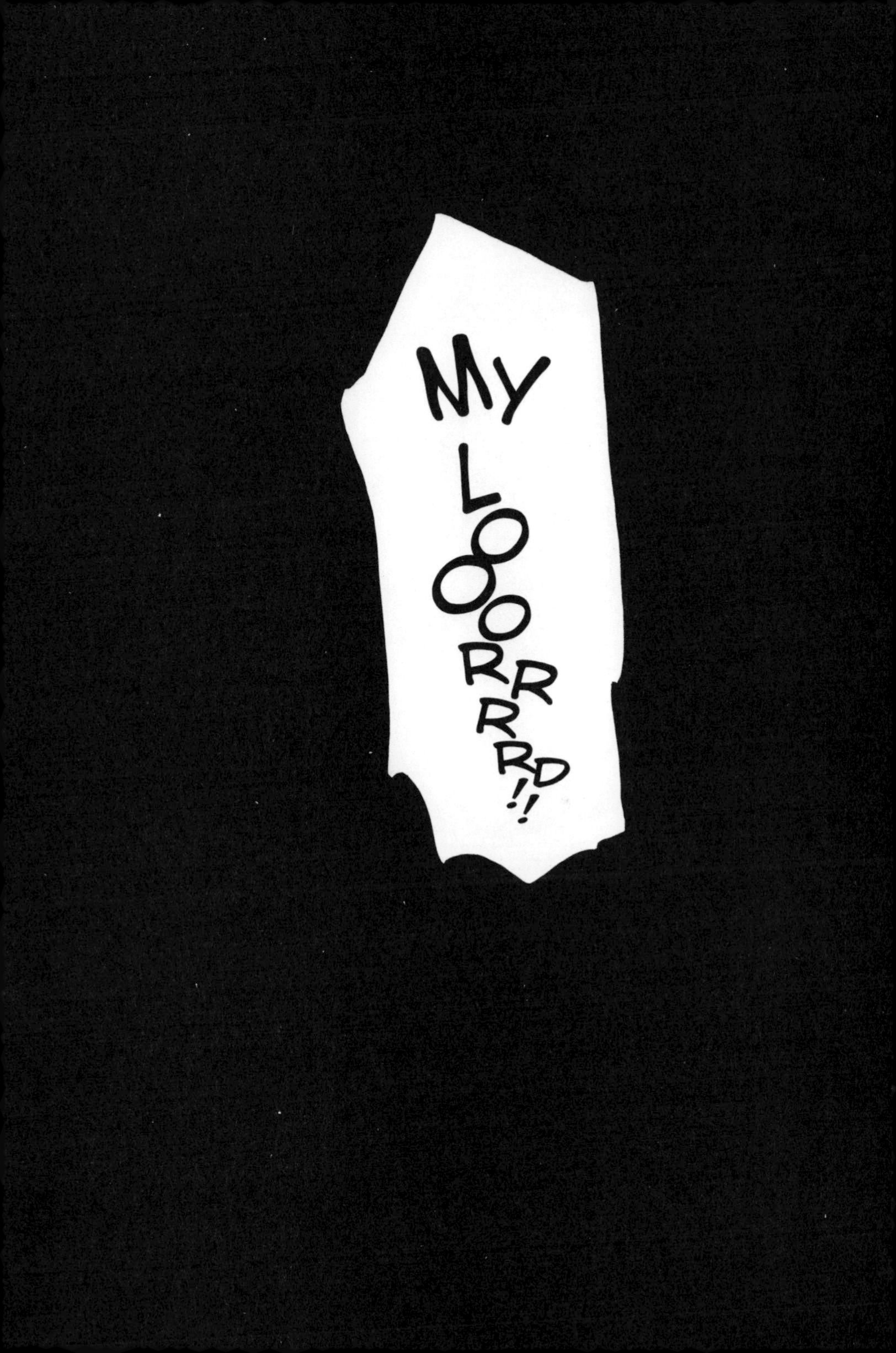
My LOOORRRRD!!

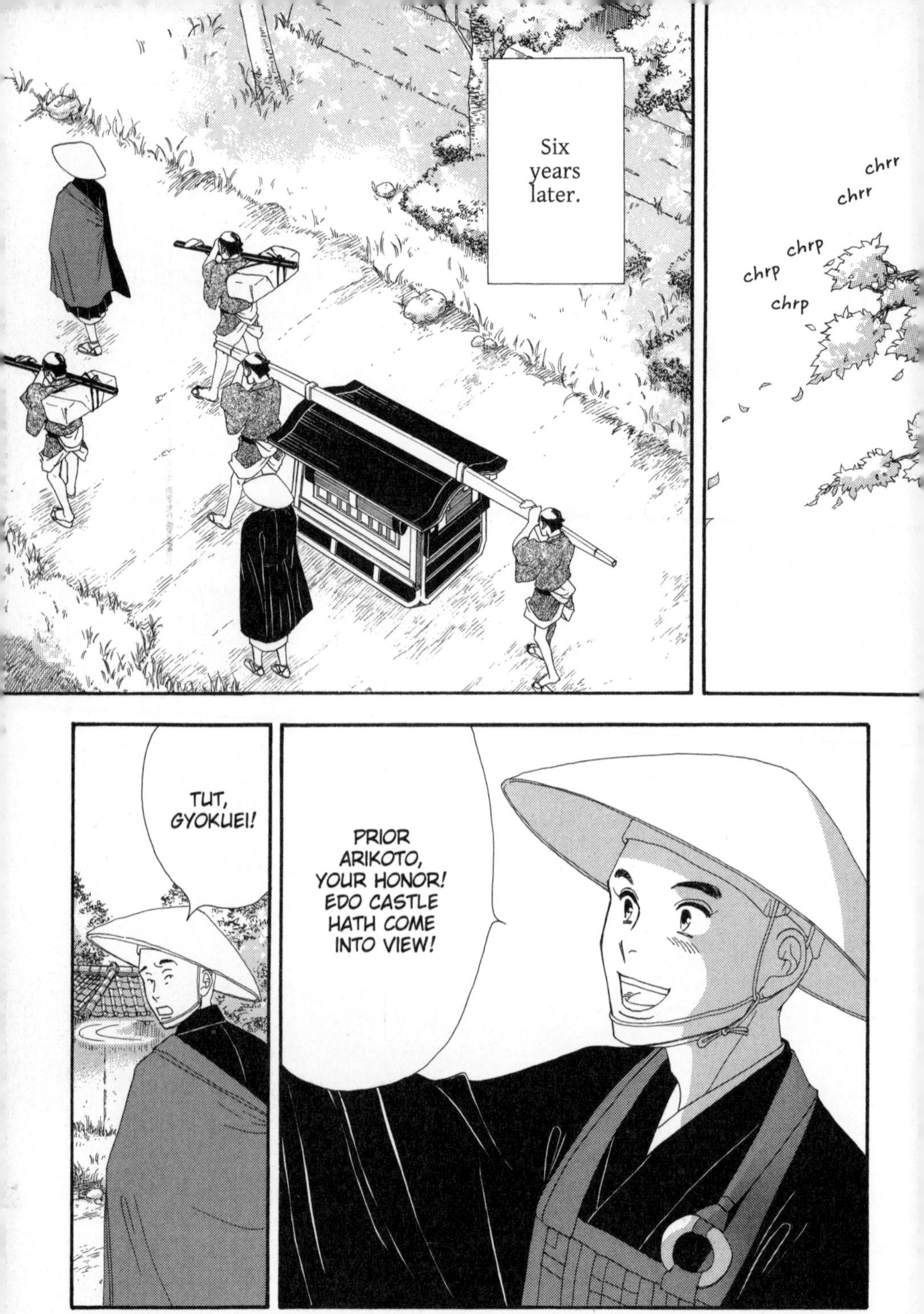
chrr
chrr
chrp
chrp
chrp
Six years later.
PRIOR ARIKOTO, YOUR HONOR! EDO CASTLE HATH COME INTO VIEW!
TUT, GYOKUEI!

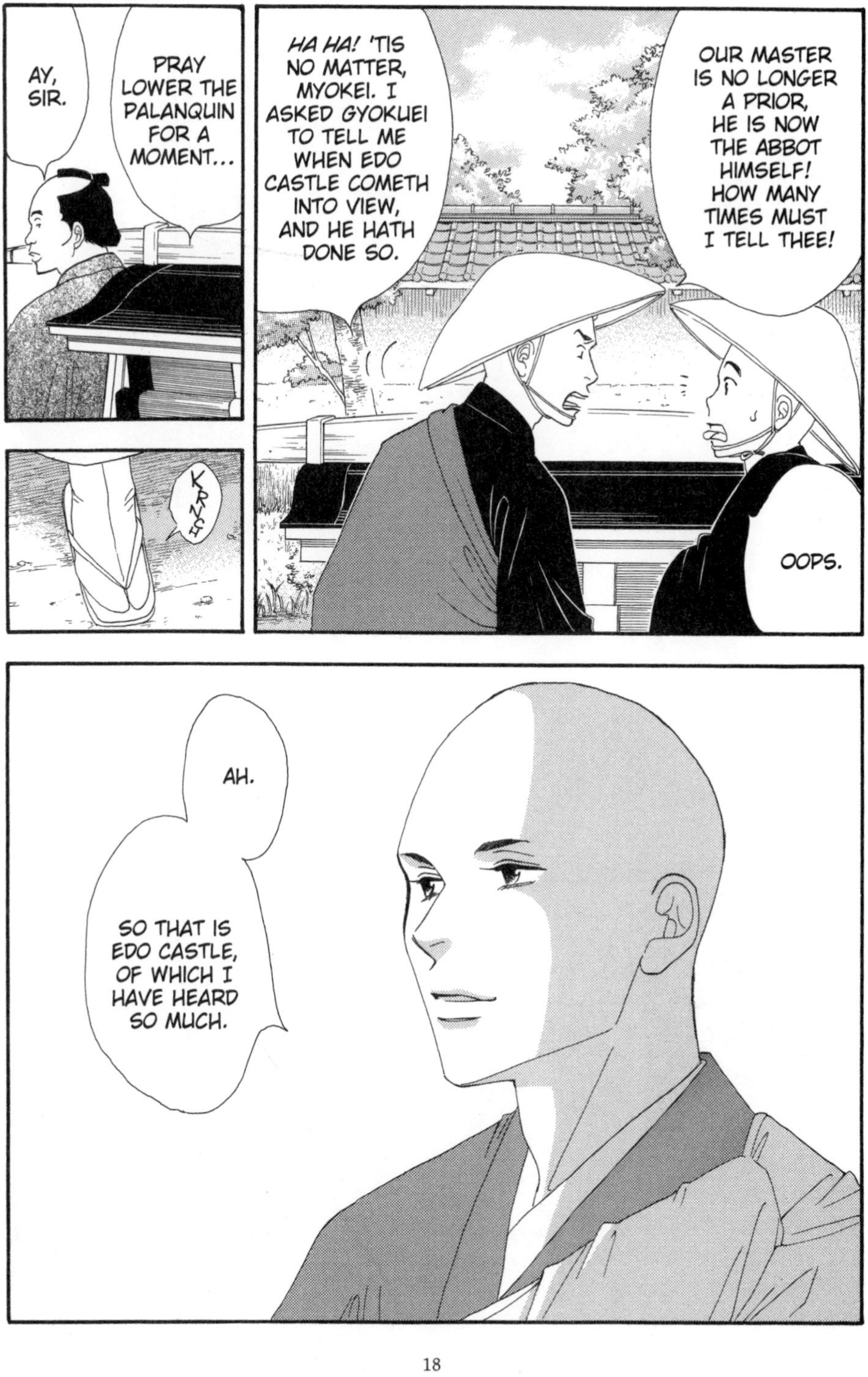
OUR MASTER IS NO LONGER A PRIOR, HE IS NOW THE ABBOT HIMSELF! HOW MANY TIMES MUST I TELL THEE!
HA HA! 'TIS NO MATTER, MYOKEI. I ASKED GYOKUEI TO TELL ME WHEN EDO CASTLE COMETH INTO VIEW, AND HE HATH DONE SO.
OOPS.
PRAY LOWER THE PALANQUIN FOR A MOMENT...
AY, SIR.
KRNCH
AH.
SO THAT IS EDO CASTLE, OF WHICH I HAVE HEARD SO MUCH.

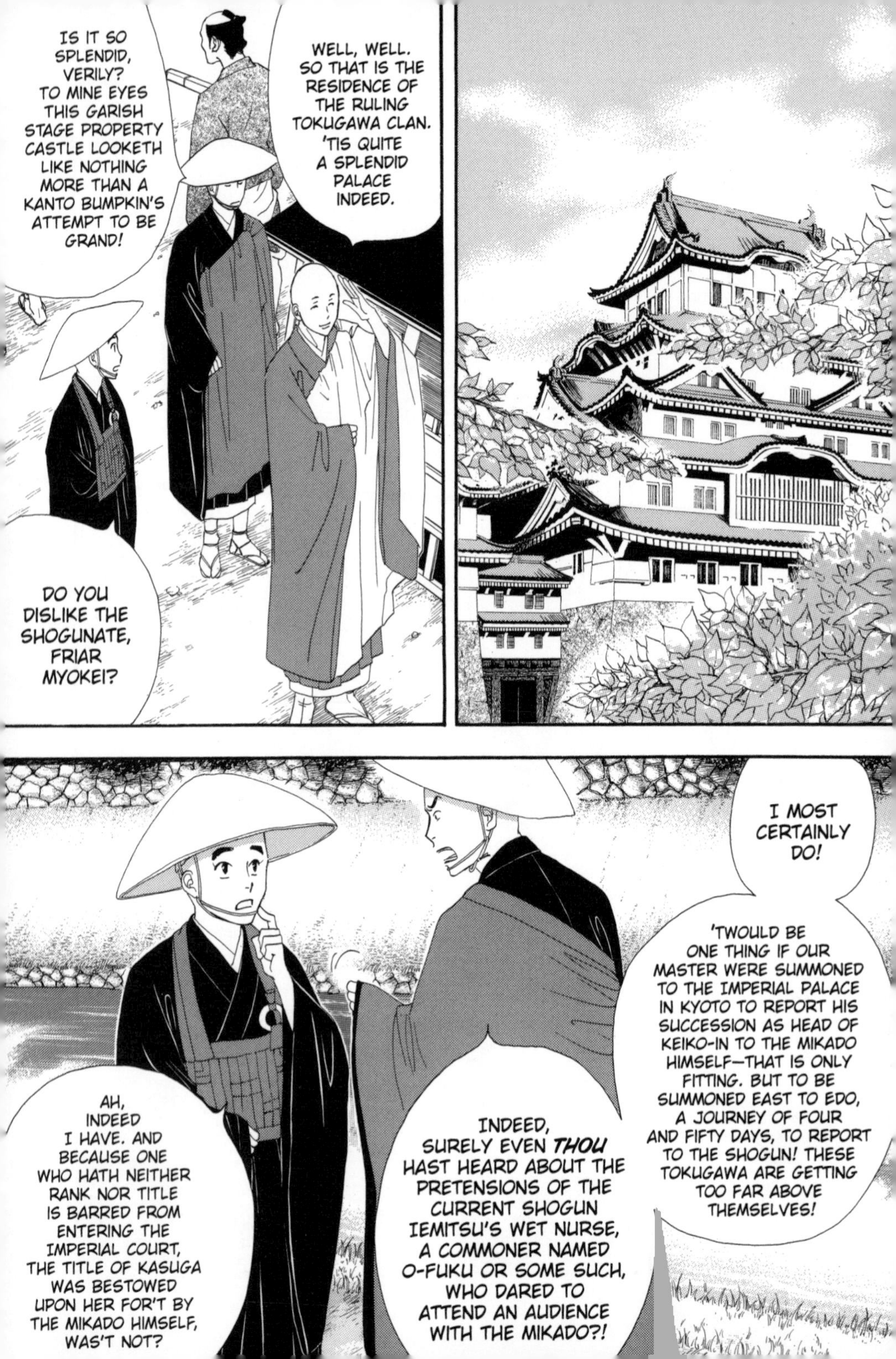

WELL, WELL. SO THAT IS THE RESIDENCE OF THE RULING TOKUGAWA CLAN. 'TIS QUITE A SPLENDID PALACE INDEED.
IS IT SO SPLENDID, VERILY? TO MINE EYES THIS GARISH STAGE PROPERTY CASTLE LOOKETH LIKE NOTHING MORE THAN A KANTO BUMPKIN'S ATTEMPT TO BE GRAND!
DO YOU DISLIKE THE SHOGUNATE, FRIAR MYOKEI?
I MOST CERTAINLY DO!
'TWOULD BE ONE THING IF OUR MASTER WERE SUMMONED TO THE IMPERIAL PALACE IN KYOTO TO REPORT HIS SUCCESSION AS HEAD OF KEIKO-IN TO THE MIKADO HIMSELF—THAT IS ONLY FITTING. BUT TO BE SUMMONED EAST TO EDO, A JOURNEY OF FOUR AND FIFTY DAYS, TO REPORT TO THE SHOGUN! THESE TOKUGAWA ARE GETTING TOO FAR ABOVE THEMSELVES!
INDEED, SURELY EVEN *THOU* HAST HEARD ABOUT THE PRETENSIONS OF THE CURRENT SHOGUN IEMITSU'S WET NURSE, A COMMONER NAMED O-FUKU OR SOME SUCH, WHO DARED TO ATTEND AN AUDIENCE WITH THE MIKADO?!
AH, INDEED I HAVE. AND BECAUSE ONE WHO HATH NEITHER RANK NOR TITLE IS BARRED FROM ENTERING THE IMPERIAL COURT, THE TITLE OF KASUGA WAS BESTOWED UPON HER FOR'T BY THE MIKADO HIMSELF, WAS'T NOT?

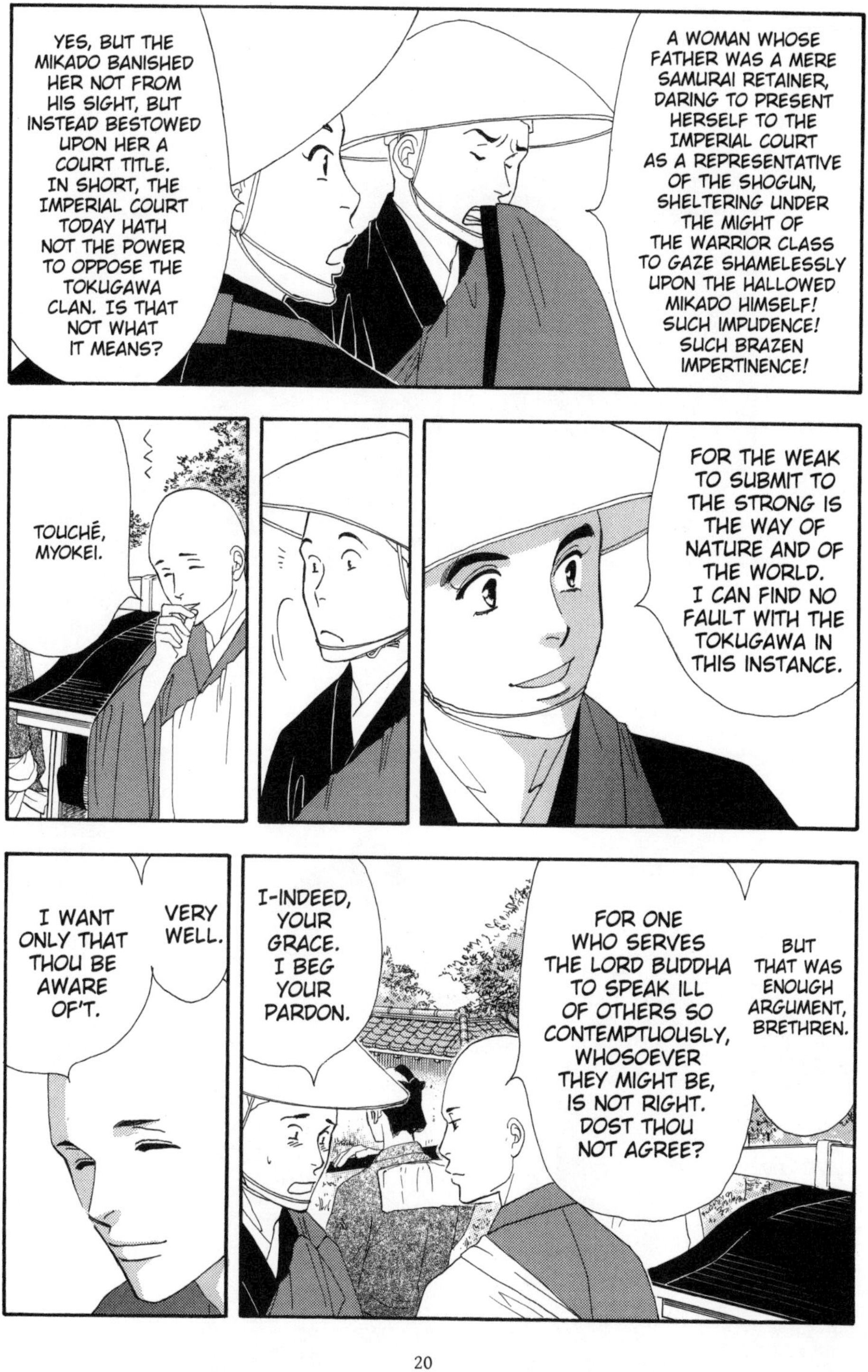
A WOMAN WHOSE FATHER WAS A MERE SAMURAI RETAINER, DARING TO PRESENT HERSELF TO THE IMPERIAL COURT AS A REPRESENTATIVE OF THE SHOGUN, SHELTERING UNDER THE MIGHT OF THE WARRIOR CLASS TO GAZE SHAMELESSLY UPON THE HALLOWED MIKADO HIMSELF! SUCH IMPUDENCE! SUCH BRAZEN IMPERTINENCE!
YES, BUT THE MIKADO BANISHED HER NOT FROM HIS SIGHT, BUT INSTEAD BESTOWED UPON HER A COURT TITLE. IN SHORT, THE IMPERIAL COURT TODAY HATH NOT THE POWER TO OPPOSE THE TOKUGAWA CLAN. IS THAT NOT WHAT IT MEANS?
FOR THE WEAK TO SUBMIT TO THE STRONG IS THE WAY OF NATURE AND OF THE WORLD. I CAN FIND NO FAULT WITH THE TOKUGAWA IN THIS INSTANCE.
TOUCHÉ, MYOKEI.
BUT THAT WAS ENOUGH ARGUMENT, BRETHREN.
FOR ONE WHO SERVES THE LORD BUDDHA TO SPEAK ILL OF OTHERS SO CONTEMPTUOUSLY, WHOSOEVER THEY MIGHT BE, IS NOT RIGHT. DOST THOU NOT AGREE?
I-INDEED, YOUR GRACE. I BEG YOUR PARDON.
VERY WELL.
I WANT ONLY THAT THOU BE AWARE OF'T.

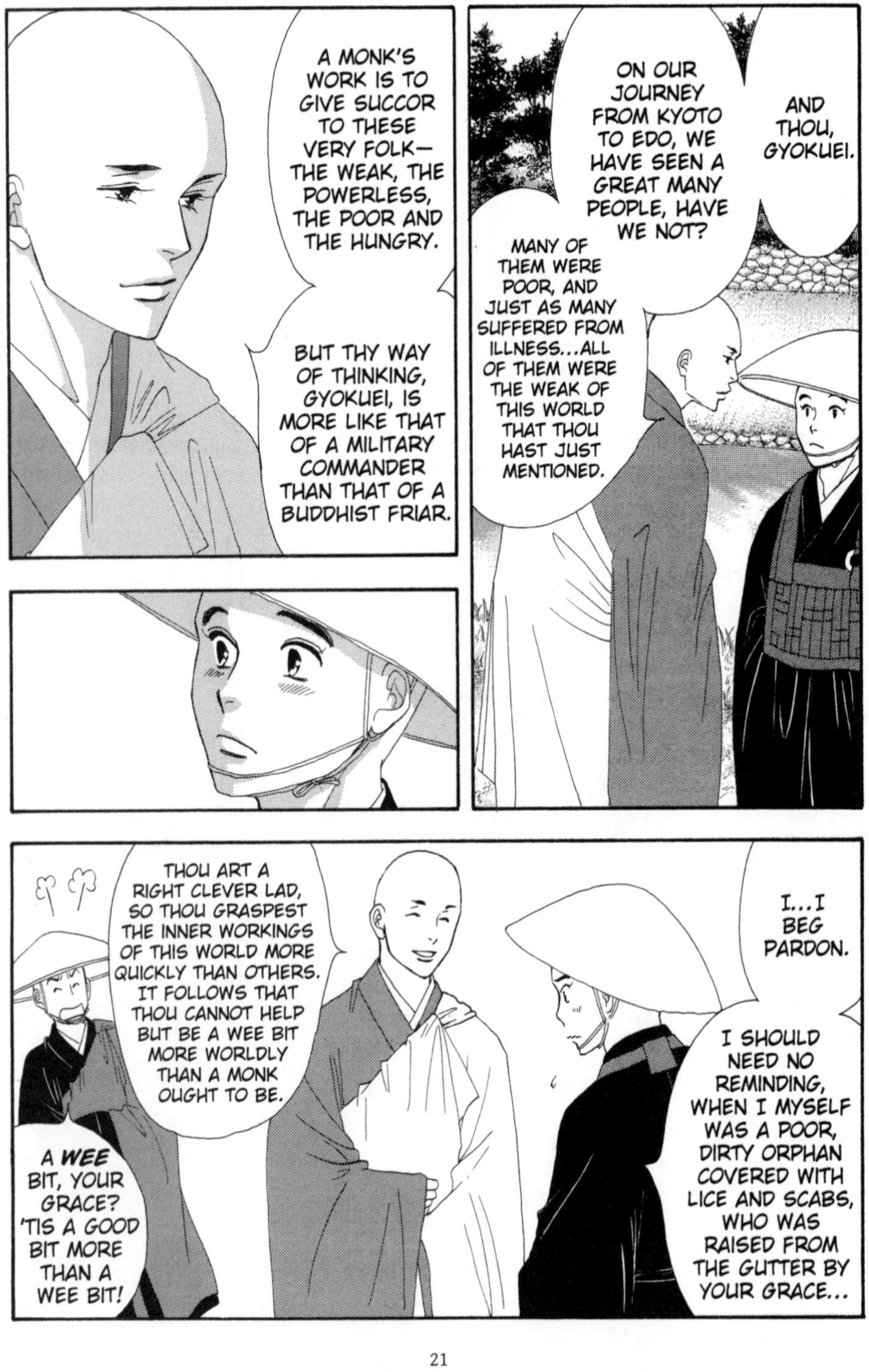
AND THOU, GYOKUEI.
ON OUR JOURNEY FROM KYOTO TO EDO, WE HAVE SEEN A GREAT MANY PEOPLE, HAVE WE NOT?
MANY OF THEM WERE POOR, AND JUST AS MANY SUFFERED FROM ILLNESS...ALL OF THEM WERE THE WEAK OF THIS WORLD THAT THOU HAST JUST MENTIONED.
A MONK'S WORK IS TO GIVE SUCCOR TO THESE VERY FOLK—THE WEAK, THE POWERLESS, THE POOR AND THE HUNGRY.
BUT THY WAY OF THINKING, GYOKUEI, IS MORE LIKE THAT OF A MILITARY COMMANDER THAN THAT OF A BUDDHIST FRIAR.
I...I BEG PARDON.
I SHOULD NEED NO REMINDING, WHEN I MYSELF WAS A POOR, DIRTY ORPHAN COVERED WITH LICE AND SCABS, WHO WAS RAISED FROM THE GUTTER BY YOUR GRACE...
THOU ART A RIGHT CLEVER LAD, SO THOU GRASPEST THE INNER WORKINGS OF THIS WORLD MORE QUICKLY THAN OTHERS. IT FOLLOWS THAT THOU CANNOT HELP BUT BE A WEE BIT MORE WORLDLY THAN A MONK OUGHT TO BE.
A *WEE* BIT, YOUR GRACE? 'TIS A GOOD BIT MORE THAN A WEE BIT!

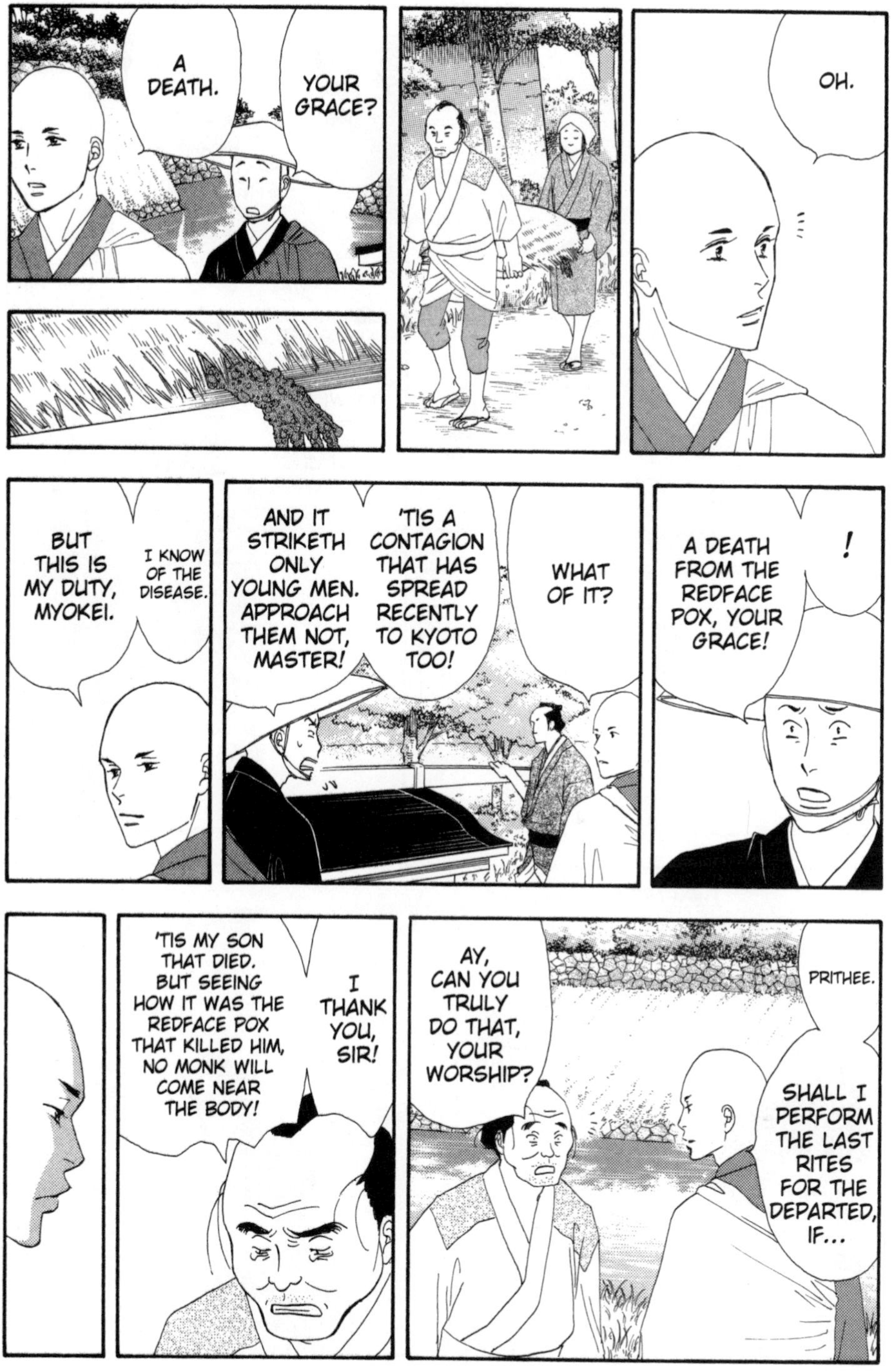
OH.
YOUR GRACE?
A DEATH.
!
A DEATH FROM THE REDFACE POX, YOUR GRACE!
WHAT OF IT?
'TIS A CONTAGION THAT HAS SPREAD RECENTLY TO KYOTO TOO!
AND IT STRIKETH ONLY YOUNG MEN. APPROACH THEM NOT, MASTER!
I KNOW OF THE DISEASE.
BUT THIS IS MY DUTY, MYOKEI.
PRITHEE.
SHALL I PERFORM THE LAST RITES FOR THE DEPARTED, IF...
AY, CAN YOU TRULY DO THAT, YOUR WORSHIP?
I THANK YOU, SIR!
'TIS MY SON THAT DIED. BUT SEEING HOW IT WAS THE REDFACE POX THAT KILLED HIM, NO MONK WILL COME NEAR THE BODY!

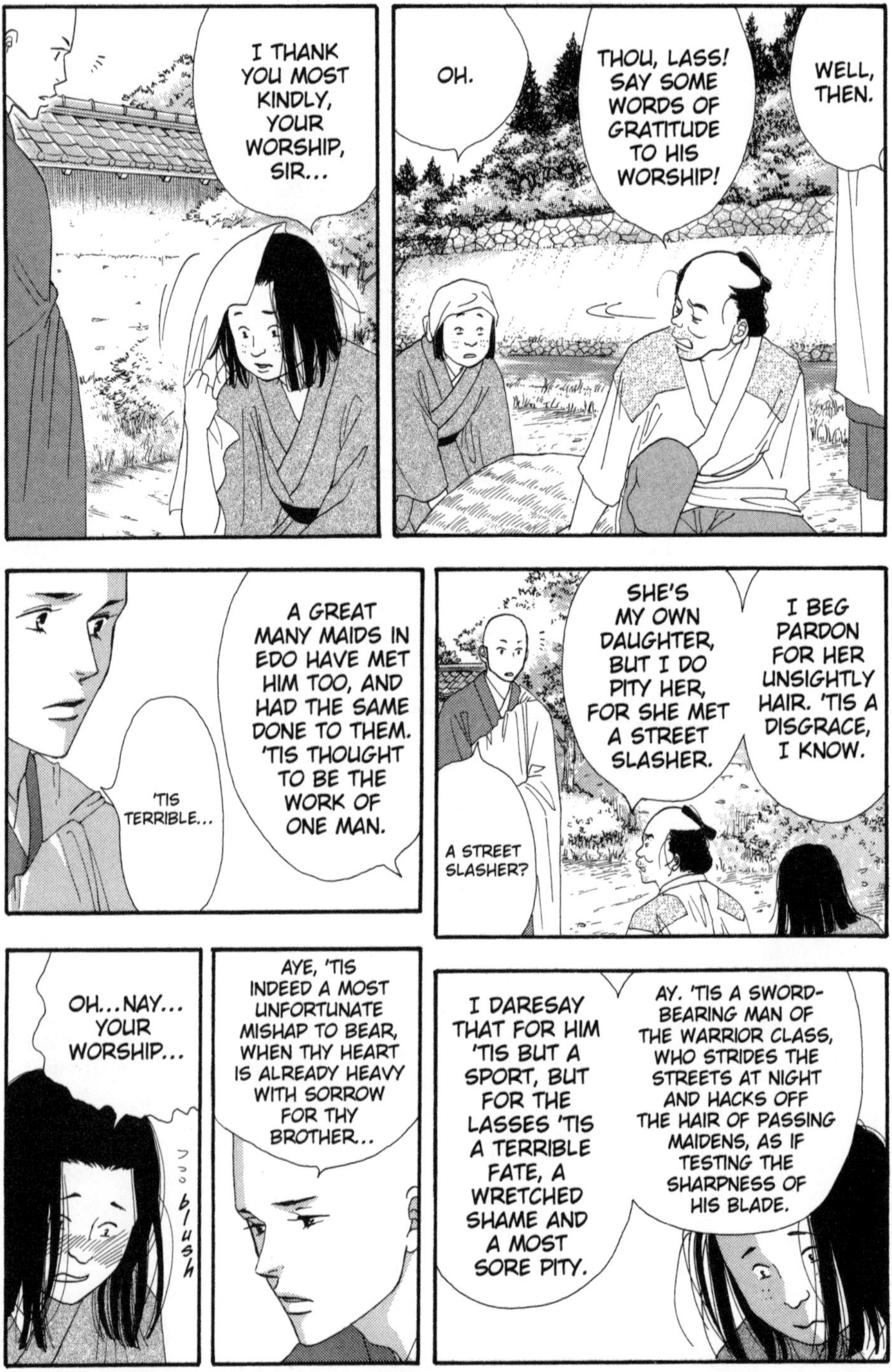
WELL, THEN.
THOU, LASS! SAY SOME WORDS OF GRATITUDE TO HIS WORSHIP!
OH.
I THANK YOU MOST KINDLY, YOUR WORSHIP, SIR...
I BEG PARDON FOR HER UNSIGHTLY HAIR. 'TIS A DISGRACE, I KNOW.
SHE'S MY OWN DAUGHTER, BUT I DO PITY HER, FOR SHE MET A STREET SLASHER.
A STREET SLASHER?
A GREAT MANY MAIDS IN EDO HAVE MET HIM TOO, AND HAD THE SAME DONE TO THEM. 'TIS THOUGHT TO BE THE WORK OF ONE MAN.
'TIS TERRIBLE...
AY. 'TIS A SWORD-BEARING MAN OF THE WARRIOR CLASS, WHO STRIDES THE STREETS AT NIGHT AND HACKS OFF THE HAIR OF PASSING MAIDENS, AS IF TESTING THE SHARPNESS OF HIS BLADE.
I DARESAY THAT FOR HIM 'TIS BUT A SPORT, BUT FOR THE LASSES 'TIS A TERRIBLE FATE, A WRETCHED SHAME AND A MOST SORE PITY.
AYE, 'TIS INDEED A MOST UNFORTUNATE MISHAP TO BEAR, WHEN THY HEART IS ALREADY HEAVY WITH SORROW FOR THY BROTHER...
OH...NAY... YOUR WORSHIP...
blush

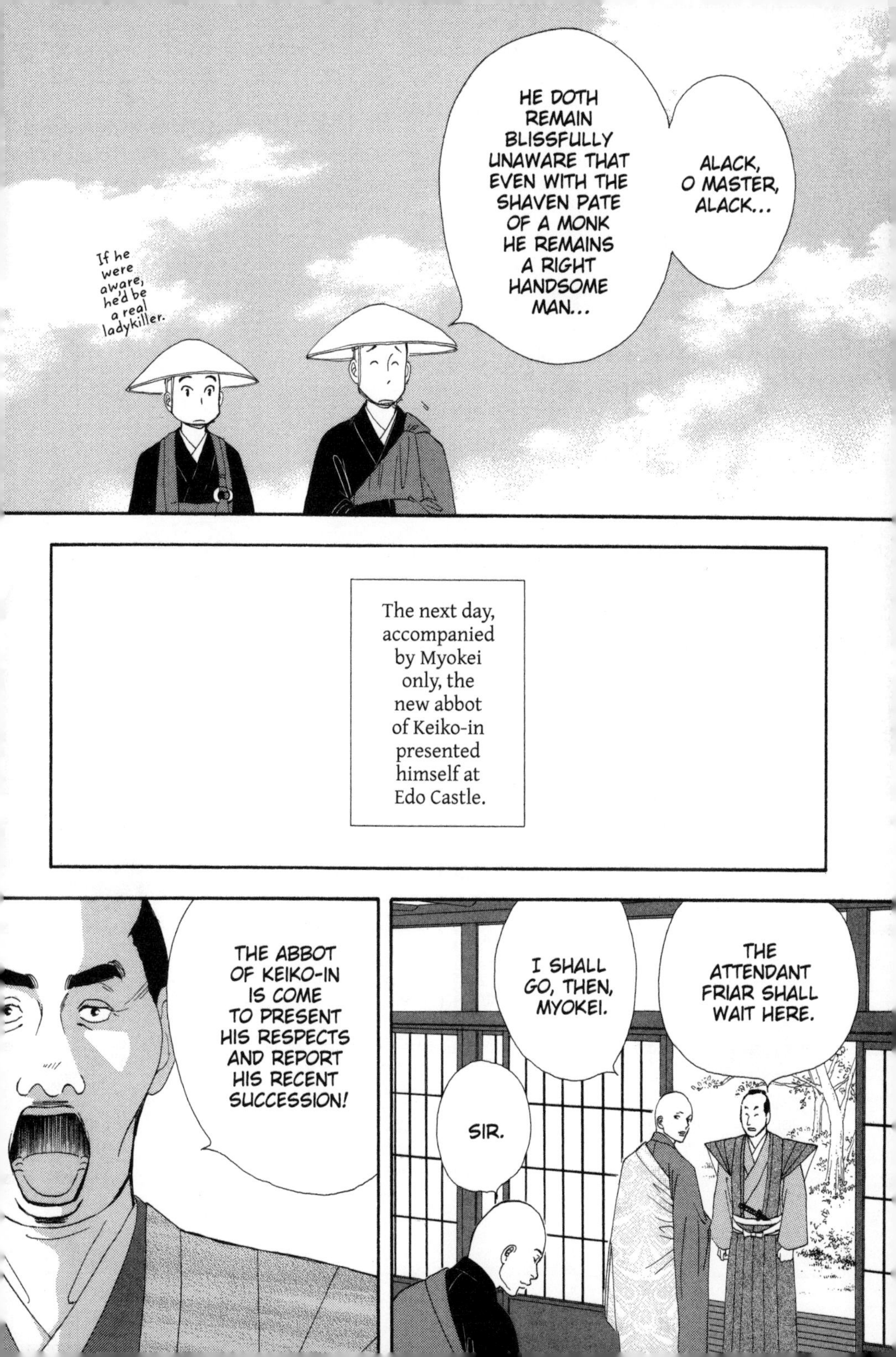
ALACK, O MASTER, ALACK...
HE DOTH REMAIN BLISSFULLY UNAWARE THAT EVEN WITH THE SHAVEN PATE OF A MONK HE REMAINS A RIGHT HANDSOME MAN...
If he were aware, he'd be a real ladykiller.
The next day, accompanied by Myokei only, the new abbot of Keiko-in presented himself at Edo Castle.
THE ATTENDANT FRIAR SHALL WAIT HERE.
I SHALL GO, THEN, MYOKEI.
SIR.
THE ABBOT OF KEIKO-IN IS COME TO PRESENT HIS RESPECTS AND REPORT HIS RECENT SUCCESSION!

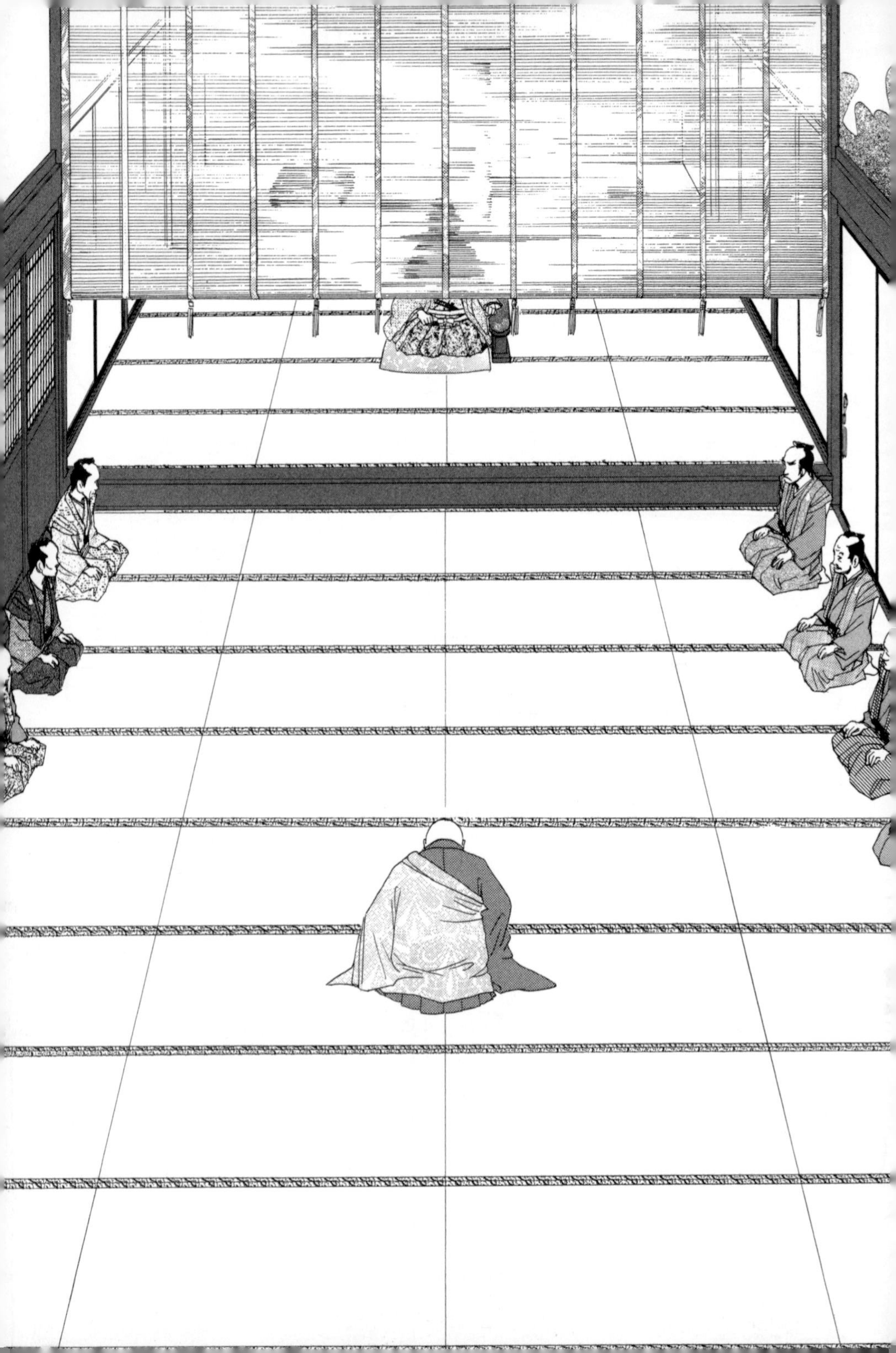

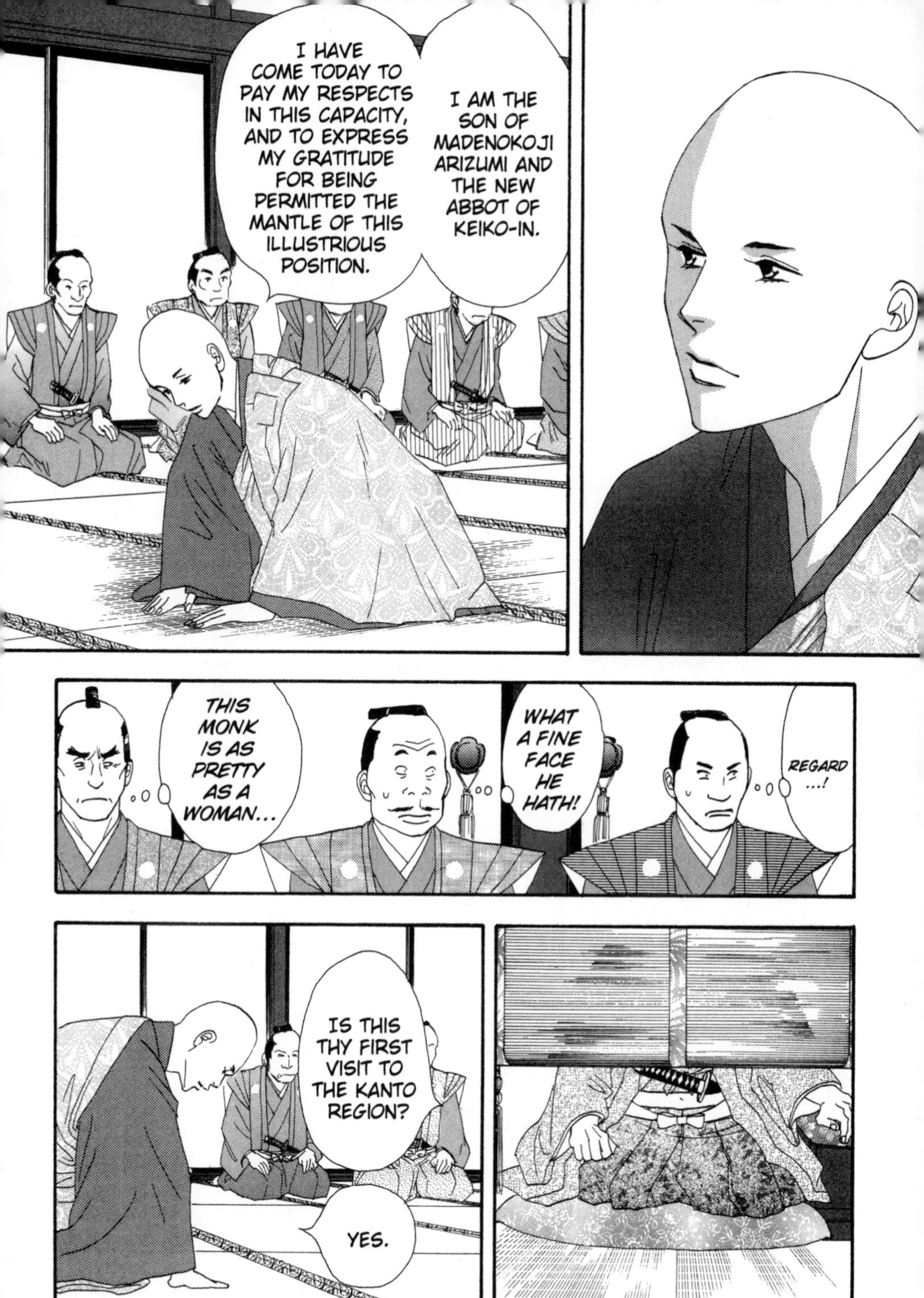
I AM THE SON OF MADENOKOJI ARIZUMI AND THE NEW ABBOT OF KEIKO-IN.
I HAVE COME TODAY TO PAY MY RESPECTS IN THIS CAPACITY, AND TO EXPRESS MY GRATITUDE FOR BEING PERMITTED THE MANTLE OF THIS ILLUSTRIOUS POSITION.
REGARD ...!
WHAT A FINE FACE HE HATH!
THIS MONK IS AS PRETTY AS A WOMAN...
IS THIS THY FIRST VISIT TO THE KANTO REGION?
YES.

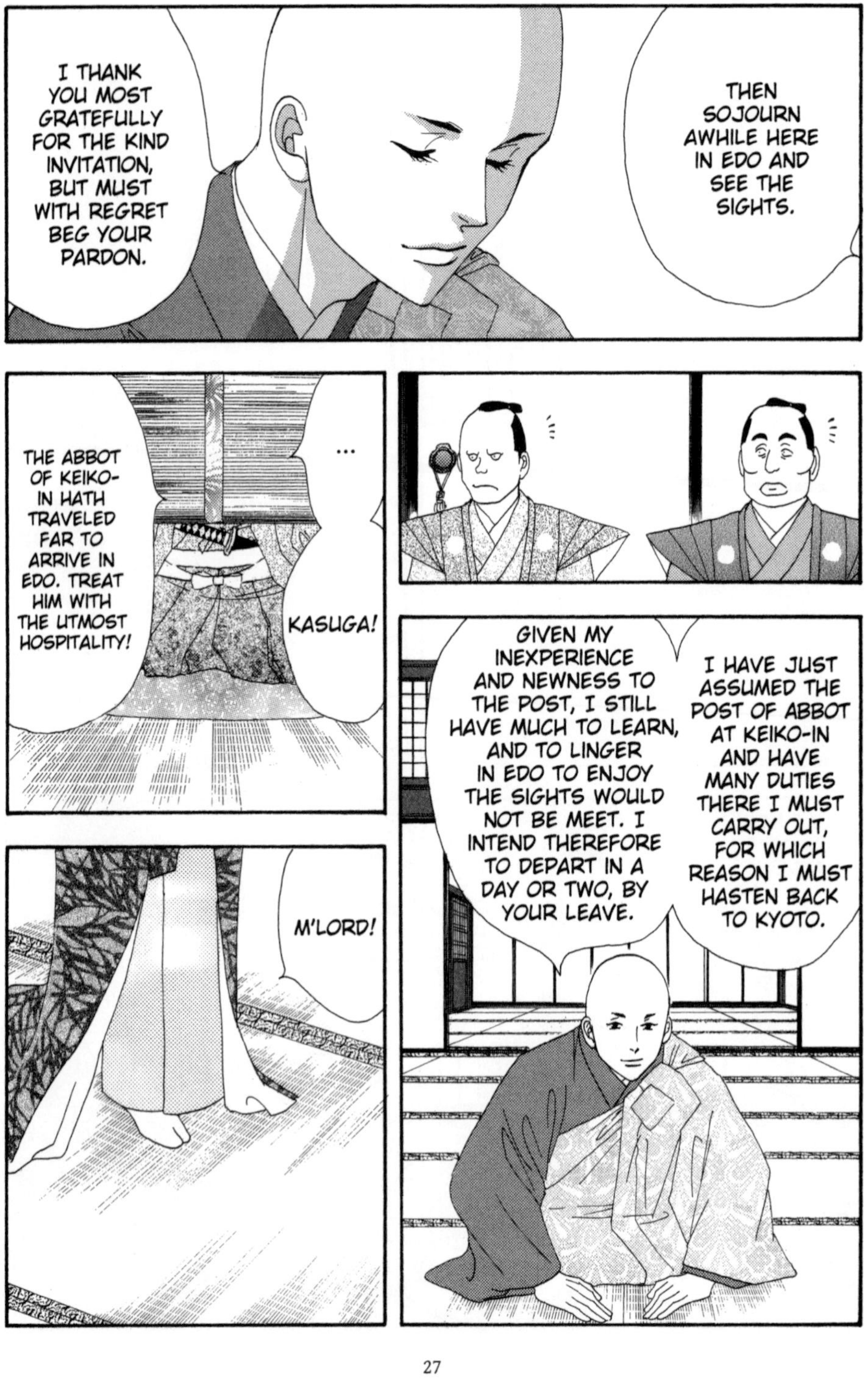

THEN SOJOURN AWHILE HERE IN EDO AND SEE THE SIGHTS.
I THANK YOU MOST GRATEFULLY FOR THE KIND INVITATION, BUT MUST WITH REGRET BEG YOUR PARDON.
...
KASUGA!
THE ABBOT OF KEIKO-IN HATH TRAVELED FAR TO ARRIVE IN EDO. TREAT HIM WITH THE UTMOST HOSPITALITY!
I HAVE JUST ASSUMED THE POST OF ABBOT AT KEIKO-IN AND HAVE MANY DUTIES THERE I MUST CARRY OUT, FOR WHICH REASON I MUST HASTEN BACK TO KYOTO.
GIVEN MY INEXPERIENCE AND NEWNESS TO THE POST, I STILL HAVE MUCH TO LEARN, AND TO LINGER IN EDO TO ENJOY THE SIGHTS WOULD NOT BE MEET. I INTEND THEREFORE TO DEPART IN A DAY OR TWO, BY YOUR LEAVE.
M'LORD!

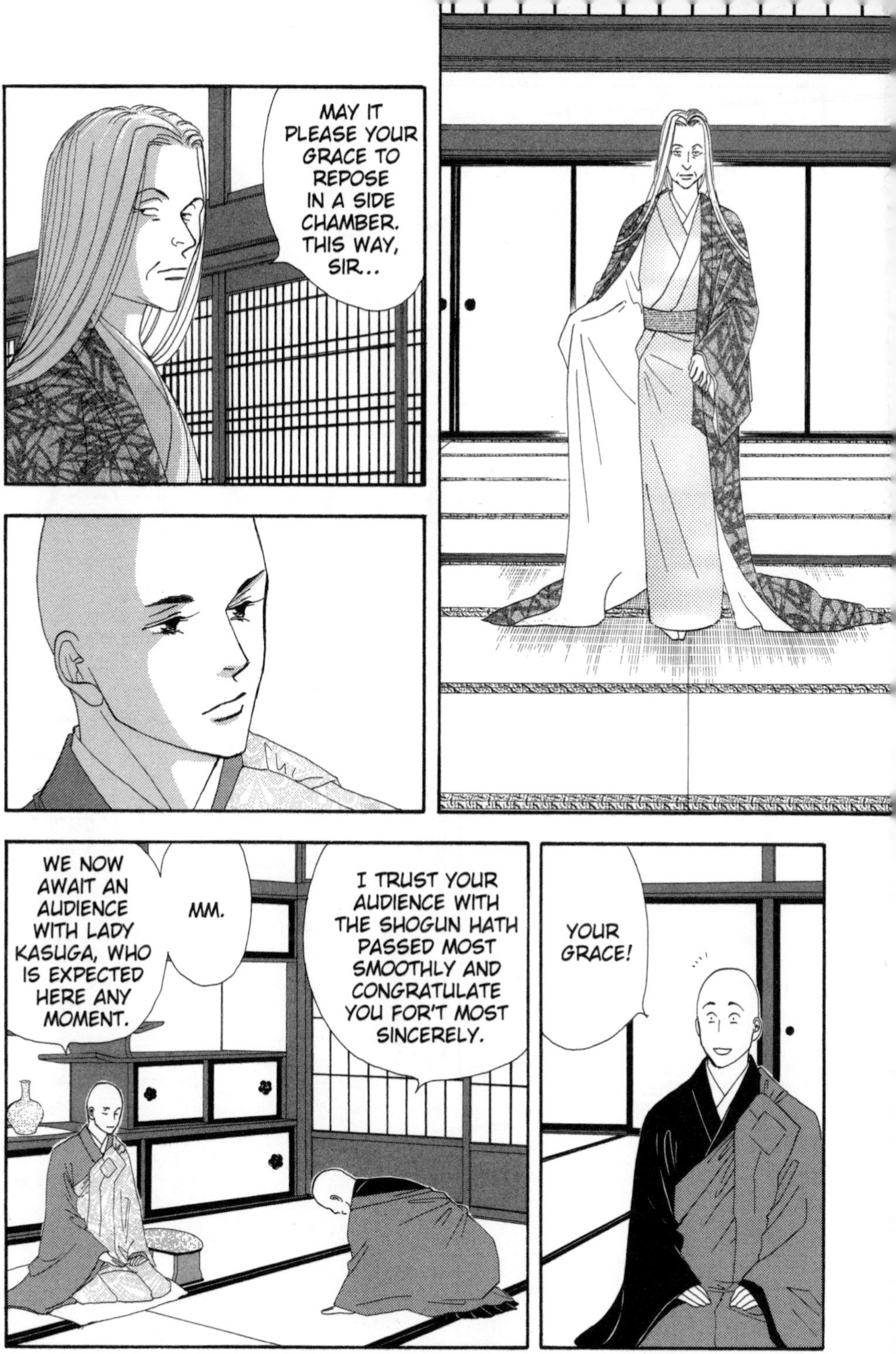
MAY IT PLEASE YOUR GRACE TO REPOSE IN A SIDE CHAMBER. THIS WAY, SIR...
YOUR GRACE!
I TRUST YOUR AUDIENCE WITH THE SHOGUN HATH PASSED MOST SMOOTHLY AND CONGRATULATE YOU FOR'T MOST SINCERELY.
MM.
WE NOW AWAIT AN AUDIENCE WITH LADY KASUGA, WHO IS EXPECTED HERE ANY MOMENT.

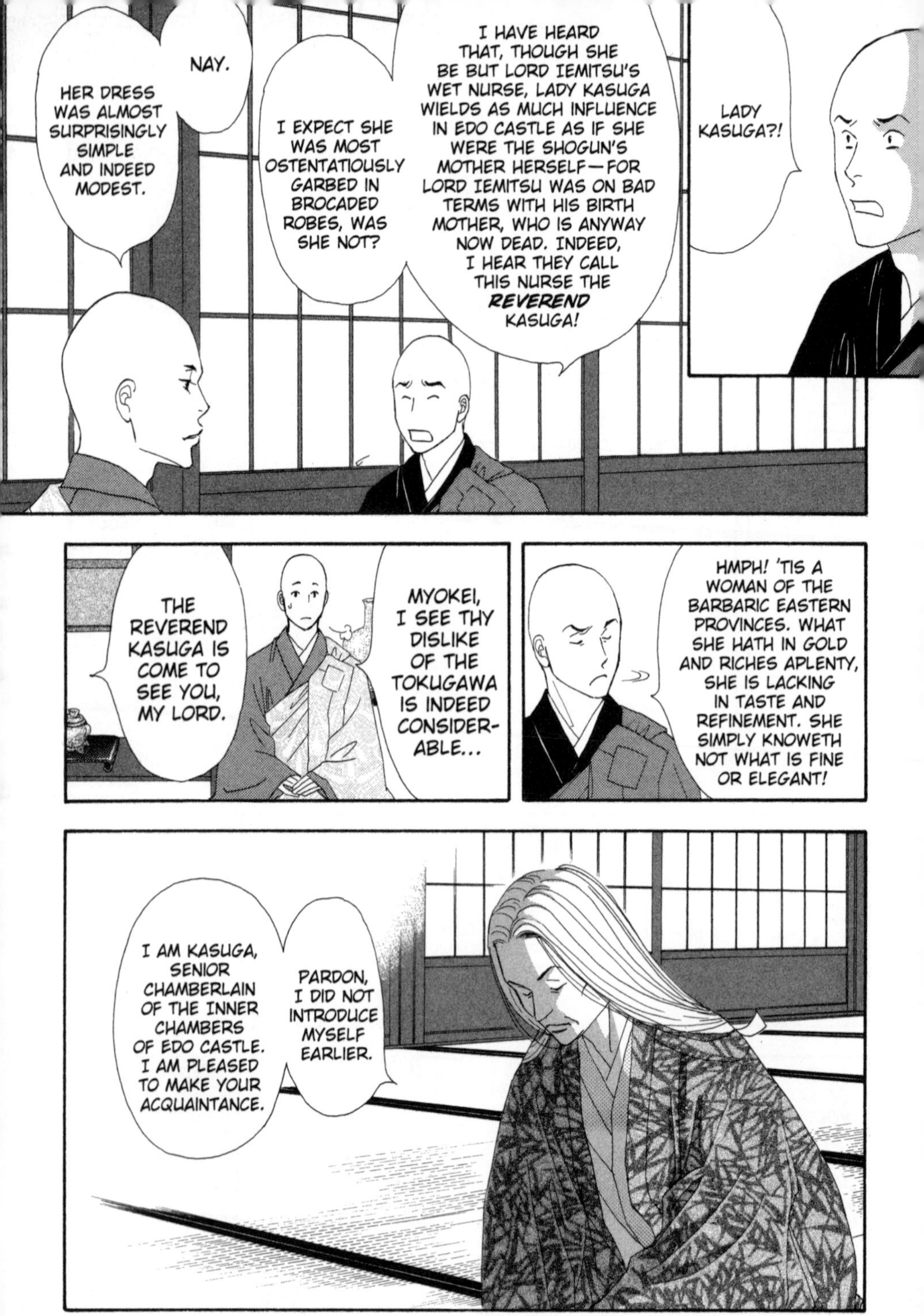
LADY KASUGA?!
I HAVE HEARD THAT, THOUGH SHE BE BUT LORD IEMITSU'S WET NURSE, LADY KASUGA WIELDS AS MUCH INFLUENCE IN EDO CASTLE AS IF SHE WERE THE SHOGUN'S MOTHER HERSELF—FOR LORD IEMITSU WAS ON BAD TERMS WITH HIS BIRTH MOTHER, WHO IS ANYWAY NOW DEAD. INDEED, I HEAR THEY CALL THIS NURSE THE *REVEREND* KASUGA!
I EXPECT SHE WAS MOST OSTENTATIOUSLY GARBED IN BROCADED ROBES, WAS SHE NOT?
NAY.
HER DRESS WAS ALMOST SURPRISINGLY SIMPLE AND INDEED MODEST.
HMPH! 'TIS A WOMAN OF THE BARBARIC EASTERN PROVINCES. WHAT SHE HATH IN GOLD AND RICHES APLENTY, SHE IS LACKING IN TASTE AND REFINEMENT. SHE SIMPLY KNOWETH NOT WHAT IS FINE OR ELEGANT!
MYOKEI, I SEE THY DISLIKE OF THE TOKUGAWA IS INDEED CONSIDER-ABLE...
THE REVEREND KASUGA IS COME TO SEE YOU, MY LORD.
PARDON, I DID NOT INTRODUCE MYSELF EARLIER.
I AM KASUGA, SENIOR CHAMBERLAIN OF THE INNER CHAMBERS OF EDO CASTLE. I AM PLEASED TO MAKE YOUR ACQUAINTANCE.

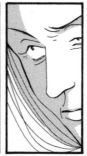

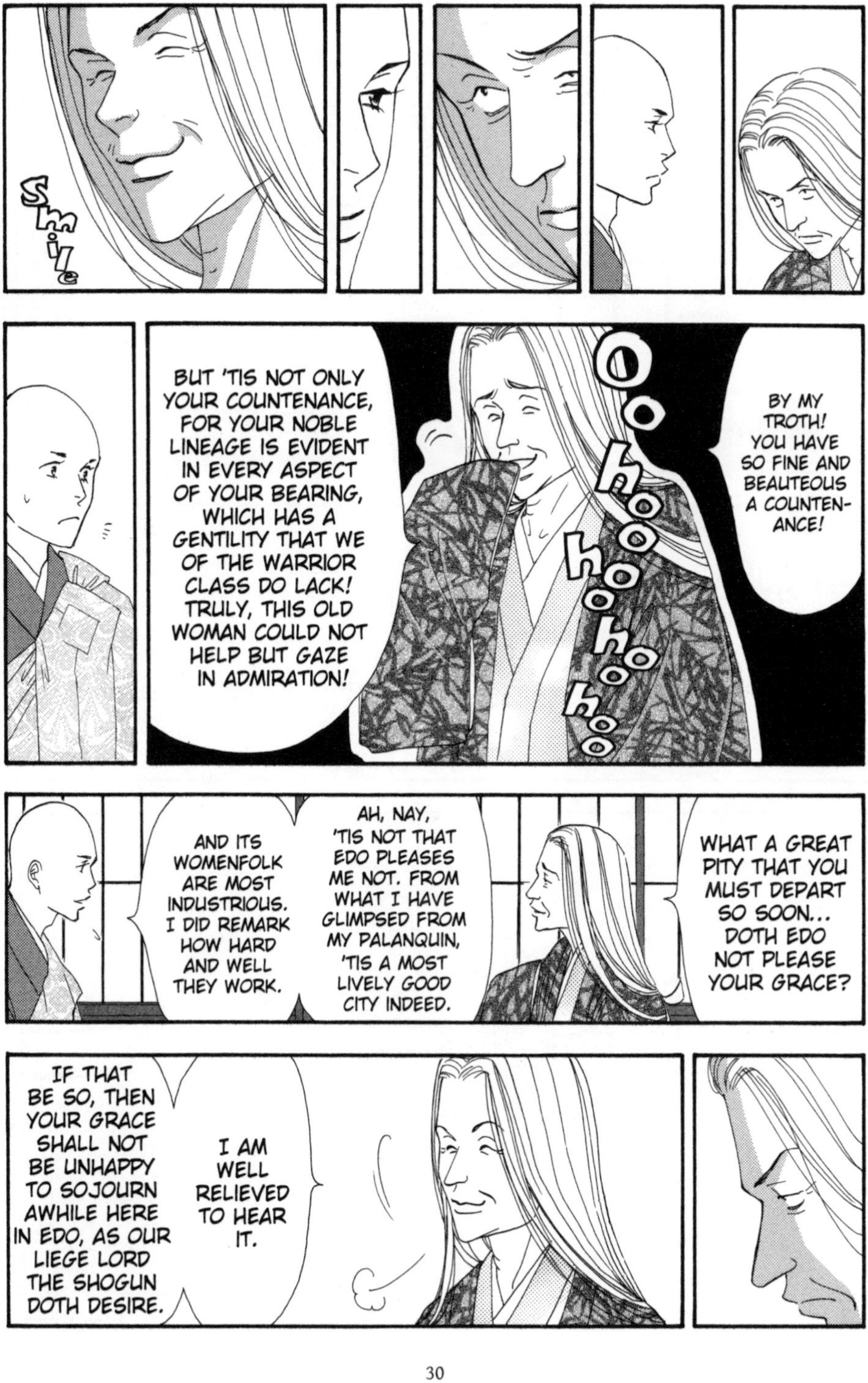
Smile
BY MY TROTH! YOU HAVE SO FINE AND BEAUTEOUS A COUNTENANCE!
Oohoohoohoohoo
BUT 'TIS NOT ONLY YOUR COUNTENANCE, FOR YOUR NOBLE LINEAGE IS EVIDENT IN EVERY ASPECT OF YOUR BEARING, WHICH HAS A GENTILITY THAT WE OF THE WARRIOR CLASS DO LACK! TRULY, THIS OLD WOMAN COULD NOT HELP BUT GAZE IN ADMIRATION!
WHAT A GREAT PITY THAT YOU MUST DEPART SO SOON... DOTH EDO NOT PLEASE YOUR GRACE?
AH, NAY, 'TIS NOT THAT EDO PLEASES ME NOT. FROM WHAT I HAVE GLIMPSED FROM MY PALANQUIN, 'TIS A MOST LIVELY GOOD CITY INDEED.
AND ITS WOMENFOLK ARE MOST INDUSTRIOUS. I DID REMARK HOW HARD AND WELL THEY WORK.
I AM WELL RELIEVED TO HEAR IT.
IF THAT BE SO, THEN YOUR GRACE SHALL NOT BE UNHAPPY TO SOJOURN AWHILE HERE IN EDO, AS OUR LIEGE LORD THE SHOGUN DOTH DESIRE.

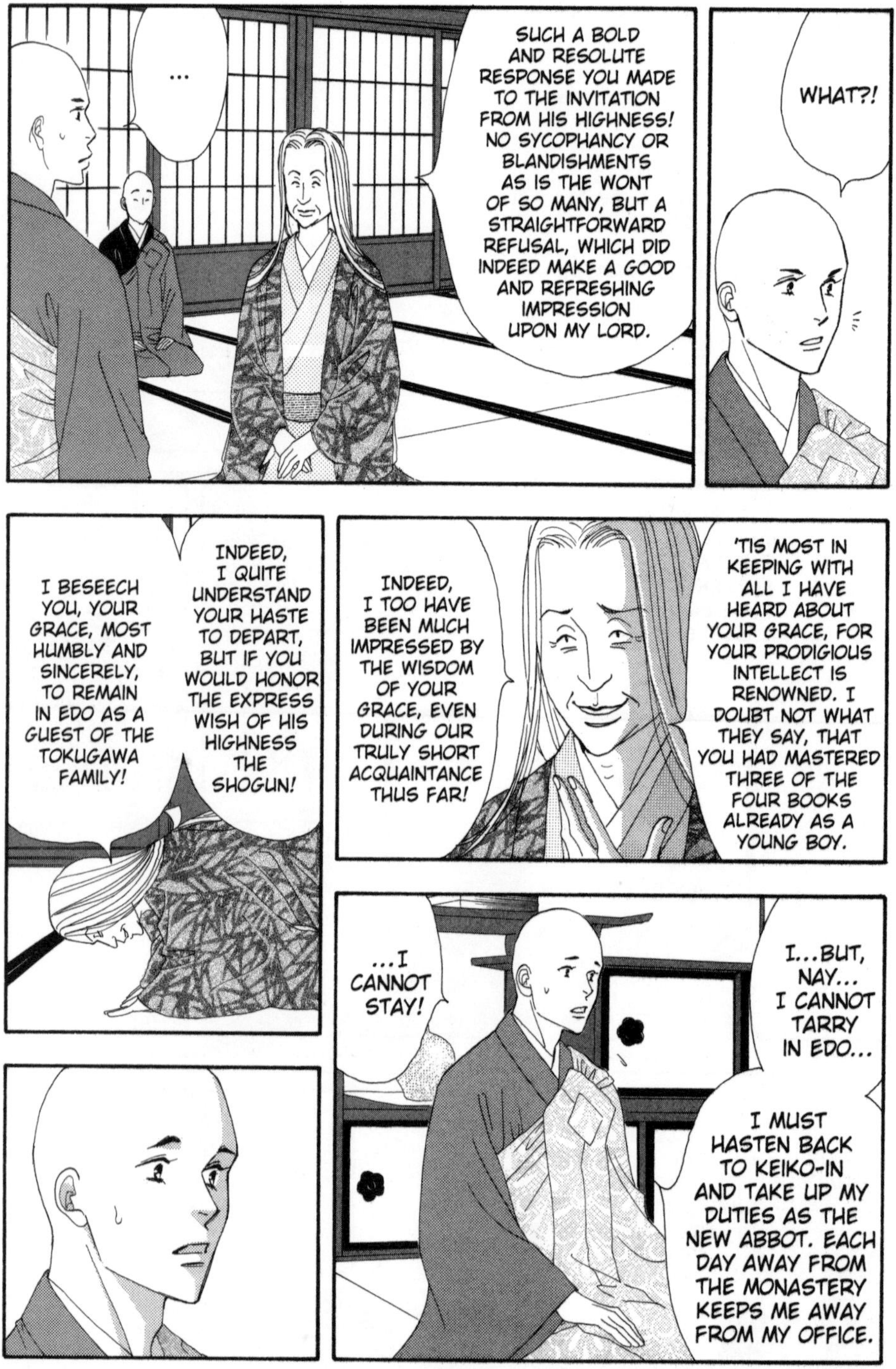
WHAT?!
SUCH A BOLD AND RESOLUTE RESPONSE YOU MADE TO THE INVITATION FROM HIS HIGHNESS! NO SYCOPHANCY OR BLANDISHMENTS AS IS THE WONT OF SO MANY, BUT A STRAIGHTFORWARD REFUSAL, WHICH DID INDEED MAKE A GOOD AND REFRESHING IMPRESSION UPON MY LORD.
...
'TIS MOST IN KEEPING WITH ALL I HAVE HEARD ABOUT YOUR GRACE, FOR YOUR PRODIGIOUS INTELLECT IS RENOWNED. I DOUBT NOT WHAT THEY SAY, THAT YOU HAD MASTERED THREE OF THE FOUR BOOKS ALREADY AS A YOUNG BOY.
INDEED, I TOO HAVE BEEN MUCH IMPRESSED BY THE WISDOM OF YOUR GRACE, EVEN DURING OUR TRULY SHORT ACQUAINTANCE THUS FAR!
INDEED, I QUITE UNDERSTAND YOUR HASTE TO DEPART, BUT IF YOU WOULD HONOR THE EXPRESS WISH OF HIS HIGHNESS THE SHOGUN!
I BESEECH YOU, YOUR GRACE, MOST HUMBLY AND SINCERELY, TO REMAIN IN EDO AS A GUEST OF THE TOKUGAWA FAMILY!
I...BUT, NAY... I CANNOT TARRY IN EDO...
...I CANNOT STAY!
I MUST HASTEN BACK TO KEIKO-IN AND TAKE UP MY DUTIES AS THE NEW ABBOT. EACH DAY AWAY FROM THE MONASTERY KEEPS ME AWAY FROM MY OFFICE.

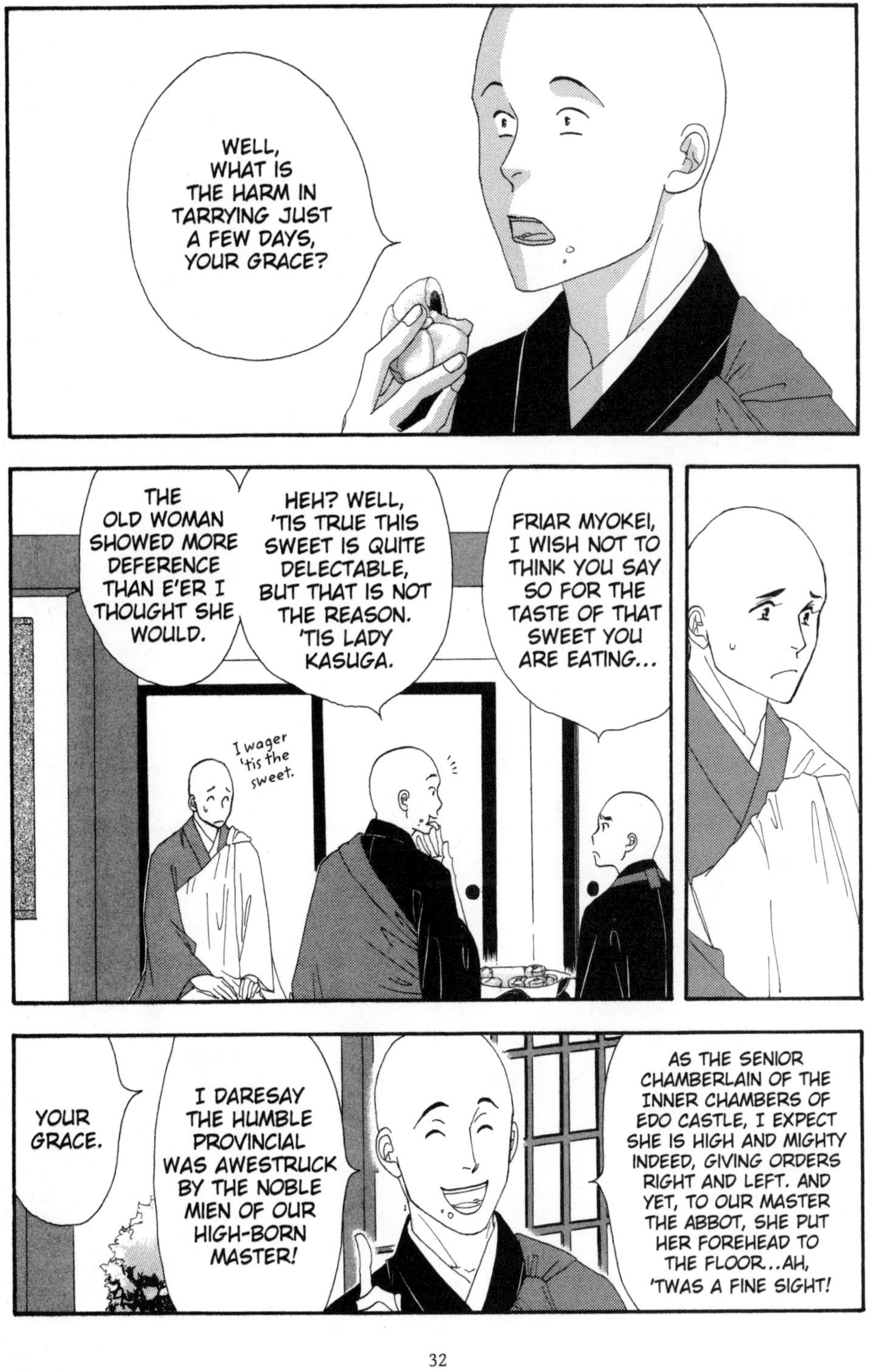
WELL, WHAT IS THE HARM IN TARRYING JUST A FEW DAYS, YOUR GRACE?
FRIAR MYOKEI, I WISH NOT TO THINK YOU SAY SO FOR THE TASTE OF THAT SWEET YOU ARE EATING...
HEH? WELL, 'TIS TRUE THIS SWEET IS QUITE DELECTABLE, BUT THAT IS NOT THE REASON. 'TIS LADY KASUGA.
THE OLD WOMAN SHOWED MORE DEFERENCE THAN E'ER I THOUGHT SHE WOULD.
I wager 'tis the sweet.
AS THE SENIOR CHAMBERLAIN OF THE INNER CHAMBERS OF EDO CASTLE, I EXPECT SHE IS HIGH AND MIGHTY INDEED, GIVING ORDERS RIGHT AND LEFT. AND YET, TO OUR MASTER THE ABBOT, SHE PUT HER FOREHEAD TO THE FLOOR...AH, 'TWAS A FINE SIGHT!
I DARESAY THE HUMBLE PROVINCIAL WAS AWESTRUCK BY THE NOBLE MIEN OF OUR HIGH-BORN MASTER!
YOUR GRACE.

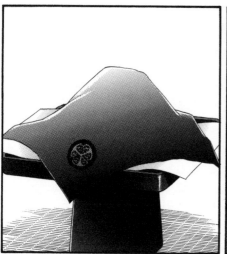

A MESSENGER IS JUST NOW COME FROM THE REVEREND KASUGA... SAYING HIS HIGHNESS DOTH DESIRE THAT YOU ACCEPT THIS.

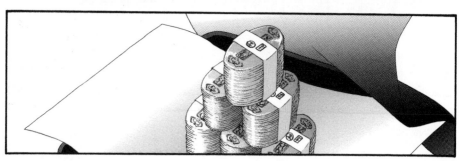

33

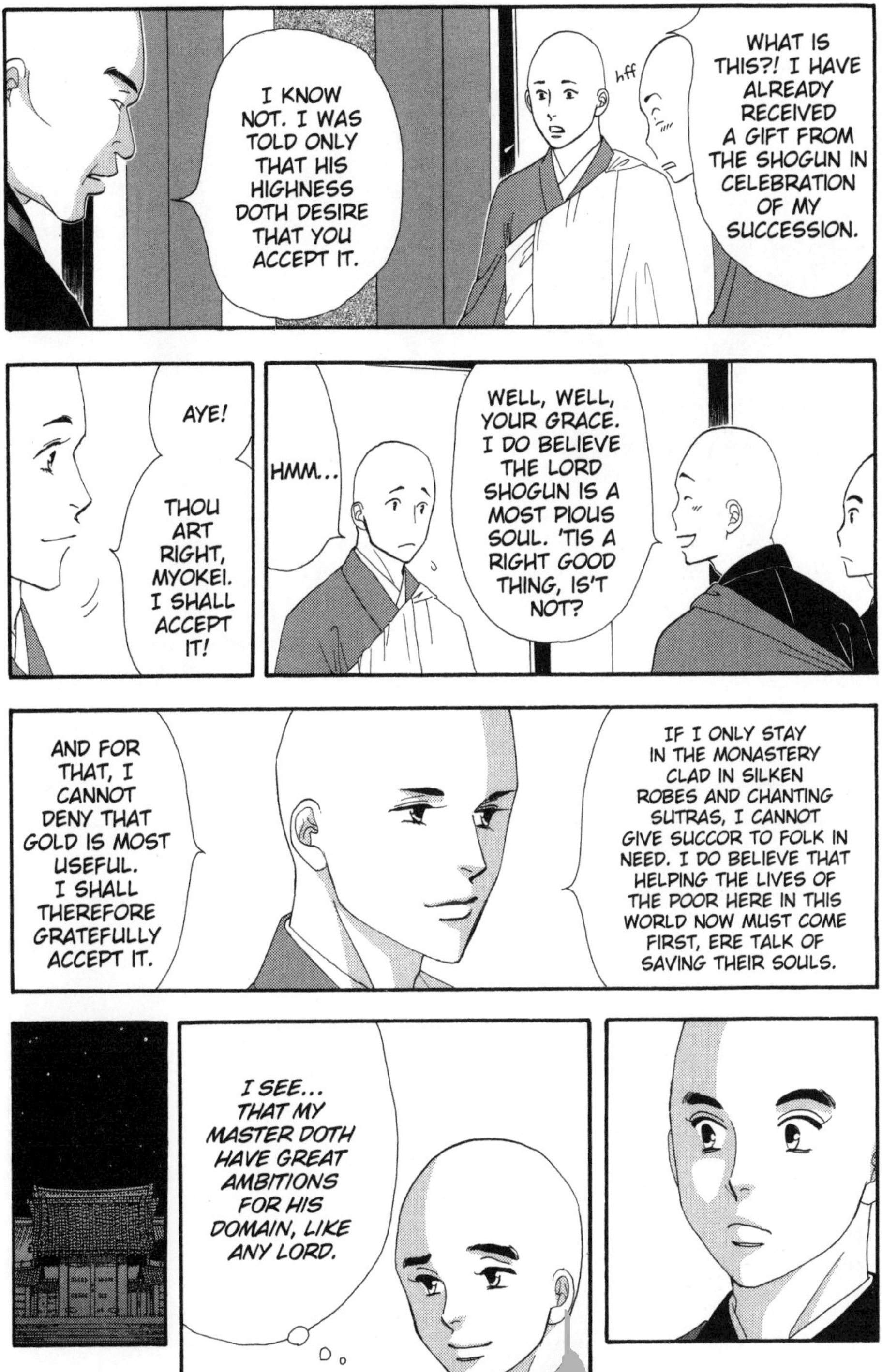
WHAT IS THIS?! I HAVE ALREADY RECEIVED A GIFT FROM THE SHOGUN IN CELEBRATION OF MY SUCCESSION.
hff
I KNOW NOT. I WAS TOLD ONLY THAT HIS HIGHNESS DOTH DESIRE THAT YOU ACCEPT IT.
WELL, WELL, YOUR GRACE. I DO BELIEVE THE LORD SHOGUN IS A MOST PIOUS SOUL. 'TIS A RIGHT GOOD THING, IS'T NOT?
HMM...
AYE!
THOU ART RIGHT, MYOKEI. I SHALL ACCEPT IT!
IF I ONLY STAY IN THE MONASTERY CLAD IN SILKEN ROBES AND CHANTING SUTRAS, I CANNOT GIVE SUCCOR TO FOLK IN NEED. I DO BELIEVE THAT HELPING THE LIVES OF THE POOR HERE IN THIS WORLD NOW MUST COME FIRST, ERE TALK OF SAVING THEIR SOULS.
AND FOR THAT, I CANNOT DENY THAT GOLD IS MOST USEFUL. I SHALL THEREFORE GRATEFULLY ACCEPT IT.
I SEE... THAT MY MASTER DOTH HAVE GREAT AMBITIONS FOR HIS DOMAIN, LIKE ANY LORD.

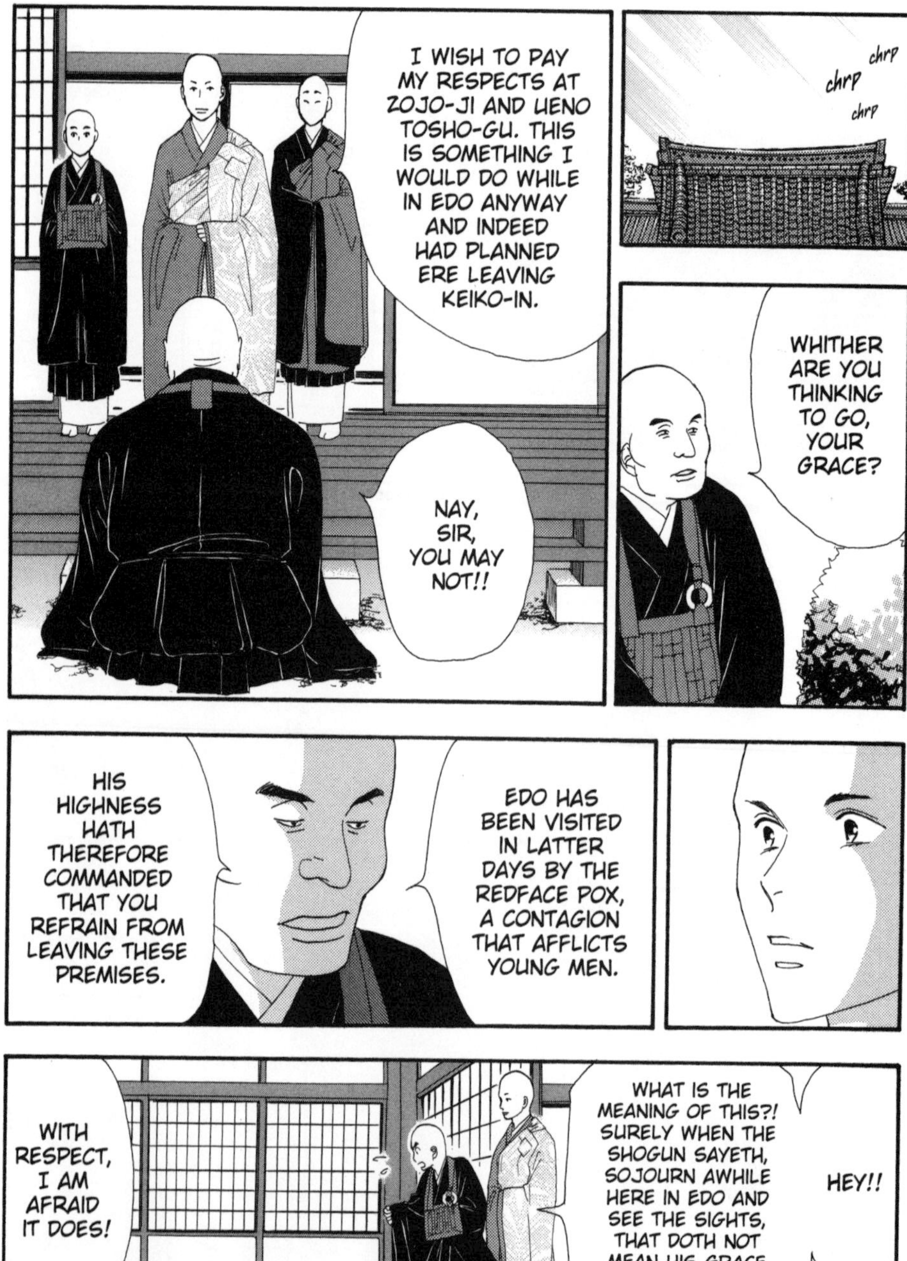
chrp
chrp
chrp
WHITHER ARE YOU THINKING TO GO, YOUR GRACE?
I WISH TO PAY MY RESPECTS AT ZOJO-JI AND UENO TOSHO-GU. THIS IS SOMETHING I WOULD DO WHILE IN EDO ANYWAY AND INDEED HAD PLANNED ERE LEAVING KEIKO-IN.
NAY, SIR, YOU MAY NOT!!
EDO HAS BEEN VISITED IN LATTER DAYS BY THE REDFACE POX, A CONTAGION THAT AFFLICTS YOUNG MEN.
HIS HIGHNESS HATH THEREFORE COMMANDED THAT YOU REFRAIN FROM LEAVING THESE PREMISES.
HEY!!
WHAT IS THE MEANING OF THIS?! SURELY WHEN THE SHOGUN SAYETH, SOJOURN AWHILE HERE IN EDO AND SEE THE SIGHTS, THAT DOTH NOT MEAN HIS GRACE IS TO SIT ON HIS HANDS IN THIS MANSION AND GAZE AT ITS WALLS!
WITH RESPECT, I AM AFRAID IT DOES!

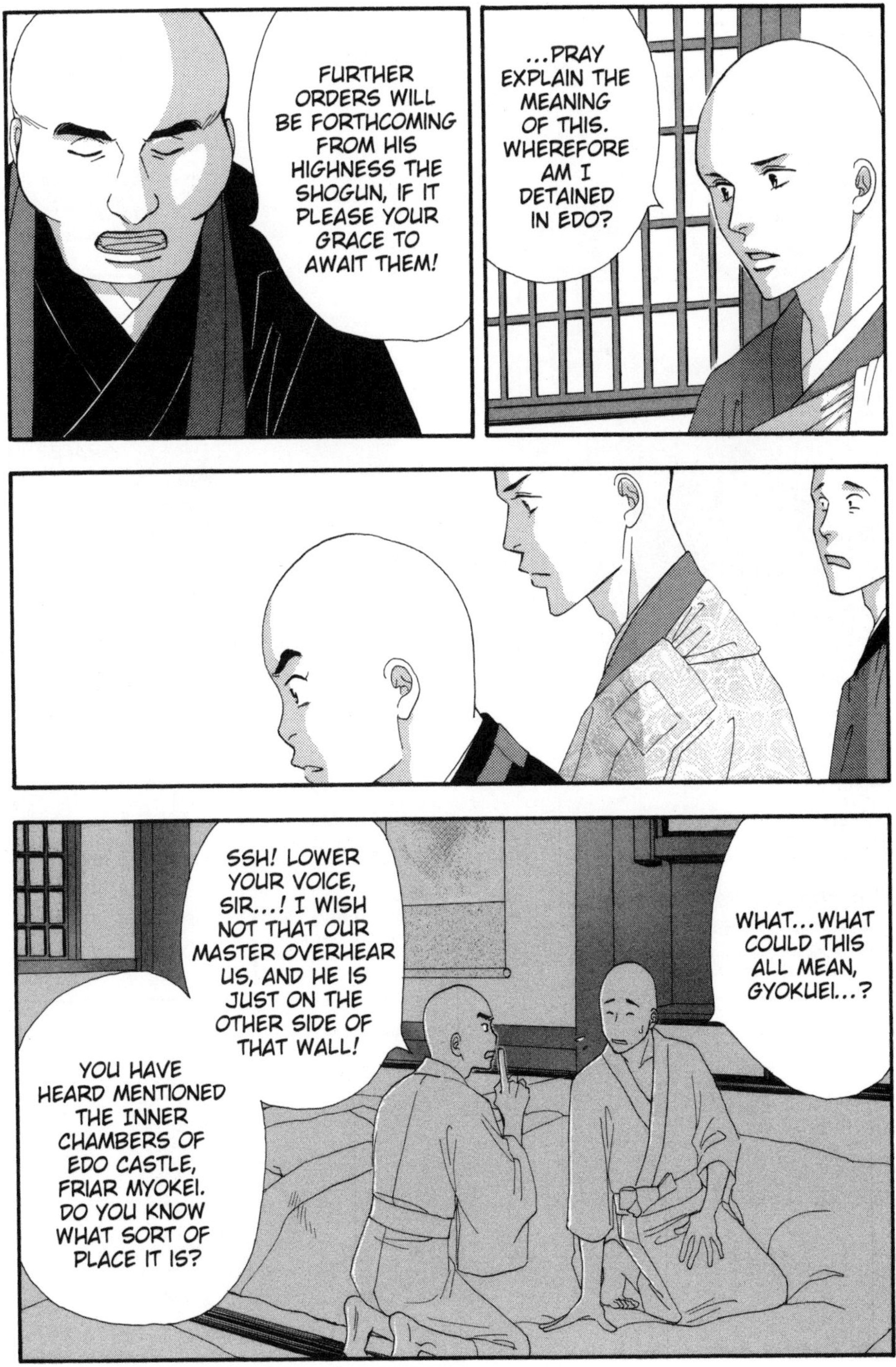
...PRAY EXPLAIN THE MEANING OF THIS. WHEREFORE AM I DETAINED IN EDO?
FURTHER ORDERS WILL BE FORTHCOMING FROM HIS HIGHNESS THE SHOGUN, IF IT PLEASE YOUR GRACE TO AWAIT THEM!
WHAT...WHAT COULD THIS ALL MEAN, GYOKUEI...?
SSH! LOWER YOUR VOICE, SIR...! I WISH NOT THAT OUR MASTER OVERHEAR US, AND HE IS JUST ON THE OTHER SIDE OF THAT WALL!
YOU HAVE HEARD MENTIONED THE INNER CHAMBERS OF EDO CASTLE, FRIAR MYOKEI. DO YOU KNOW WHAT SORT OF PLACE IT IS?

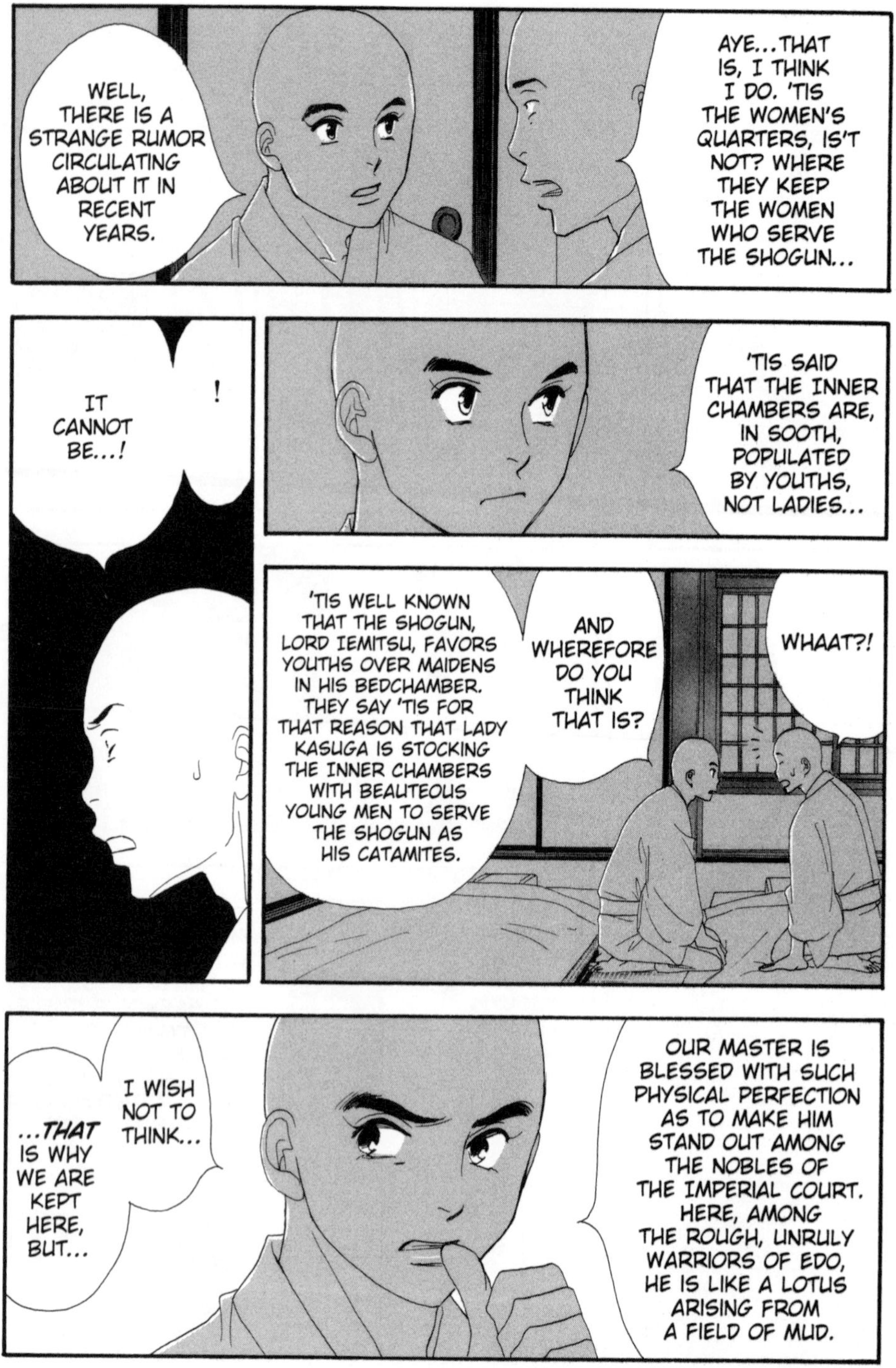
AYE...THAT IS, I THINK I DO. 'TIS THE WOMEN'S QUARTERS, IS'T NOT? WHERE THEY KEEP THE WOMEN WHO SERVE THE SHOGUN...
WELL, THERE IS A STRANGE RUMOR CIRCULATING ABOUT IT IN RECENT YEARS.
'TIS SAID THAT THE INNER CHAMBERS ARE, IN SOOTH, POPULATED BY YOUTHS, NOT LADIES...
WHAAT?!
AND WHEREFORE DO YOU THINK THAT IS?
'TIS WELL KNOWN THAT THE SHOGUN, LORD IEMITSU, FAVORS YOUTHS OVER MAIDENS IN HIS BEDCHAMBER. THEY SAY 'TIS FOR THAT REASON THAT LADY KASUGA IS STOCKING THE INNER CHAMBERS WITH BEAUTEOUS YOUNG MEN TO SERVE THE SHOGUN AS HIS CATAMITES.
!
IT CANNOT BE...!
OUR MASTER IS BLESSED WITH SUCH PHYSICAL PERFECTION AS TO MAKE HIM STAND OUT AMONG THE NOBLES OF THE IMPERIAL COURT. HERE, AMONG THE ROUGH, UNRULY WARRIORS OF EDO, HE IS LIKE A LOTUS ARISING FROM A FIELD OF MUD.
I WISH NOT TO THINK...
...THAT IS WHY WE ARE KEPT HERE, BUT...

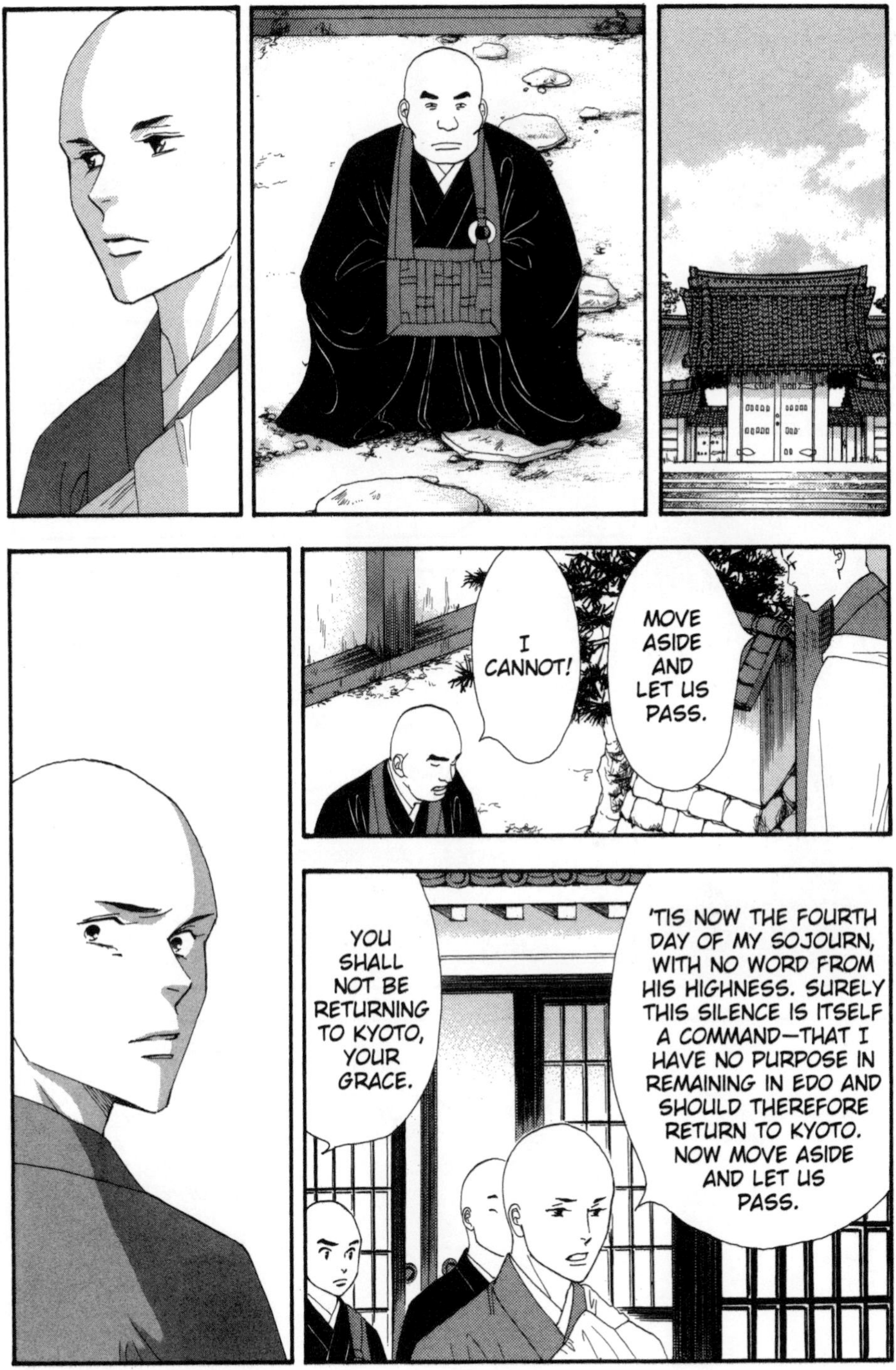
MOVE ASIDE AND LET US PASS.
I CANNOT!
'TIS NOW THE FOURTH DAY OF MY SOJOURN, WITH NO WORD FROM HIS HIGHNESS. SURELY THIS SILENCE IS ITSELF A COMMAND—THAT I HAVE NO PURPOSE IN REMAINING IN EDO AND SHOULD THEREFORE RETURN TO KYOTO. NOW MOVE ASIDE AND LET US PASS.
YOU SHALL NOT BE RETURNING TO KYOTO, YOUR GRACE.

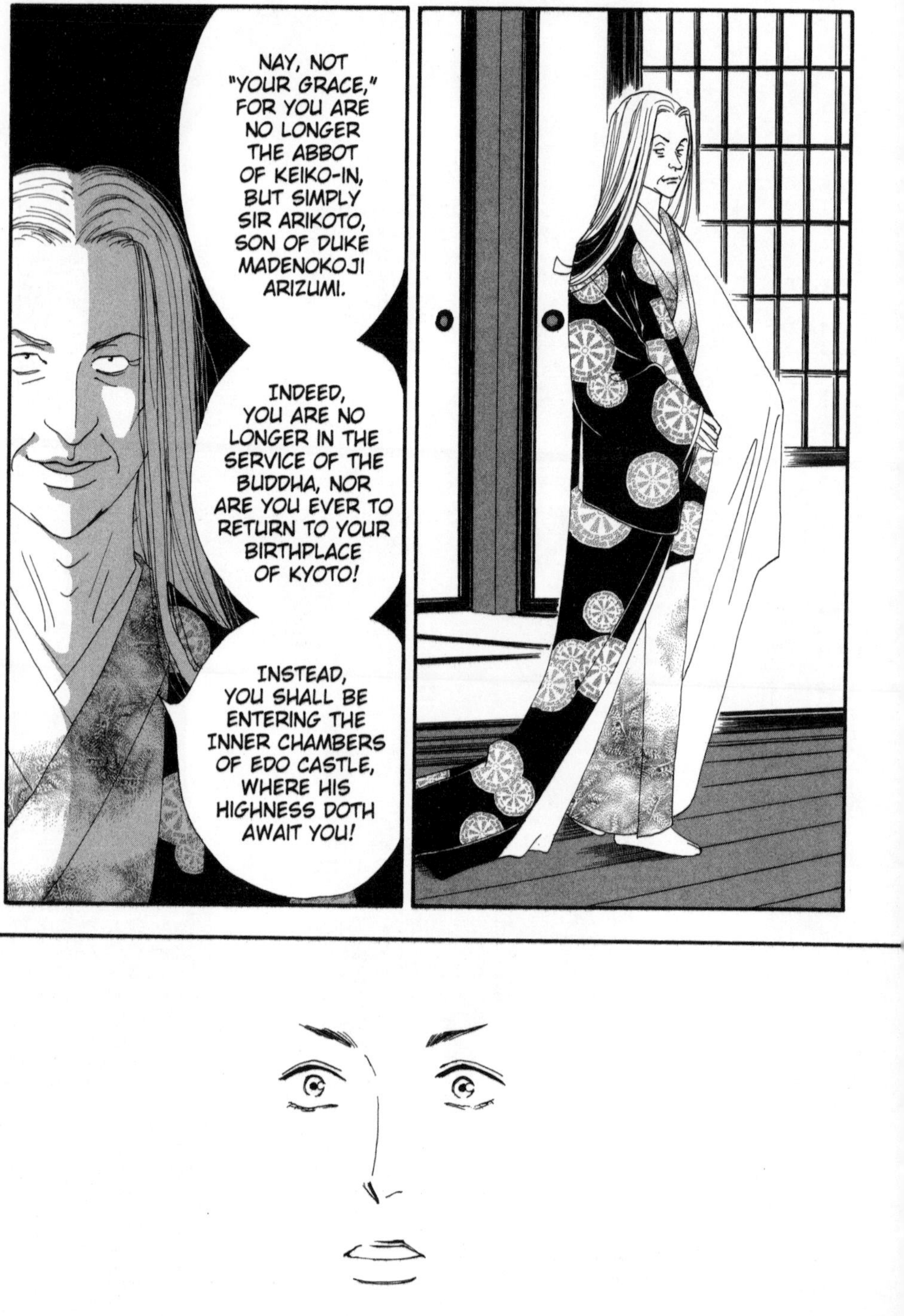
NAY, NOT "YOUR GRACE," FOR YOU ARE NO LONGER THE ABBOT OF KEIKO-IN, BUT SIMPLY SIR ARIKOTO, SON OF DUKE MADENOKOJI ARIZUMI.
INDEED, YOU ARE NO LONGER IN THE SERVICE OF THE BUDDHA, NOR ARE YOU EVER TO RETURN TO YOUR BIRTHPLACE OF KYOTO!
INSTEAD, YOU SHALL BE ENTERING THE INNER CHAMBERS OF EDO CASTLE, WHERE HIS HIGHNESS DOTH AWAIT YOU!

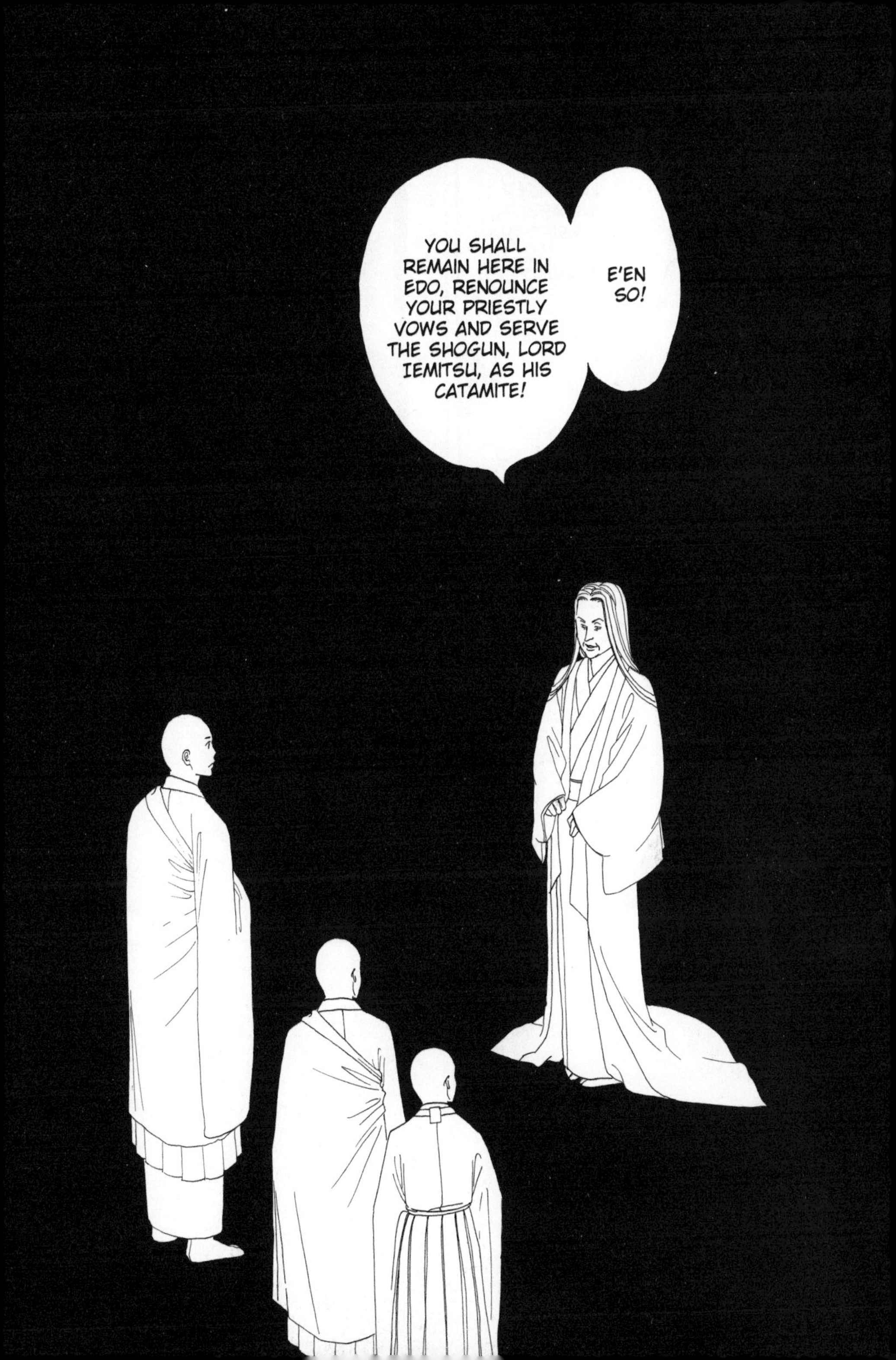
YOU SHALL REMAIN HERE IN EDO, RENOUNCE YOUR PRIESTLY VOWS AND SERVE THE SHOGUN, LORD IEMITSU, AS HIS CATAMITE!
E'EN SO!

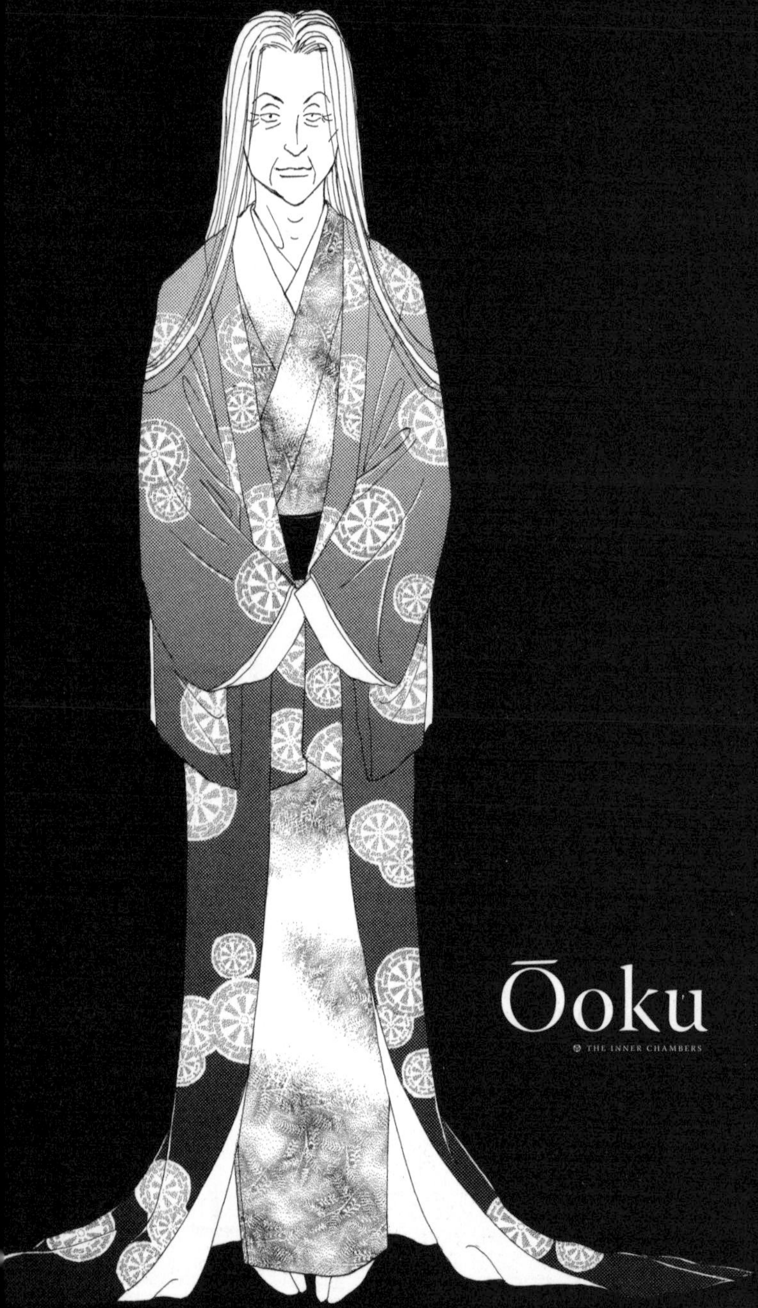

Ōoku

THE INNER CHAMBERS

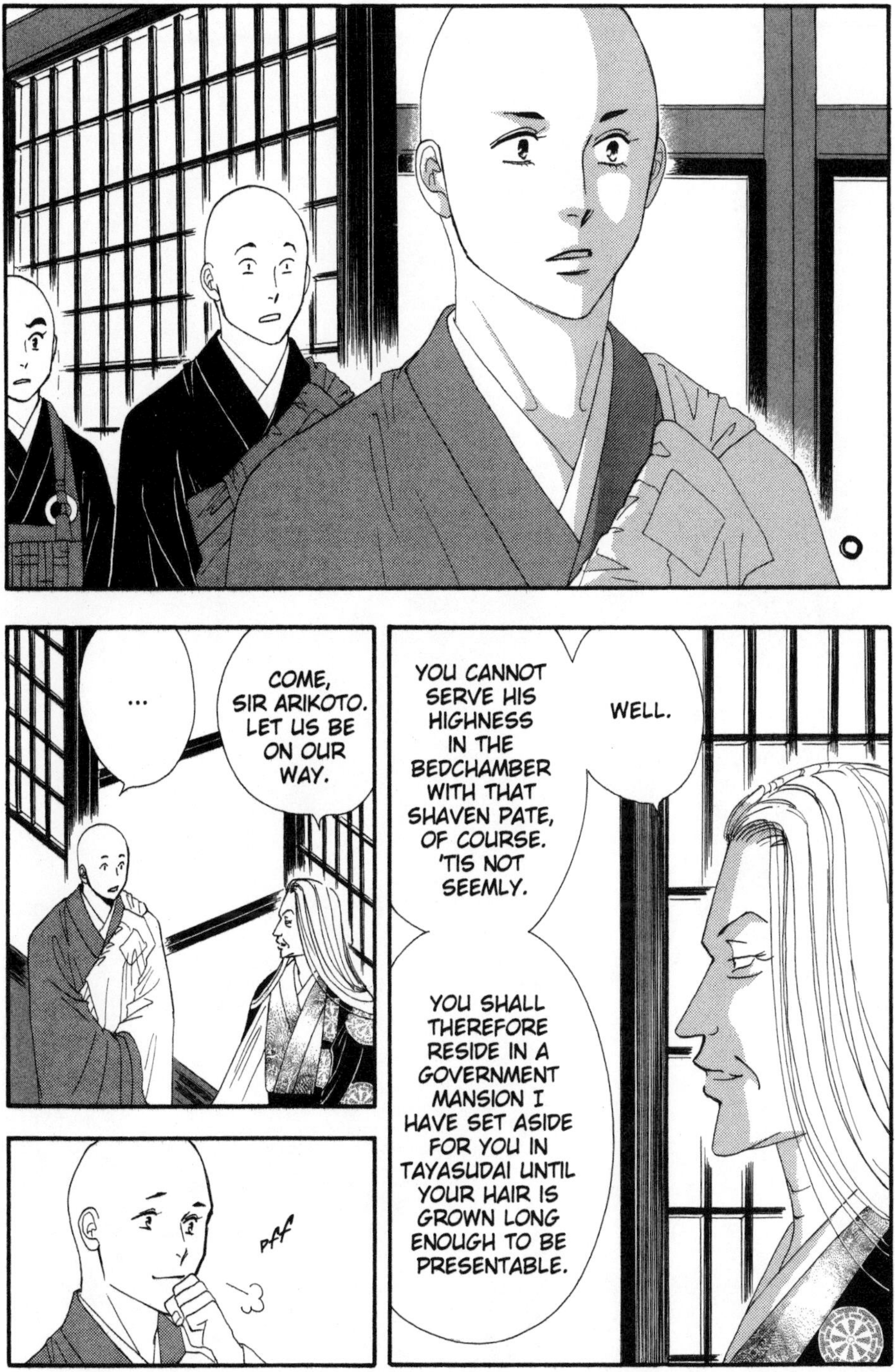
WELL.
YOU CANNOT SERVE HIS HIGHNESS IN THE BEDCHAMBER WITH THAT SHAVEN PATE, OF COURSE. 'TIS NOT SEEMLY.
YOU SHALL THEREFORE RESIDE IN A GOVERNMENT MANSION I HAVE SET ASIDE FOR YOU IN TAYASUDAI UNTIL YOUR HAIR IS GROWN LONG ENOUGH TO BE PRESENTABLE.
COME, SIR ARIKOTO. LET US BE ON OUR WAY.
...
pff

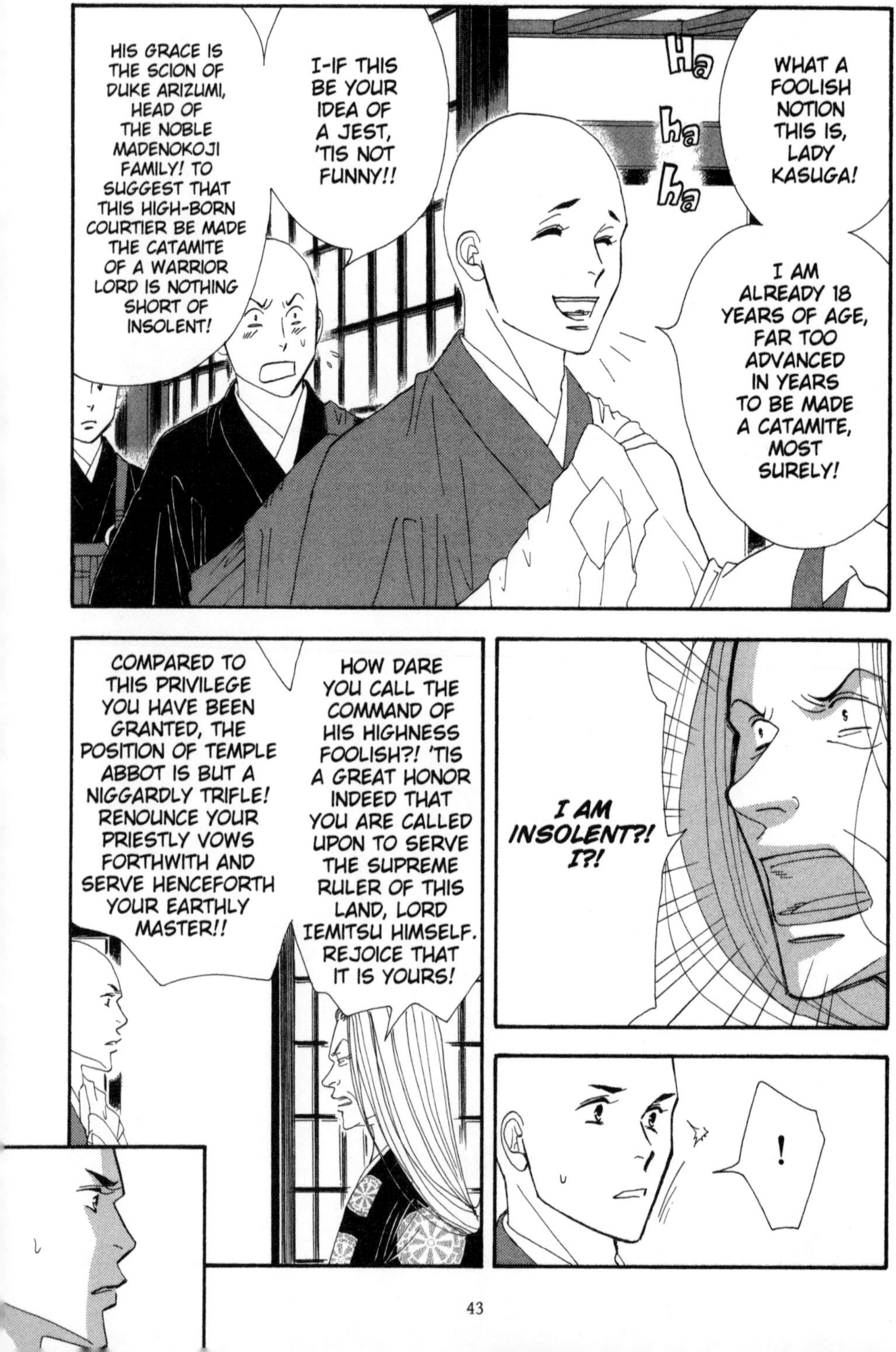
WHAT A FOOLISH NOTION THIS IS, LADY KASUGA!
Ha ha ha
I AM ALREADY 18 YEARS OF AGE, FAR TOO ADVANCED IN YEARS TO BE MADE A CATAMITE, MOST SURELY!
I-IF THIS BE YOUR IDEA OF A JEST, 'TIS NOT FUNNY!!
HIS GRACE IS THE SCION OF DUKE ARIZUMI, HEAD OF THE NOBLE MADENOKOJI FAMILY! TO SUGGEST THAT THIS HIGH-BORN COURTIER BE MADE THE CATAMITE OF A WARRIOR LORD IS NOTHING SHORT OF INSOLENT!
I AM INSOLENT?! I?!
!
HOW DARE YOU CALL THE COMMAND OF HIS HIGHNESS FOOLISH?! 'TIS A GREAT HONOR INDEED THAT YOU ARE CALLED UPON TO SERVE THE SUPREME RULER OF THIS LAND, LORD IEMITSU HIMSELF. REJOICE THAT IT IS YOURS!
COMPARED TO THIS PRIVILEGE YOU HAVE BEEN GRANTED, THE POSITION OF TEMPLE ABBOT IS BUT A NIGGARDLY TRIFLE! RENOUNCE YOUR PRIESTLY VOWS FORTHWITH AND SERVE HENCEFORTH YOUR EARTHLY MASTER!!

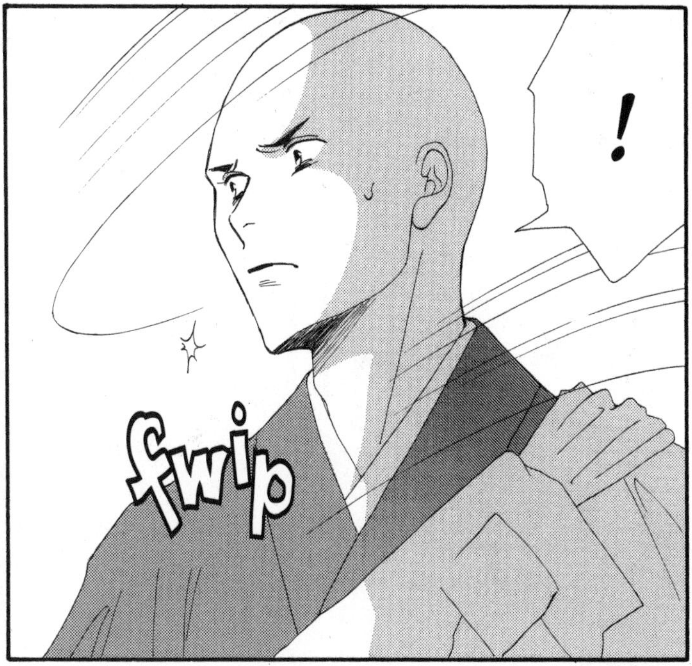
!
fwip
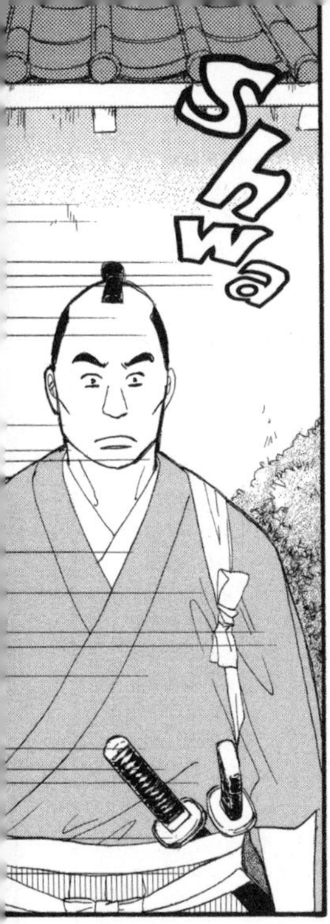
shwa
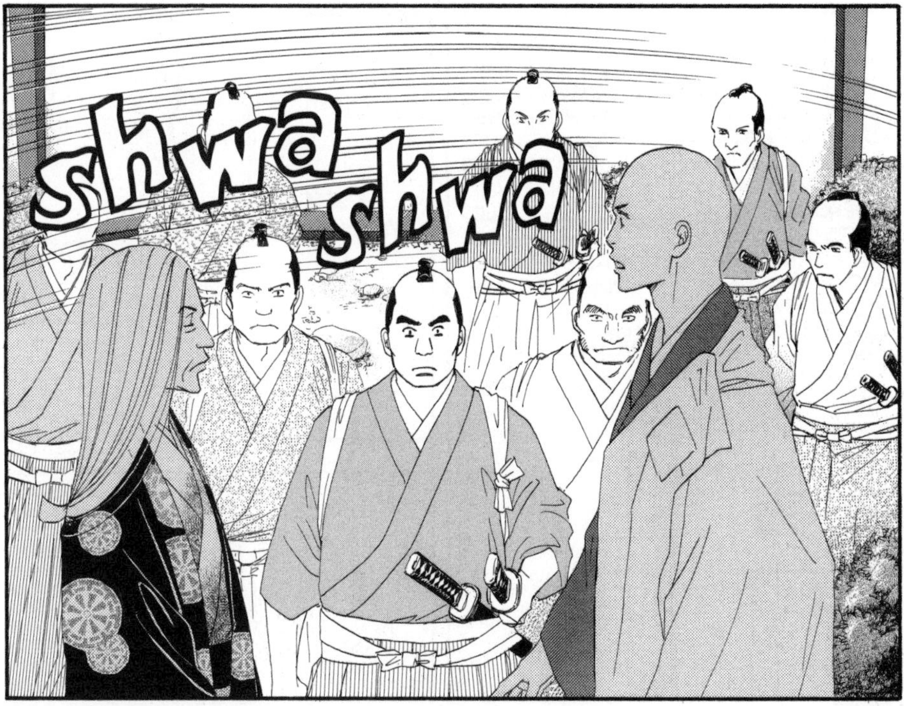
shwa
shwa

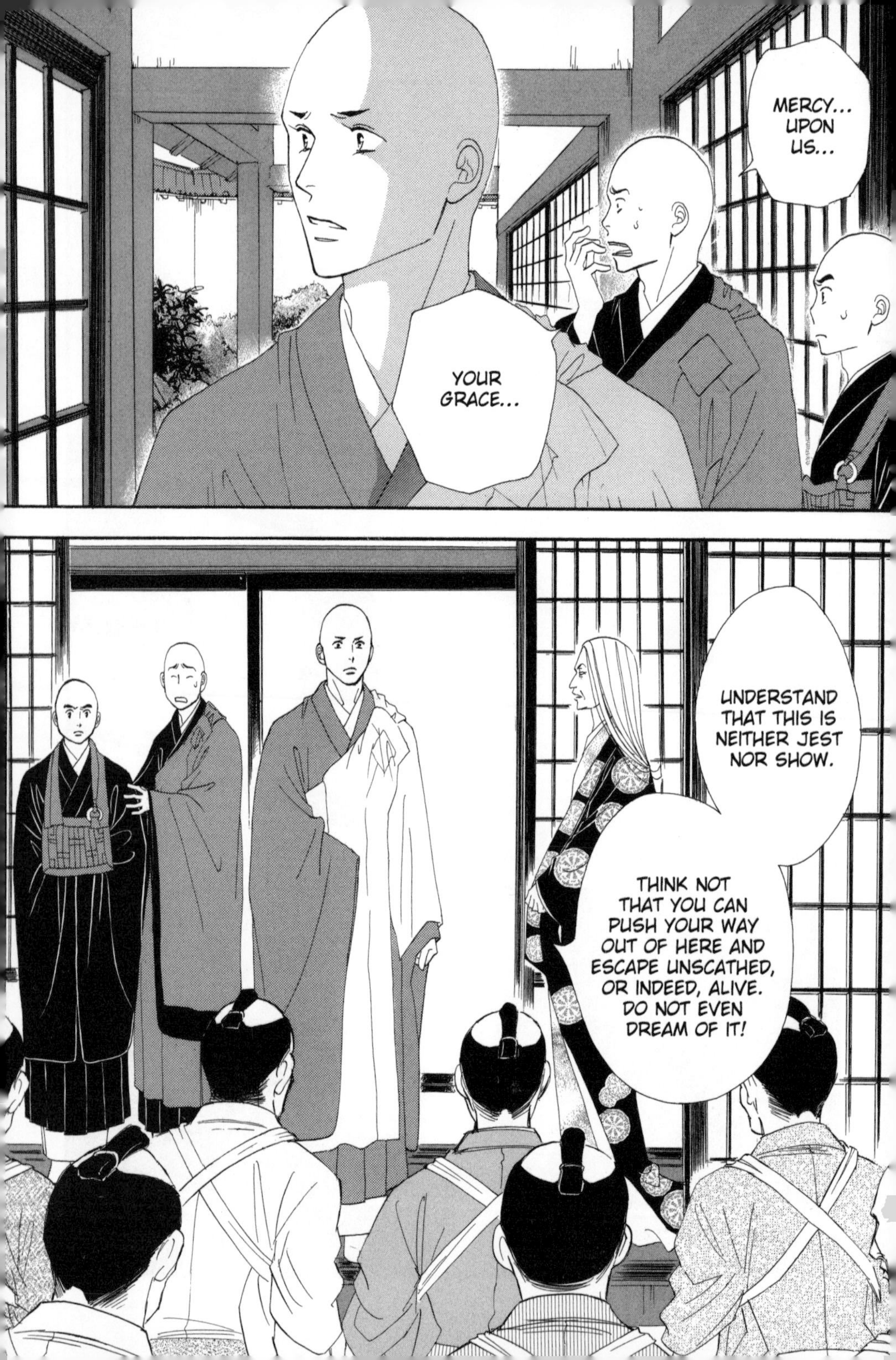
MERCY... UPON US...
YOUR GRACE...
UNDERSTAND THAT THIS IS NEITHER JEST NOR SHOW.
THINK NOT THAT YOU CAN PUSH YOUR WAY OUT OF HERE AND ESCAPE UNSCATHED, OR INDEED, ALIVE. DO NOT EVEN DREAM OF IT!

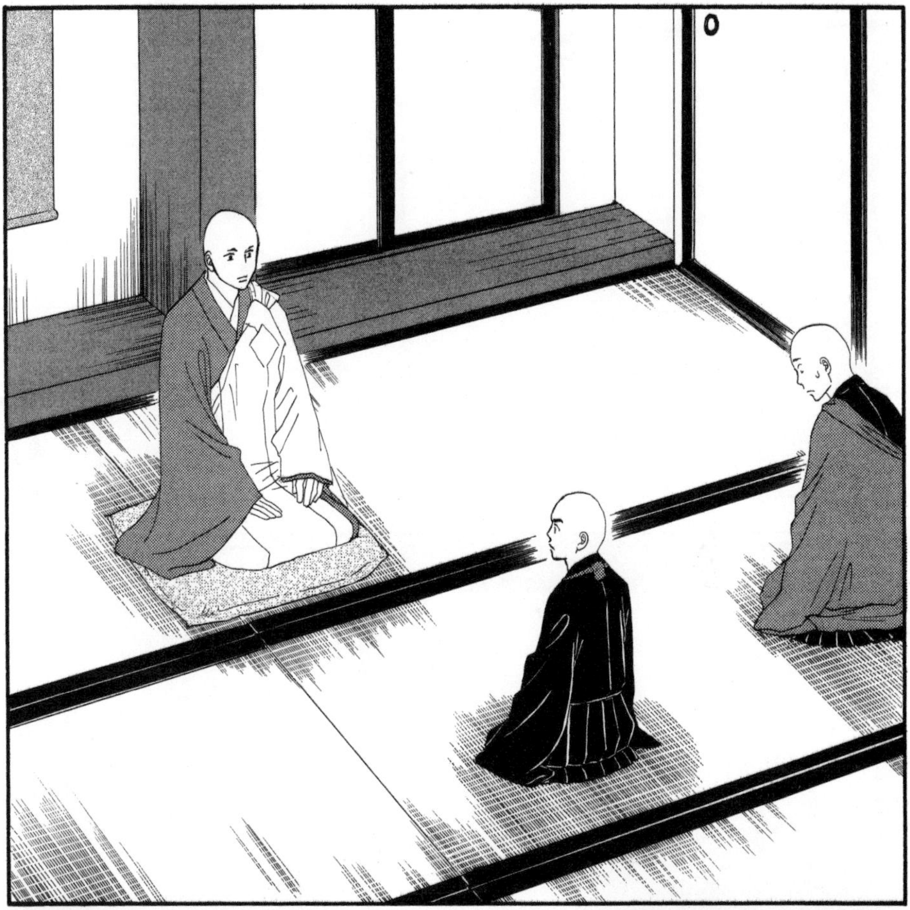
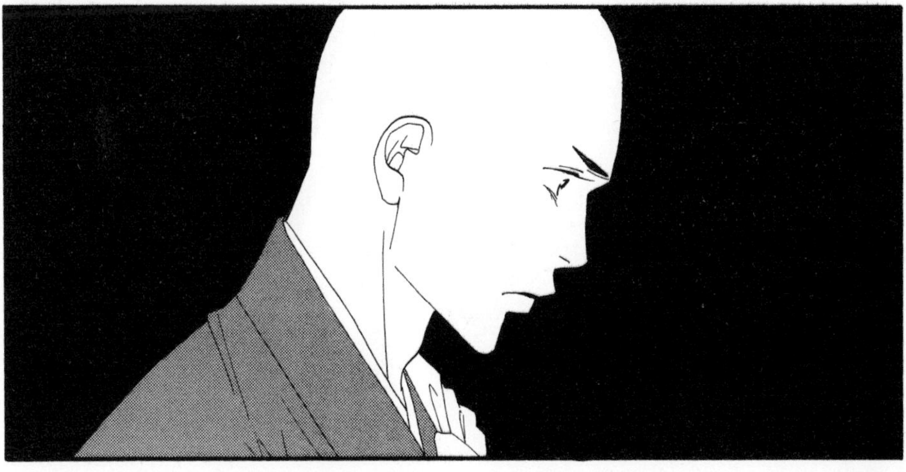

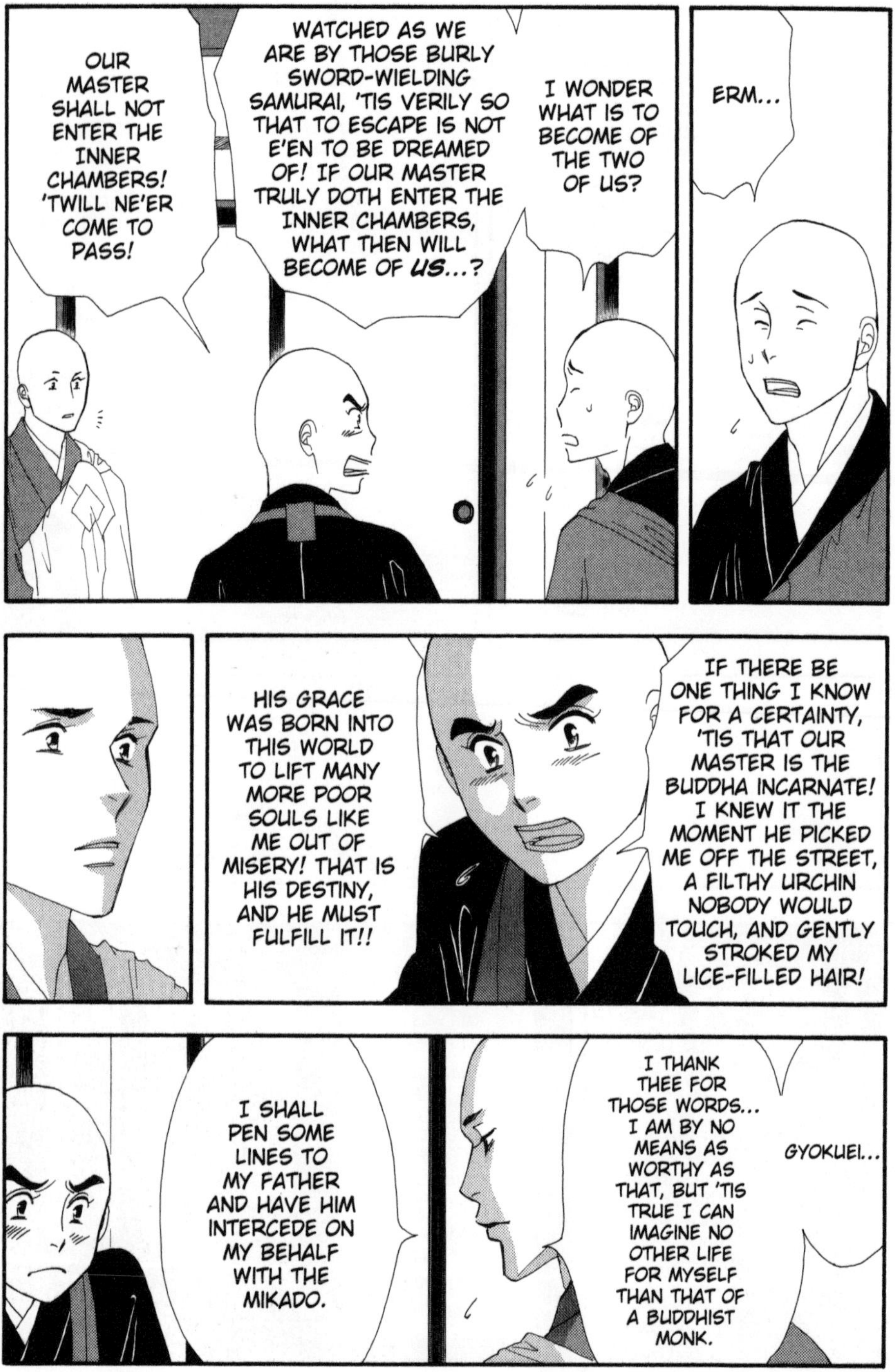
ERM...
I WONDER WHAT IS TO BECOME OF THE TWO OF US?
WATCHED AS WE ARE BY THOSE BURLY SWORD-WIELDING SAMURAI, 'TIS VERILY SO THAT TO ESCAPE IS NOT E'EN TO BE DREAMED OF! IF OUR MASTER TRULY DOTH ENTER THE INNER CHAMBERS, WHAT THEN WILL BECOME OF *US*...?
OUR MASTER SHALL NOT ENTER THE INNER CHAMBERS! 'TWILL NE'ER COME TO PASS!
IF THERE BE ONE THING I KNOW FOR A CERTAINTY, 'TIS THAT OUR MASTER IS THE BUDDHA INCARNATE! I KNEW IT THE MOMENT HE PICKED ME OFF THE STREET, A FILTHY URCHIN NOBODY WOULD TOUCH, AND GENTLY STROKED MY LICE-FILLED HAIR!
HIS GRACE WAS BORN INTO THIS WORLD TO LIFT MANY MORE POOR SOULS LIKE ME OUT OF MISERY! THAT IS HIS DESTINY, AND HE MUST FULFILL IT!!
GYOKUEI...
I THANK THEE FOR THOSE WORDS... I AM BY NO MEANS AS WORTHY AS THAT, BUT 'TIS TRUE I CAN IMAGINE NO OTHER LIFE FOR MYSELF THAN THAT OF A BUDDHIST MONK.
I SHALL PEN SOME LINES TO MY FATHER AND HAVE HIM INTERCEDE ON MY BEHALF WITH THE MIKADO.

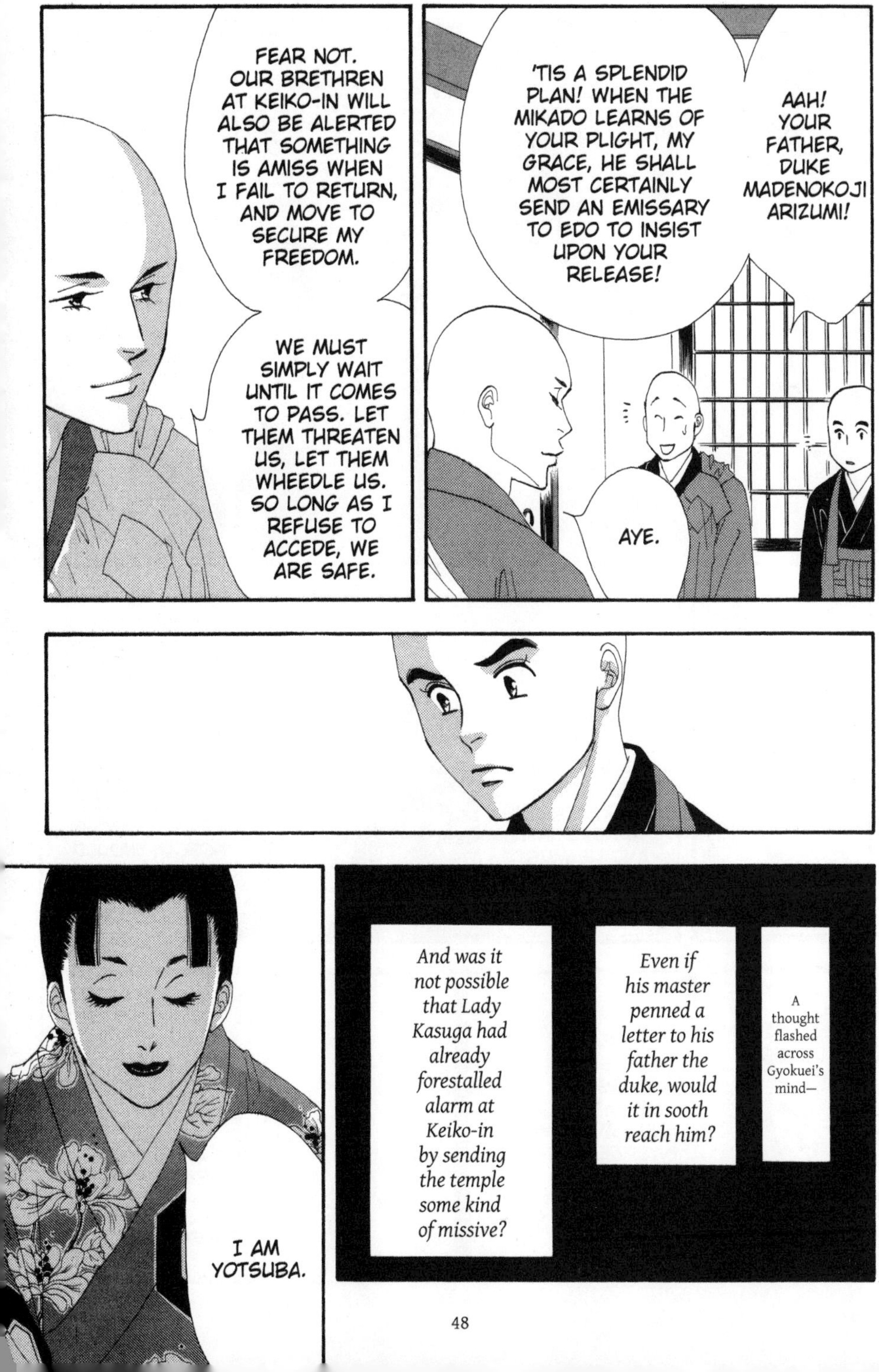
AAH! YOUR FATHER, DUKE MADENOKOJI ARIZUMI!
'TIS A SPLENDID PLAN! WHEN THE MIKADO LEARNS OF YOUR PLIGHT, MY GRACE, HE SHALL MOST CERTAINLY SEND AN EMISSARY TO EDO TO INSIST UPON YOUR RELEASE!
AYE.
FEAR NOT. OUR BRETHREN AT KEIKO-IN WILL ALSO BE ALERTED THAT SOMETHING IS AMISS WHEN I FAIL TO RETURN, AND MOVE TO SECURE MY FREEDOM.
WE MUST SIMPLY WAIT UNTIL IT COMES TO PASS. LET THEM THREATEN US, LET THEM WHEEDLE US. SO LONG AS I REFUSE TO ACCEDE, WE ARE SAFE.
A thought flashed across Gyokuei's mind—
Even if his master penned a letter to his father the duke, would it in sooth reach him?
And was it not possible that Lady Kasuga had already forestalled alarm at Keiko-in by sending the temple some kind of missive?
I AM YOTSUBA.

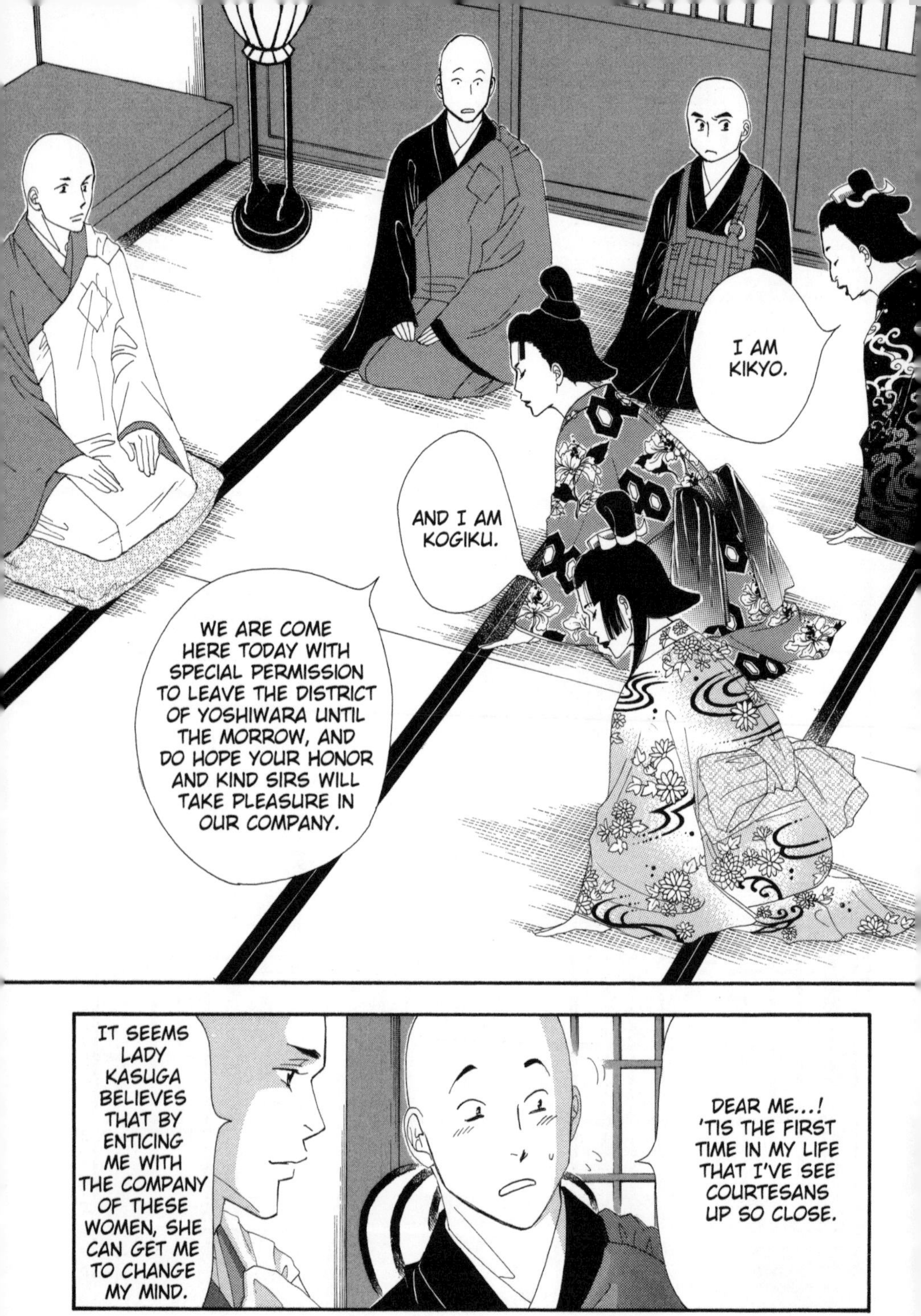
I AM KIKYO.
AND I AM KOGIKU.
WE ARE COME HERE TODAY WITH SPECIAL PERMISSION TO LEAVE THE DISTRICT OF YOSHIWARA UNTIL THE MORROW, AND DO HOPE YOUR HONOR AND KIND SIRS WILL TAKE PLEASURE IN OUR COMPANY.
DEAR ME...! 'TIS THE FIRST TIME IN MY LIFE THAT I'VE SEE COURTESANS UP SO CLOSE.
IT SEEMS LADY KASUGA BELIEVES THAT BY ENTICING ME WITH THE COMPANY OF THESE WOMEN, SHE CAN GET ME TO CHANGE MY MIND.

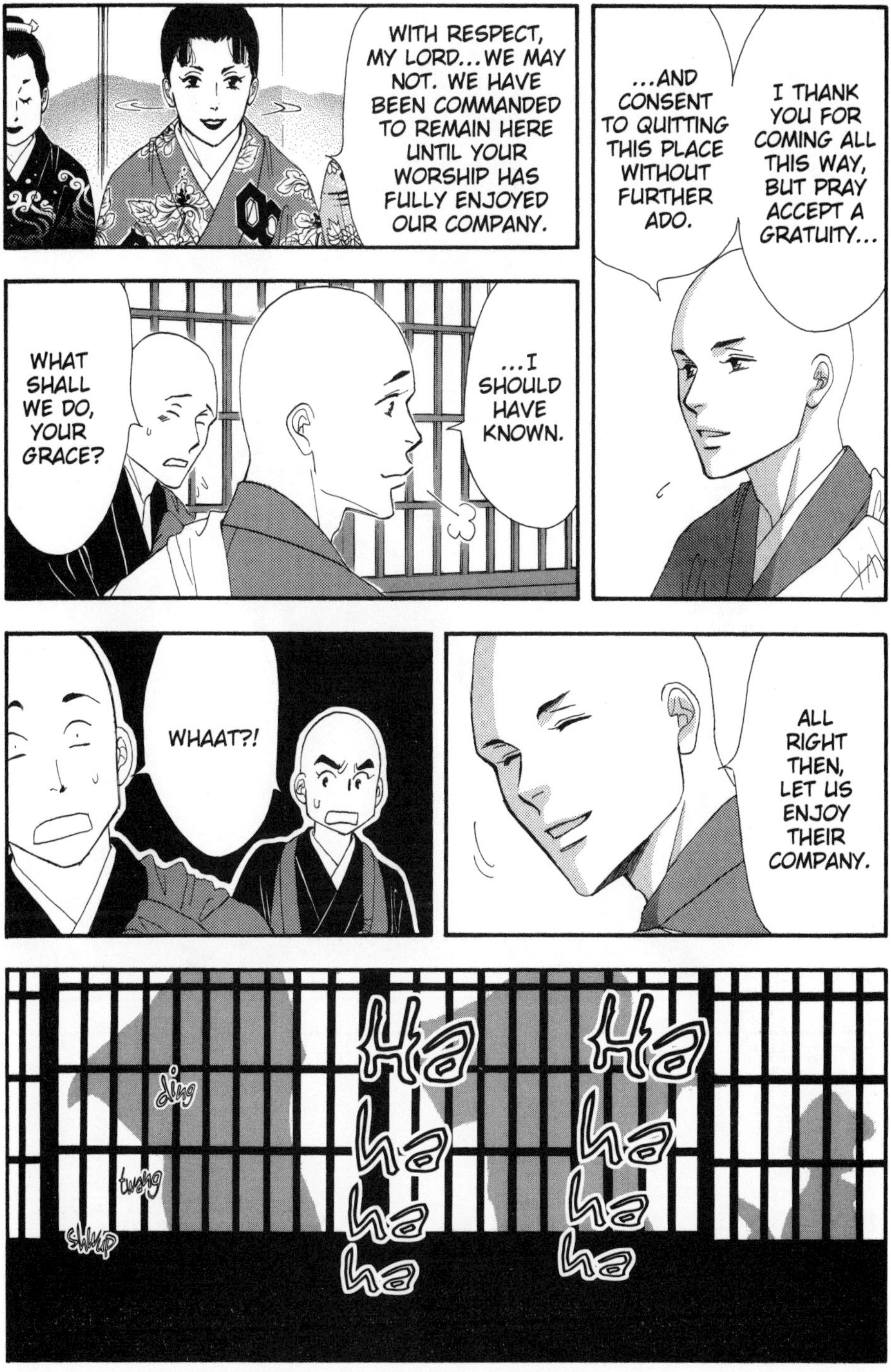
I THANK YOU FOR COMING ALL THIS WAY, BUT PRAY ACCEPT A GRATUITY...
...AND CONSENT TO QUITTING THIS PLACE WITHOUT FURTHER ADO.
WITH RESPECT, MY LORD...WE MAY NOT. WE HAVE BEEN COMMANDED TO REMAIN HERE UNTIL YOUR WORSHIP HAS FULLY ENJOYED OUR COMPANY.
...I SHOULD HAVE KNOWN.
WHAT SHALL WE DO, YOUR GRACE?
ALL RIGHT THEN, LET US ENJOY THEIR COMPANY.
WHAAT?!
Ha ha ha ha
Ha ha ha ha
ding
twang
shwup

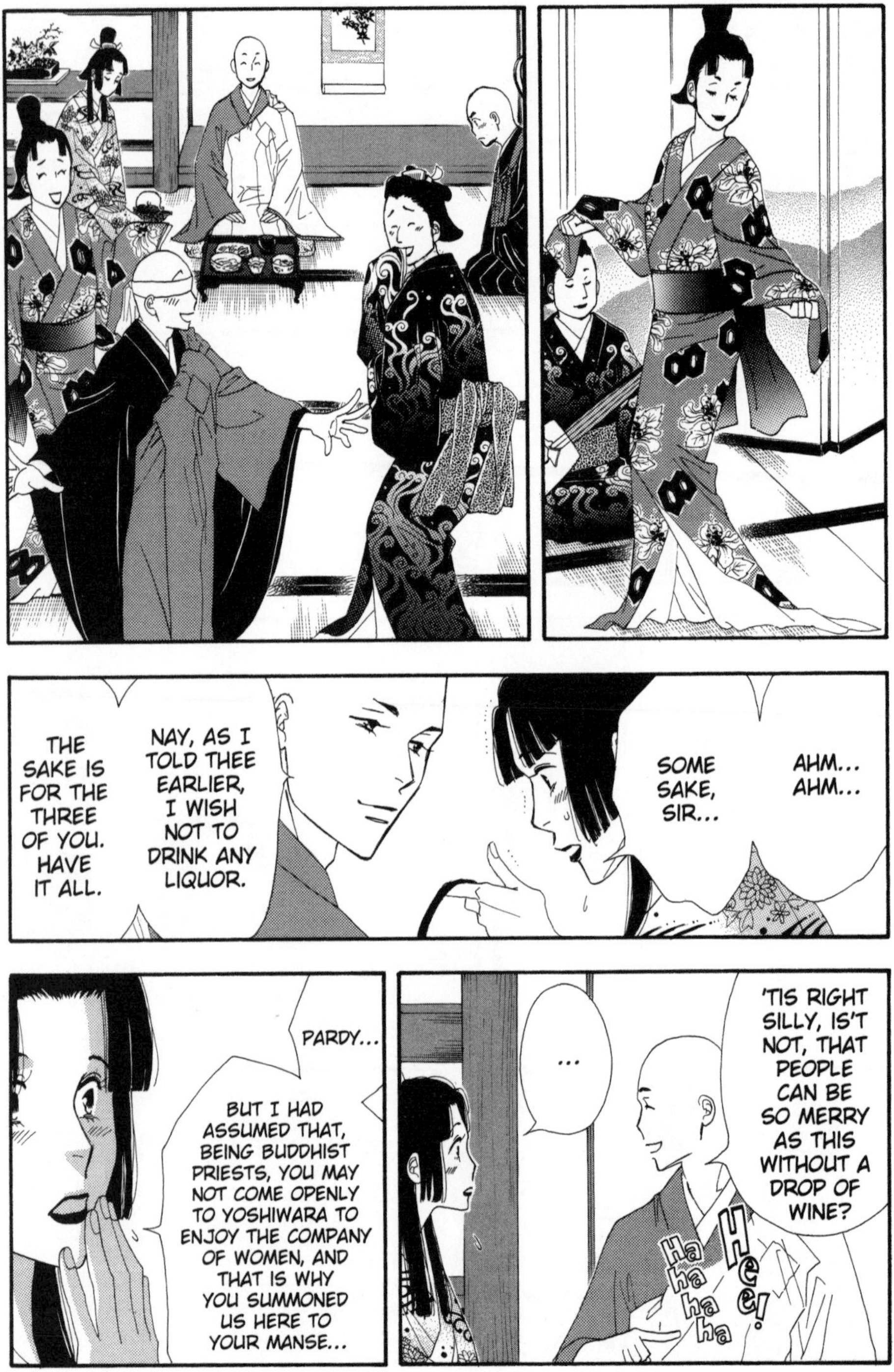
AHM... AHM...
SOME SAKE, SIR...
NAY, AS I TOLD THEE EARLIER, I WISH NOT TO DRINK ANY LIQUOR.
THE SAKE IS FOR THE THREE OF YOU. HAVE IT ALL.
'TIS RIGHT SILLY, IS'T NOT, THAT PEOPLE CAN BE SO MERRY AS THIS WITHOUT A DROP OF WINE?
He he!
Ha ha ha ha ha ha
...
PARDY...
BUT I HAD ASSUMED THAT, BEING BUDDHIST PRIESTS, YOU MAY NOT COME OPENLY TO YOSHIWARA TO ENJOY THE COMPANY OF WOMEN, AND THAT IS WHY YOU SUMMONED US HERE TO YOUR MANSE...

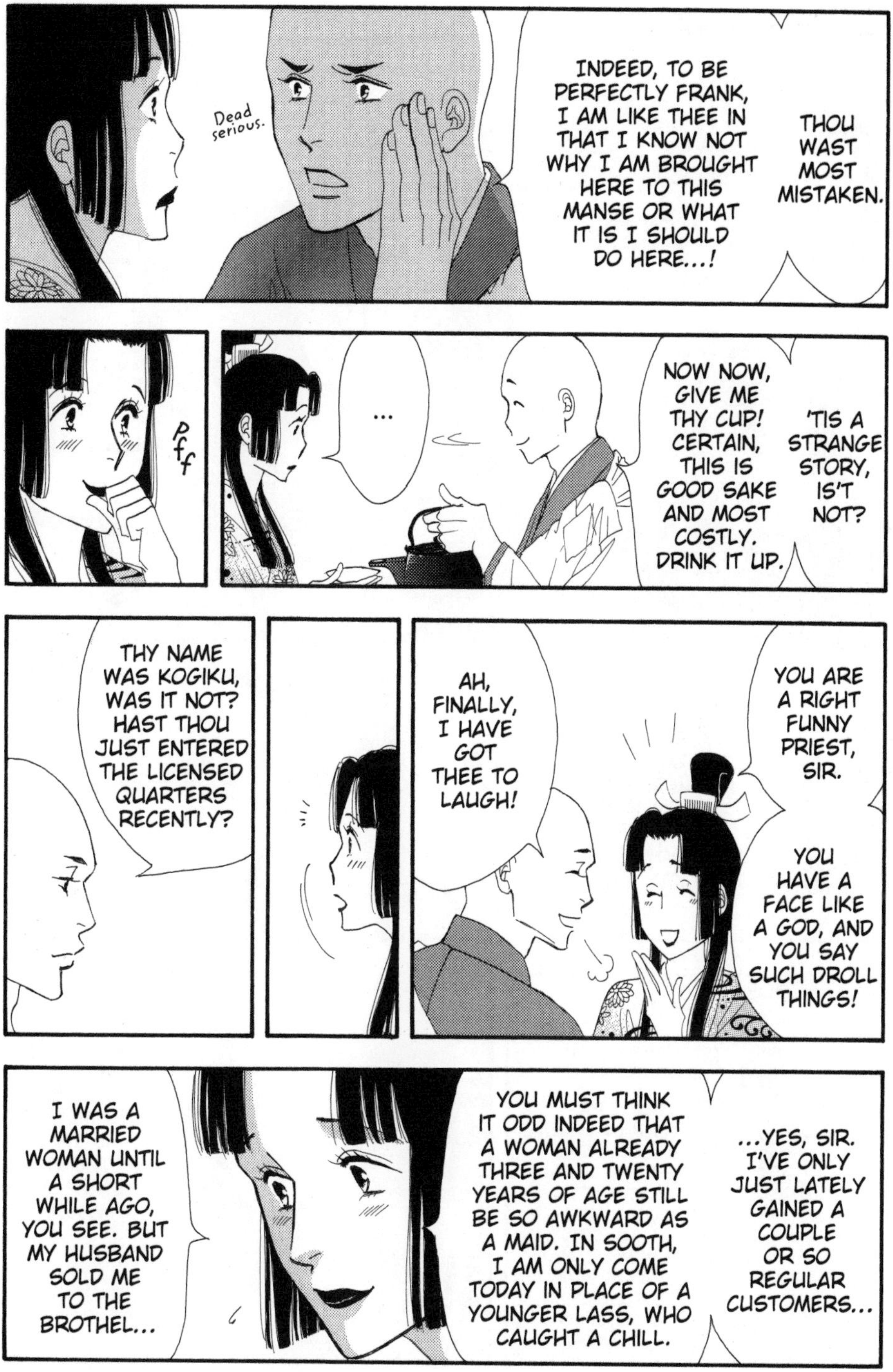
THOU WAST MOST MISTAKEN.
INDEED, TO BE PERFECTLY FRANK, I AM LIKE THEE IN THAT I KNOW NOT WHY I AM BROUGHT HERE TO THIS MANSE OR WHAT IT IS I SHOULD DO HERE...!
Dead serious.
'TIS A STRANGE STORY, IS'T NOT?
NOW NOW, GIVE ME THY CUP! CERTAIN, THIS IS GOOD SAKE AND MOST COSTLY. DRINK IT UP.
...
Pff
YOU ARE A RIGHT FUNNY PRIEST, SIR.
YOU HAVE A FACE LIKE A GOD, AND YOU SAY SUCH DROLL THINGS!
AH, FINALLY, I HAVE GOT THEE TO LAUGH!
THY NAME WAS KOGIKU, WAS IT NOT? HAST THOU JUST ENTERED THE LICENSED QUARTERS RECENTLY?
...YES, SIR. I'VE ONLY JUST LATELY GAINED A COUPLE OR SO REGULAR CUSTOMERS...
YOU MUST THINK IT ODD INDEED THAT A WOMAN ALREADY THREE AND TWENTY YEARS OF AGE STILL BE SO AWKWARD AS A MAID. IN SOOTH, I AM ONLY COME TODAY IN PLACE OF A YOUNGER LASS, WHO CAUGHT A CHILL.
I WAS A MARRIED WOMAN UNTIL A SHORT WHILE AGO, YOU SEE. BUT MY HUSBAND SOLD ME TO THE BROTHEL...

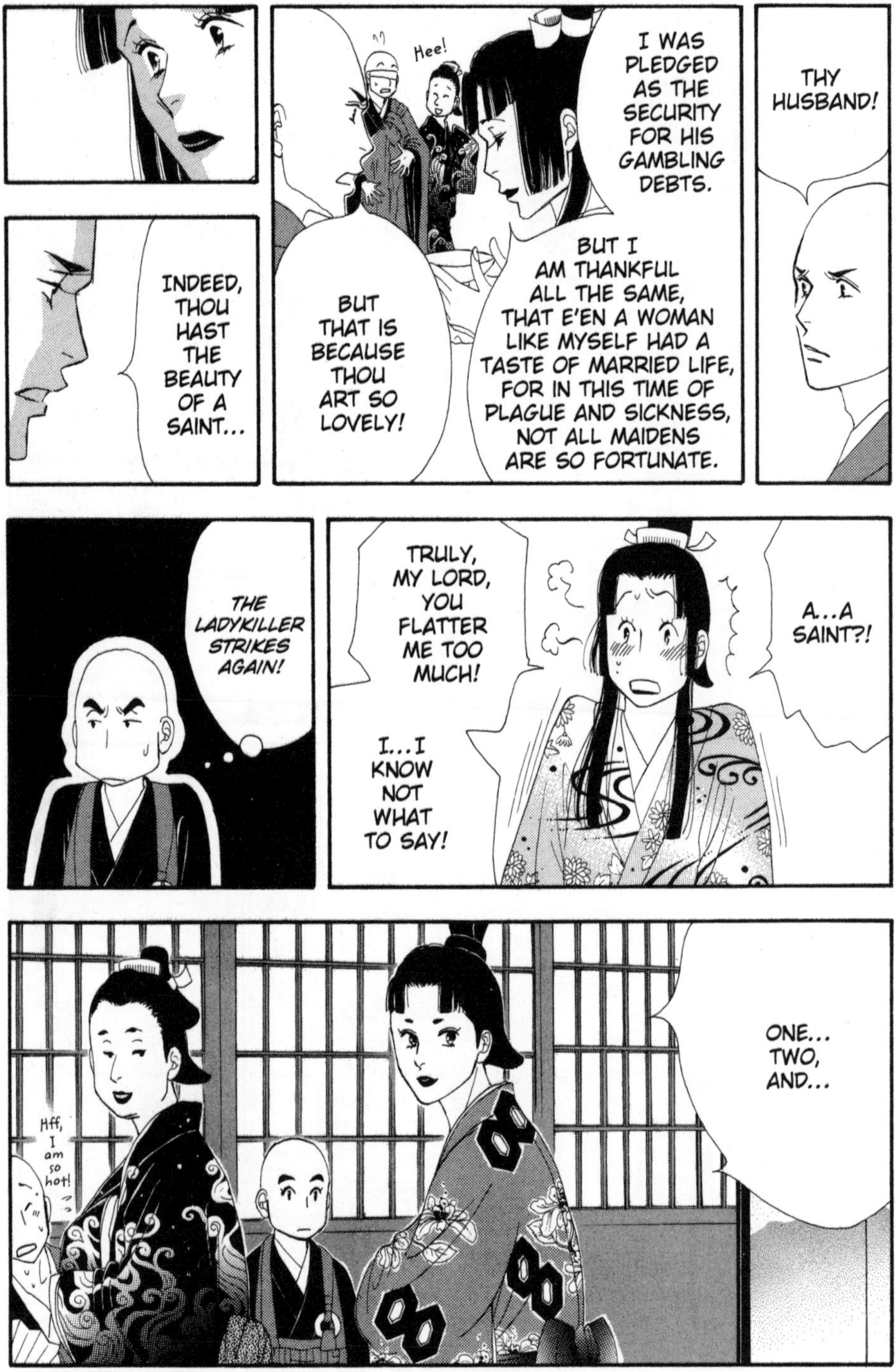
THY HUSBAND!
I WAS PLEDGED AS THE SECURITY FOR HIS GAMBLING DEBTS.
Hee!
BUT I AM THANKFUL ALL THE SAME, THAT E'EN A WOMAN LIKE MYSELF HAD A TASTE OF MARRIED LIFE, FOR IN THIS TIME OF PLAGUE AND SICKNESS, NOT ALL MAIDENS ARE SO FORTUNATE.
BUT THAT IS BECAUSE THOU ART SO LOVELY!
INDEED, THOU HAST THE BEAUTY OF A SAINT...
A...A SAINT?!
TRULY, MY LORD, YOU FLATTER ME TOO MUCH!
I...I KNOW NOT WHAT TO SAY!
THE LADYKILLER STRIKES AGAIN!
ONE... TWO, AND...
Hff, I am so hot!

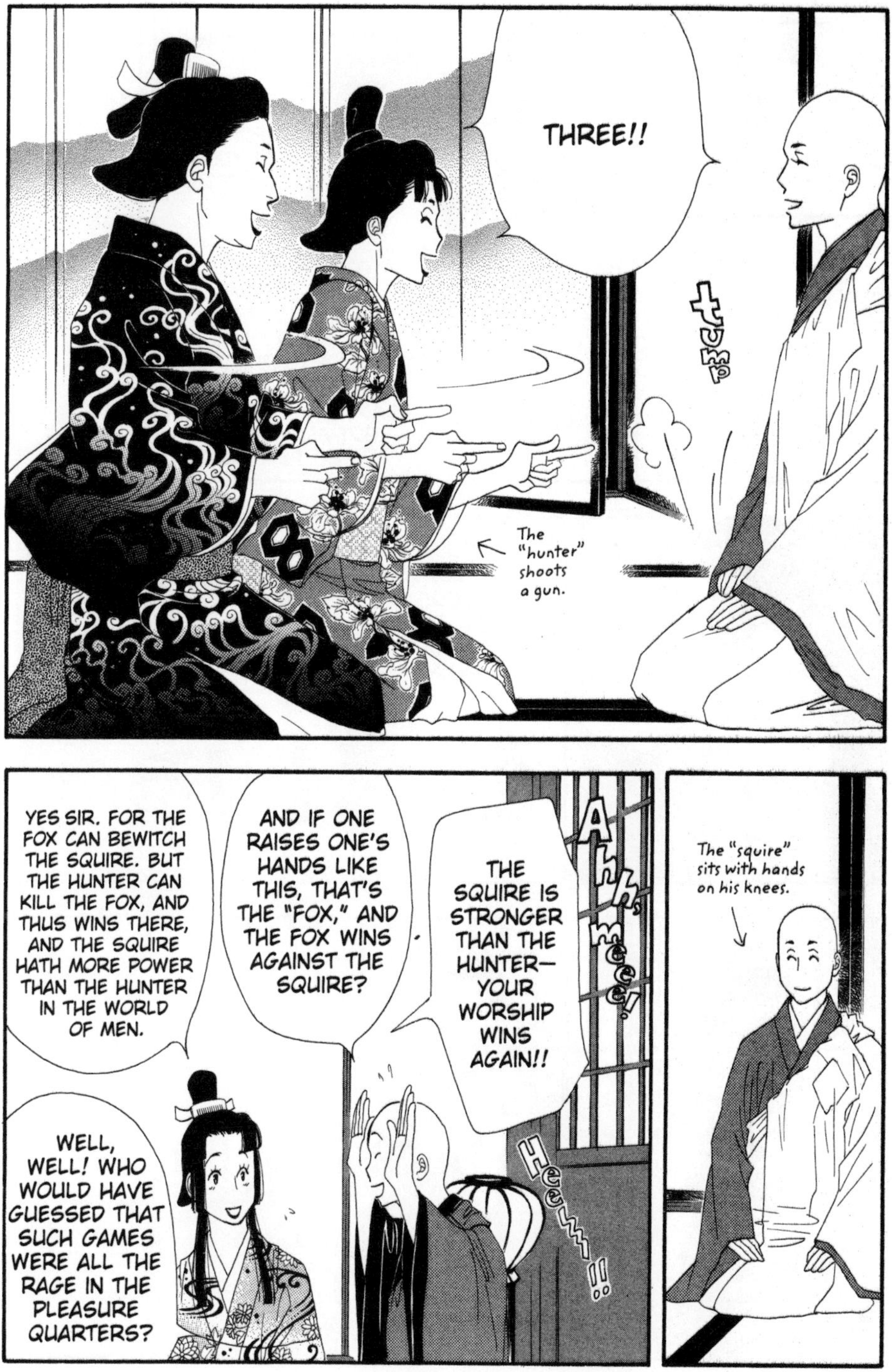
THREE!!
tump
The "hunter" shoots a gun.
The "squire" sits with hands on his knees.
THE SQUIRE IS STRONGER THAN THE HUNTER— YOUR WORSHIP WINS AGAIN!!
Ahh, mee!
AND IF ONE RAISES ONE'S HANDS LIKE THIS, THAT'S THE "FOX," AND THE FOX WINS AGAINST THE SQUIRE?
YES SIR. FOR THE FOX CAN BEWITCH THE SQUIRE. BUT THE HUNTER CAN KILL THE FOX, AND THUS WINS THERE, AND THE SQUIRE HATH MORE POWER THAN THE HUNTER IN THE WORLD OF MEN.
Heeww!!
WELL, WELL! WHO WOULD HAVE GUESSED THAT SUCH GAMES WERE ALL THE RAGE IN THE PLEASURE QUARTERS?

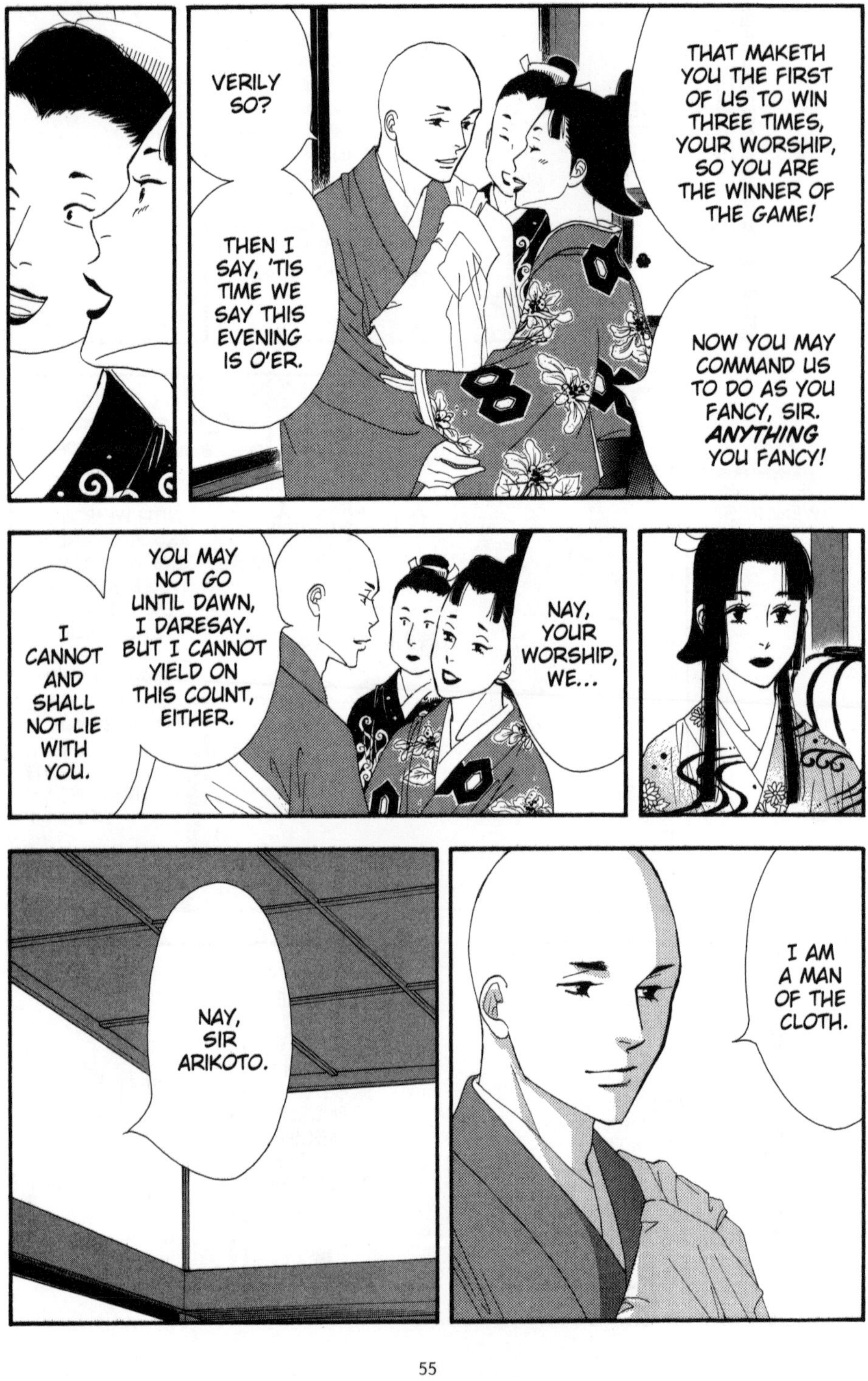
THAT MAKETH YOU THE FIRST OF US TO WIN THREE TIMES, YOUR WORSHIP, SO YOU ARE THE WINNER OF THE GAME!
NOW YOU MAY COMMAND US TO DO AS YOU FANCY, SIR. *ANYTHING* YOU FANCY!
VERILY SO?
THEN I SAY, 'TIS TIME WE SAY THIS EVENING IS O'ER.
NAY, YOUR WORSHIP, WE...
YOU MAY NOT GO UNTIL DAWN, I DARESAY. BUT I CANNOT YIELD ON THIS COUNT, EITHER.
I CANNOT AND SHALL NOT LIE WITH YOU.
I AM A MAN OF THE CLOTH.
NAY, SIR ARIKOTO.

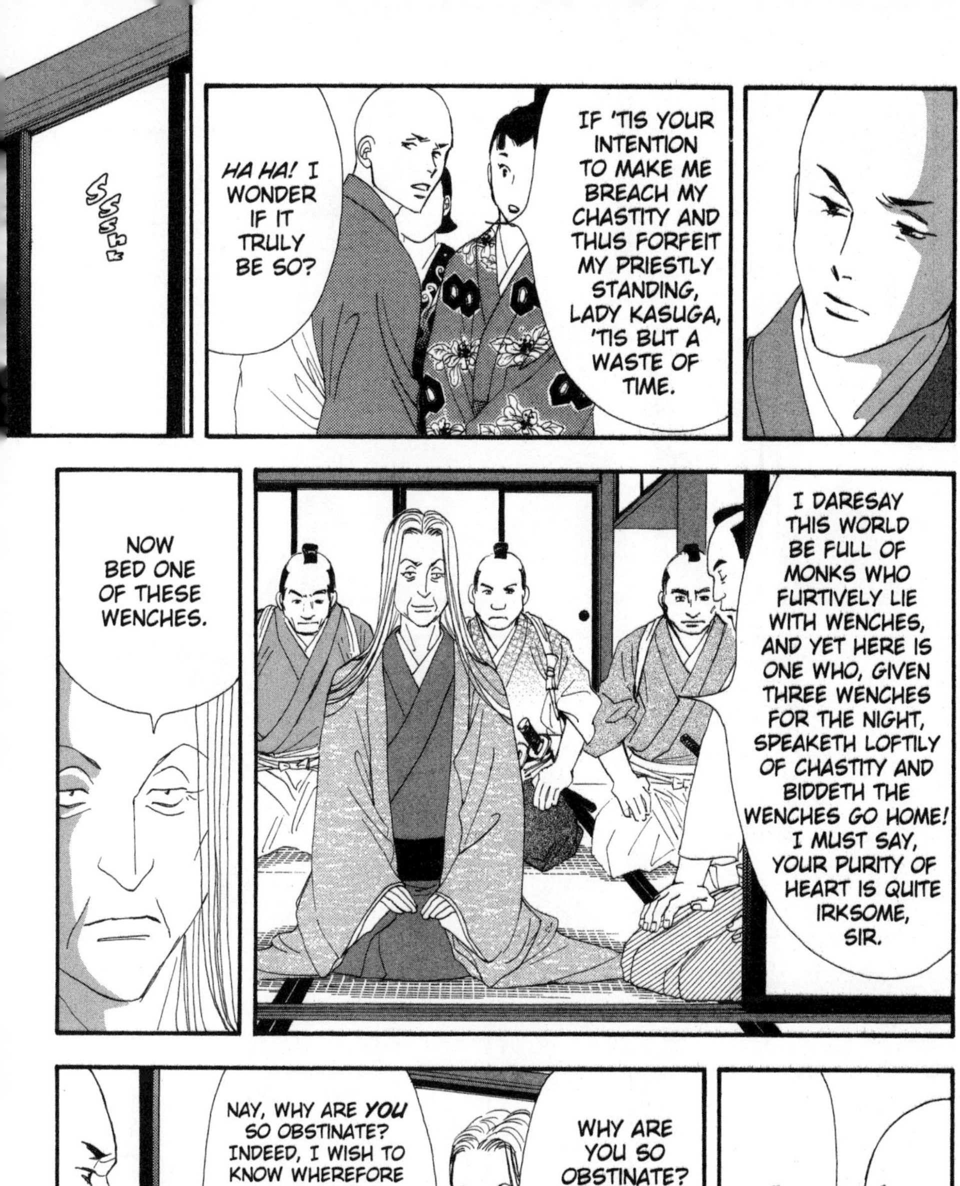
IF 'TIS YOUR INTENTION TO MAKE ME BREACH MY CHASTITY AND THUS FORFEIT MY PRIESTLY STANDING, LADY KASUGA, 'TIS BUT A WASTE OF TIME.
HA HA! I WONDER IF IT TRULY BE SO?
SSSHK
I DARESAY THIS WORLD BE FULL OF MONKS WHO FURTIVELY LIE WITH WENCHES, AND YET HERE IS ONE WHO, GIVEN THREE WENCHES FOR THE NIGHT, SPEAKETH LOFTILY OF CHASTITY AND BIDDETH THE WENCHES GO HOME! I MUST SAY, YOUR PURITY OF HEART IS QUITE IRKSOME, SIR.
NOW BED ONE OF THESE WENCHES.
I REFUSE!
WHY ARE YOU SO OBSTINATE? A WOMAN'S BODY IS A THING OF PLEASURE. TAKE ONE TO ENJOY.
NAY, WHY ARE *YOU* SO OBSTINATE? INDEED, I WISH TO KNOW WHEREFORE YOU GO TO SUCH LENGTHS TO FORCE ONE WHO HATH MOST WILLINGLY TAKEN PRIESTLY VOWS TO RENOUNCE THOSE VOWS?!

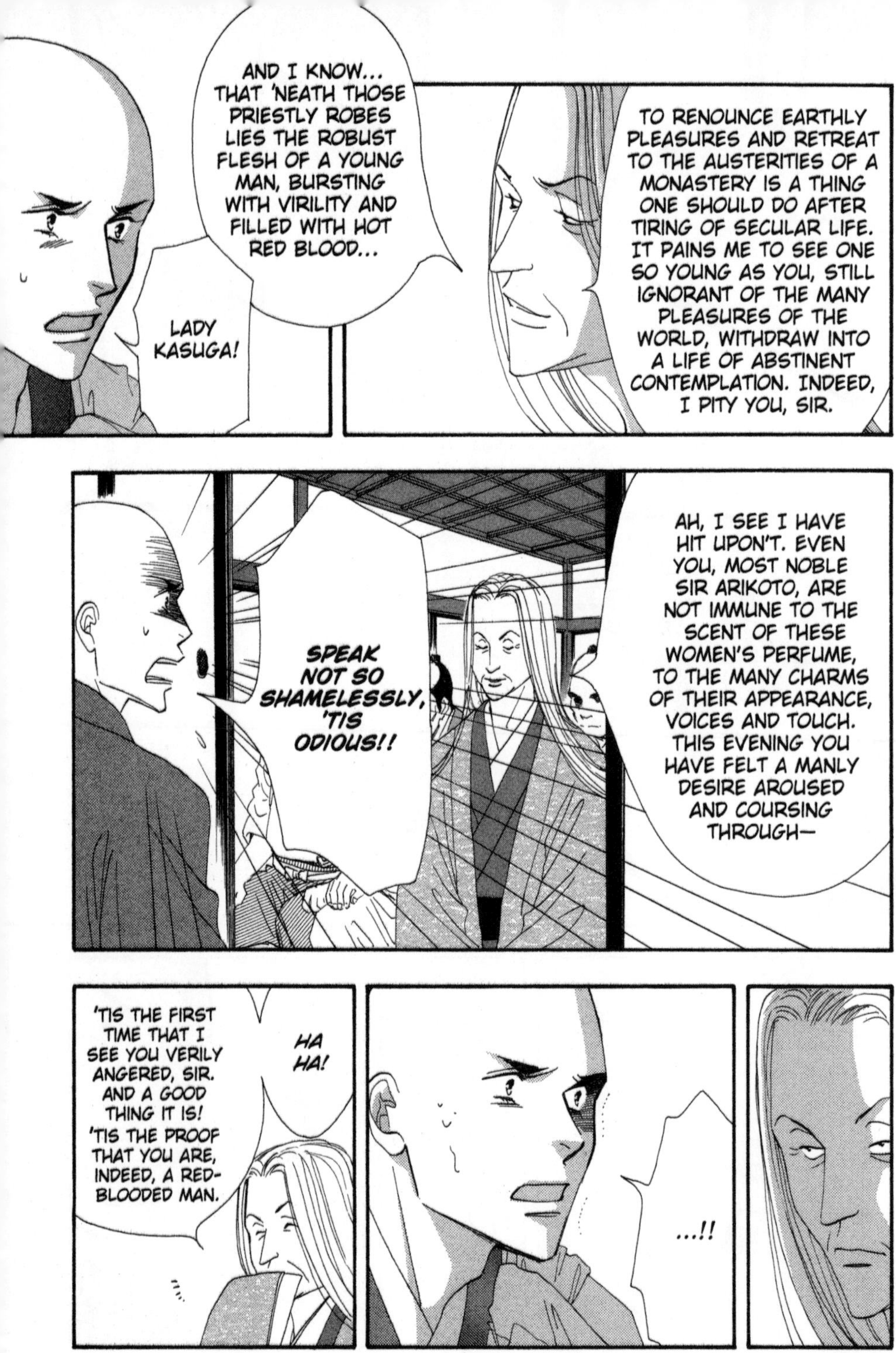
TO RENOUNCE EARTHLY PLEASURES AND RETREAT TO THE AUSTERITIES OF A MONASTERY IS A THING ONE SHOULD DO AFTER TIRING OF SECULAR LIFE. IT PAINS ME TO SEE ONE SO YOUNG AS YOU, STILL IGNORANT OF THE MANY PLEASURES OF THE WORLD, WITHDRAW INTO A LIFE OF ABSTINENT CONTEMPLATION. INDEED, I PITY YOU, SIR.
AND I KNOW... THAT 'NEATH THOSE PRIESTLY ROBES LIES THE ROBUST FLESH OF A YOUNG MAN, BURSTING WITH VIRILITY AND FILLED WITH HOT RED BLOOD...
LADY KASUGA!
AH, I SEE I HAVE HIT UPON'T. EVEN YOU, MOST NOBLE SIR ARIKOTO, ARE NOT IMMUNE TO THE SCENT OF THESE WOMEN'S PERFUME, TO THE MANY CHARMS OF THEIR APPEARANCE, VOICES AND TOUCH. THIS EVENING YOU HAVE FELT A MANLY DESIRE AROUSED AND COURSING THROUGH—
SPEAK NOT SO SHAMELESSLY, 'TIS ODIOUS!!
...!!
HA HA!
'TIS THE FIRST TIME THAT I SEE YOU VERILY ANGERED, SIR. AND A GOOD THING IT IS! 'TIS THE PROOF THAT YOU ARE, INDEED, A RED-BLOODED MAN.

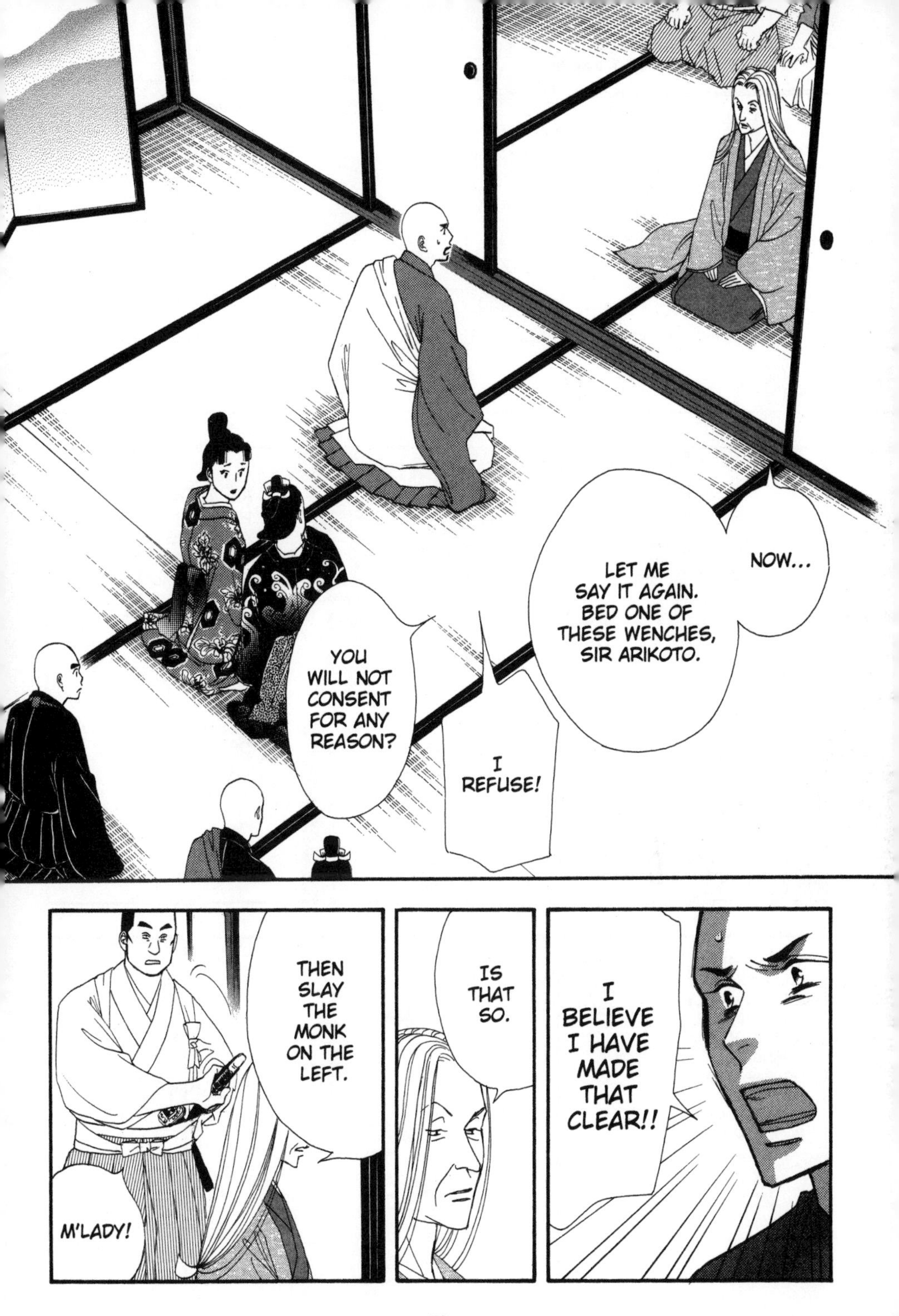
NOW...
LET ME SAY IT AGAIN. BED ONE OF THESE WENCHES, SIR ARIKOTO.
I REFUSE!
YOU WILL NOT CONSENT FOR ANY REASON?
I BELIEVE I HAVE MADE THAT CLEAR!!
IS THAT SO.
THEN SLAY THE MONK ON THE LEFT.
M'LADY!

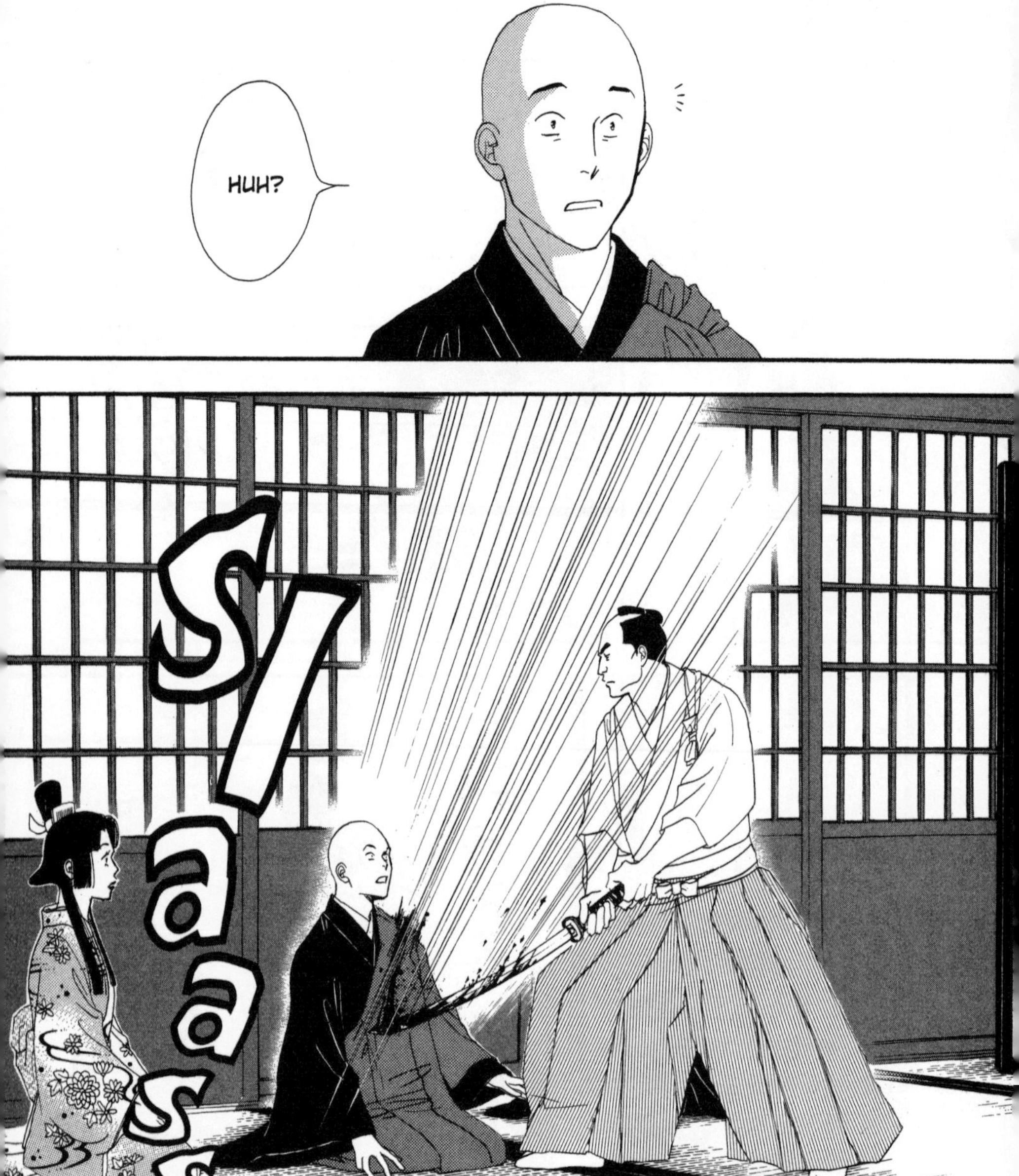
HUH?
Slaasshh

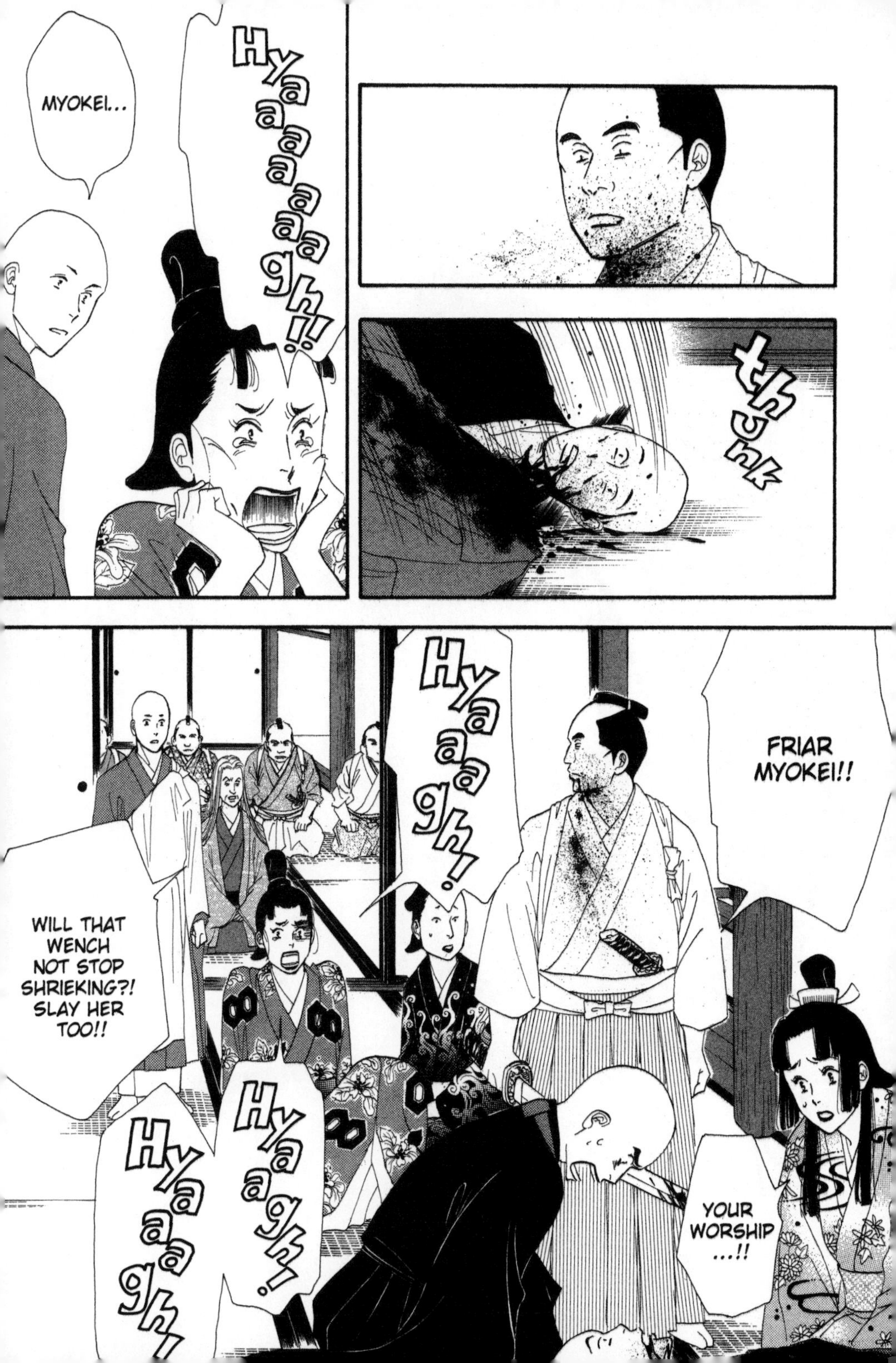
thunk
Hyaaaaaaagh!!
MYOKEI...
FRIAR MYOKEI!!
Hyaaagh!
YOUR WORSHIP ...!!
WILL THAT WENCH NOT STOP SHRIEKING?! SLAY HER TOO!!
Hyaagh!
Hyaaagh!

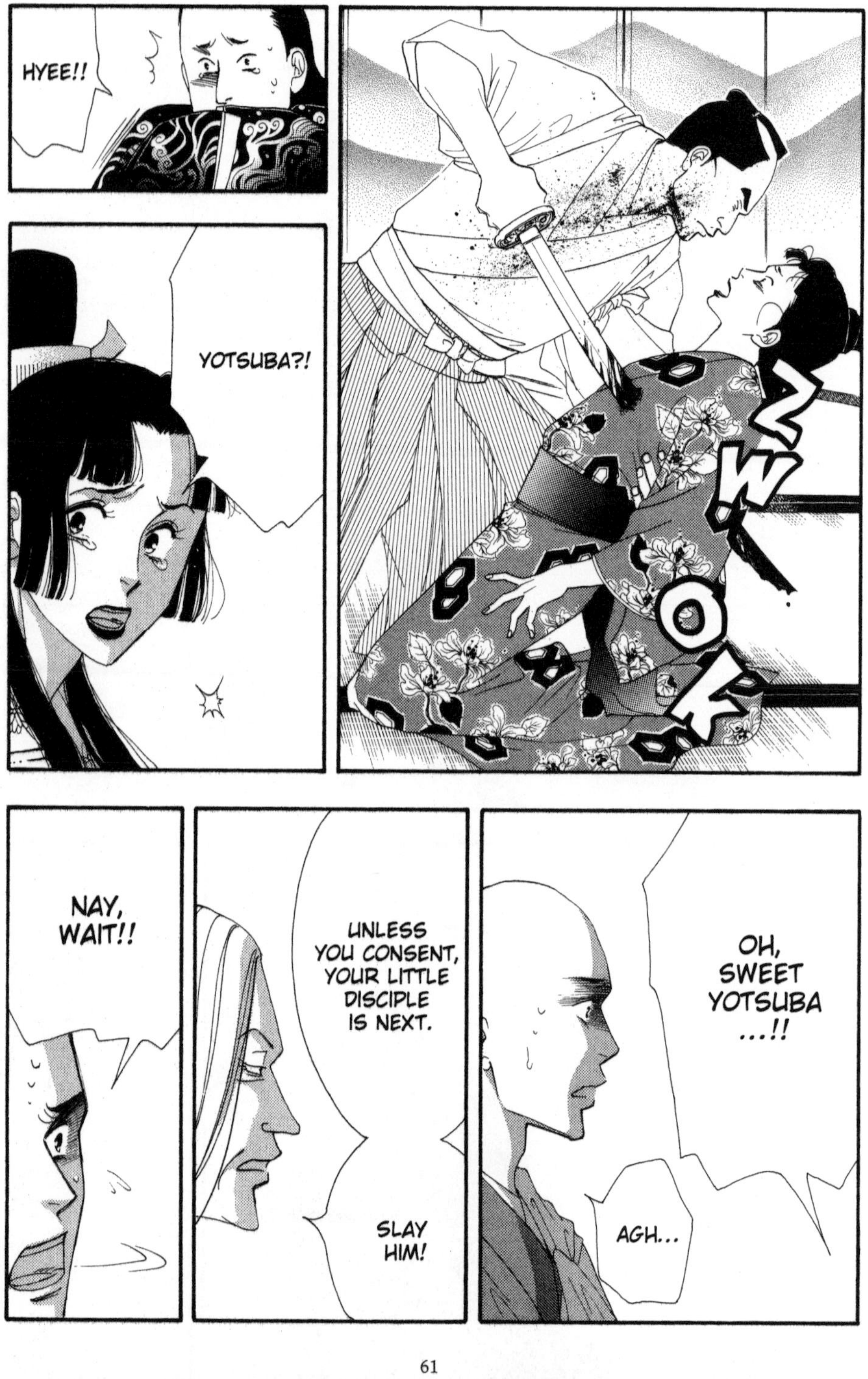
ZWOK
HYEE!!
YOTSUBA?!
OH, SWEET YOTSUBA ...!!
AGH...
UNLESS YOU CONSENT, YOUR LITTLE DISCIPLE IS NEXT.
SLAY HIM!
NAY, WAIT!!

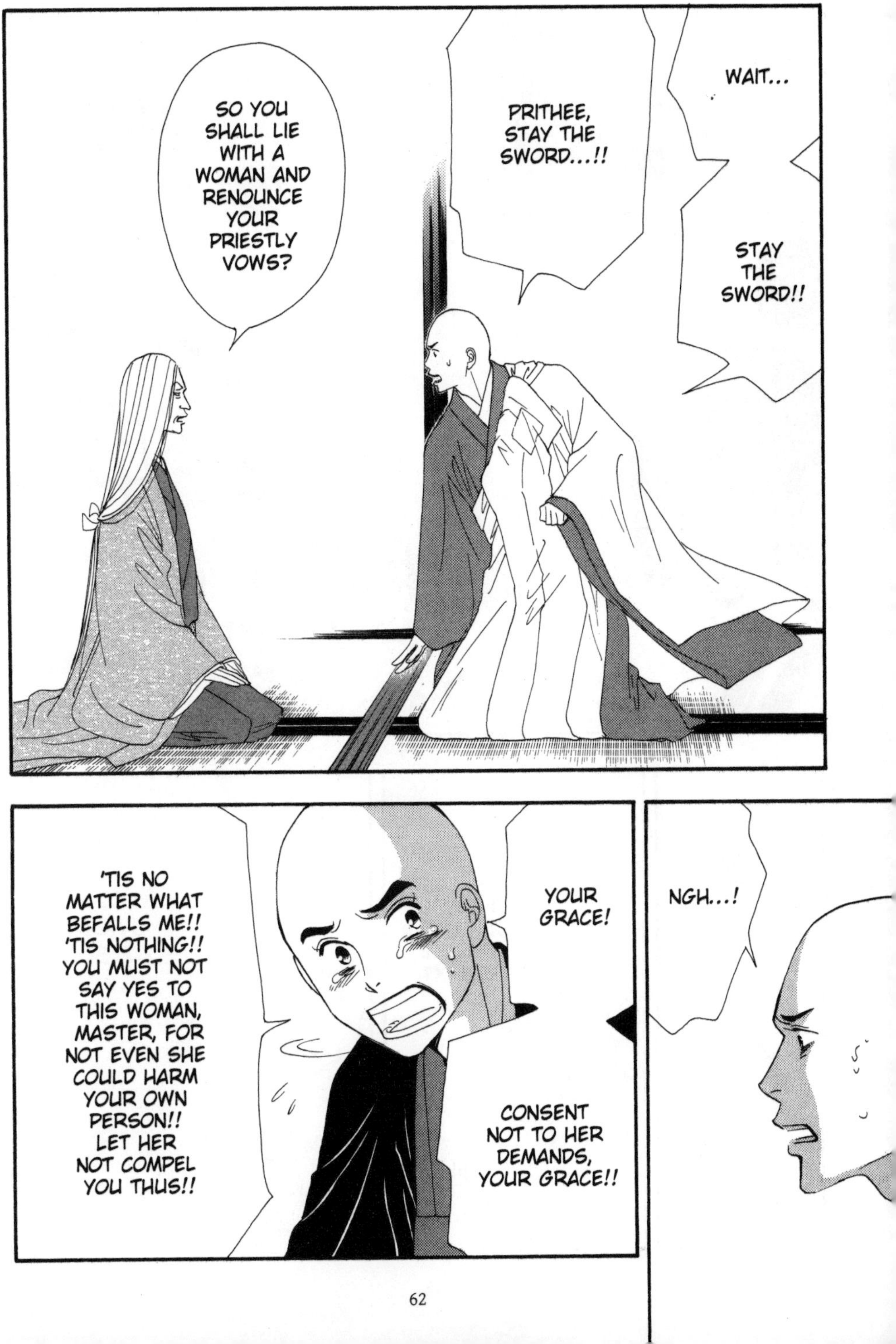
WAIT...
STAY THE SWORD!!
PRITHEE, STAY THE SWORD...!!
SO YOU SHALL LIE WITH A WOMAN AND RENOUNCE YOUR PRIESTLY VOWS?
NGH...!
YOUR GRACE!
CONSENT NOT TO HER DEMANDS, YOUR GRACE!!
'TIS NO MATTER WHAT BEFALLS ME!! 'TIS NOTHING!! YOU MUST NOT SAY YES TO THIS WOMAN, MASTER, FOR NOT EVEN SHE COULD HARM YOUR OWN PERSON!! LET HER NOT COMPEL YOU THUS!!

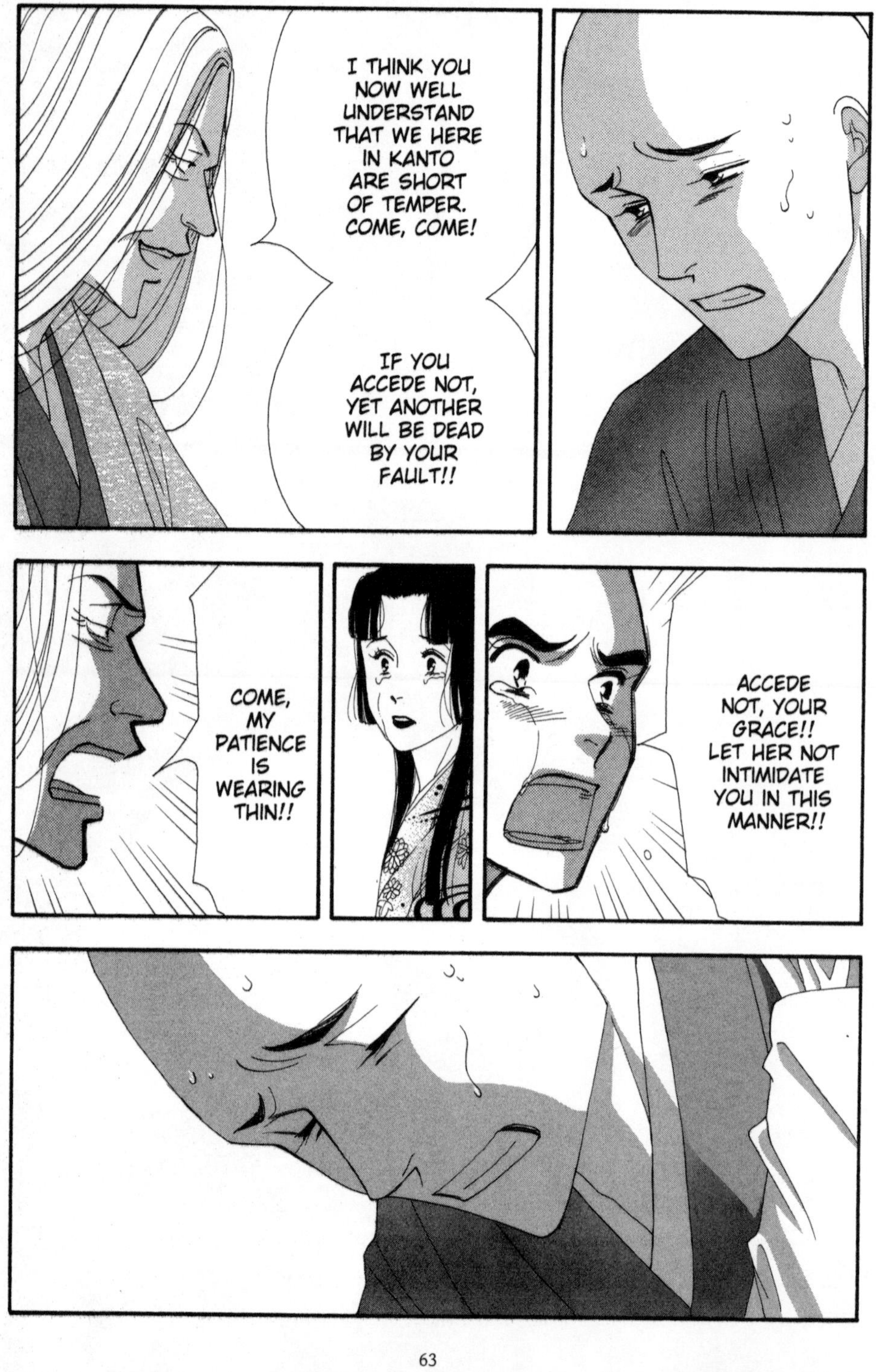
I THINK YOU NOW WELL UNDERSTAND THAT WE HERE IN KANTO ARE SHORT OF TEMPER. COME, COME!
IF YOU ACCEDE NOT, YET ANOTHER WILL BE DEAD BY YOUR FAULT!!
ACCEDE NOT, YOUR GRACE!! LET HER NOT INTIMIDATE YOU IN THIS MANNER!!
COME, MY PATIENCE IS WEARING THIN!!

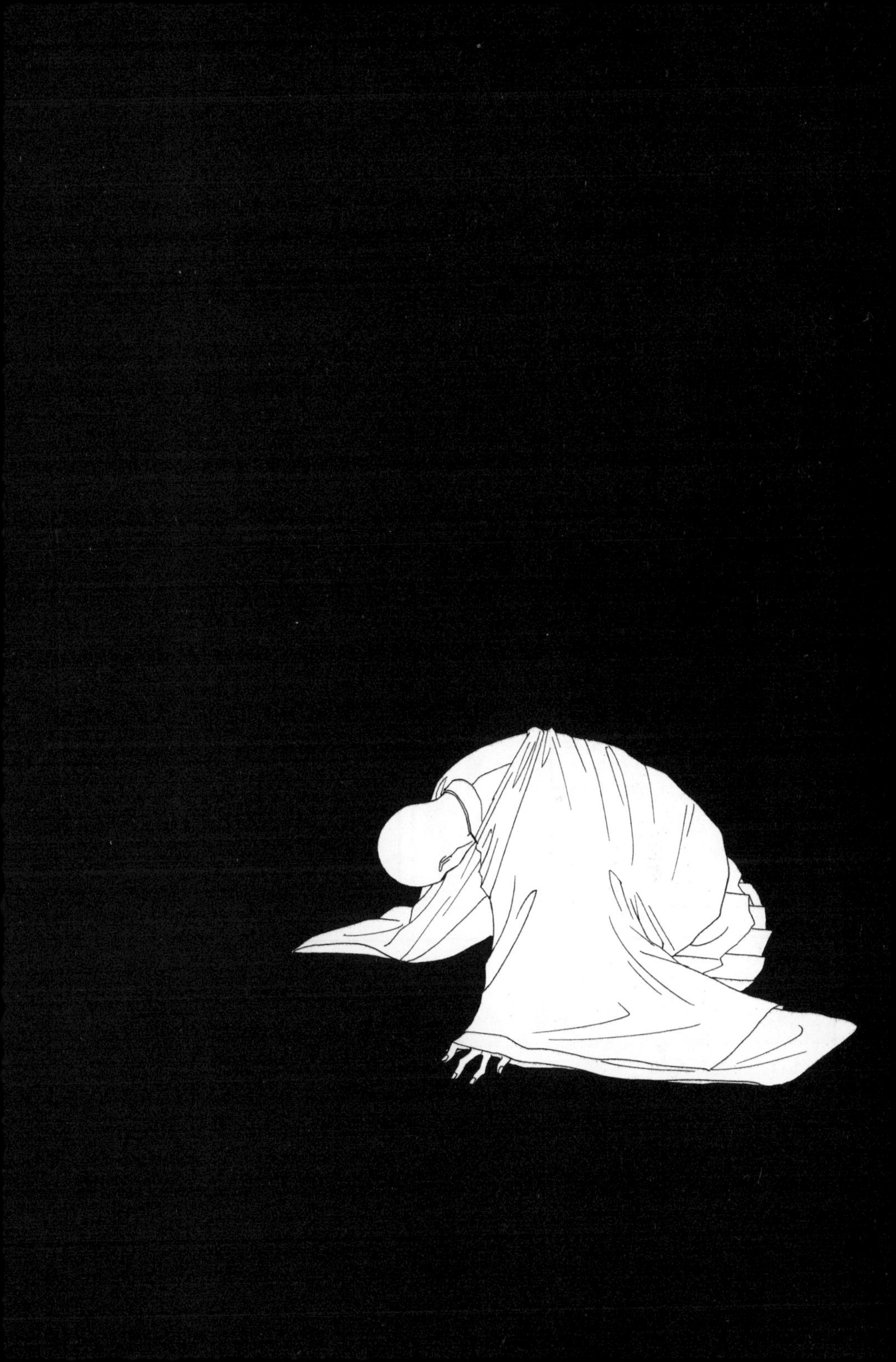

SPEAK NOT, MY LORD.

...KOGIKU.

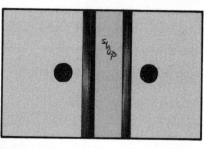

SNAP

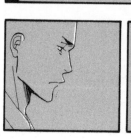

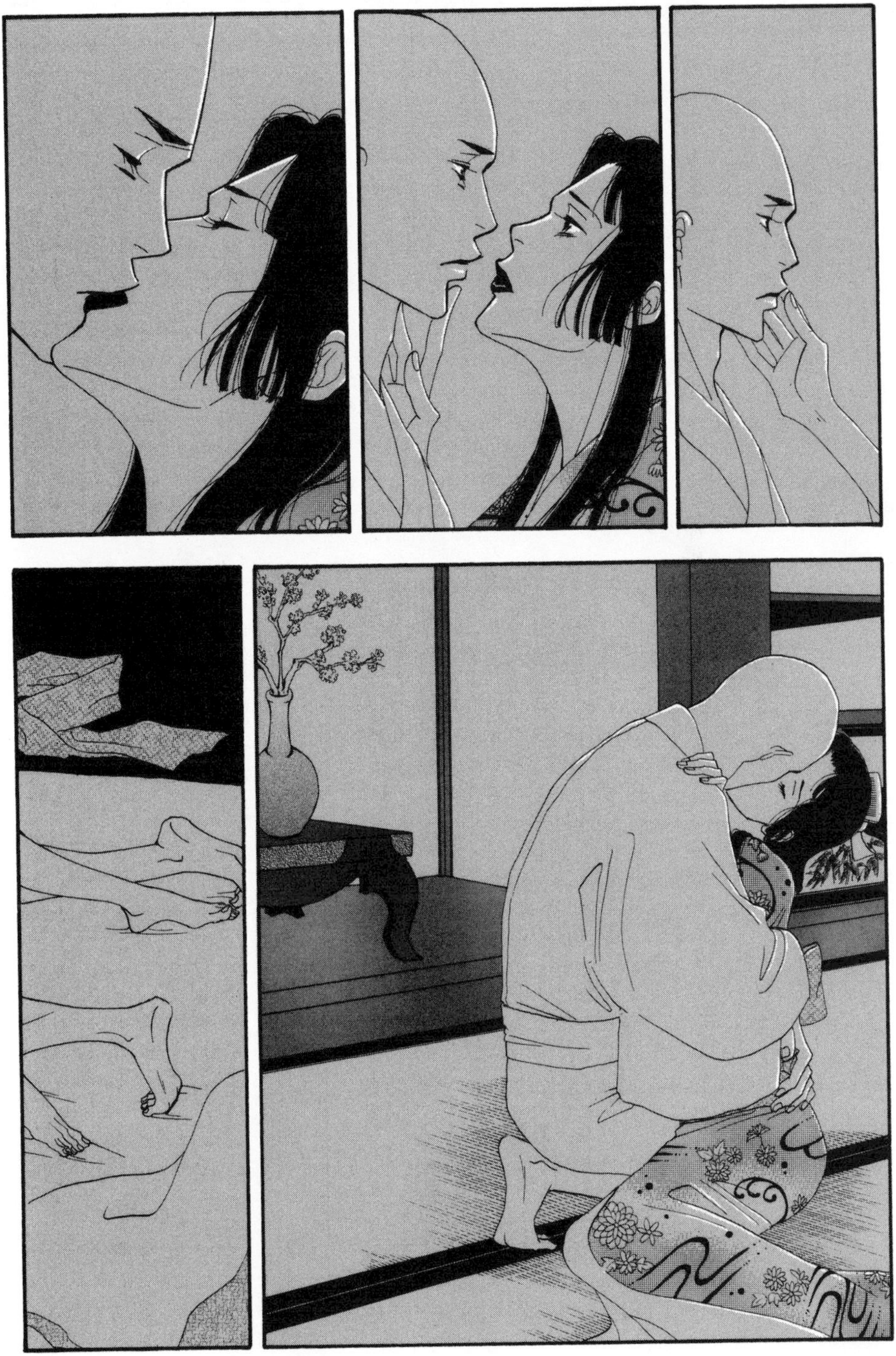

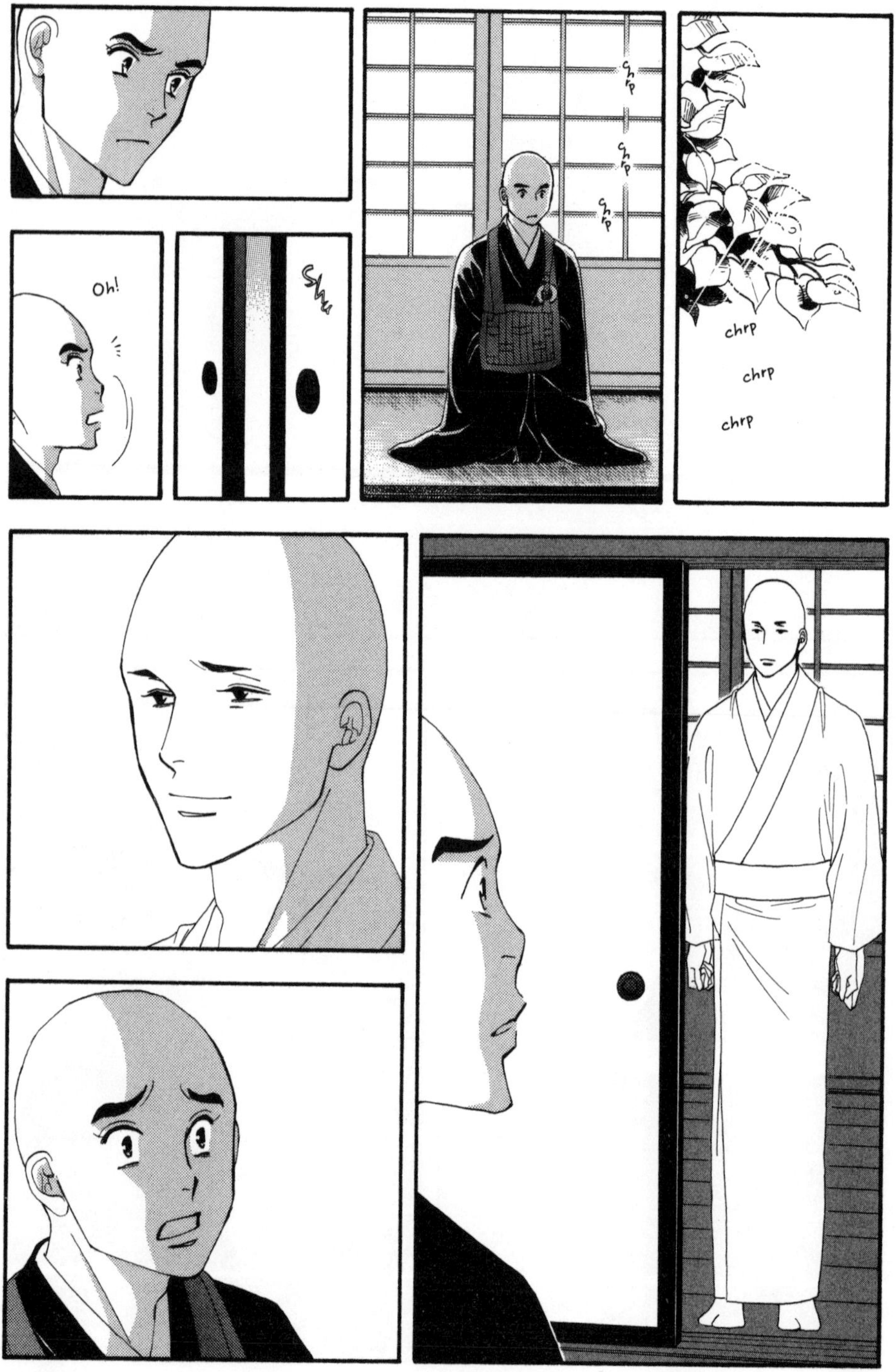
chrp
chrp
chrp
chrp
chrp
chrp
Oh!

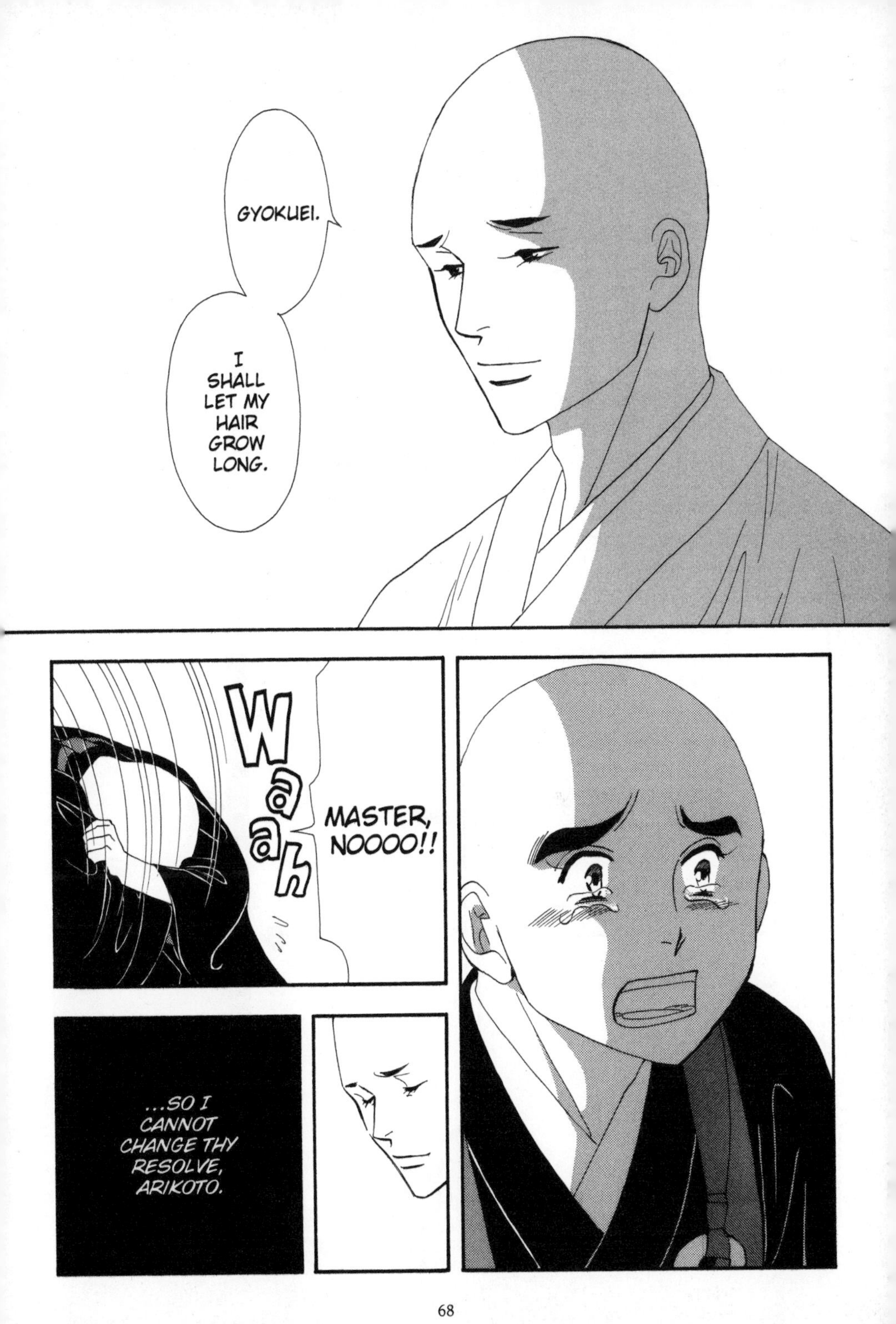
GYOKUEI.
I SHALL LET MY HAIR GROW LONG.
Waah
MASTER, NOOOO!!
...SO I CANNOT CHANGE THY RESOLVE, ARIKOTO.

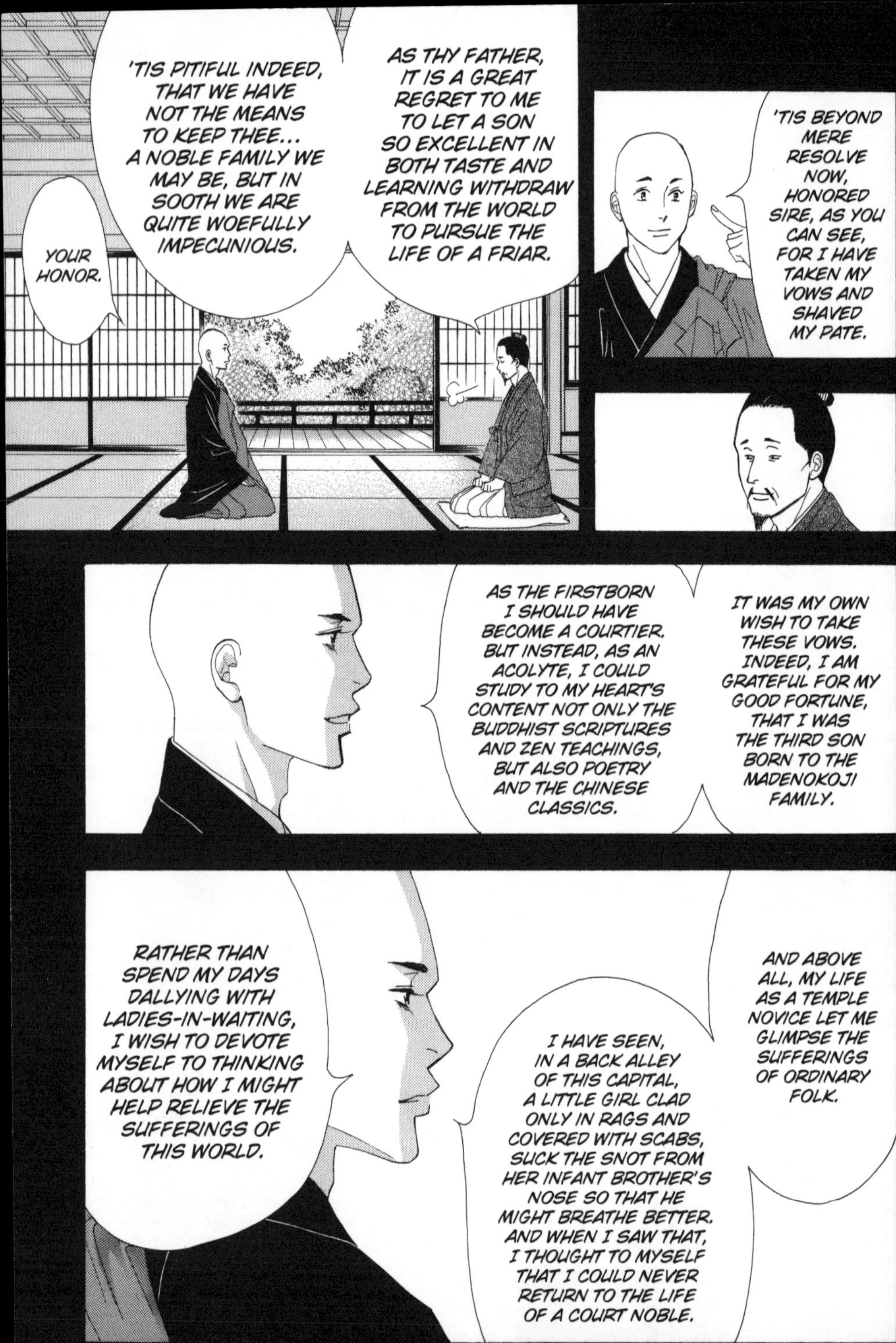
'TIS BEYOND MERE RESOLVE NOW, HONORED SIRE, AS YOU CAN SEE, FOR I HAVE TAKEN MY VOWS AND SHAVED MY PATE.
AS THY FATHER, IT IS A GREAT REGRET TO ME TO LET A SON SO EXCELLENT IN BOTH TASTE AND LEARNING WITHDRAW FROM THE WORLD TO PURSUE THE LIFE OF A FRIAR.
'TIS PITIFUL INDEED, THAT WE HAVE NOT THE MEANS TO KEEP THEE... A NOBLE FAMILY WE MAY BE, BUT IN SOOTH WE ARE QUITE WOEFULLY IMPECUNIOUS.
YOUR HONOR.
IT WAS MY OWN WISH TO TAKE THESE VOWS. INDEED, I AM GRATEFUL FOR MY GOOD FORTUNE, THAT I WAS THE THIRD SON BORN TO THE MADENOKOJI FAMILY.
AS THE FIRSTBORN I SHOULD HAVE BECOME A COURTIER. BUT INSTEAD, AS AN ACOLYTE, I COULD STUDY TO MY HEART'S CONTENT NOT ONLY THE BUDDHIST SCRIPTURES AND ZEN TEACHINGS, BUT ALSO POETRY AND THE CHINESE CLASSICS.
AND ABOVE ALL, MY LIFE AS A TEMPLE NOVICE LET ME GLIMPSE THE SUFFERINGS OF ORDINARY FOLK.
I HAVE SEEN, IN A BACK ALLEY OF THIS CAPITAL, A LITTLE GIRL CLAD ONLY IN RAGS AND COVERED WITH SCABS, SUCK THE SNOT FROM HER INFANT BROTHER'S NOSE SO THAT HE MIGHT BREATHE BETTER. AND WHEN I SAW THAT, I THOUGHT TO MYSELF THAT I COULD NEVER RETURN TO THE LIFE OF A COURT NOBLE.
RATHER THAN SPEND MY DAYS DALLYING WITH LADIES-IN-WAITING, I WISH TO DEVOTE MYSELF TO THINKING ABOUT HOW I MIGHT HELP RELIEVE THE SUFFERINGS OF THIS WORLD.

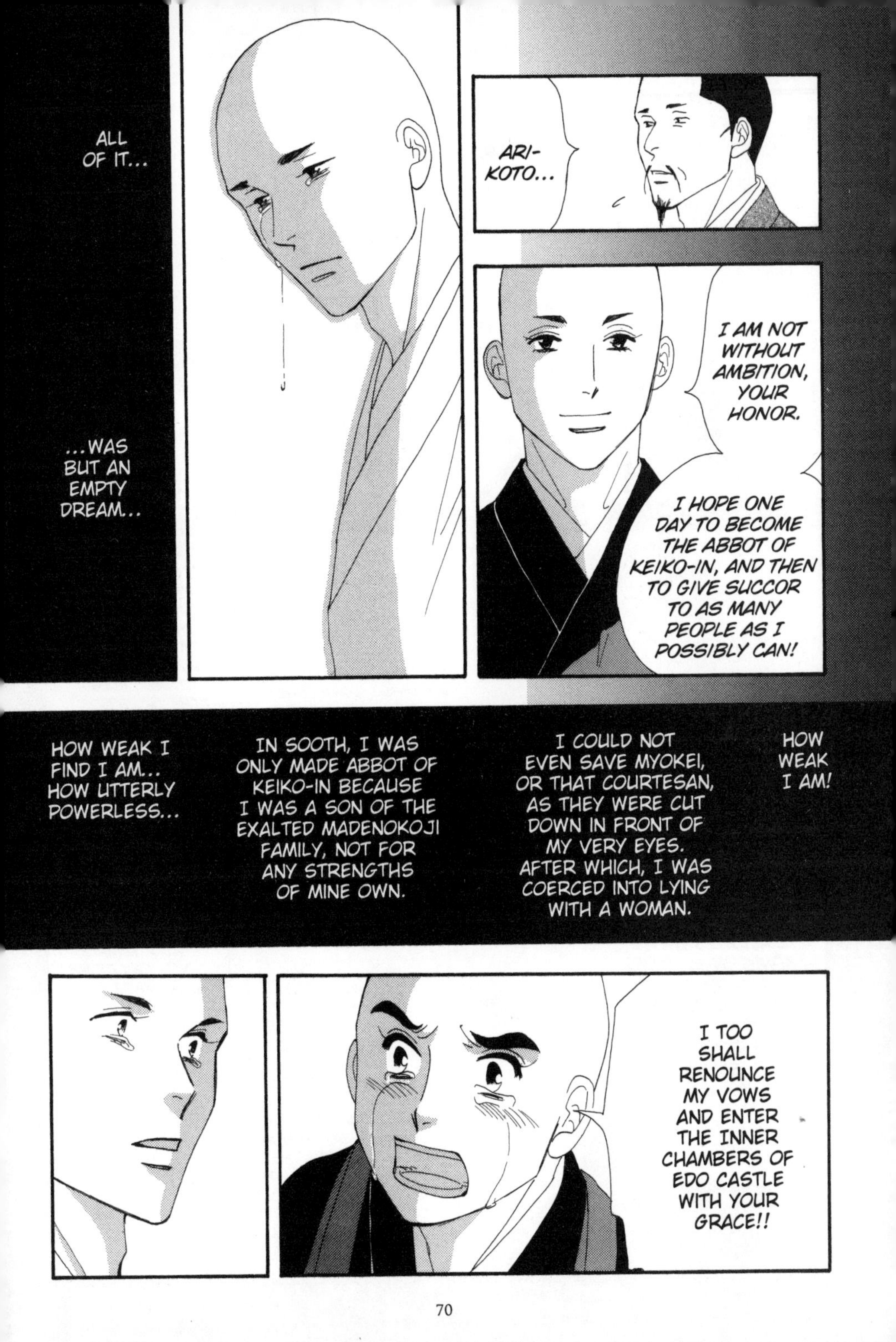
ARI-KOTO...
I AM NOT WITHOUT AMBITION, YOUR HONOR.
I HOPE ONE DAY TO BECOME THE ABBOT OF KEIKO-IN, AND THEN TO GIVE SUCCOR TO AS MANY PEOPLE AS I POSSIBLY CAN!
ALL OF IT...
...WAS BUT AN EMPTY DREAM...
HOW WEAK I AM!
I COULD NOT EVEN SAVE MYOKEI, OR THAT COURTESAN, AS THEY WERE CUT DOWN IN FRONT OF MY VERY EYES. AFTER WHICH, I WAS COERCED INTO LYING WITH A WOMAN.
IN SOOTH, I WAS ONLY MADE ABBOT OF KEIKO-IN BECAUSE I WAS A SON OF THE EXALTED MADENOKOJI FAMILY, NOT FOR ANY STRENGTHS OF MINE OWN.
HOW WEAK I FIND I AM... HOW UTTERLY POWERLESS...
I TOO SHALL RENOUNCE MY VOWS AND ENTER THE INNER CHAMBERS OF EDO CASTLE WITH YOUR GRACE!!

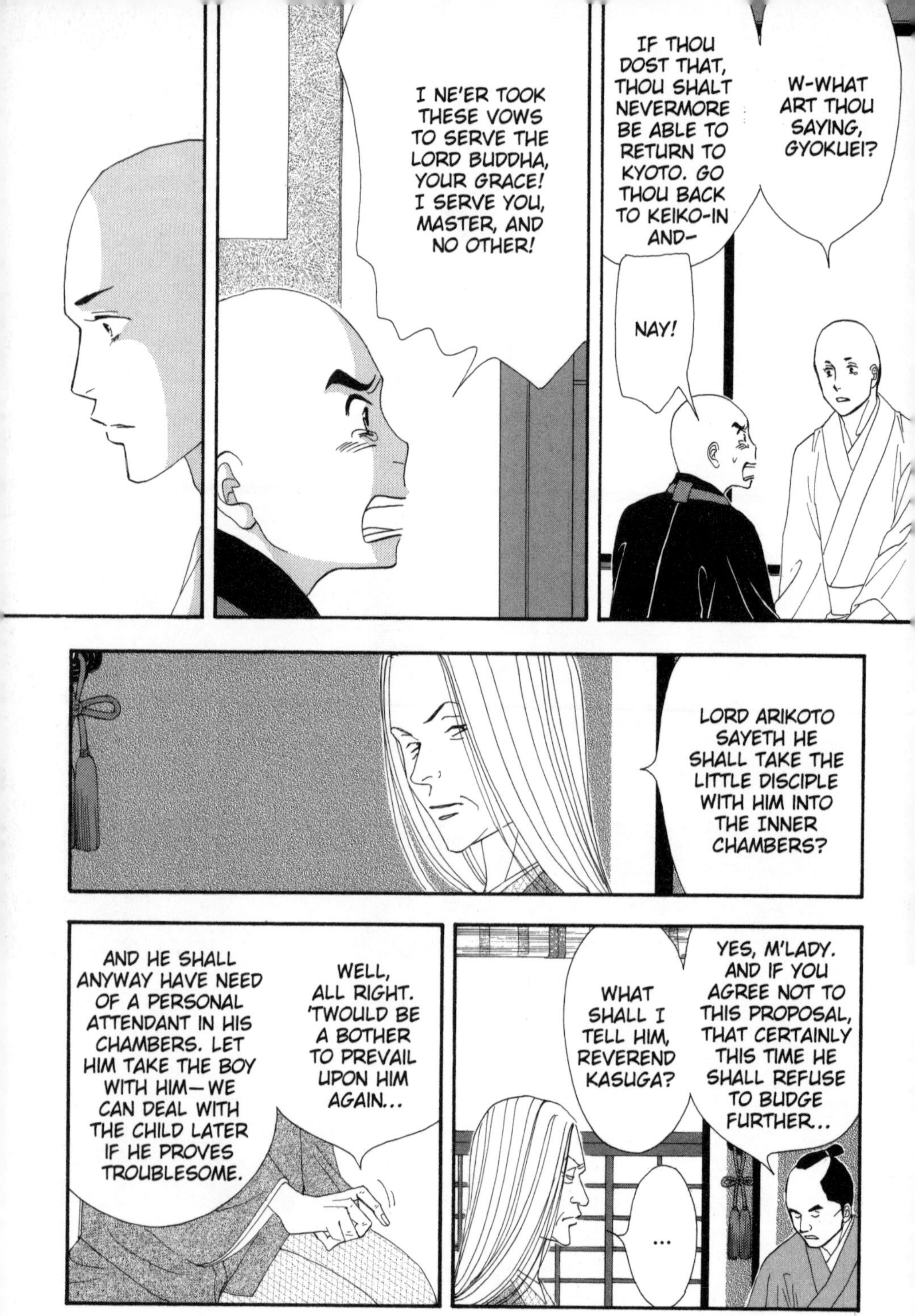
W-WHAT ART THOU SAYING, GYOKUEI?
IF THOU DOST THAT, THOU SHALT NEVERMORE BE ABLE TO RETURN TO KYOTO. GO THOU BACK TO KEIKO-IN AND–
NAY!
I NE'ER TOOK THESE VOWS TO SERVE THE LORD BUDDHA, YOUR GRACE! I SERVE YOU, MASTER, AND NO OTHER!
LORD ARIKOTO SAYETH HE SHALL TAKE THE LITTLE DISCIPLE WITH HIM INTO THE INNER CHAMBERS?
YES, M'LADY. AND IF YOU AGREE NOT TO THIS PROPOSAL, THAT CERTAINLY THIS TIME HE SHALL REFUSE TO BUDGE FURTHER...
WHAT SHALL I TELL HIM, REVEREND KASUGA?
...
WELL, ALL RIGHT. 'TWOULD BE A BOTHER TO PREVAIL UPON HIM AGAIN...
AND HE SHALL ANYWAY HAVE NEED OF A PERSONAL ATTENDANT IN HIS CHAMBERS. LET HIM TAKE THE BOY WITH HIM—WE CAN DEAL WITH THE CHILD LATER IF HE PROVES TROUBLESOME.

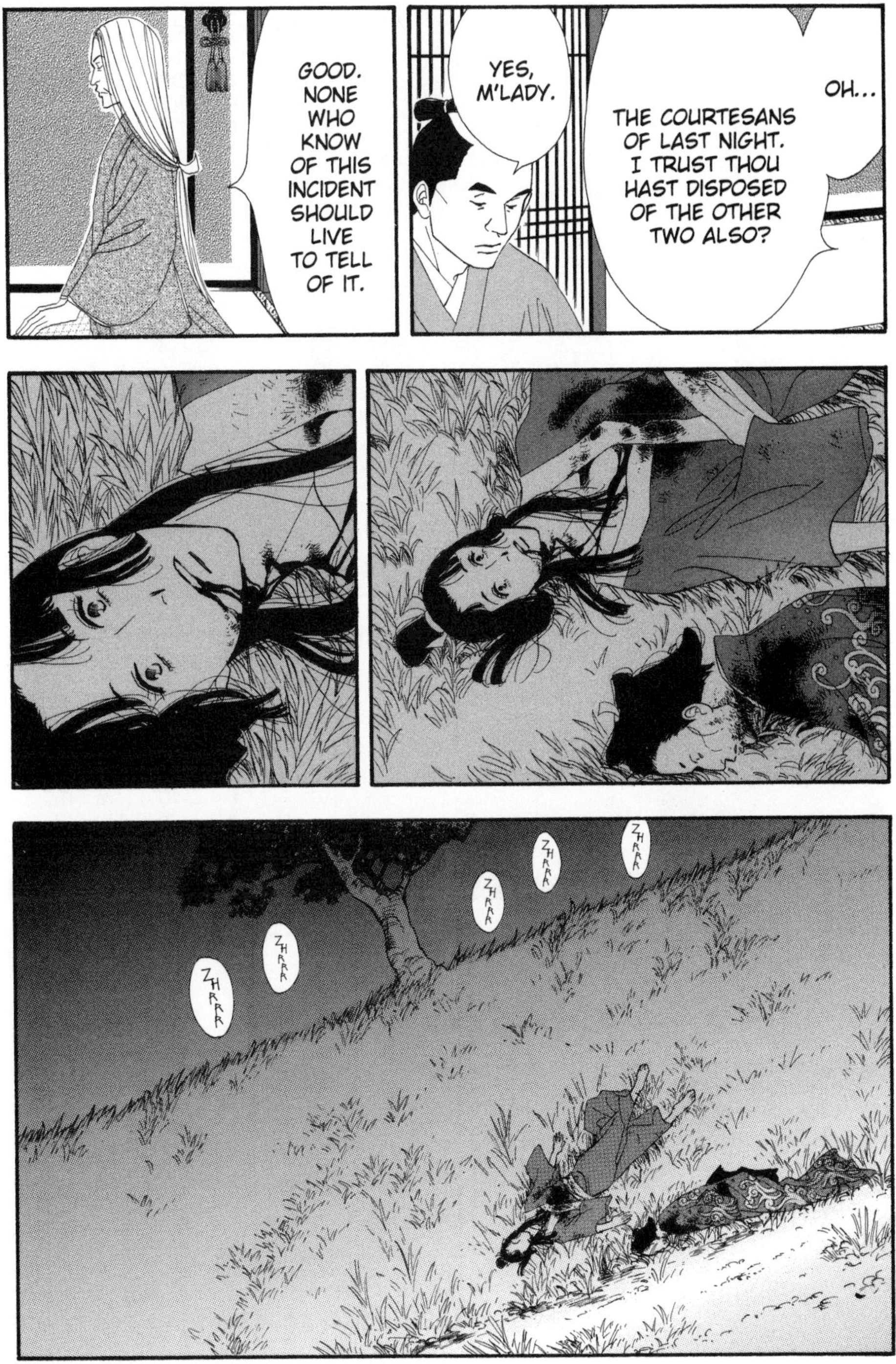
OH...
THE COURTESANS OF LAST NIGHT. I TRUST THOU HAST DISPOSED OF THE OTHER TWO ALSO?
YES, M'LADY.
GOOD. NONE WHO KNOW OF THIS INCIDENT SHOULD LIVE TO TELL OF IT.
ZHRRR
ZHRRR
ZHRRR
ZHRRR
ZHRRR

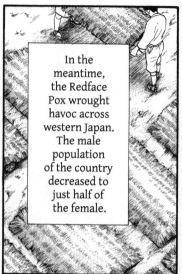

Six months later.
Arikoto and Gyokuei remained in the government mansion provided by Lady Kasuga in Tayasudai, waiting for their hair to grow long enough to be presentable.
In the meantime, the Redface Pox wrought havoc across western Japan. The male population of the country decreased to just half of the female.
chirr chirr
MASTER ARIKOTO.
WE HAVE ARRIVED IN THE INNER CHAMBERS OF EDO CASTLE.

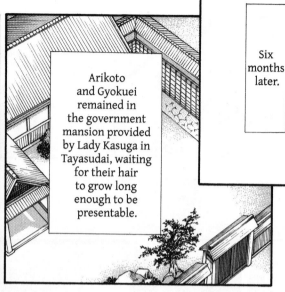

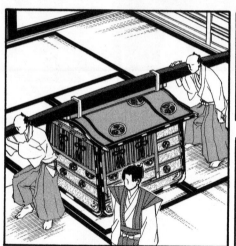

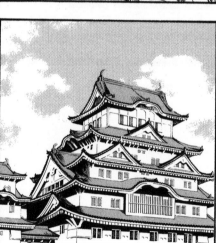

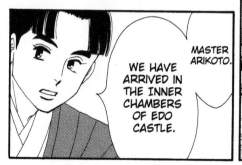

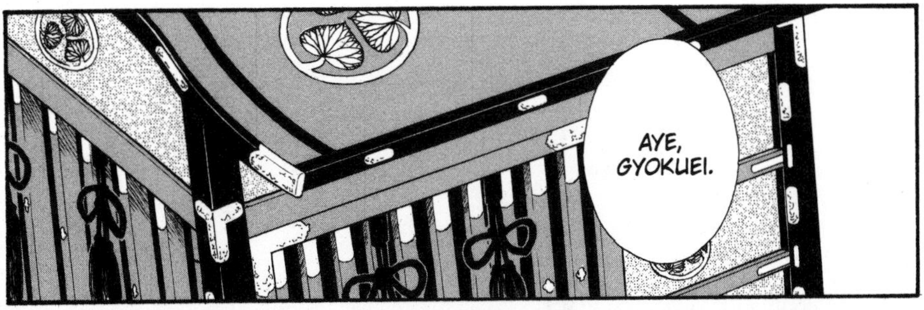
AYE, GYOKUEI.

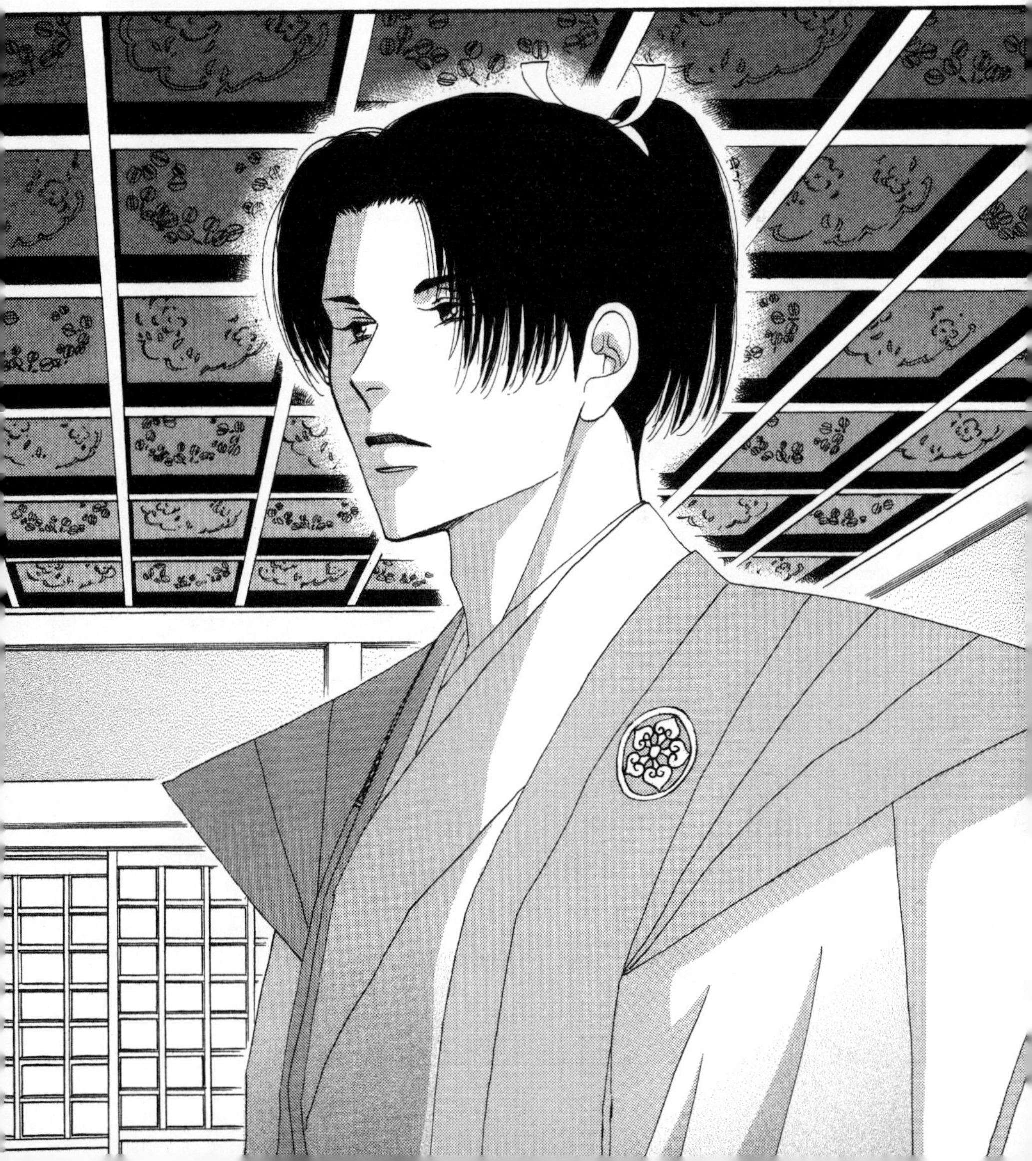

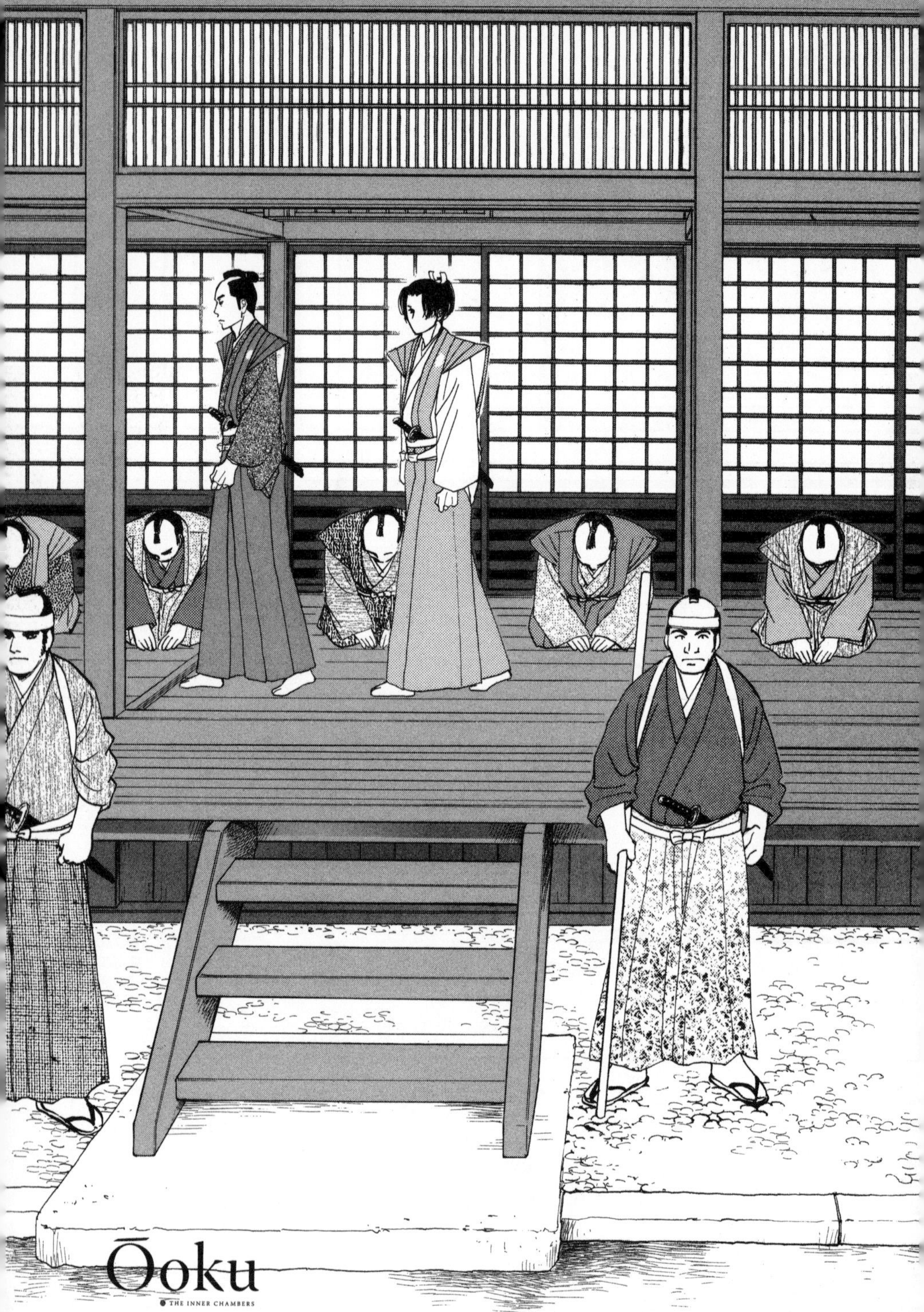

Ōoku
THE INNER CHAMBERS

NNGH...!

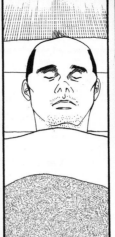

chrp

chrp

chrp

YASUKE! YASUKE...!

HOW CANST THOU LEAVE THY AGED MOTHER BEHIND LIKE THIS, THOU WRETCHED SON?!

FAAATHERR!!

Waaaaah!!

WAAAAGH!! PAPPYYYYY!!

Gyaagh!

gyaagh!

Gyaaagh!

...

hic

76

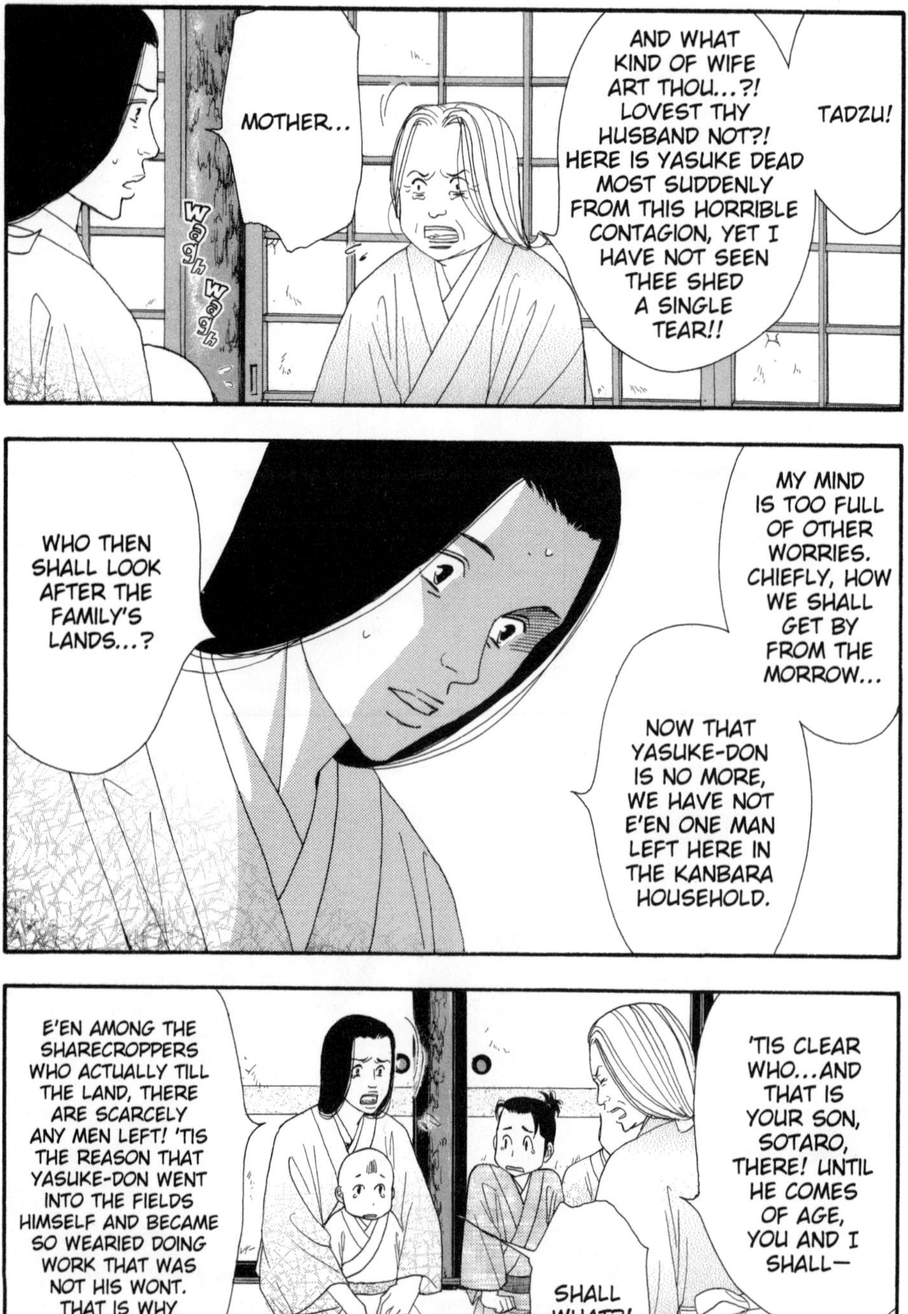
TADZU!
AND WHAT KIND OF WIFE ART THOU...?! LOVEST THY HUSBAND NOT?! HERE IS YASUKE DEAD MOST SUDDENLY FROM THIS HORRIBLE CONTAGION, YET I HAVE NOT SEEN THEE SHED A SINGLE TEAR!!
MOTHER...
Wagh wagh
MY MIND IS TOO FULL OF OTHER WORRIES. CHIEFLY, HOW WE SHALL GET BY FROM THE MORROW...
NOW THAT YASUKE-DON IS NO MORE, WE HAVE NOT E'EN ONE MAN LEFT HERE IN THE KANBARA HOUSEHOLD.
WHO THEN SHALL LOOK AFTER THE FAMILY'S LANDS...?
'TIS CLEAR WHO...AND THAT IS YOUR SON, SOTARO, THERE! UNTIL HE COMES OF AGE, YOU AND I SHALL—
SHALL WHAT?!
E'EN AMONG THE SHARECROPPERS WHO ACTUALLY TILL THE LAND, THERE ARE SCARCELY ANY MEN LEFT! 'TIS THE REASON THAT YASUKE-DON WENT INTO THE FIELDS HIMSELF AND BECAME SO WEARIED DOING WORK THAT WAS NOT HIS WONT. THAT IS WHY HE FELL ILL, I'M SURE OF'T...!!

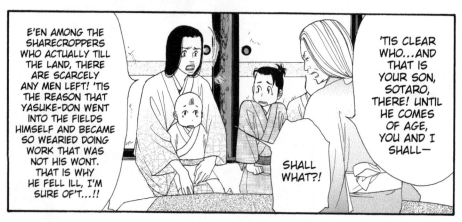

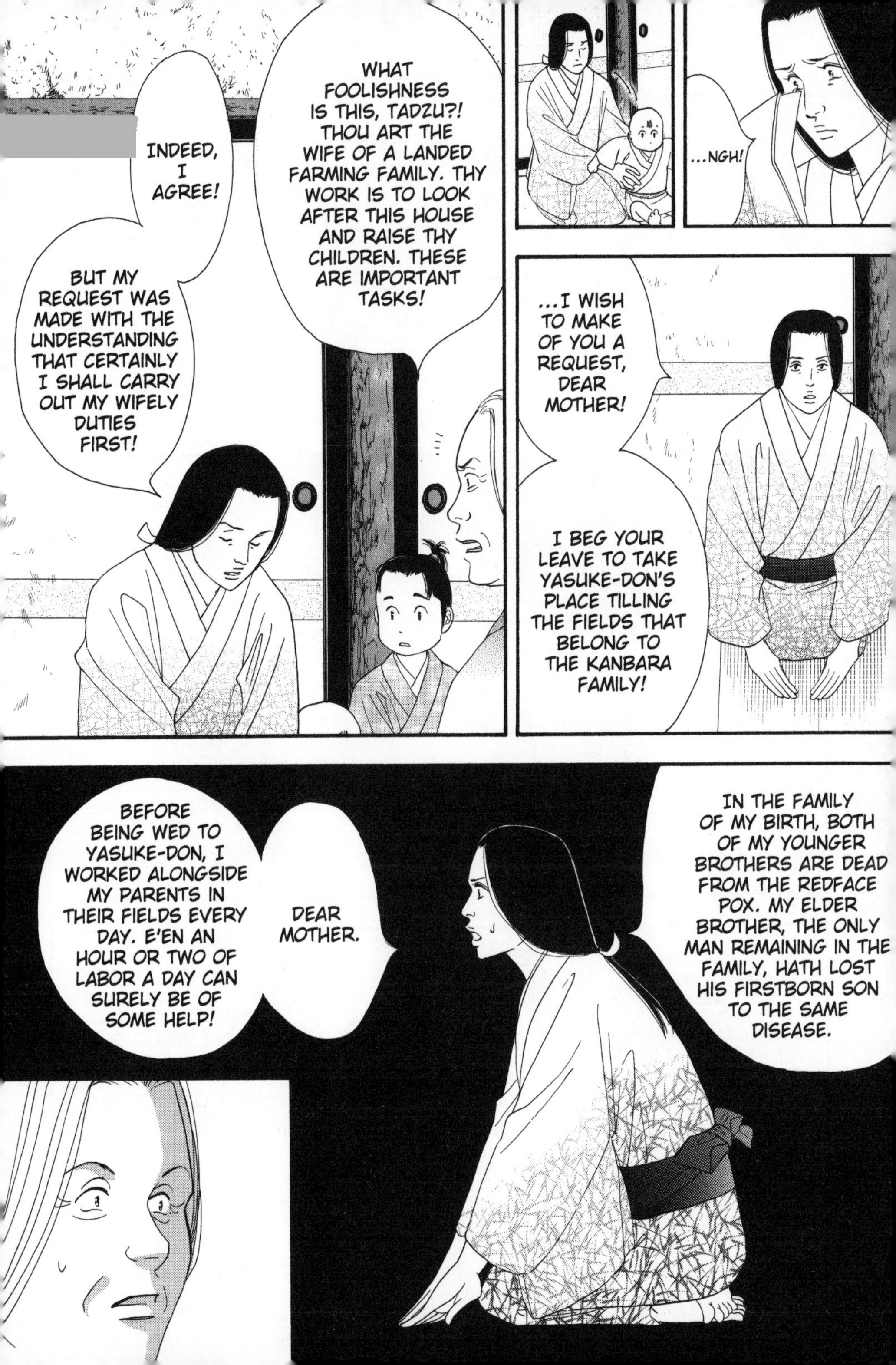
...NGH!
...I WISH TO MAKE OF YOU A REQUEST, DEAR MOTHER!
I BEG YOUR LEAVE TO TAKE YASUKE-DON'S PLACE TILLING THE FIELDS THAT BELONG TO THE KANBARA FAMILY!
WHAT FOOLISHNESS IS THIS, TADZU?! THOU ART THE WIFE OF A LANDED FARMING FAMILY. THY WORK IS TO LOOK AFTER THIS HOUSE AND RAISE THY CHILDREN. THESE ARE IMPORTANT TASKS!
INDEED, I AGREE!
BUT MY REQUEST WAS MADE WITH THE UNDERSTANDING THAT CERTAINLY I SHALL CARRY OUT MY WIFELY DUTIES FIRST!
IN THE FAMILY OF MY BIRTH, BOTH OF MY YOUNGER BROTHERS ARE DEAD FROM THE REDFACE POX. MY ELDER BROTHER, THE ONLY MAN REMAINING IN THE FAMILY, HATH LOST HIS FIRSTBORN SON TO THE SAME DISEASE.
DEAR MOTHER.
BEFORE BEING WED TO YASUKE-DON, I WORKED ALONGSIDE MY PARENTS IN THEIR FIELDS EVERY DAY. E'EN AN HOUR OR TWO OF LABOR A DAY CAN SURELY BE OF SOME HELP!

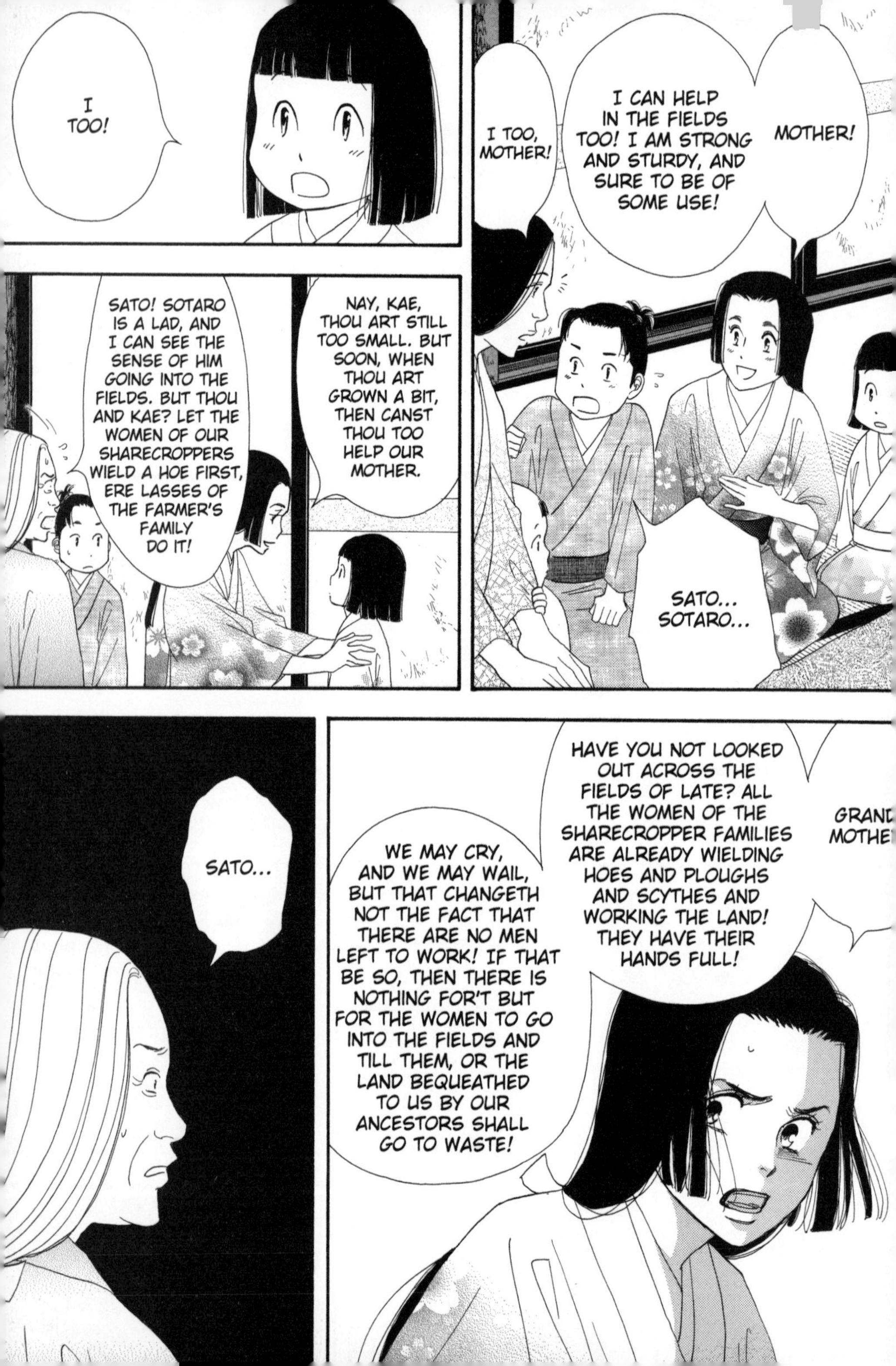

MOTHER!
I CAN HELP IN THE FIELDS TOO! I AM STRONG AND STURDY, AND SURE TO BE OF SOME USE!
I TOO, MOTHER!
SATO... SOTARO...
I TOO!
NAY, KAE, THOU ART STILL TOO SMALL. BUT SOON, WHEN THOU ART GROWN A BIT, THEN CANST THOU TOO HELP OUR MOTHER.
SATO! SOTARO IS A LAD, AND I CAN SEE THE SENSE OF HIM GOING INTO THE FIELDS. BUT THOU AND KAE? LET THE WOMEN OF OUR SHARECROPPERS WIELD A HOE FIRST, ERE LASSES OF THE FARMER'S FAMILY DO IT!
GRAND MOTHE
HAVE YOU NOT LOOKED OUT ACROSS THE FIELDS OF LATE? ALL THE WOMEN OF THE SHARECROPPER FAMILIES ARE ALREADY WIELDING HOES AND PLOUGHS AND SCYTHES AND WORKING THE LAND! THEY HAVE THEIR HANDS FULL!
WE MAY CRY, AND WE MAY WAIL, BUT THAT CHANGETH NOT THE FACT THAT THERE ARE NO MEN LEFT TO WORK! IF THAT BE SO, THEN THERE IS NOTHING FOR'T BUT FOR THE WOMEN TO GO INTO THE FIELDS AND TILL THEM, OR THE LAND BEQUEATHED TO US BY OUR ANCESTORS SHALL GO TO WASTE!
SATO...

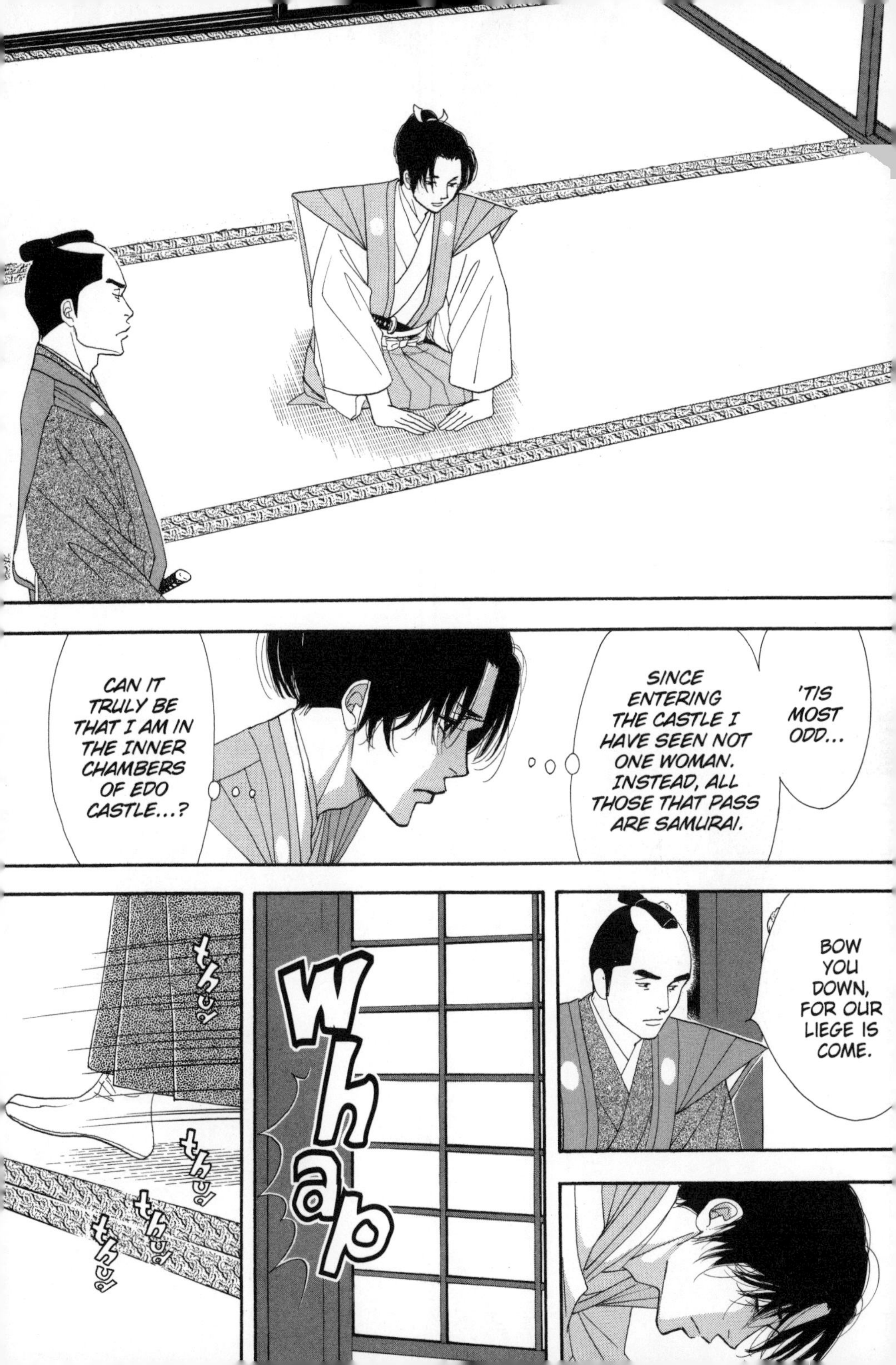

'TIS MOST ODD...
SINCE ENTERING THE CASTLE I HAVE SEEN NOT ONE WOMAN. INSTEAD, ALL THOSE THAT PASS ARE SAMURAI.
CAN IT TRULY BE THAT I AM IN THE INNER CHAMBERS OF EDO CASTLE...?
BOW YOU DOWN, FOR OUR LIEGE IS COME.
Whap
thud
thud
thud
thud

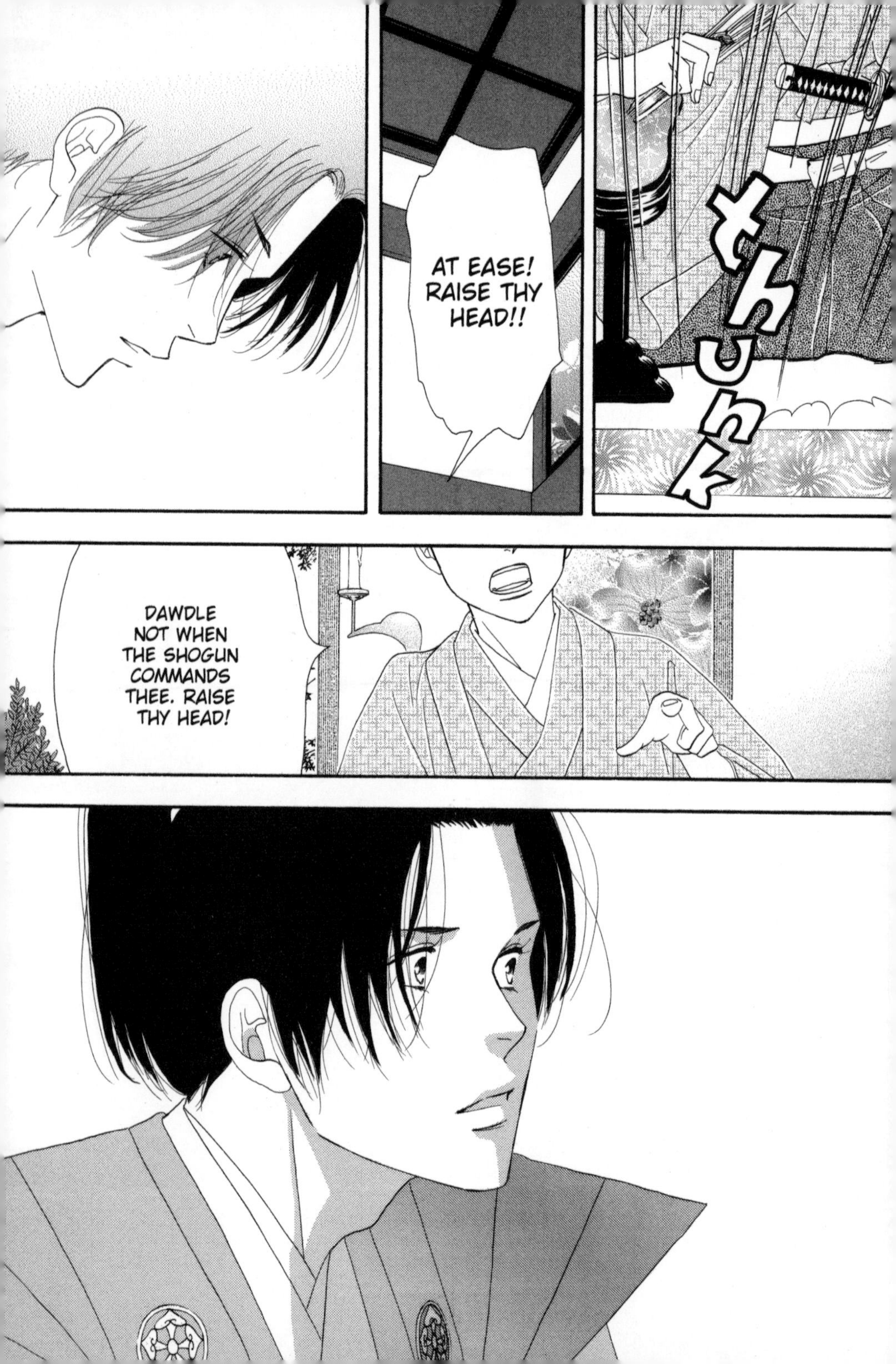
AT EASE! RAISE THY HEAD!!
DAWDLE NOT WHEN THE SHOGUN COMMANDS THEE. RAISE THY HEAD!

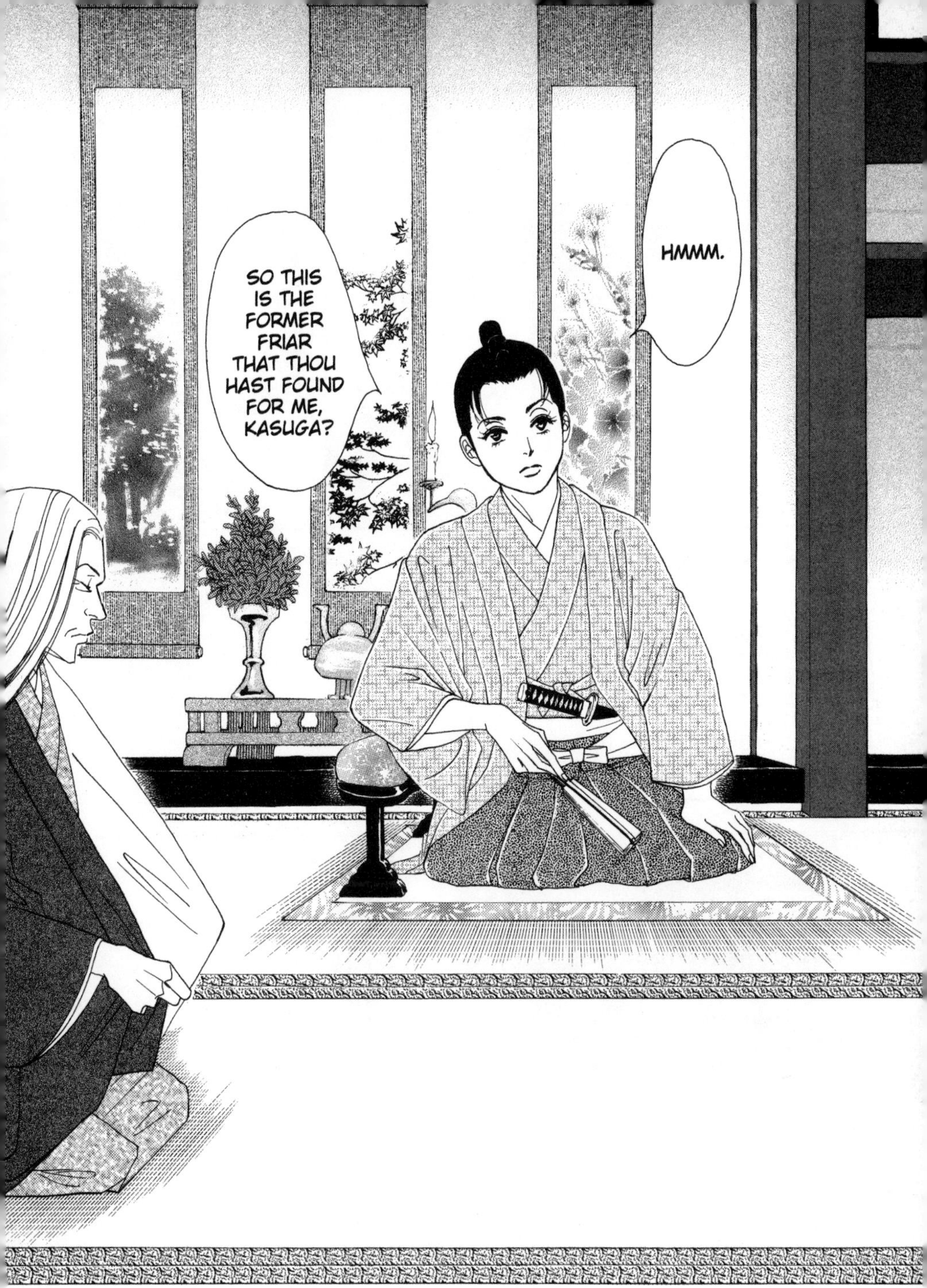
HMMM.
SO THIS IS THE FORMER FRIAR THAT THOU HAST FOUND FOR ME, KASUGA?

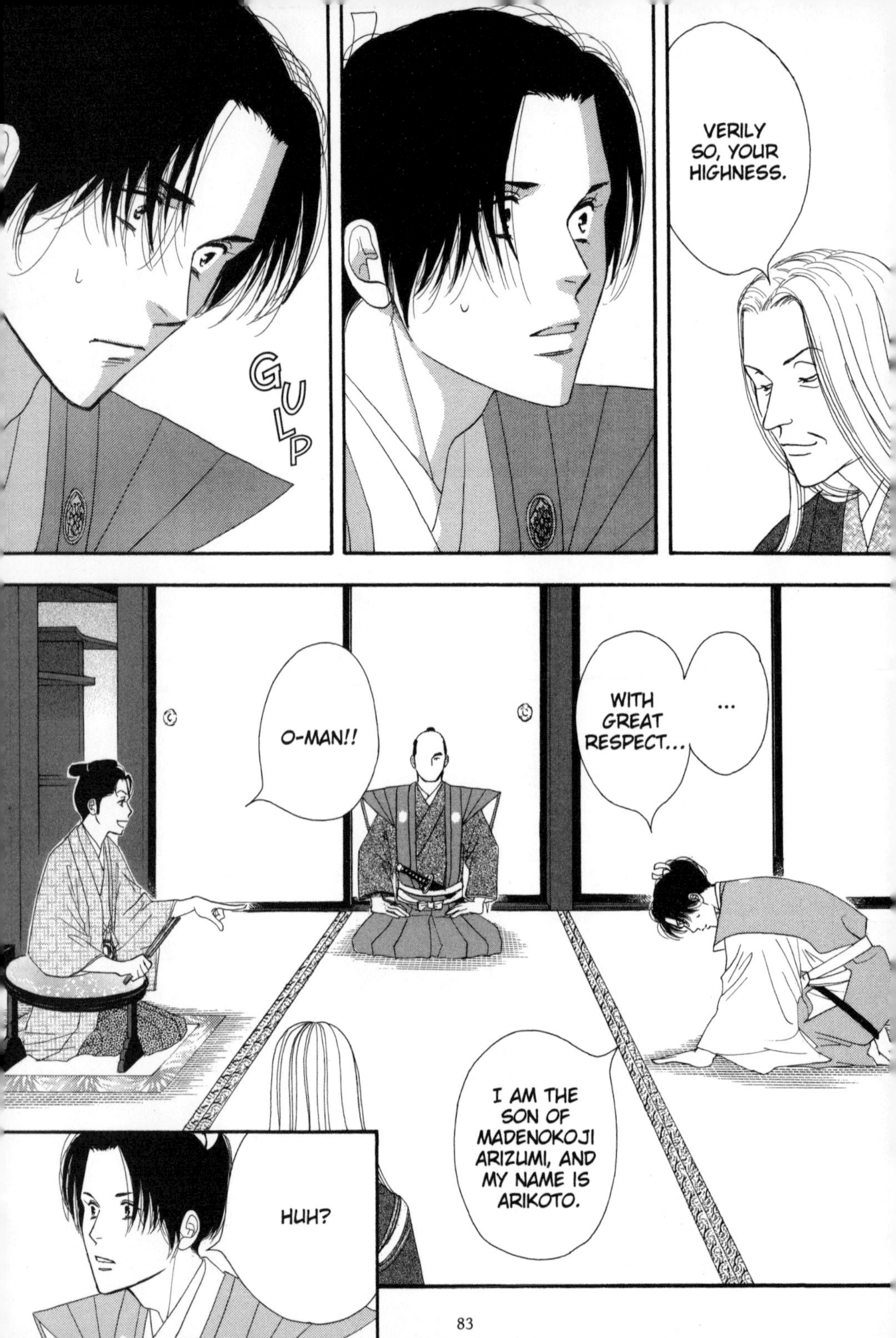
VERILY SO, YOUR HIGHNESS.
GULP
...
WITH GREAT RESPECT...
O-MAN!!
I AM THE SON OF MADENOKOJI ARIZUMI, AND MY NAME IS ARIKOTO.
HUH?

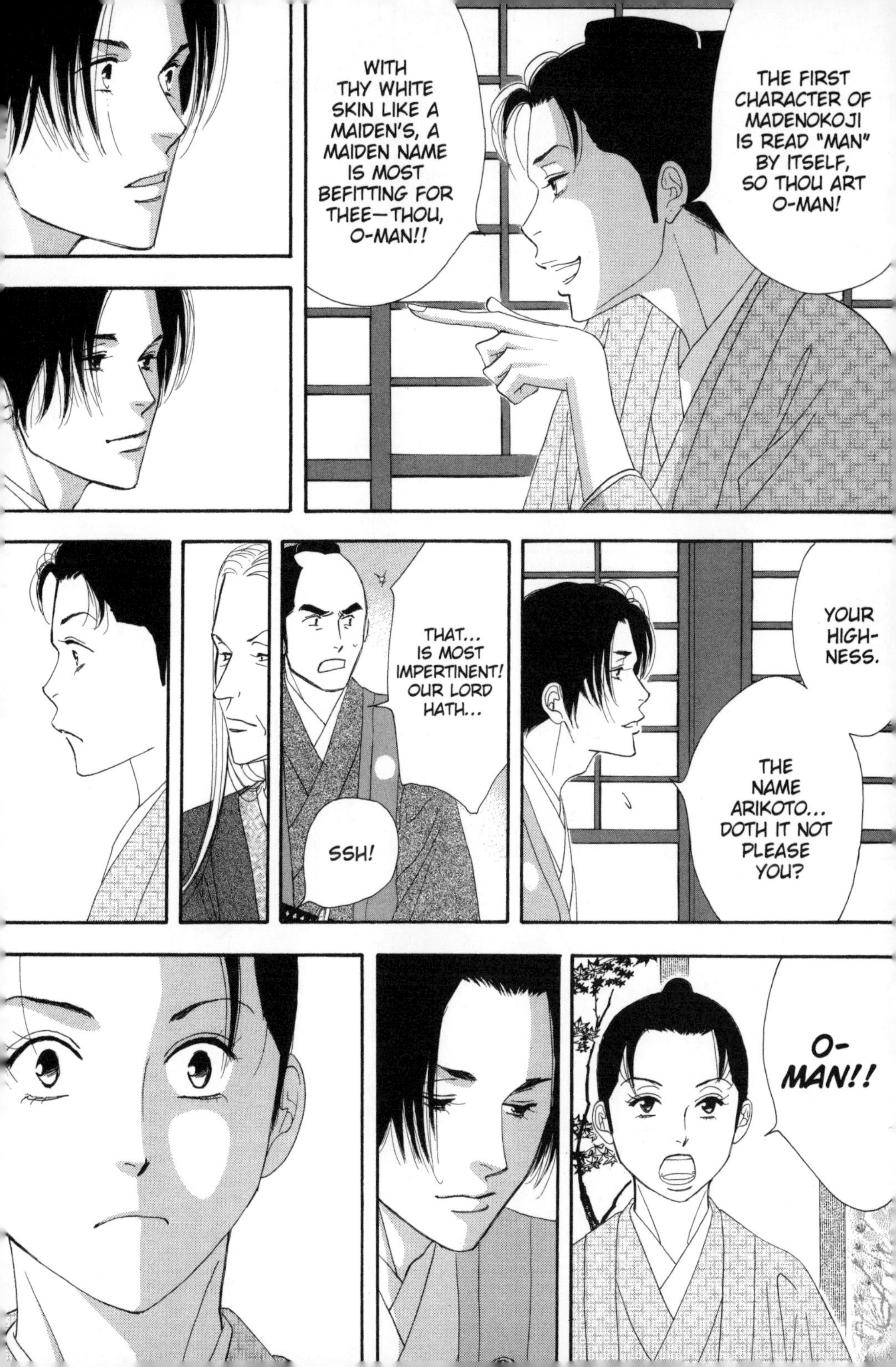
THE FIRST CHARACTER OF MADENOKOJI IS READ "MAN" BY ITSELF, SO THOU ART O-MAN!
WITH THY WHITE SKIN LIKE A MAIDEN'S, A MAIDEN NAME IS MOST BEFITTING FOR THEE—THOU, O-MAN!!
YOUR HIGHNESS.
THE NAME ARIKOTO... DOTH IT NOT PLEASE YOU?
THAT... IS MOST IMPERTINENT! OUR LORD HATH...
SSH!
O-MAN!!

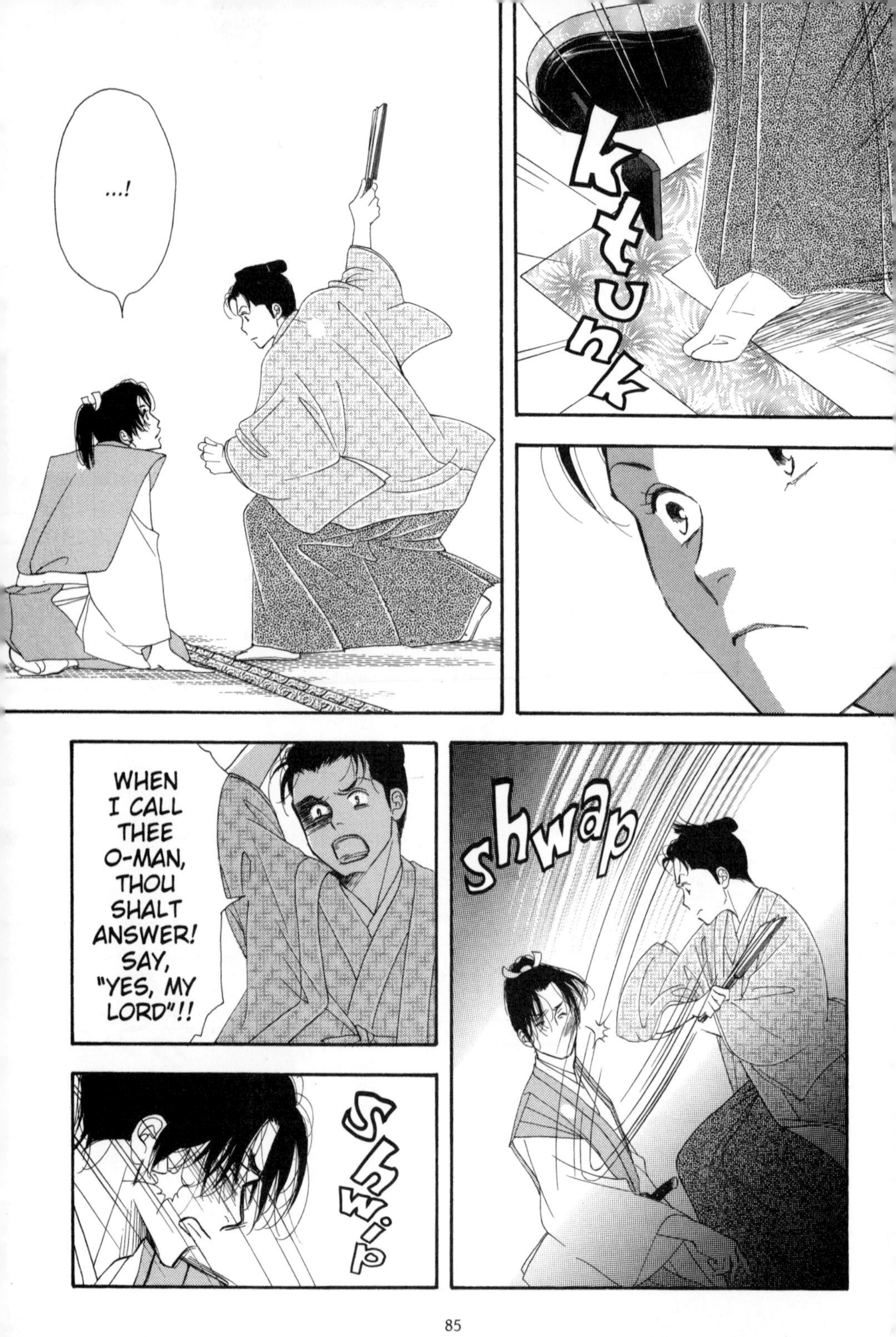
ktunk
...!
shwap
WHEN I CALL THEE O-MAN, THOU SHALT ANSWER! SAY, "YES, MY LORD"!!
shwip

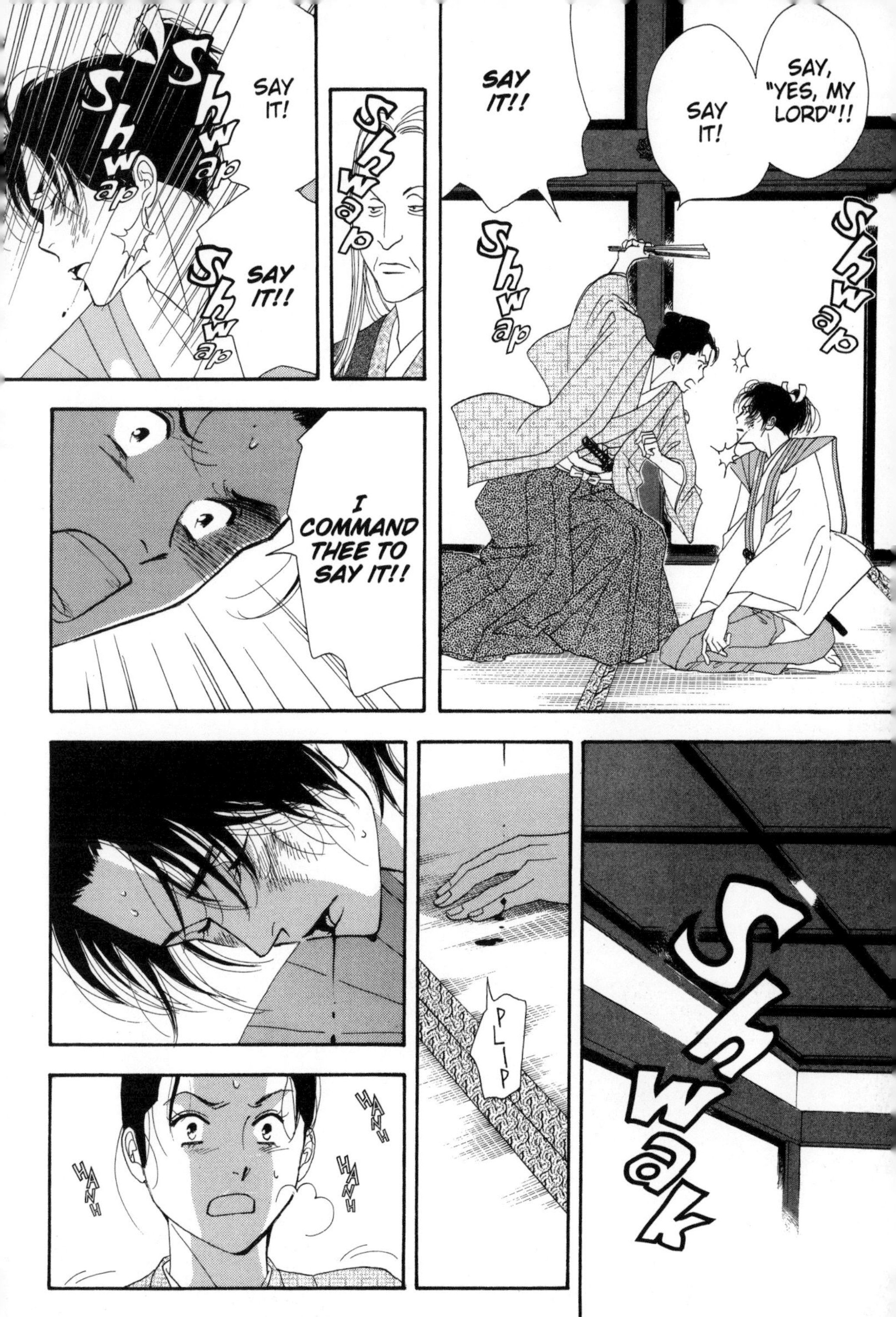
SAY, "YES, MY LORD"!!
SAY IT!
SAY IT!!
Shwap
Shwap
Shwap
Shwap
SAY IT!
Shwap
SAY IT!!
I COMMAND THEE TO SAY IT!!
Shwak
PLIP
HANH
HANH
HANH

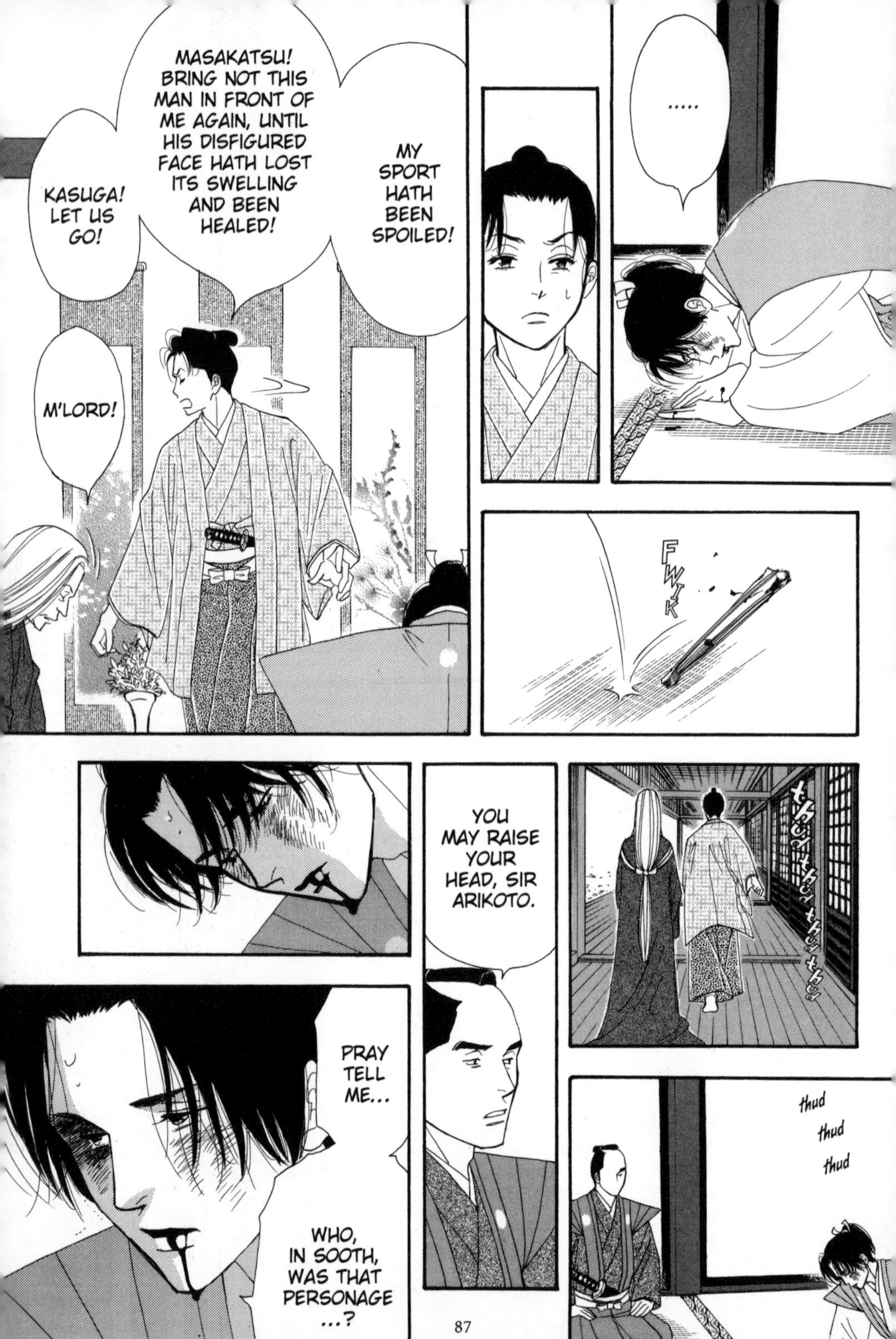
.....
FWIK
MY SPORT HATH BEEN SPOILED!
MASAKATSU! BRING NOT THIS MAN IN FRONT OF ME AGAIN, UNTIL HIS DISFIGURED FACE HATH LOST ITS SWELLING AND BEEN HEALED!
KASUGA! LET US GO!
M'LORD!
thud
thud
thud
YOU MAY RAISE YOUR HEAD, SIR ARIKOTO.
PRAY TELL ME...
WHO, IN SOOTH, WAS THAT PERSONAGE ...?

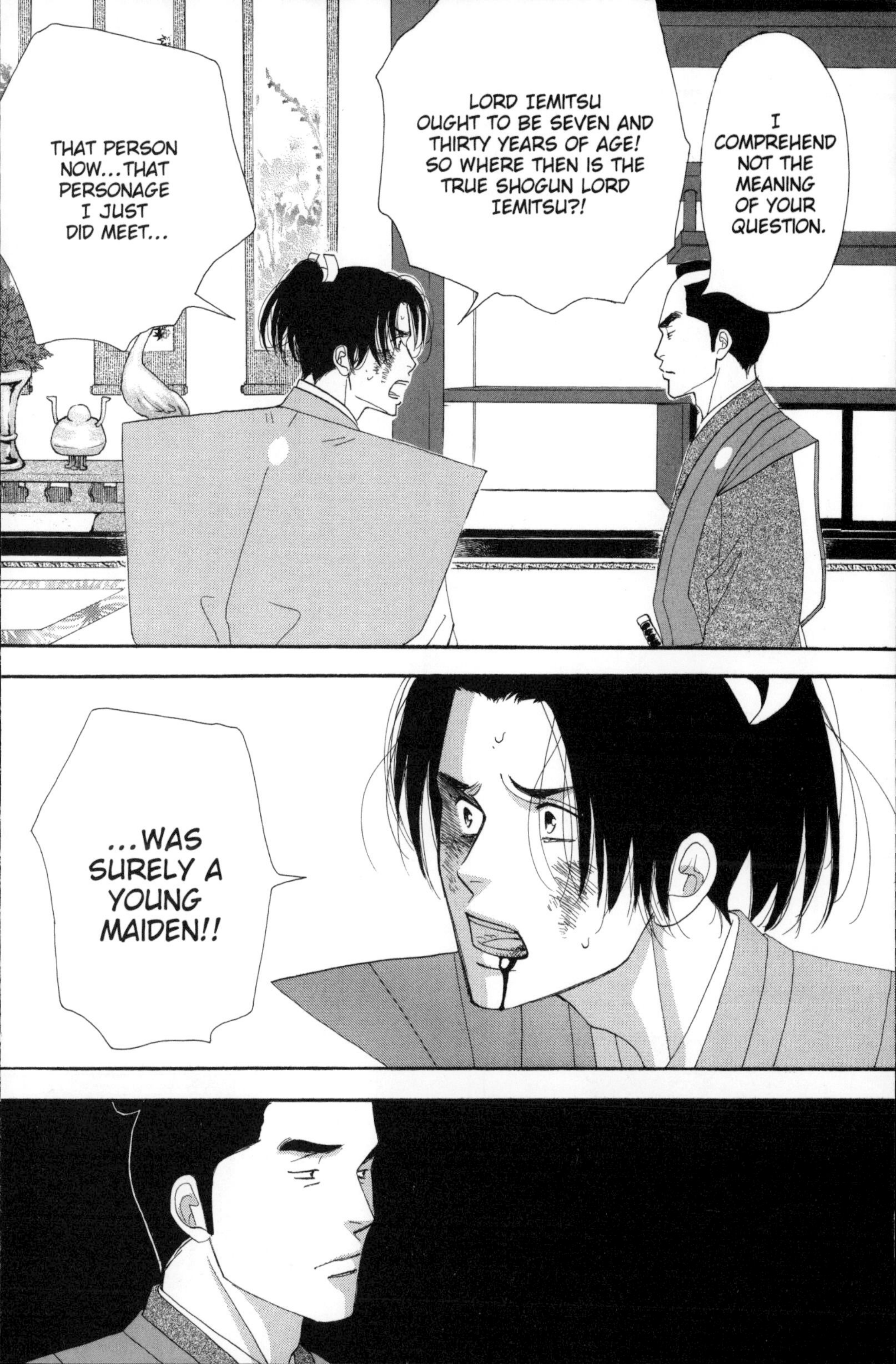
I COMPREHEND NOT THE MEANING OF YOUR QUESTION.
LORD IEMITSU OUGHT TO BE SEVEN AND THIRTY YEARS OF AGE! SO WHERE THEN IS THE TRUE SHOGUN LORD IEMITSU?!
THAT PERSON NOW...THAT PERSONAGE I JUST DID MEET...
...WAS SURELY A YOUNG MAIDEN!!

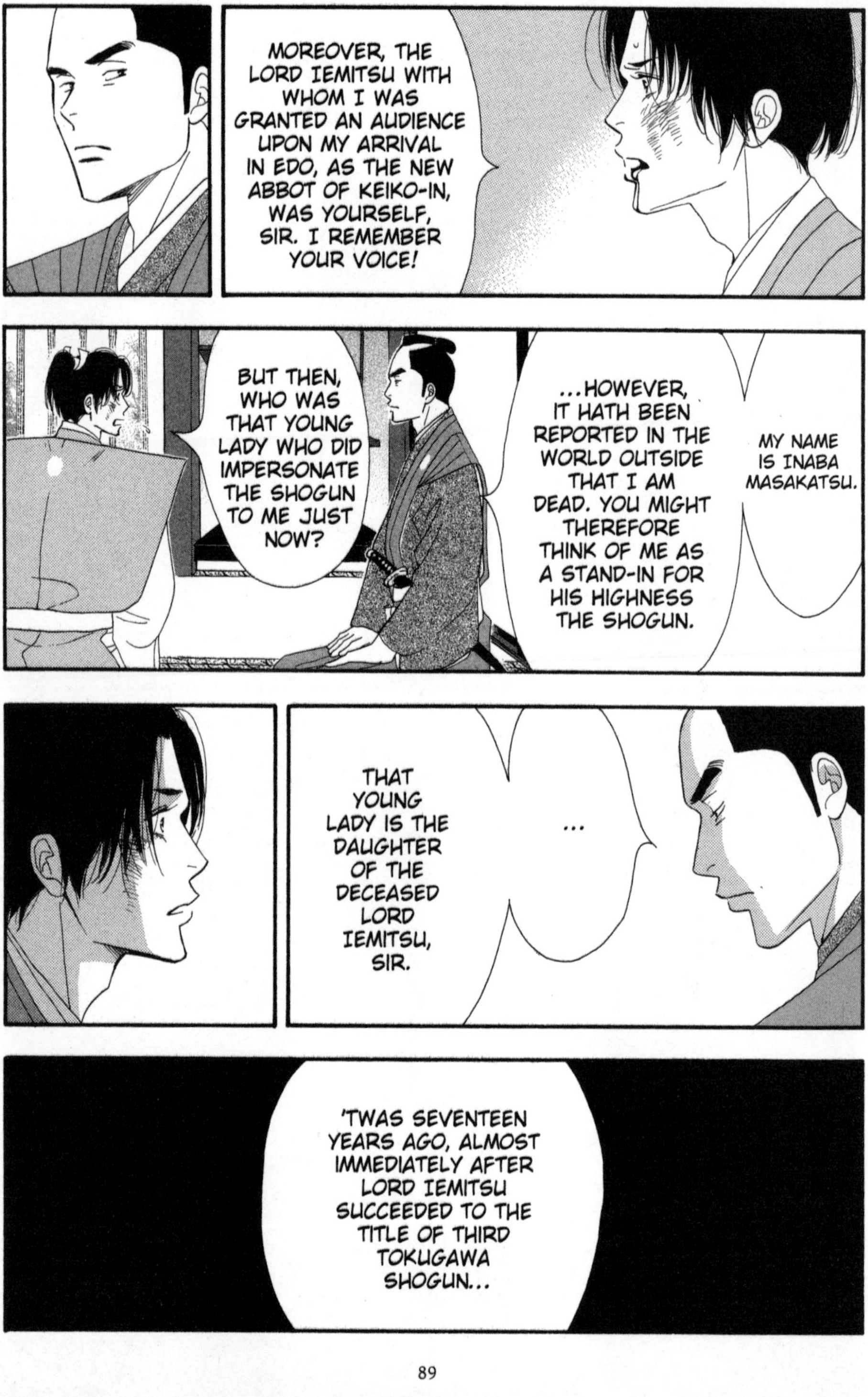
MOREOVER, THE LORD IEMITSU WITH WHOM I WAS GRANTED AN AUDIENCE UPON MY ARRIVAL IN EDO, AS THE NEW ABBOT OF KEIKO-IN, WAS YOURSELF, SIR. I REMEMBER YOUR VOICE!
MY NAME IS INABA MASAKATSU.
...HOWEVER, IT HATH BEEN REPORTED IN THE WORLD OUTSIDE THAT I AM DEAD. YOU MIGHT THEREFORE THINK OF ME AS A STAND-IN FOR HIS HIGHNESS THE SHOGUN.
BUT THEN, WHO WAS THAT YOUNG LADY WHO DID IMPERSONATE THE SHOGUN TO ME JUST NOW?
...
THAT YOUNG LADY IS THE DAUGHTER OF THE DECEASED LORD IEMITSU, SIR.
'TWAS SEVENTEEN YEARS AGO, ALMOST IMMEDIATELY AFTER LORD IEMITSU SUCCEEDED TO THE TITLE OF THIRD TOKUGAWA SHOGUN...

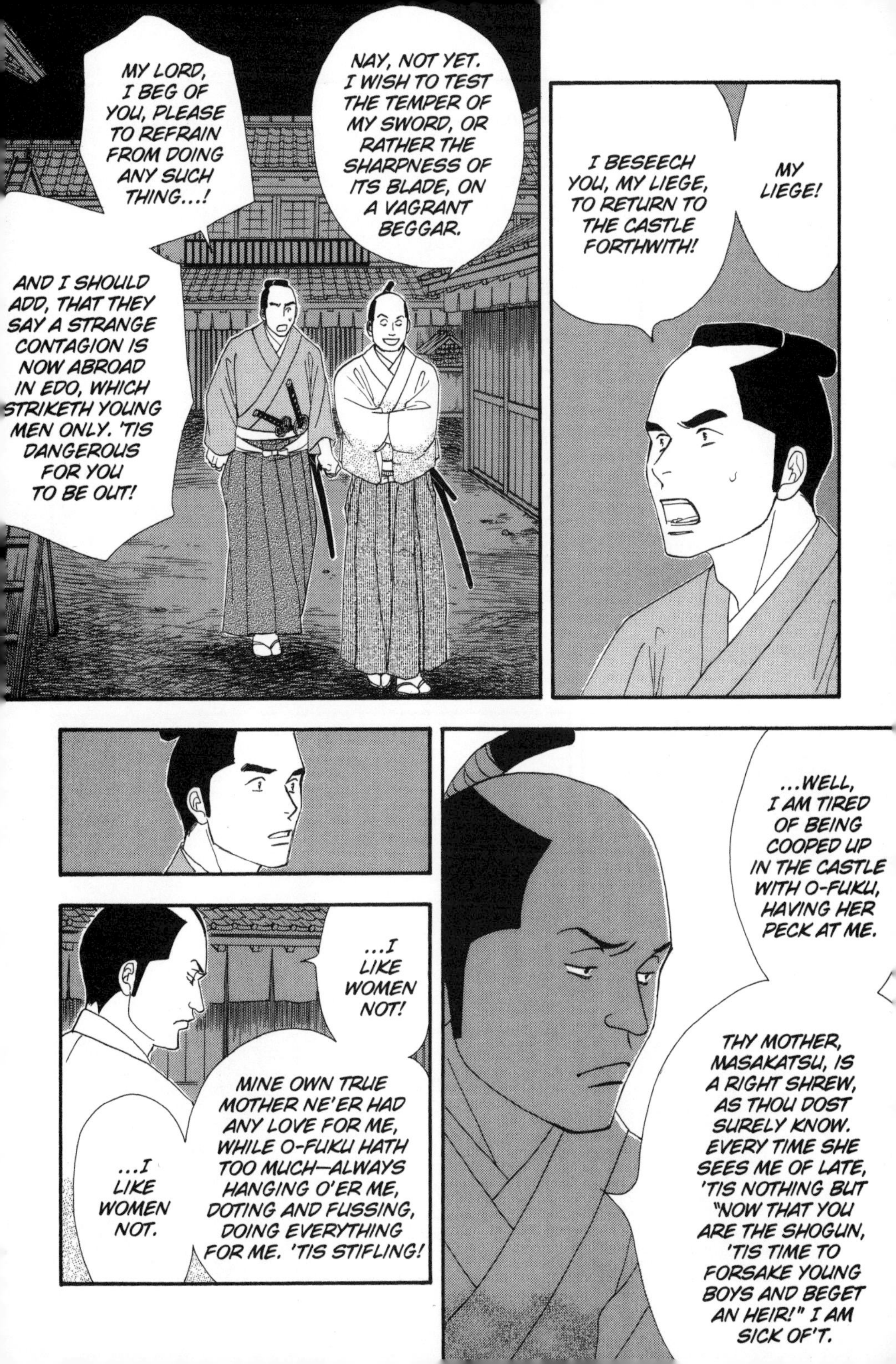
MY LIEGE!
I BESEECH YOU, MY LIEGE, TO RETURN TO THE CASTLE FORTHWITH!
NAY, NOT YET. I WISH TO TEST THE TEMPER OF MY SWORD, OR RATHER THE SHARPNESS OF ITS BLADE, ON A VAGRANT BEGGAR.
MY LORD, I BEG OF YOU, PLEASE TO REFRAIN FROM DOING ANY SUCH THING...!
AND I SHOULD ADD, THAT THEY SAY A STRANGE CONTAGION IS NOW ABROAD IN EDO, WHICH STRIKETH YOUNG MEN ONLY. 'TIS DANGEROUS FOR YOU TO BE OUT!
...WELL, I AM TIRED OF BEING COOPED UP IN THE CASTLE WITH O-FUKU, HAVING HER PECK AT ME.
THY MOTHER, MASAKATSU, IS A RIGHT SHREW, AS THOU DOST SURELY KNOW. EVERY TIME SHE SEES ME OF LATE, 'TIS NOTHING BUT "NOW THAT YOU ARE THE SHOGUN, 'TIS TIME TO FORSAKE YOUNG BOYS AND BEGET AN HEIR!" I AM SICK OF'T.
...I LIKE WOMEN NOT!
MINE OWN TRUE MOTHER NE'ER HAD ANY LOVE FOR ME, WHILE O-FUKU HATH TOO MUCH—ALWAYS HANGING O'ER ME, DOTING AND FUSSING, DOING EVERYTHING FOR ME. 'TIS STIFLING!
...I LIKE WOMEN NOT.

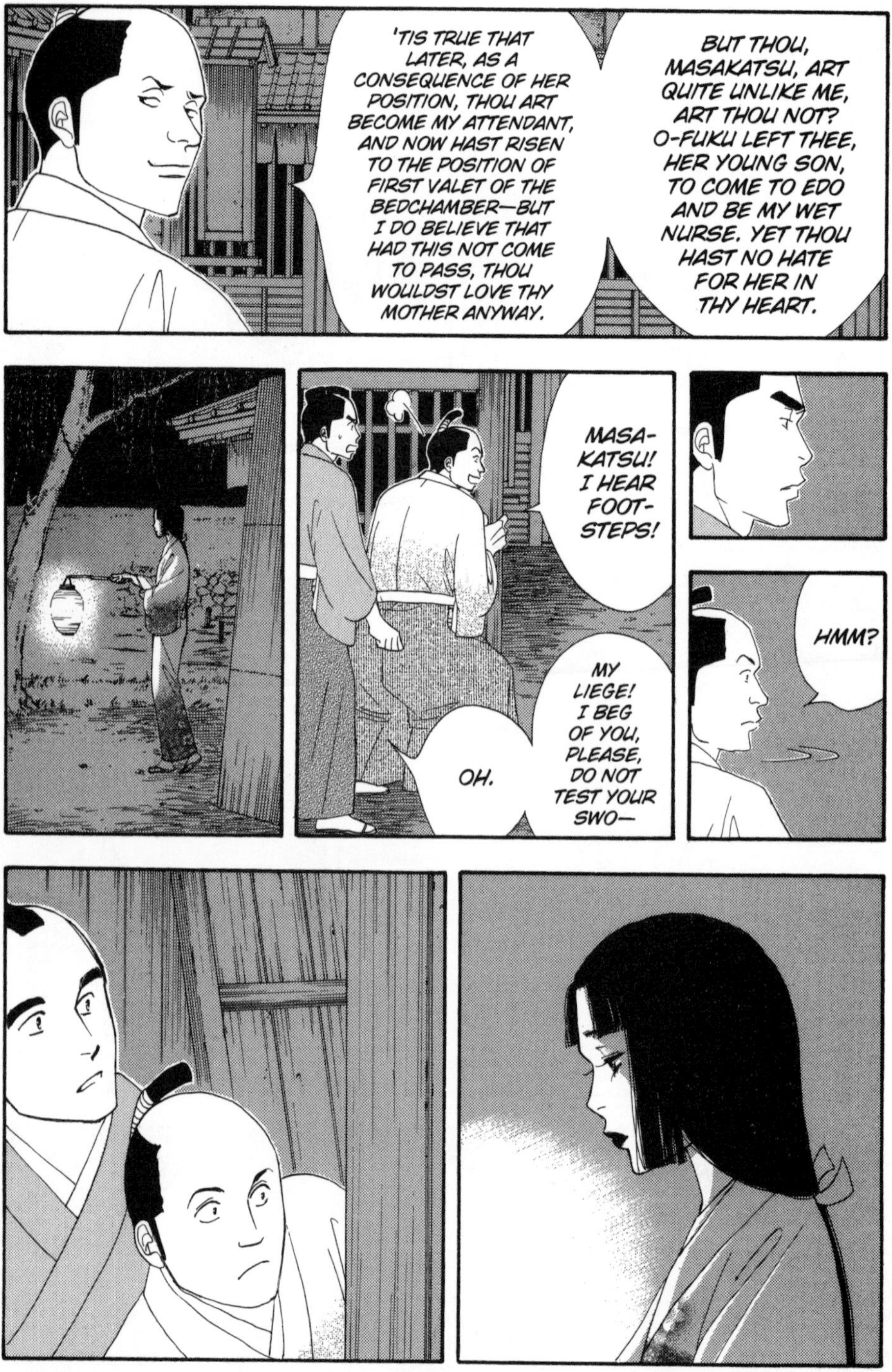
BUT THOU, MASAKATSU, ART QUITE UNLIKE ME, ART THOU NOT? O-FUKU LEFT THEE, HER YOUNG SON, TO COME TO EDO AND BE MY WET NURSE. YET THOU HAST NO HATE FOR HER IN THY HEART.
'TIS TRUE THAT LATER, AS A CONSEQUENCE OF HER POSITION, THOU ART BECOME MY ATTENDANT, AND NOW HAST RISEN TO THE POSITION OF FIRST VALET OF THE BEDCHAMBER—BUT I DO BELIEVE THAT HAD THIS NOT COME TO PASS, THOU WOULDST LOVE THY MOTHER ANYWAY.
HMM?
MASA-KATSU! I HEAR FOOT-STEPS!
MY LIEGE! I BEG OF YOU, PLEASE, DO NOT TEST YOUR SWO—
OH.

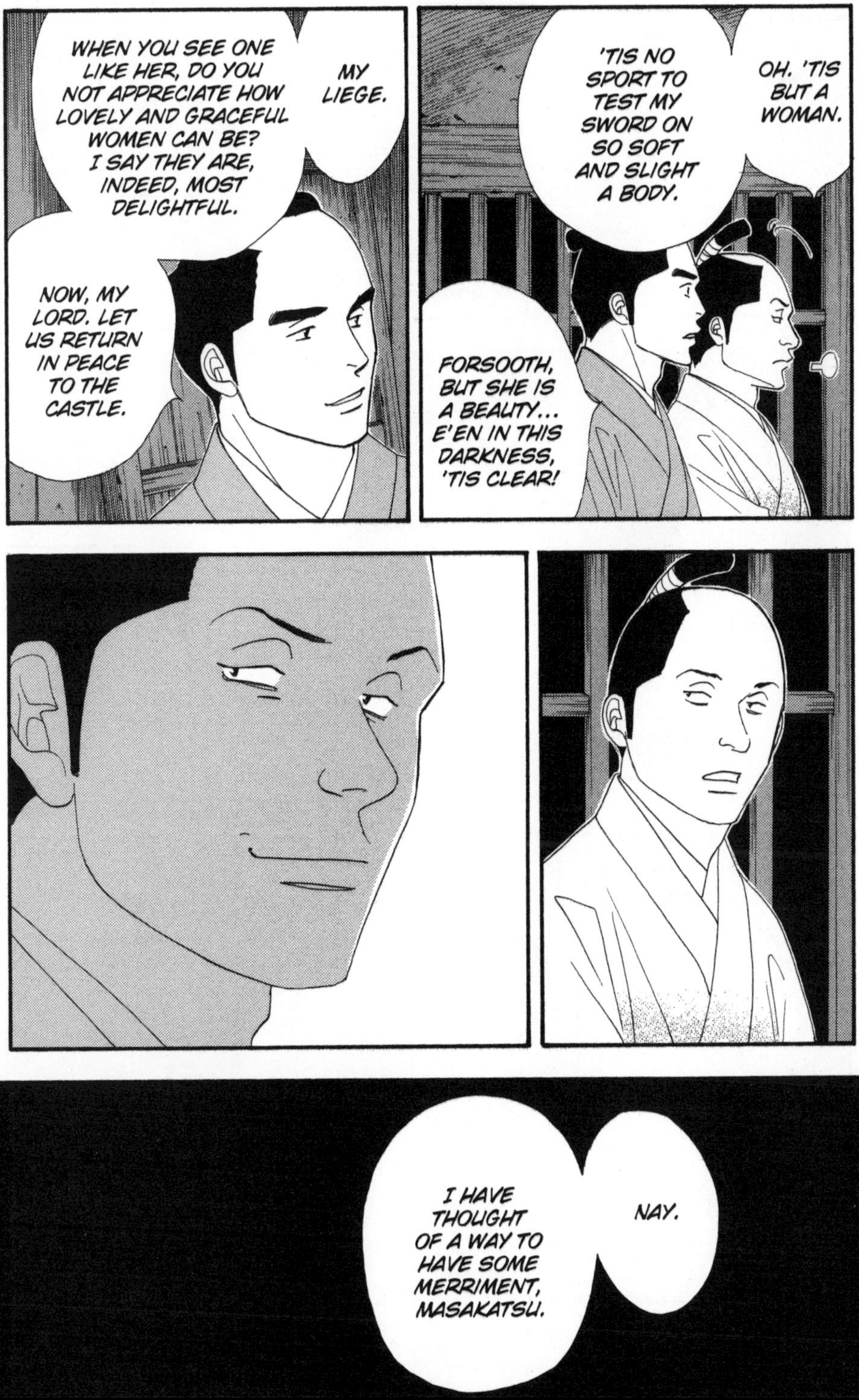
OH. 'TIS BUT A WOMAN.
'TIS NO SPORT TO TEST MY SWORD ON SO SOFT AND SLIGHT A BODY.
FORSOOTH, BUT SHE IS A BEAUTY... E'EN IN THIS DARKNESS, 'TIS CLEAR!
MY LIEGE.
WHEN YOU SEE ONE LIKE HER, DO YOU NOT APPRECIATE HOW LOVELY AND GRACEFUL WOMEN CAN BE? I SAY THEY ARE, INDEED, MOST DELIGHTFUL.
NOW, MY LORD. LET US RETURN IN PEACE TO THE CASTLE.
NAY.
I HAVE THOUGHT OF A WAY TO HAVE SOME MERRIMENT, MASAKATSU.

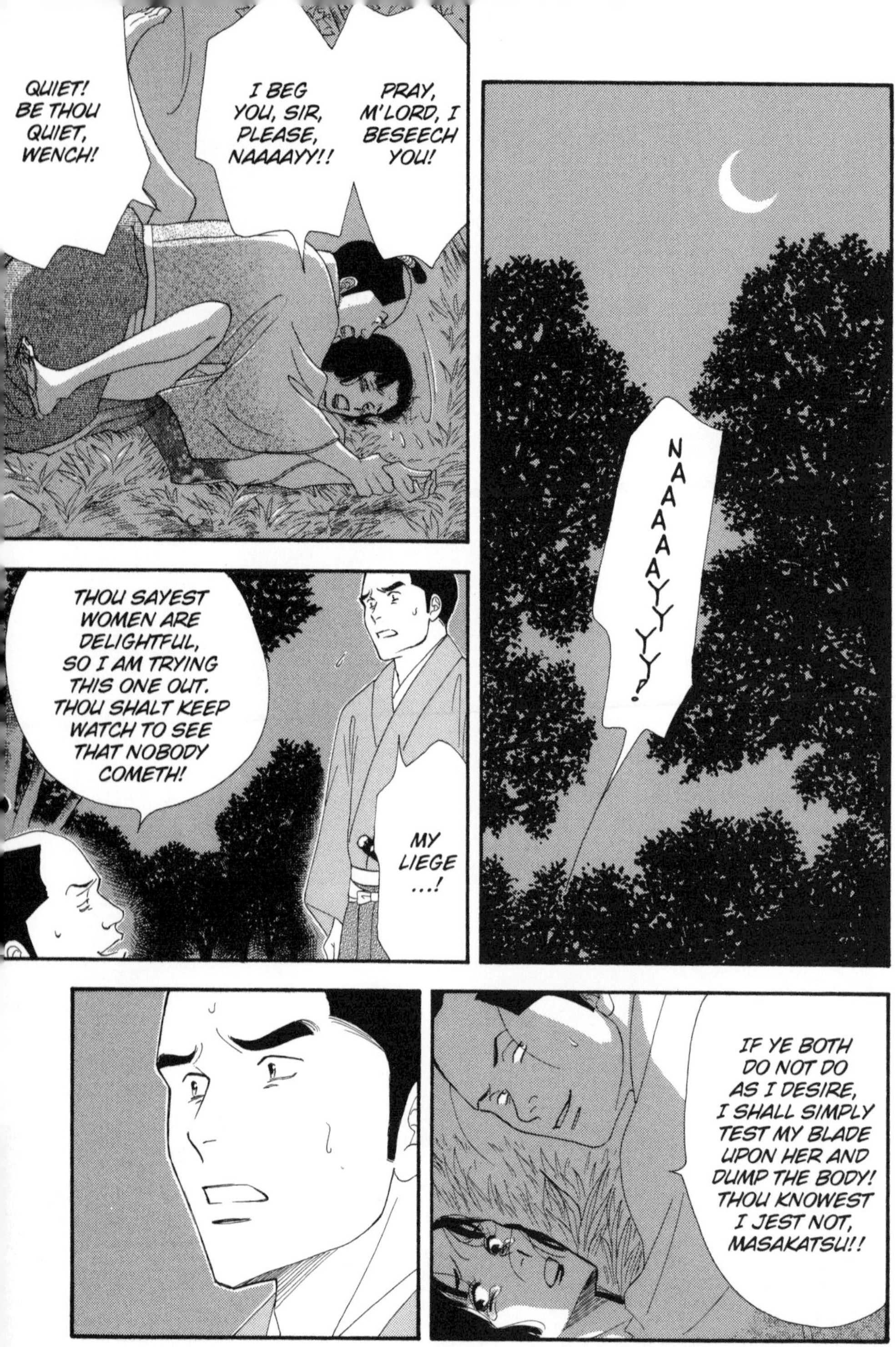
NAAAAAYYYY!
PRAY, M'LORD, I BESEECH YOU!
I BEG YOU, SIR, PLEASE, NAAAAYY!!
QUIET! BE THOU QUIET, WENCH!
THOU SAYEST WOMEN ARE DELIGHTFUL, SO I AM TRYING THIS ONE OUT. THOU SHALT KEEP WATCH TO SEE THAT NOBODY COMETH!
MY LIEGE ...!
IF YE BOTH DO NOT DO AS I DESIRE, I SHALL SIMPLY TEST MY BLADE UPON HER AND DUMP THE BODY! THOU KNOWEST I JEST NOT, MASAKATSU!!

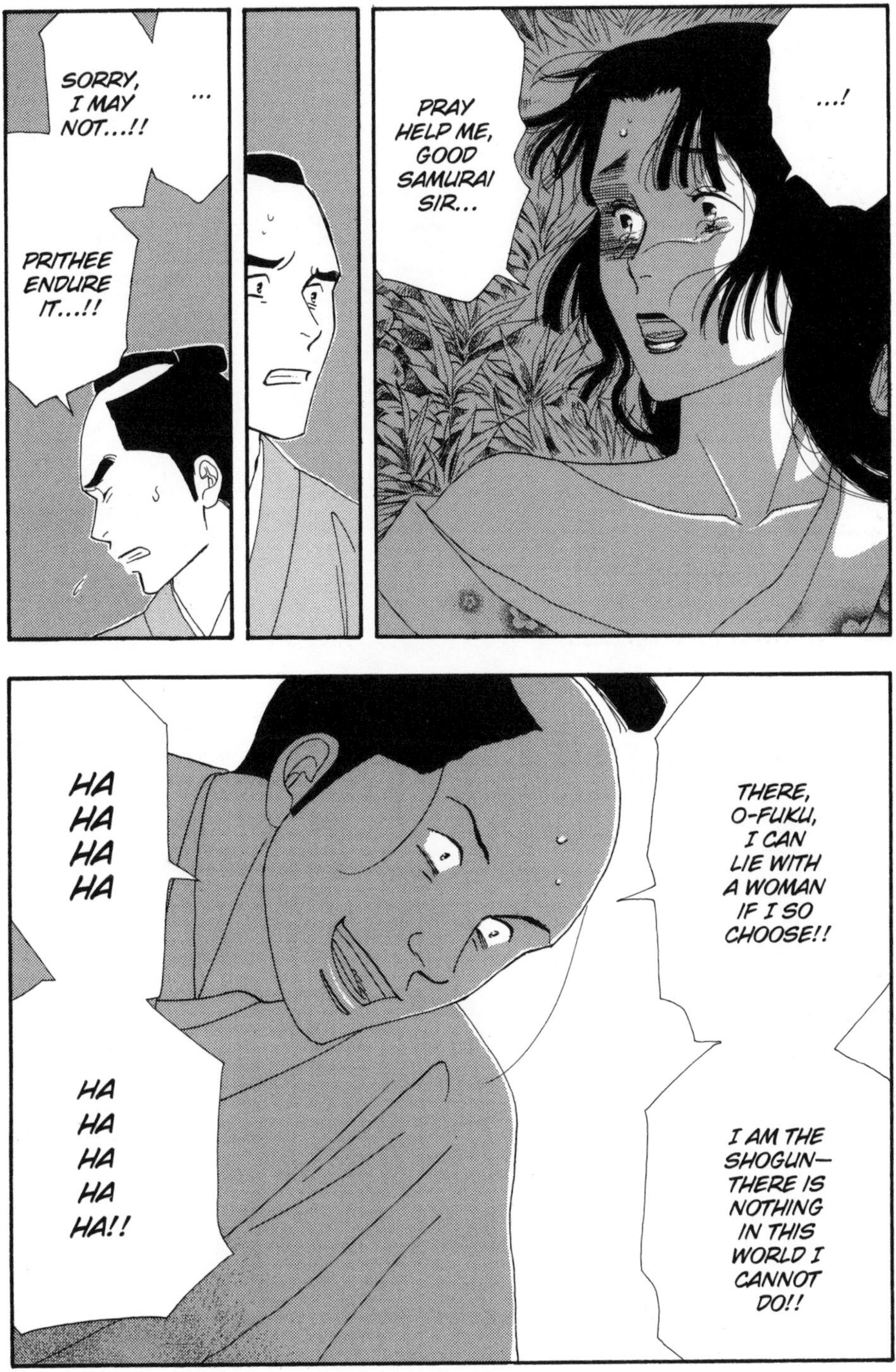
...!
PRAY HELP ME, GOOD SAMURAI SIR...
...
SORRY, I MAY NOT...!!
PRITHEE ENDURE IT...!!
THERE, O-FUKU, I CAN LIE WITH A WOMAN IF I SO CHOOSE!!
I AM THE SHOGUN— THERE IS NOTHING IN THIS WORLD I CANNOT DO!!
HA HA HA HA
HA HA HA HA HA!!

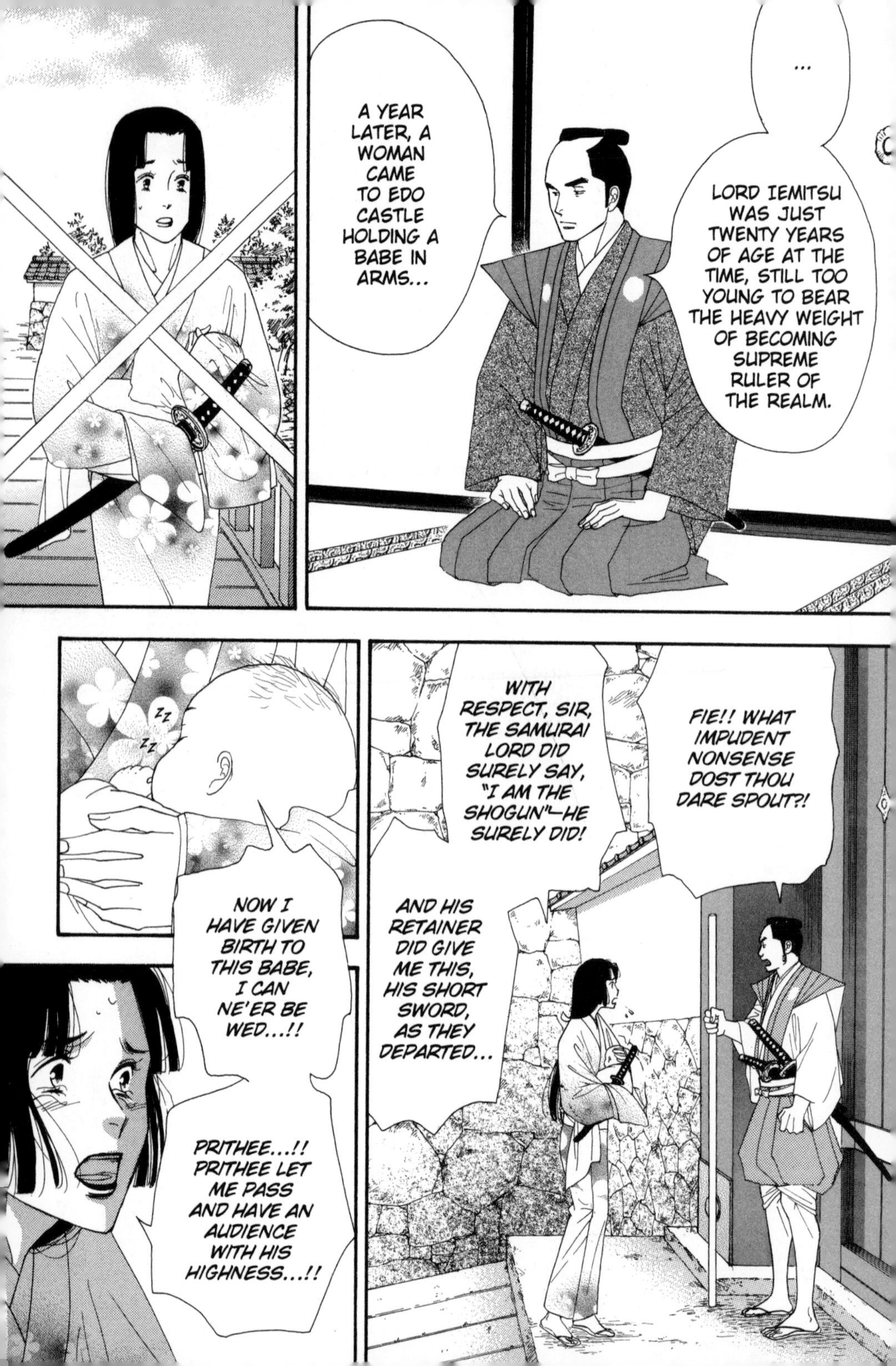
...
LORD IEMITSU WAS JUST TWENTY YEARS OF AGE AT THE TIME, STILL TOO YOUNG TO BEAR THE HEAVY WEIGHT OF BECOMING SUPREME RULER OF THE REALM.
A YEAR LATER, A WOMAN CAME TO EDO CASTLE HOLDING A BABE IN ARMS...
FIE!! WHAT IMPUDENT NONSENSE DOST THOU DARE SPOUT?!
WITH RESPECT, SIR, THE SAMURAI LORD DID SURELY SAY, "I AM THE SHOGUN"—HE SURELY DID!
AND HIS RETAINER DID GIVE ME THIS, HIS SHORT SWORD, AS THEY DEPARTED...
ZZ
ZZ
NOW I HAVE GIVEN BIRTH TO THIS BABE, I CAN NE'ER BE WED...!!
PRITHEE...!! PRITHEE LET ME PASS AND HAVE AN AUDIENCE WITH HIS HIGHNESS...!!

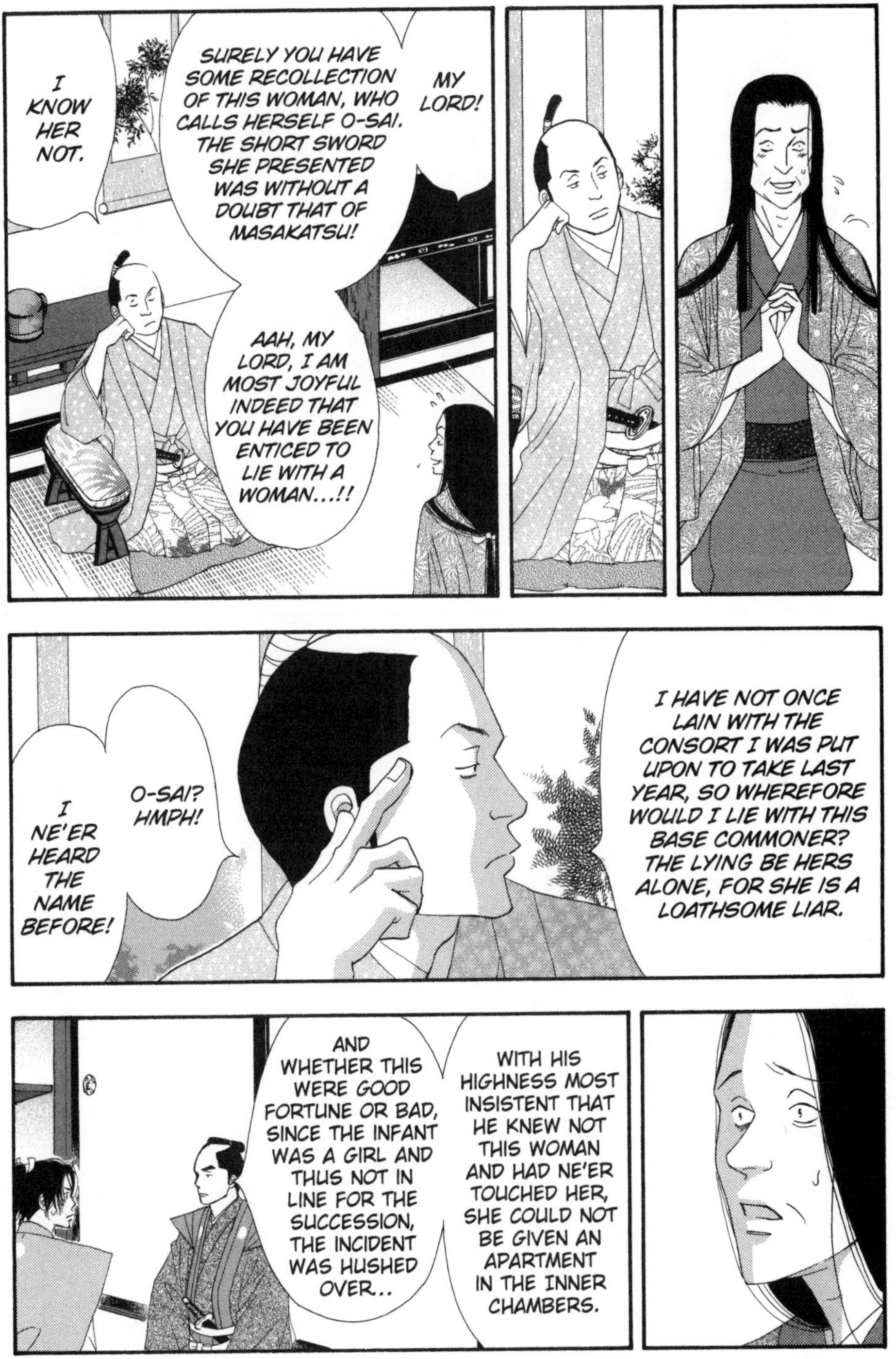
MY LORD!
SURELY YOU HAVE SOME RECOLLECTION OF THIS WOMAN, WHO CALLS HERSELF O-SAI. THE SHORT SWORD SHE PRESENTED WAS WITHOUT A DOUBT THAT OF MASAKATSU!
I KNOW HER NOT.
AAH, MY LORD, I AM MOST JOYFUL INDEED THAT YOU HAVE BEEN ENTICED TO LIE WITH A WOMAN...!!
I HAVE NOT ONCE LAIN WITH THE CONSORT I WAS PUT UPON TO TAKE LAST YEAR, SO WHEREFORE WOULD I LIE WITH THIS BASE COMMONER? THE LYING BE HERS ALONE, FOR SHE IS A LOATHSOME LIAR.
O-SAI? HMPH!
I NE'ER HEARD THE NAME BEFORE!
WITH HIS HIGHNESS MOST INSISTENT THAT HE KNEW NOT THIS WOMAN AND HAD NE'ER TOUCHED HER, SHE COULD NOT BE GIVEN AN APARTMENT IN THE INNER CHAMBERS.
AND WHETHER THIS WERE GOOD FORTUNE OR BAD, SINCE THE INFANT WAS A GIRL AND THUS NOT IN LINE FOR THE SUCCESSION, THE INCIDENT WAS HUSHED OVER...

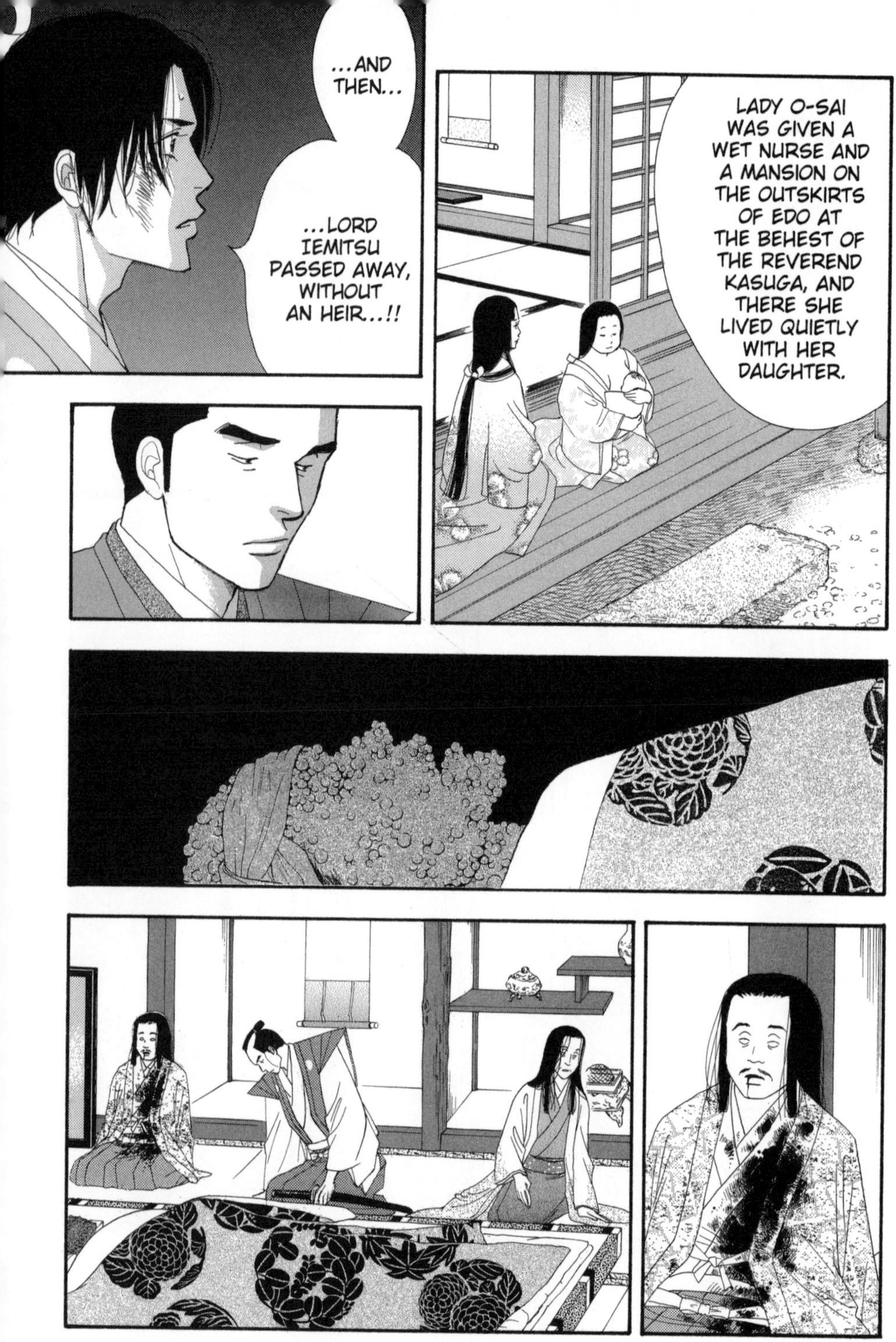
LADY O-SAI WAS GIVEN A WET NURSE AND A MANSION ON THE OUTSKIRTS OF EDO AT THE BEHEST OF THE REVEREND KASUGA, AND THERE SHE LIVED QUIETLY WITH HER DAUGHTER.
...AND THEN...
...LORD IEMITSU PASSED AWAY, WITHOUT AN HEIR...!!

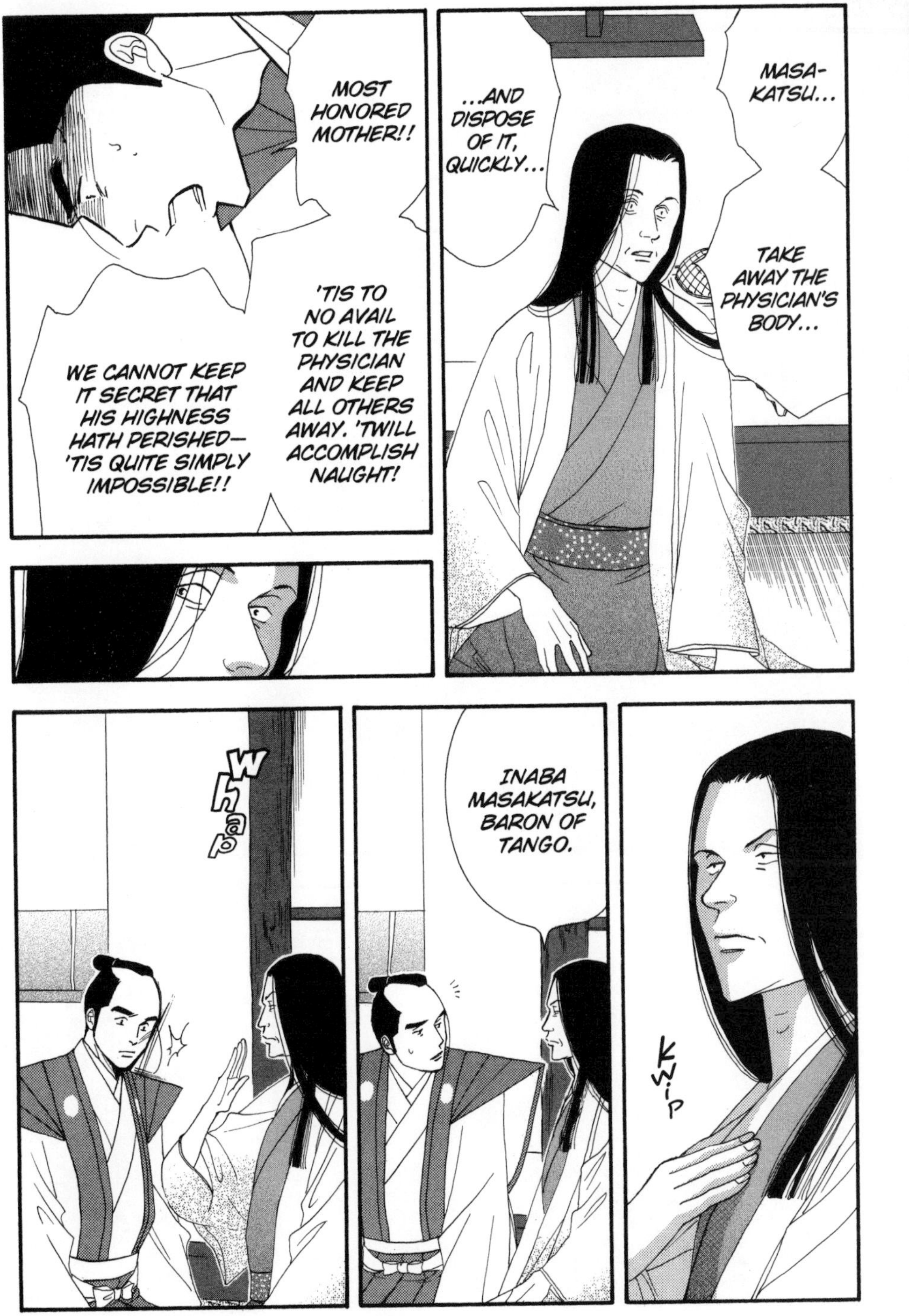
MASA-KATSU...
TAKE AWAY THE PHYSICIAN'S BODY...
...AND DISPOSE OF IT, QUICKLY...
MOST HONORED MOTHER!!
'TIS TO NO AVAIL TO KILL THE PHYSICIAN AND KEEP ALL OTHERS AWAY. 'TWILL ACCOMPLISH NAUGHT!
WE CANNOT KEEP IT SECRET THAT HIS HIGHNESS HATH PERISHED— 'TIS QUITE SIMPLY IMPOSSIBLE!!
KWIP
INABA MASAKATSU, BARON OF TANGO.
WHAP

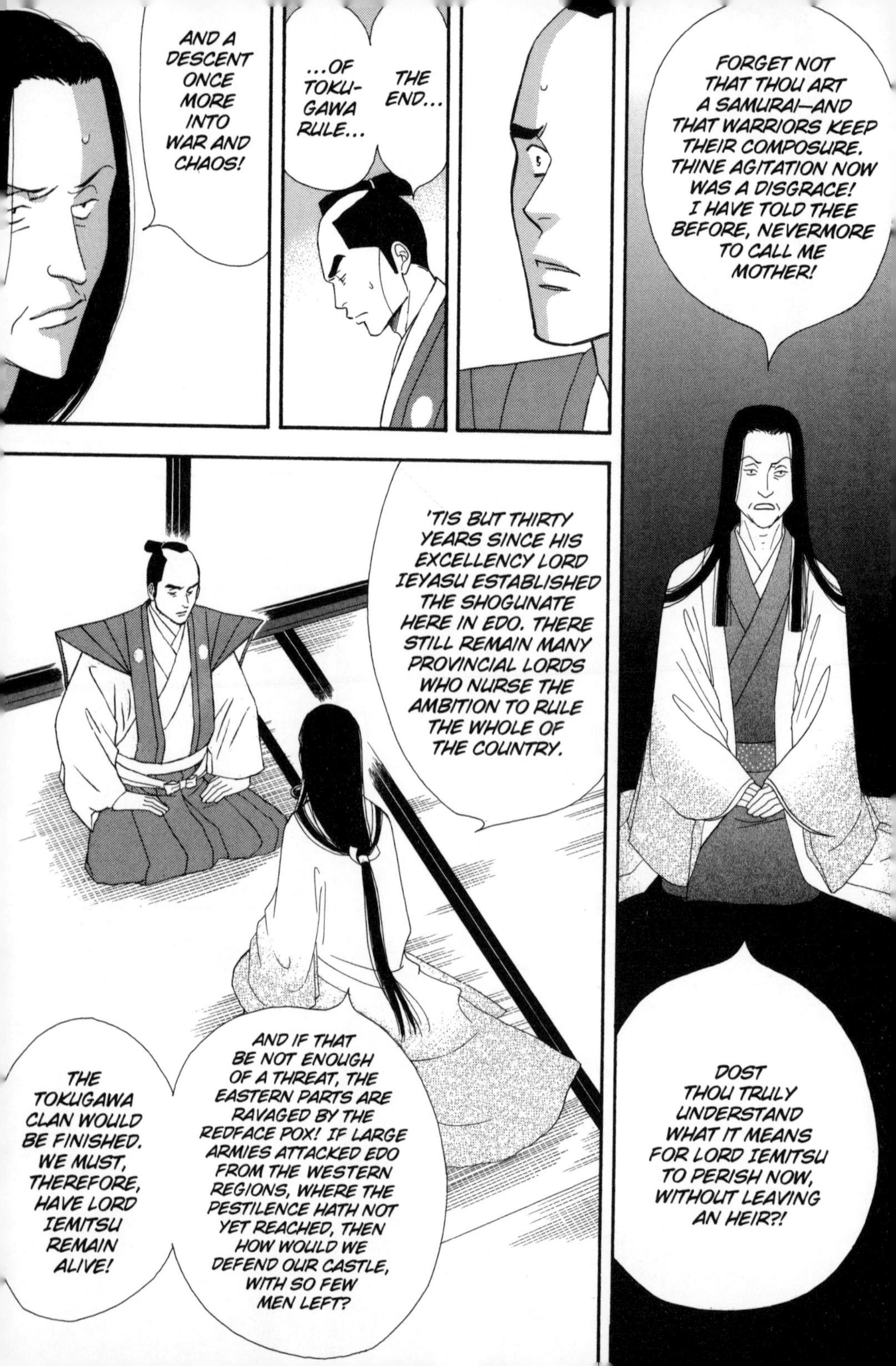
FORGET NOT THAT THOU ART A SAMURAI—AND THAT WARRIORS KEEP THEIR COMPOSURE. THINE AGITATION NOW WAS A DISGRACE! I HAVE TOLD THEE BEFORE, NEVERMORE TO CALL ME MOTHER!
DOST THOU TRULY UNDERSTAND WHAT IT MEANS FOR LORD IEMITSU TO PERISH NOW, WITHOUT LEAVING AN HEIR?!
THE END...
...OF TOKUGAWA RULE...
AND A DESCENT ONCE MORE INTO WAR AND CHAOS!
'TIS BUT THIRTY YEARS SINCE HIS EXCELLENCY LORD IEYASU ESTABLISHED THE SHOGUNATE HERE IN EDO. THERE STILL REMAIN MANY PROVINCIAL LORDS WHO NURSE THE AMBITION TO RULE THE WHOLE OF THE COUNTRY.
AND IF THAT BE NOT ENOUGH OF A THREAT, THE EASTERN PARTS ARE RAVAGED BY THE REDFACE POX! IF LARGE ARMIES ATTACKED EDO FROM THE WESTERN REGIONS, WHERE THE PESTILENCE HATH NOT YET REACHED, THEN HOW WOULD WE DEFEND OUR CASTLE, WITH SO FEW MEN LEFT?
THE TOKUGAWA CLAN WOULD BE FINISHED. WE MUST, THEREFORE, HAVE LORD IEMITSU REMAIN ALIVE!

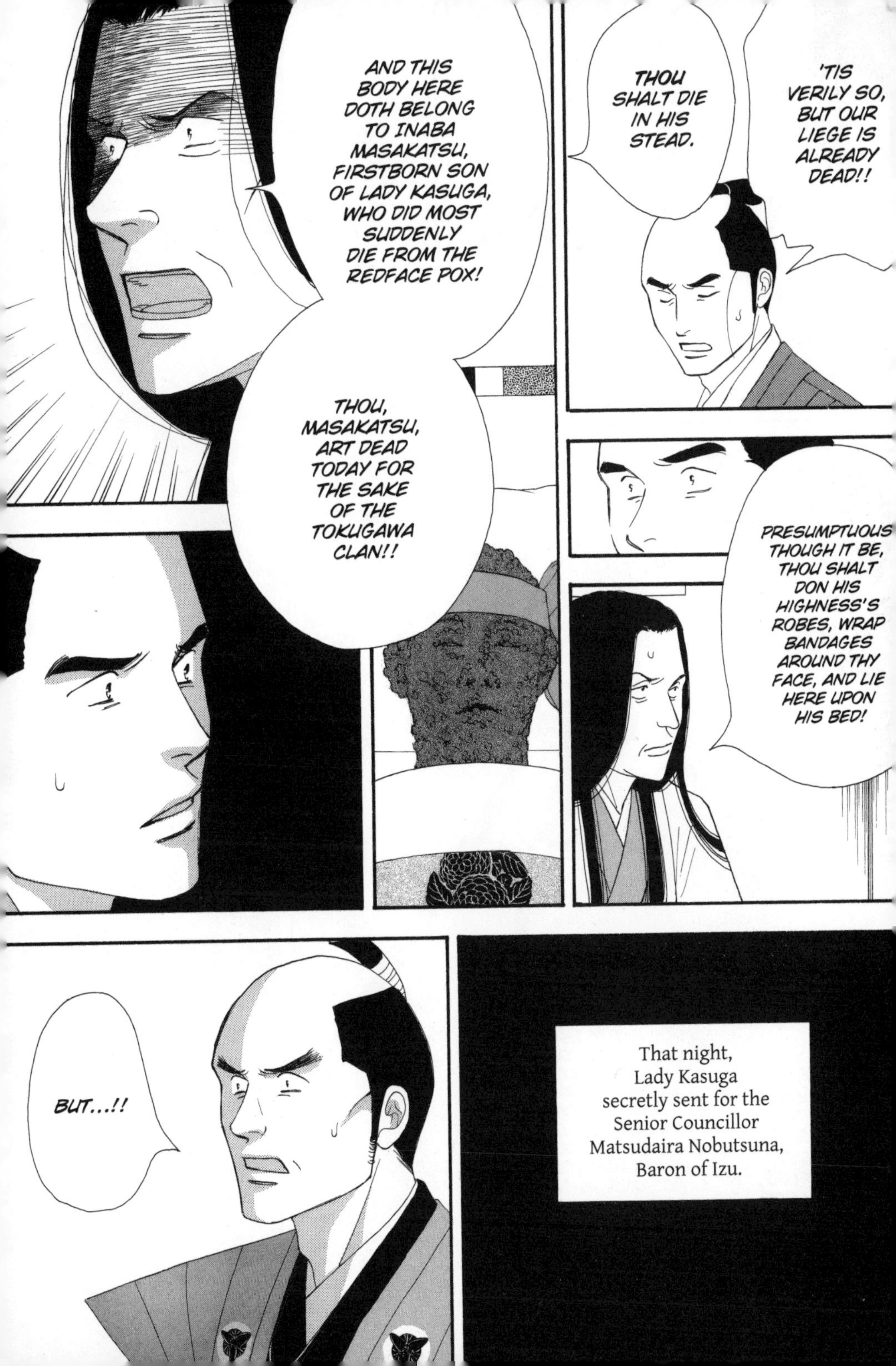
'TIS VERILY SO, BUT OUR LIEGE IS ALREADY DEAD!!
THOU SHALT DIE IN HIS STEAD.
AND THIS BODY HERE DOTH BELONG TO INABA MASAKATSU, FIRSTBORN SON OF LADY KASUGA, WHO DID MOST SUDDENLY DIE FROM THE REDFACE POX!
THOU, MASAKATSU, ART DEAD TODAY FOR THE SAKE OF THE TOKUGAWA CLAN!!
PRESUMPTUOUS THOUGH IT BE, THOU SHALT DON HIS HIGHNESS'S ROBES, WRAP BANDAGES AROUND THY FACE, AND LIE HERE UPON HIS BED!
That night, Lady Kasuga secretly sent for the Senior Councillor Matsudaira Nobutsuna, Baron of Izu.
BUT...!!

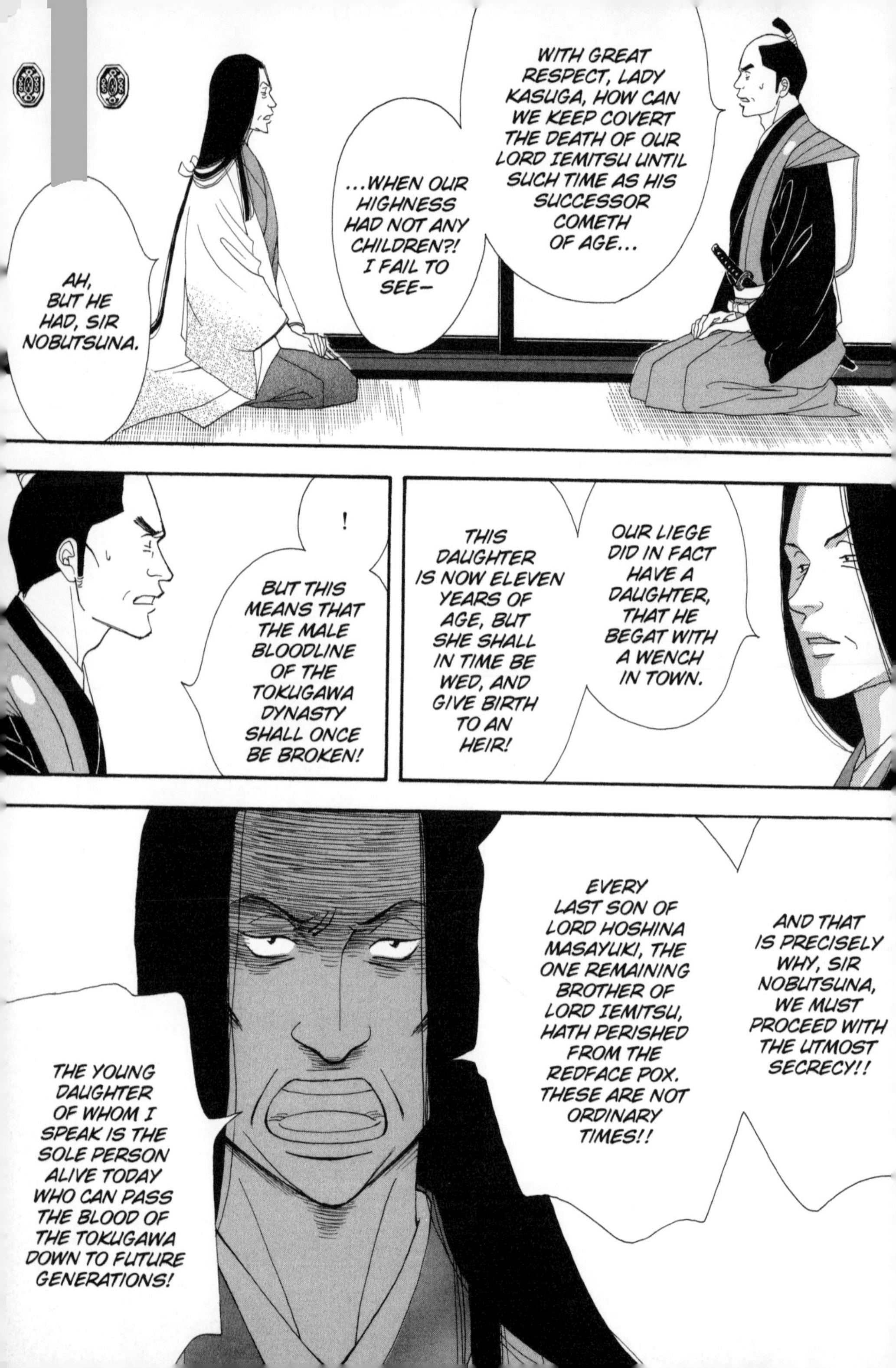
WITH GREAT RESPECT, LADY KASUGA, HOW CAN WE KEEP COVERT THE DEATH OF OUR LORD IEMITSU UNTIL SUCH TIME AS HIS SUCCESSOR COMETH OF AGE...
...WHEN OUR HIGHNESS HAD NOT ANY CHILDREN?! I FAIL TO SEE–
AH, BUT HE HAD, SIR NOBUTSUNA.
OUR LIEGE DID IN FACT HAVE A DAUGHTER, THAT HE BEGAT WITH A WENCH IN TOWN.
THIS DAUGHTER IS NOW ELEVEN YEARS OF AGE, BUT SHE SHALL IN TIME BE WED, AND GIVE BIRTH TO AN HEIR!
!
BUT THIS MEANS THAT THE MALE BLOODLINE OF THE TOKUGAWA DYNASTY SHALL ONCE BE BROKEN!
AND THAT IS PRECISELY WHY, SIR NOBUTSUNA, WE MUST PROCEED WITH THE UTMOST SECRECY!!
EVERY LAST SON OF LORD HOSHINA MASAYUKI, THE ONE REMAINING BROTHER OF LORD IEMITSU, HATH PERISHED FROM THE REDFACE POX. THESE ARE NOT ORDINARY TIMES!!
THE YOUNG DAUGHTER OF WHOM I SPEAK IS THE SOLE PERSON ALIVE TODAY WHO CAN PASS THE BLOOD OF THE TOKUGAWA DOWN TO FUTURE GENERATIONS!

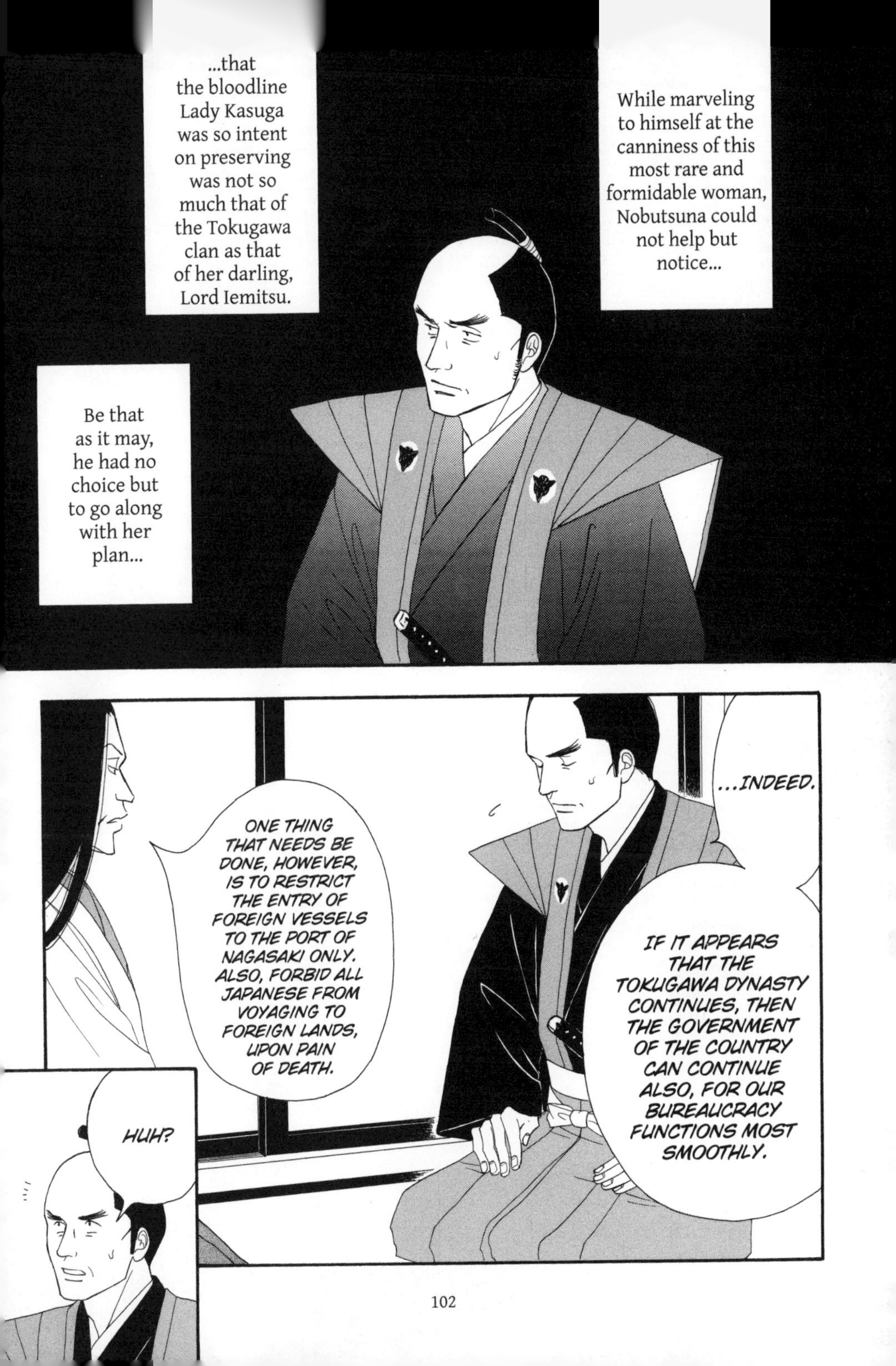
While marveling to himself at the canniness of this most rare and formidable woman, Nobutsuna could not help but notice...
...that the bloodline Lady Kasuga was so intent on preserving was not so much that of the Tokugawa clan as that of her darling, Lord Iemitsu.
Be that as it may, he had no choice but to go along with her plan...
...INDEED.
IF IT APPEARS THAT THE TOKUGAWA DYNASTY CONTINUES, THEN THE GOVERNMENT OF THE COUNTRY CAN CONTINUE ALSO, FOR OUR BUREAUCRACY FUNCTIONS MOST SMOOTHLY.
ONE THING THAT NEEDS BE DONE, HOWEVER, IS TO RESTRICT THE ENTRY OF FOREIGN VESSELS TO THE PORT OF NAGASAKI ONLY. ALSO, FORBID ALL JAPANESE FROM VOYAGING TO FOREIGN LANDS, UPON PAIN OF DEATH.
HUH?

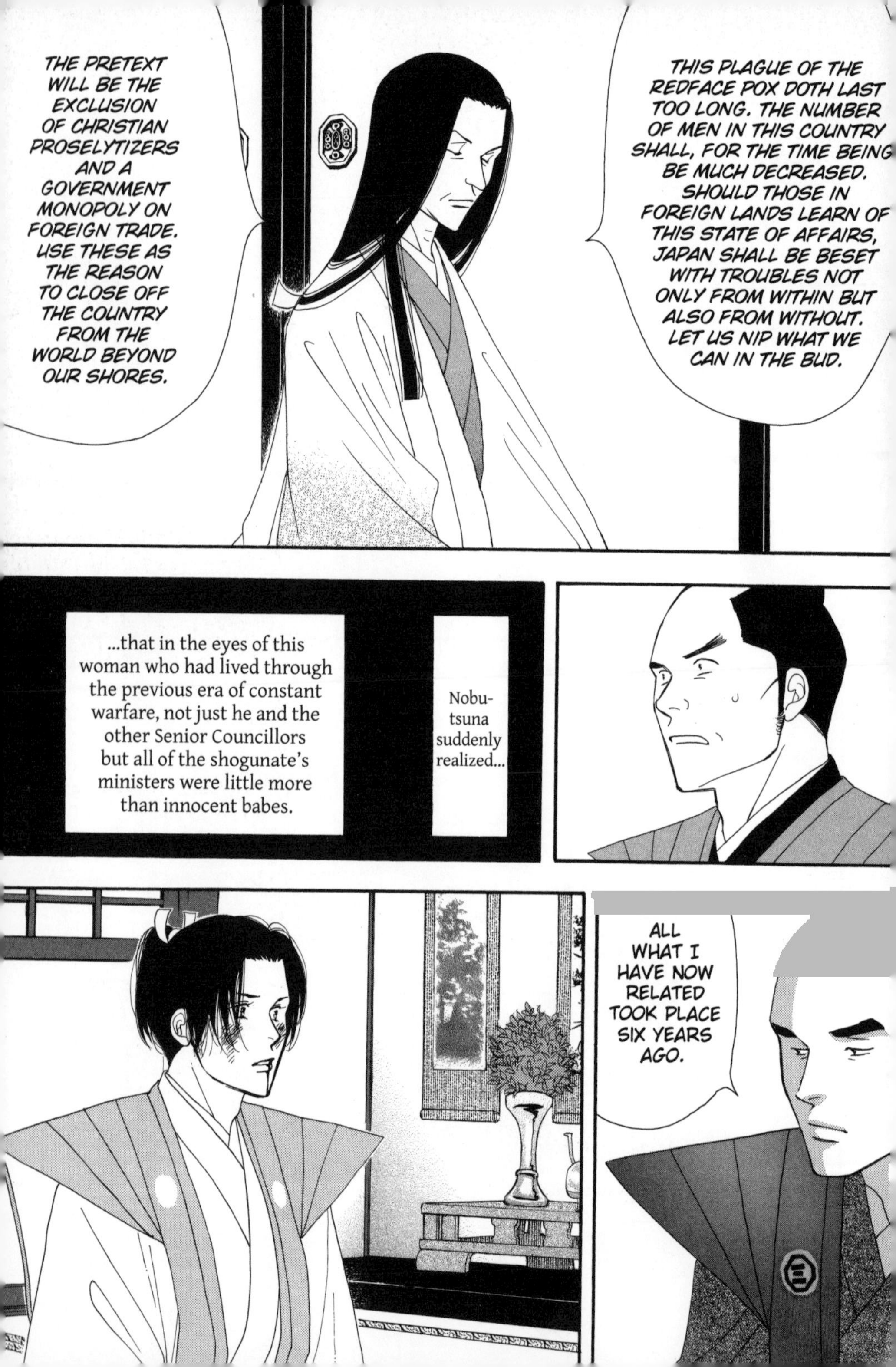
THIS PLAGUE OF THE REDFACE POX DOTH LAST TOO LONG. THE NUMBER OF MEN IN THIS COUNTRY SHALL, FOR THE TIME BEING BE MUCH DECREASED. SHOULD THOSE IN FOREIGN LANDS LEARN OF THIS STATE OF AFFAIRS, JAPAN SHALL BE BESET WITH TROUBLES NOT ONLY FROM WITHIN BUT ALSO FROM WITHOUT. LET US NIP WHAT WE CAN IN THE BUD.
THE PRETEXT WILL BE THE EXCLUSION OF CHRISTIAN PROSELYTIZERS AND A GOVERNMENT MONOPOLY ON FOREIGN TRADE. USE THESE AS THE REASON TO CLOSE OFF THE COUNTRY FROM THE WORLD BEYOND OUR SHORES.
Nobutsuna suddenly realized...
...that in the eyes of this woman who had lived through the previous era of constant warfare, not just he and the other Senior Councillors but all of the shogunate's ministers were little more than innocent babes.
ALL WHAT I HAVE NOW RELATED TOOK PLACE SIX YEARS AGO.

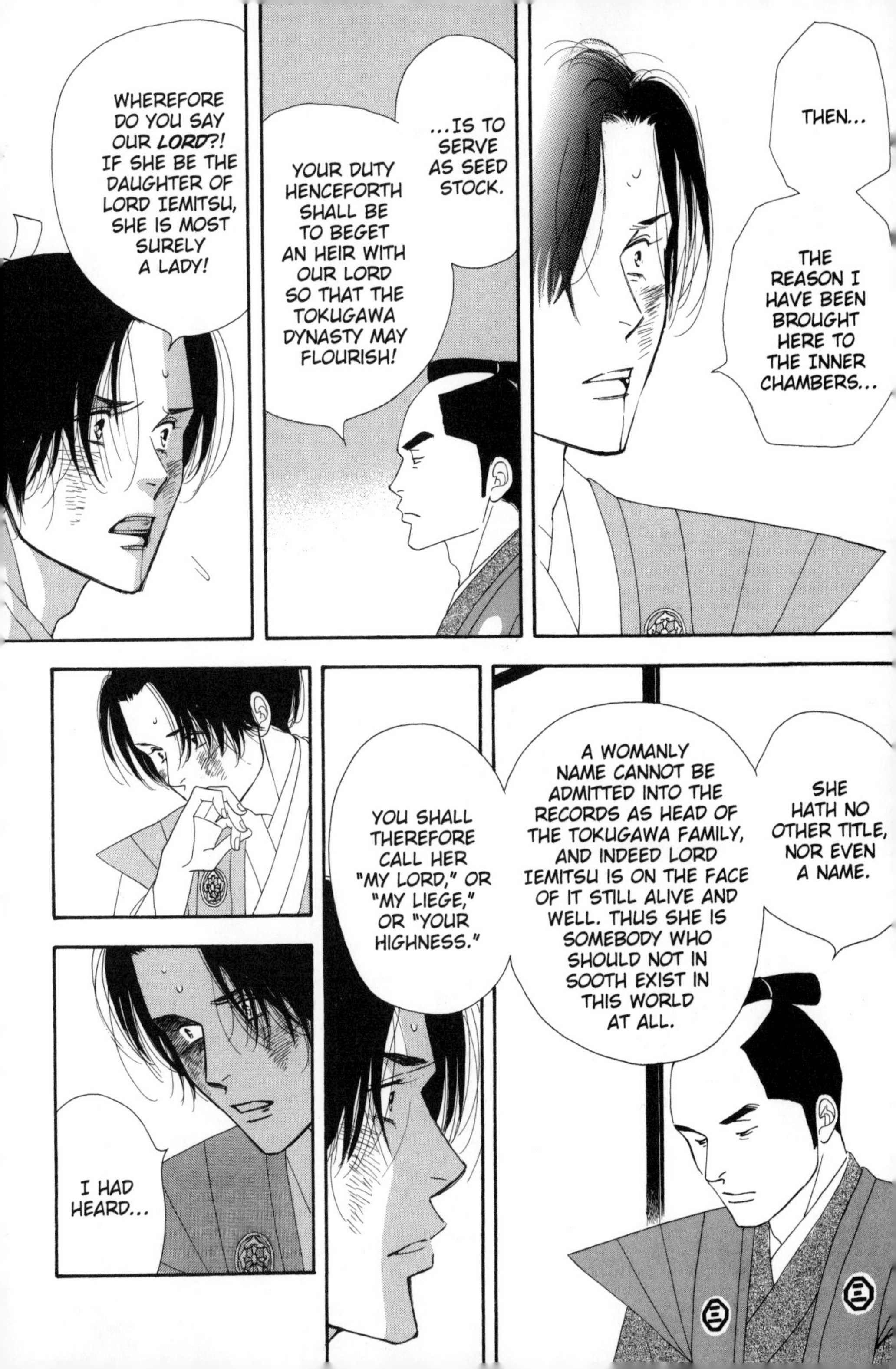
THEN...
THE REASON I HAVE BEEN BROUGHT HERE TO THE INNER CHAMBERS...
...IS TO SERVE AS SEED STOCK.
YOUR DUTY HENCEFORTH SHALL BE TO BEGET AN HEIR WITH OUR LORD SO THAT THE TOKUGAWA DYNASTY MAY FLOURISH!
WHEREFORE DO YOU SAY OUR *LORD*?! IF SHE BE THE DAUGHTER OF LORD IEMITSU, SHE IS MOST SURELY A LADY!
SHE HATH NO OTHER TITLE, NOR EVEN A NAME.
A WOMANLY NAME CANNOT BE ADMITTED INTO THE RECORDS AS HEAD OF THE TOKUGAWA FAMILY, AND INDEED LORD IEMITSU IS ON THE FACE OF IT STILL ALIVE AND WELL. THUS SHE IS SOMEBODY WHO SHOULD NOT IN SOOTH EXIST IN THIS WORLD AT ALL.
YOU SHALL THEREFORE CALL HER "MY LORD," OR "MY LIEGE," OR "YOUR HIGHNESS."
I HAD HEARD...

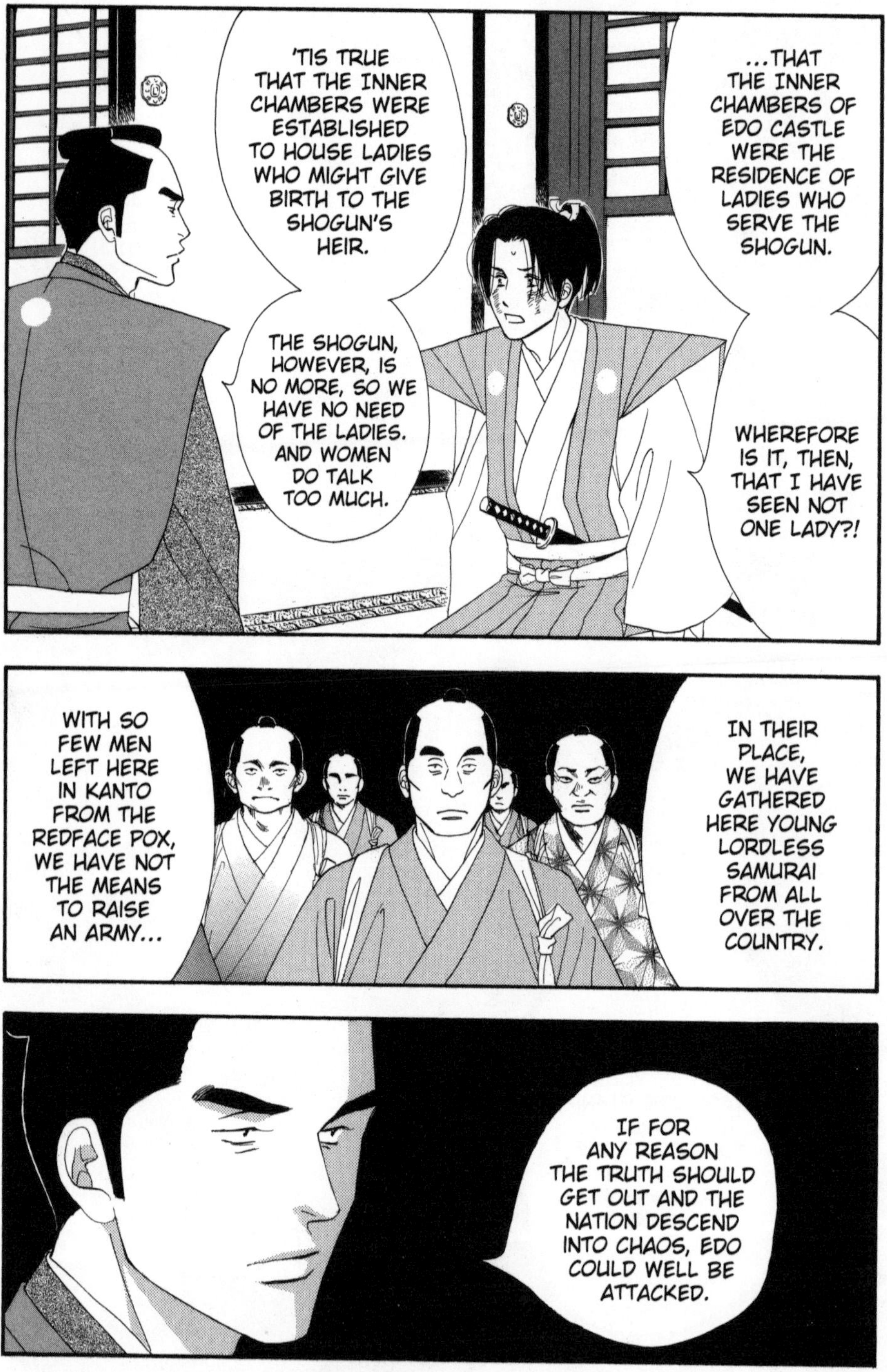
...THAT THE INNER CHAMBERS OF EDO CASTLE WERE THE RESIDENCE OF LADIES WHO SERVE THE SHOGUN.
WHEREFORE IS IT, THEN, THAT I HAVE SEEN NOT ONE LADY?!
'TIS TRUE THAT THE INNER CHAMBERS WERE ESTABLISHED TO HOUSE LADIES WHO MIGHT GIVE BIRTH TO THE SHOGUN'S HEIR.
THE SHOGUN, HOWEVER, IS NO MORE, SO WE HAVE NO NEED OF THE LADIES. AND WOMEN DO TALK TOO MUCH.
IN THEIR PLACE, WE HAVE GATHERED HERE YOUNG LORDLESS SAMURAI FROM ALL OVER THE COUNTRY.
WITH SO FEW MEN LEFT HERE IN KANTO FROM THE REDFACE POX, WE HAVE NOT THE MEANS TO RAISE AN ARMY...
IF FOR ANY REASON THE TRUTH SHOULD GET OUT AND THE NATION DESCEND INTO CHAOS, EDO COULD WELL BE ATTACKED.

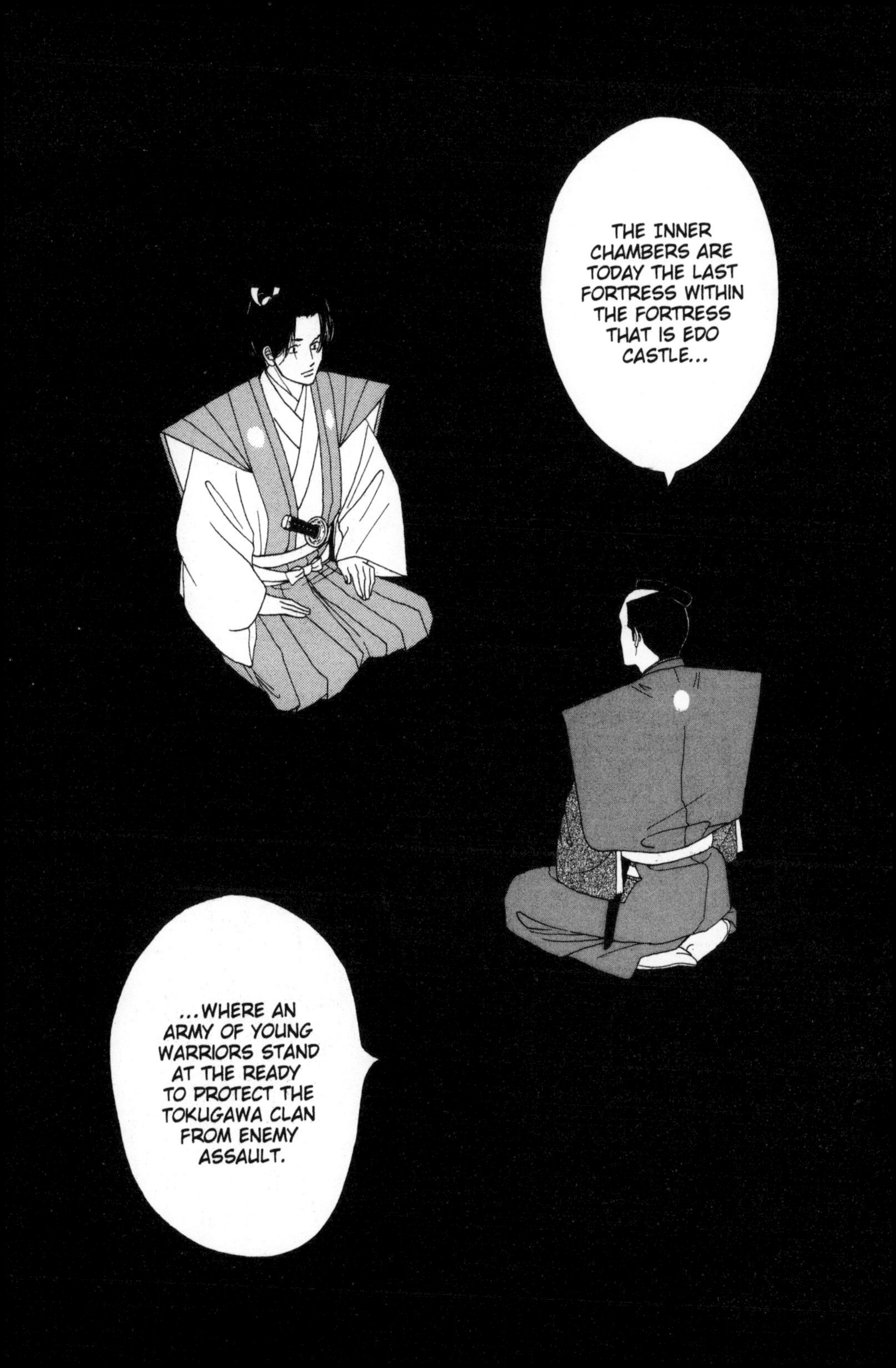
THE INNER CHAMBERS ARE TODAY THE LAST FORTRESS WITHIN THE FORTRESS THAT IS EDO CASTLE...
...WHERE AN ARMY OF YOUNG WARRIORS STAND AT THE READY TO PROTECT THE TOKUGAWA CLAN FROM ENEMY ASSAULT.

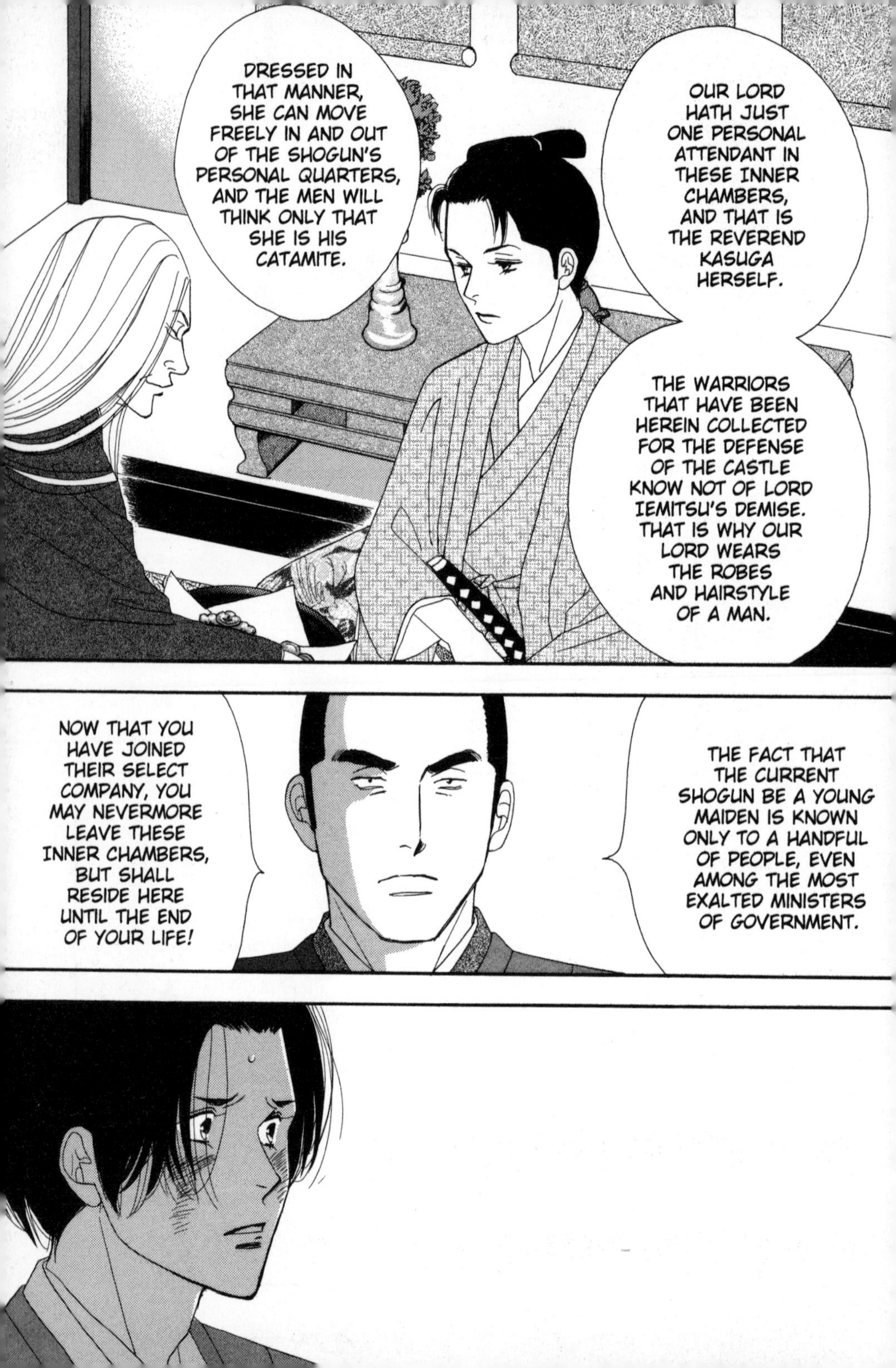
OUR LORD HATH JUST ONE PERSONAL ATTENDANT IN THESE INNER CHAMBERS, AND THAT IS THE REVEREND KASUGA HERSELF.
THE WARRIORS THAT HAVE BEEN HEREIN COLLECTED FOR THE DEFENSE OF THE CASTLE KNOW NOT OF LORD IEMITSU'S DEMISE. THAT IS WHY OUR LORD WEARS THE ROBES AND HAIRSTYLE OF A MAN.
DRESSED IN THAT MANNER, SHE CAN MOVE FREELY IN AND OUT OF THE SHOGUN'S PERSONAL QUARTERS, AND THE MEN WILL THINK ONLY THAT SHE IS HIS CATAMITE.
THE FACT THAT THE CURRENT SHOGUN BE A YOUNG MAIDEN IS KNOWN ONLY TO A HANDFUL OF PEOPLE, EVEN AMONG THE MOST EXALTED MINISTERS OF GOVERNMENT.
NOW THAT YOU HAVE JOINED THEIR SELECT COMPANY, YOU MAY NEVERMORE LEAVE THESE INNER CHAMBERS, BUT SHALL RESIDE HERE UNTIL THE END OF YOUR LIFE!

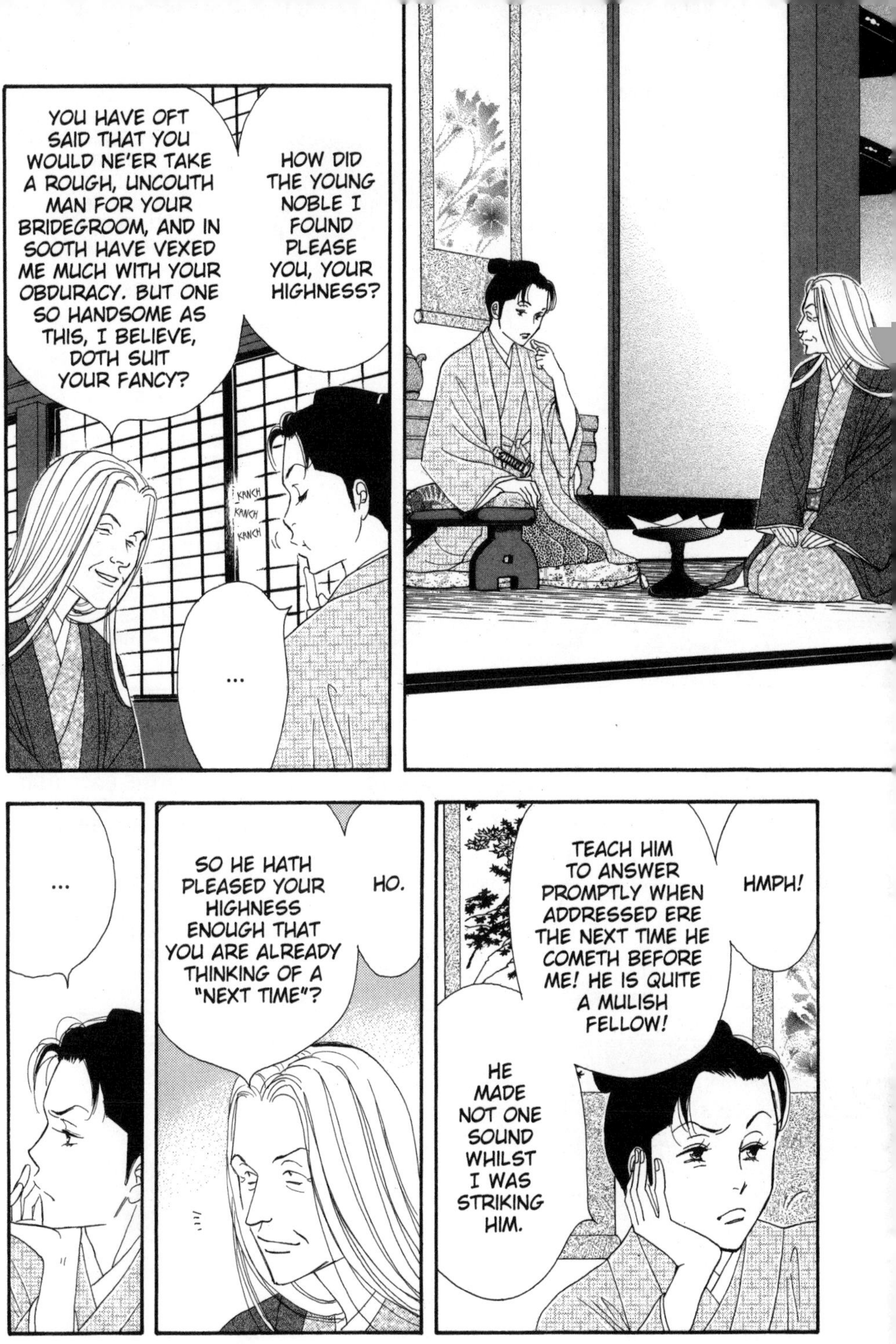
HOW DID THE YOUNG NOBLE I FOUND PLEASE YOU, YOUR HIGHNESS?
YOU HAVE OFT SAID THAT YOU WOULD NE'ER TAKE A ROUGH, UNCOUTH MAN FOR YOUR BRIDEGROOM, AND IN SOOTH HAVE VEXED ME MUCH WITH YOUR OBDURACY. BUT ONE SO HANDSOME AS THIS, I BELIEVE, DOTH SUIT YOUR FANCY?
KANCH KANCH KANCH
...
HMPH!
TEACH HIM TO ANSWER PROMPTLY WHEN ADDRESSED ERE THE NEXT TIME HE COMETH BEFORE ME! HE IS QUITE A MULISH FELLOW!
HE MADE NOT ONE SOUND WHILST I WAS STRIKING HIM.
HO.
SO HE HATH PLEASED YOUR HIGHNESS ENOUGH THAT YOU ARE ALREADY THINKING OF A "NEXT TIME"?
...

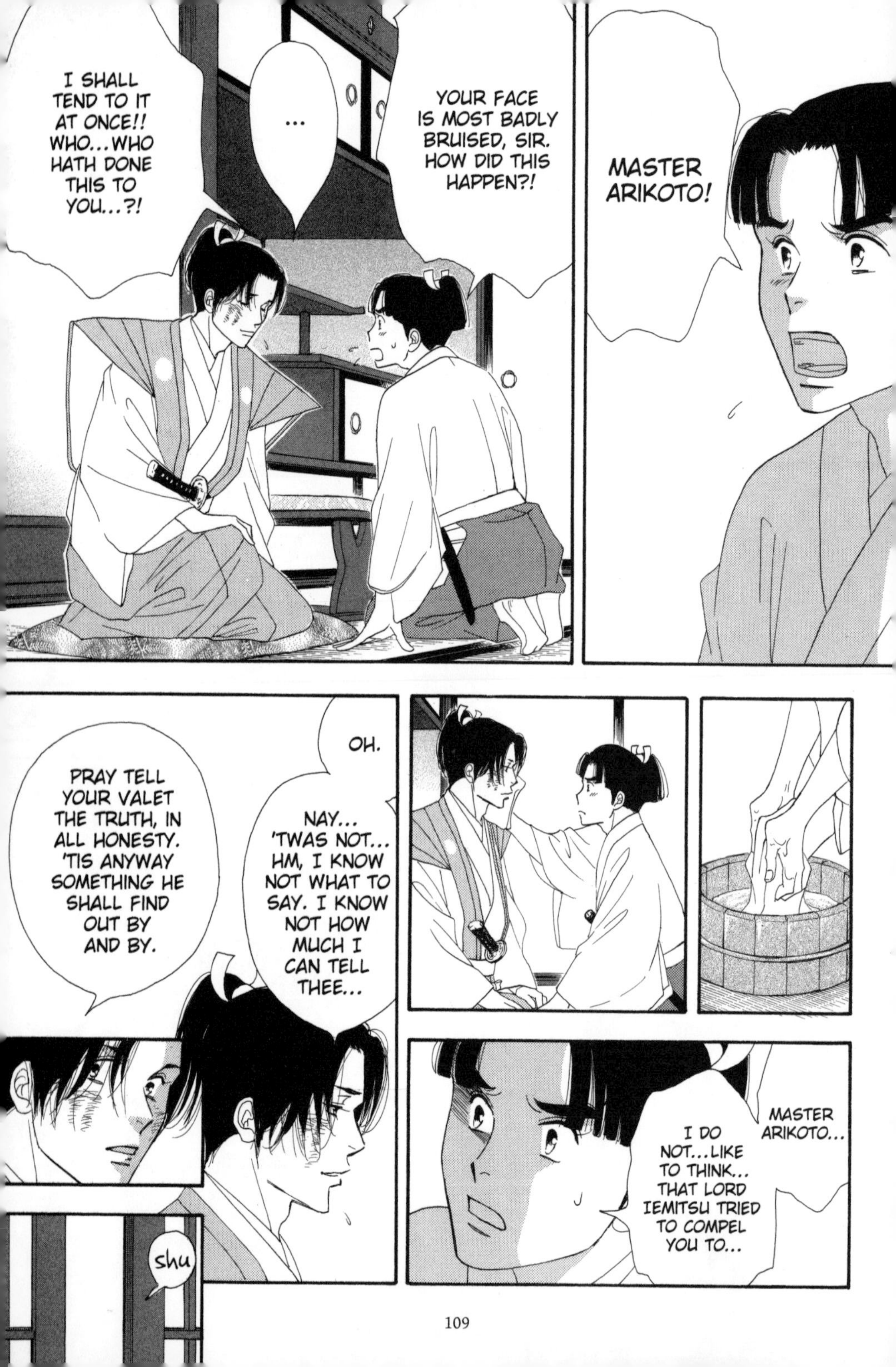
MASTER ARIKOTO!
YOUR FACE IS MOST BADLY BRUISED, SIR. HOW DID THIS HAPPEN?!
...
I SHALL TEND TO IT AT ONCE!! WHO...WHO HATH DONE THIS TO YOU...?!
OH.
NAY... 'TWAS NOT... HM, I KNOW NOT WHAT TO SAY. I KNOW NOT HOW MUCH I CAN TELL THEE...
PRAY TELL YOUR VALET THE TRUTH, IN ALL HONESTY. 'TIS ANYWAY SOMETHING HE SHALL FIND OUT BY AND BY.
shu
MASTER ARIKOTO...
I DO NOT...LIKE TO THINK... THAT LORD IEMITSU TRIED TO COMPEL YOU TO...

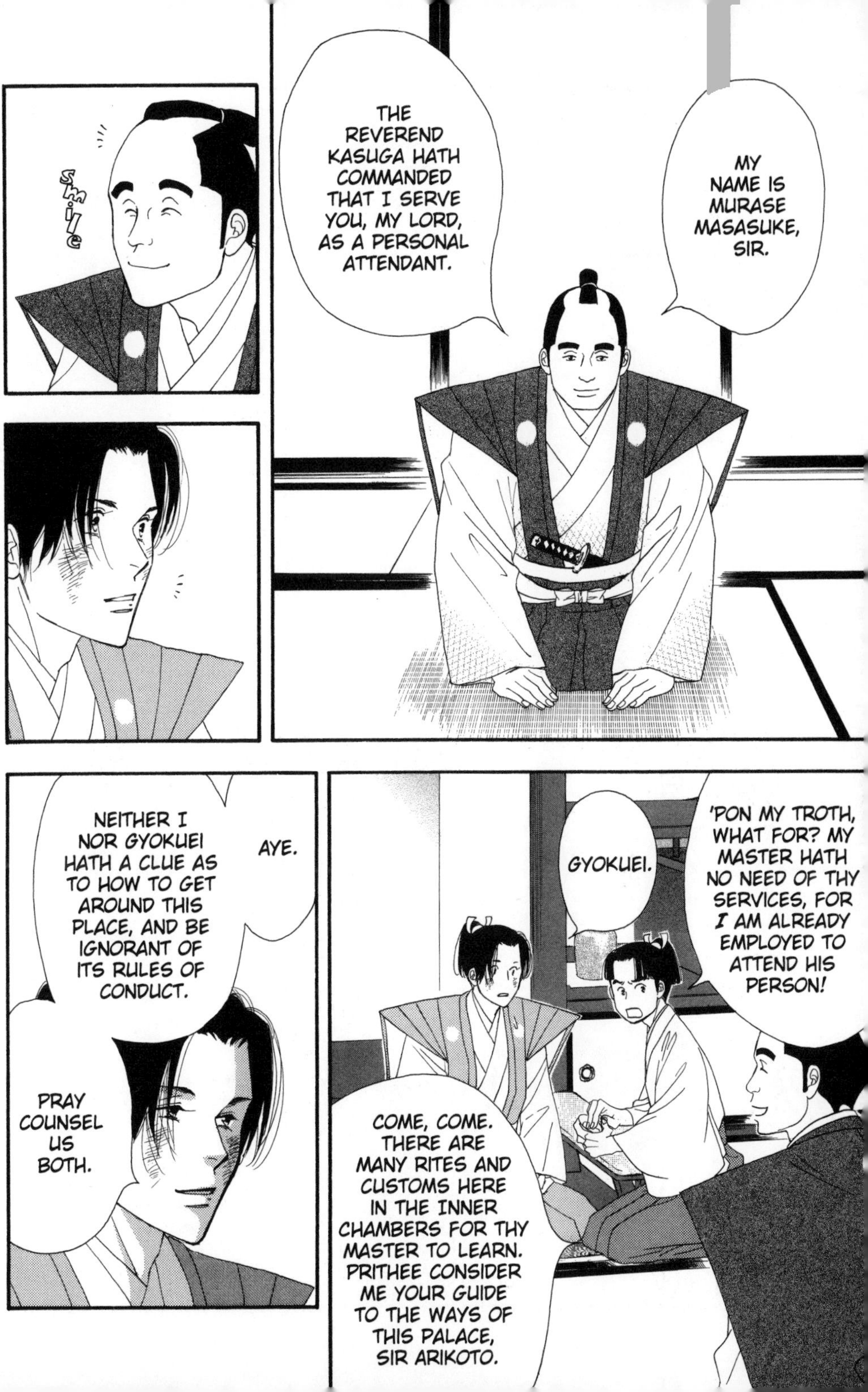
MY NAME IS MURASE MASASUKE, SIR.
THE REVEREND KASUGA HATH COMMANDED THAT I SERVE YOU, MY LORD, AS A PERSONAL ATTENDANT.
Smile
'PON MY TROTH, WHAT FOR? MY MASTER HATH NO NEED OF THY SERVICES, FOR I AM ALREADY EMPLOYED TO ATTEND HIS PERSON!
GYOKUEI.
COME, COME. THERE ARE MANY RITES AND CUSTOMS HERE IN THE INNER CHAMBERS FOR THY MASTER TO LEARN. PRITHEE CONSIDER ME YOUR GUIDE TO THE WAYS OF THIS PALACE, SIR ARIKOTO.
AYE.
NEITHER I NOR GYOKUEI HATH A CLUE AS TO HOW TO GET AROUND THIS PLACE, AND BE IGNORANT OF ITS RULES OF CONDUCT.
PRAY COUNSEL US BOTH.

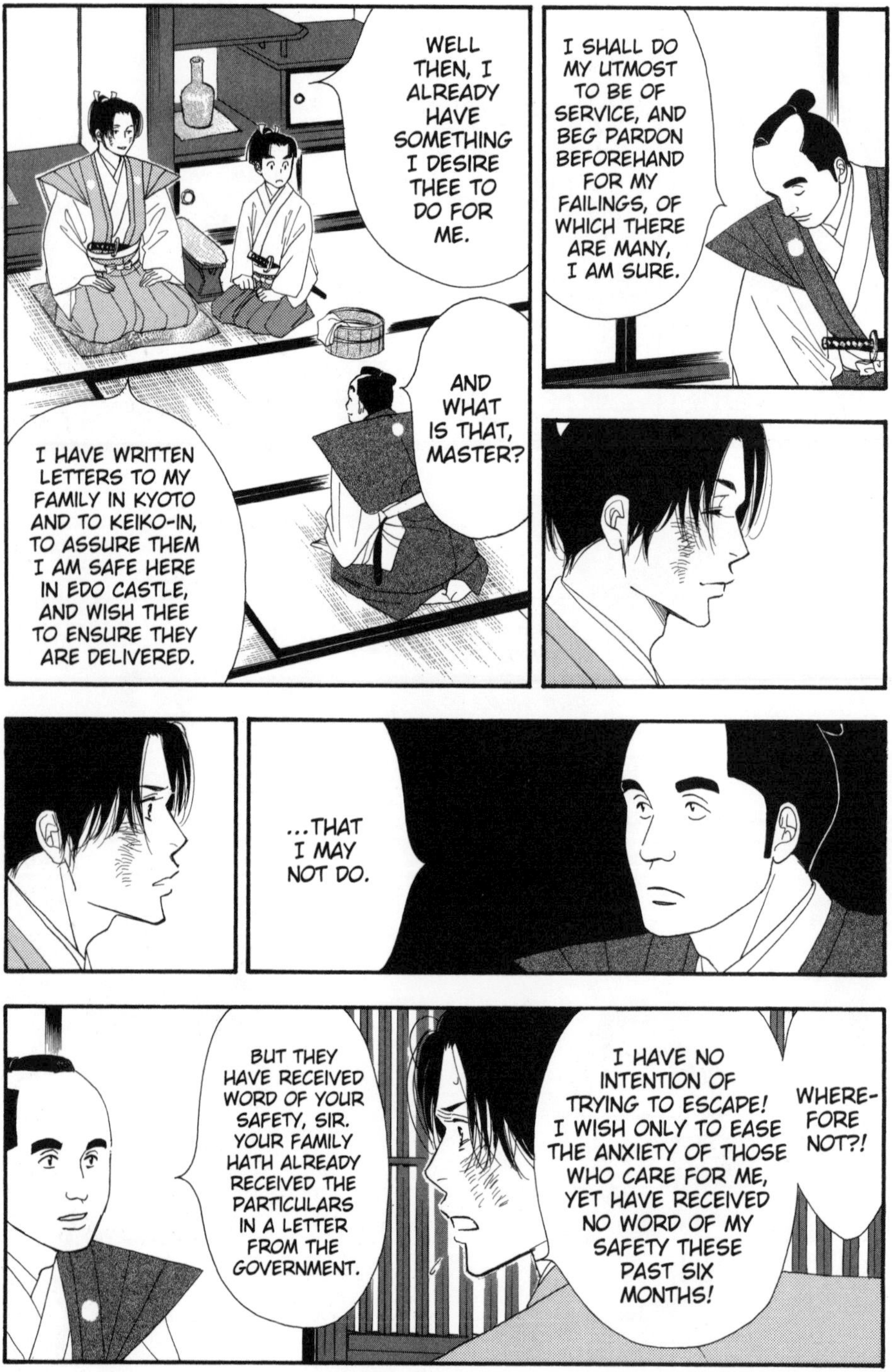
I SHALL DO MY UTMOST TO BE OF SERVICE, AND BEG PARDON BEFOREHAND FOR MY FAILINGS, OF WHICH THERE ARE MANY, I AM SURE.
WELL THEN, I ALREADY HAVE SOMETHING I DESIRE THEE TO DO FOR ME.
AND WHAT IS THAT, MASTER?
I HAVE WRITTEN LETTERS TO MY FAMILY IN KYOTO AND TO KEIKO-IN, TO ASSURE THEM I AM SAFE HERE IN EDO CASTLE, AND WISH THEE TO ENSURE THEY ARE DELIVERED.
...THAT I MAY NOT DO.
WHERE-FORE NOT?!
I HAVE NO INTENTION OF TRYING TO ESCAPE! I WISH ONLY TO EASE THE ANXIETY OF THOSE WHO CARE FOR ME, YET HAVE RECEIVED NO WORD OF MY SAFETY THESE PAST SIX MONTHS!
BUT THEY HAVE RECEIVED WORD OF YOUR SAFETY, SIR. YOUR FAMILY HATH ALREADY RECEIVED THE PARTICULARS IN A LETTER FROM THE GOVERNMENT.

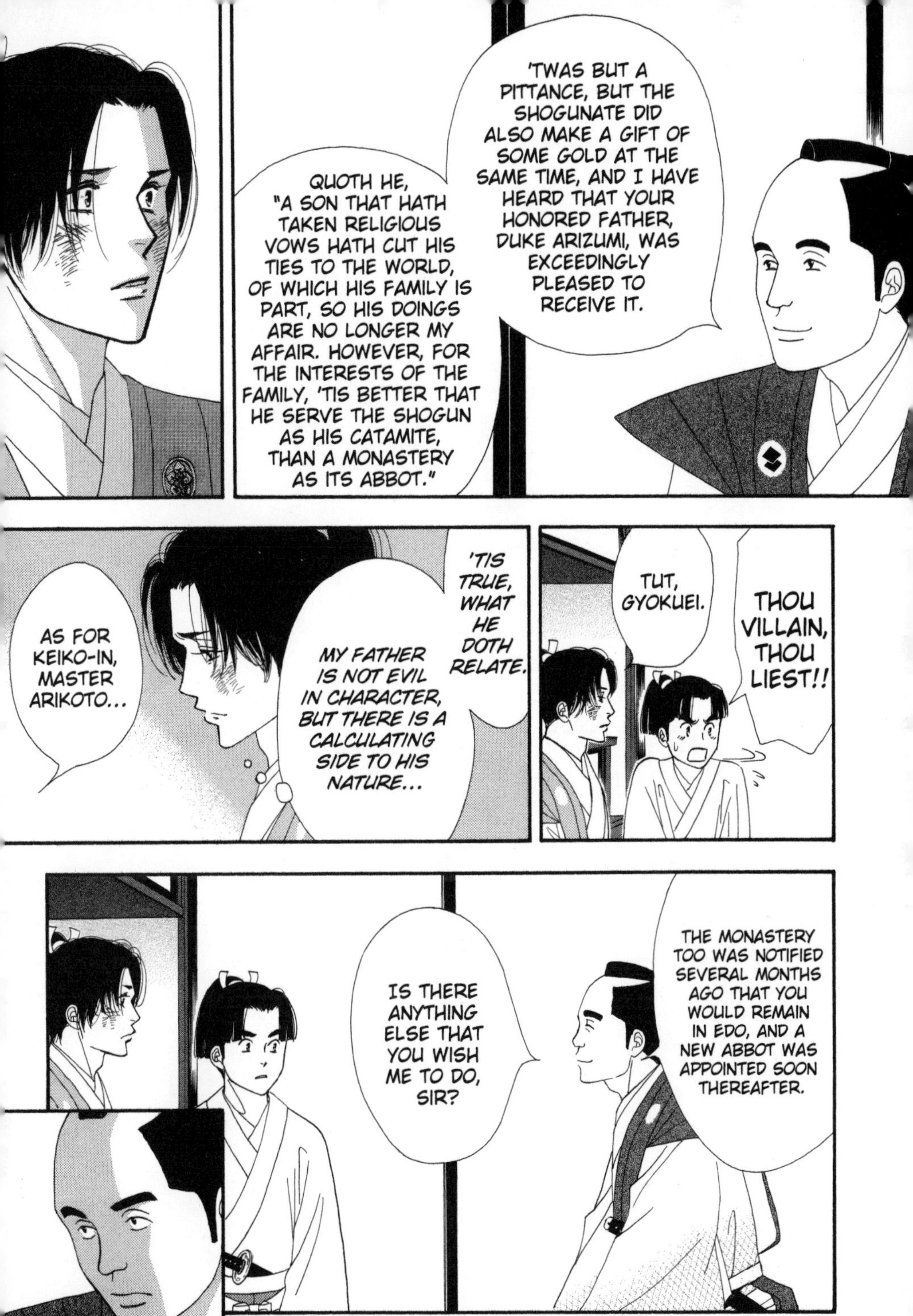
'TWAS BUT A PITTANCE, BUT THE SHOGUNATE DID ALSO MAKE A GIFT OF SOME GOLD AT THE SAME TIME, AND I HAVE HEARD THAT YOUR HONORED FATHER, DUKE ARIZUMI, WAS EXCEEDINGLY PLEASED TO RECEIVE IT.
QUOTH HE, "A SON THAT HATH TAKEN RELIGIOUS VOWS HATH CUT HIS TIES TO THE WORLD, OF WHICH HIS FAMILY IS PART, SO HIS DOINGS ARE NO LONGER MY AFFAIR. HOWEVER, FOR THE INTERESTS OF THE FAMILY, 'TIS BETTER THAT HE SERVE THE SHOGUN AS HIS CATAMITE, THAN A MONASTERY AS ITS ABBOT."
THOU VILLAIN, THOU LIEST!!
TUT, GYOKUEI.
'TIS TRUE, WHAT HE DOTH RELATE.
MY FATHER IS NOT EVIL IN CHARACTER, BUT THERE IS A CALCULATING SIDE TO HIS NATURE...
AS FOR KEIKO-IN, MASTER ARIKOTO...
THE MONASTERY TOO WAS NOTIFIED SEVERAL MONTHS AGO THAT YOU WOULD REMAIN IN EDO, AND A NEW ABBOT WAS APPOINTED SOON THEREAFTER.
IS THERE ANYTHING ELSE THAT YOU WISH ME TO DO, SIR?

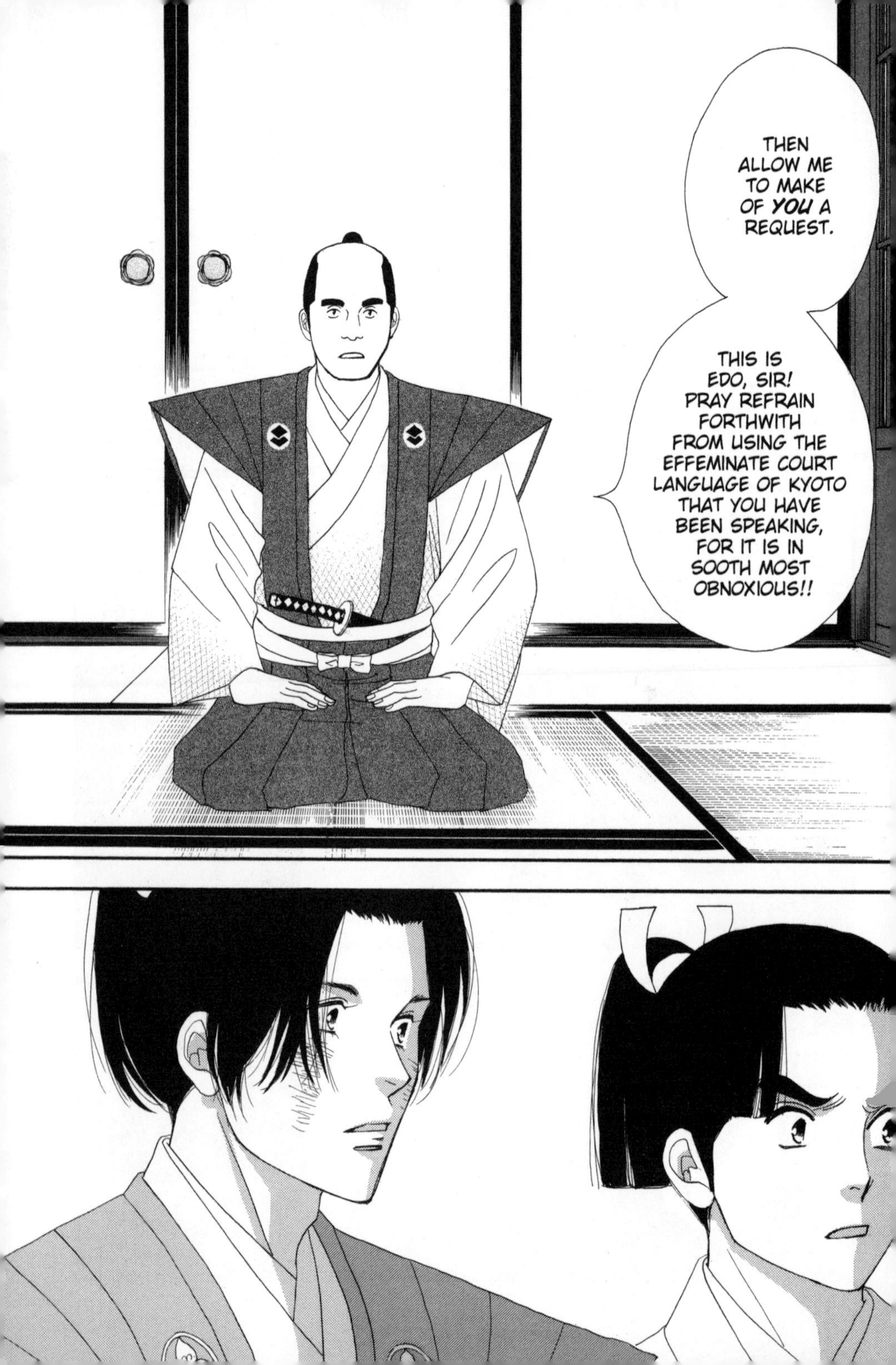
THEN ALLOW ME TO MAKE OF *YOU* A REQUEST.
THIS IS EDO, SIR! PRAY REFRAIN FORTHWITH FROM USING THE EFFEMINATE COURT LANGUAGE OF KYOTO THAT YOU HAVE BEEN SPEAKING, FOR IT IS IN SOOTH MOST OBNOXIOUS!!

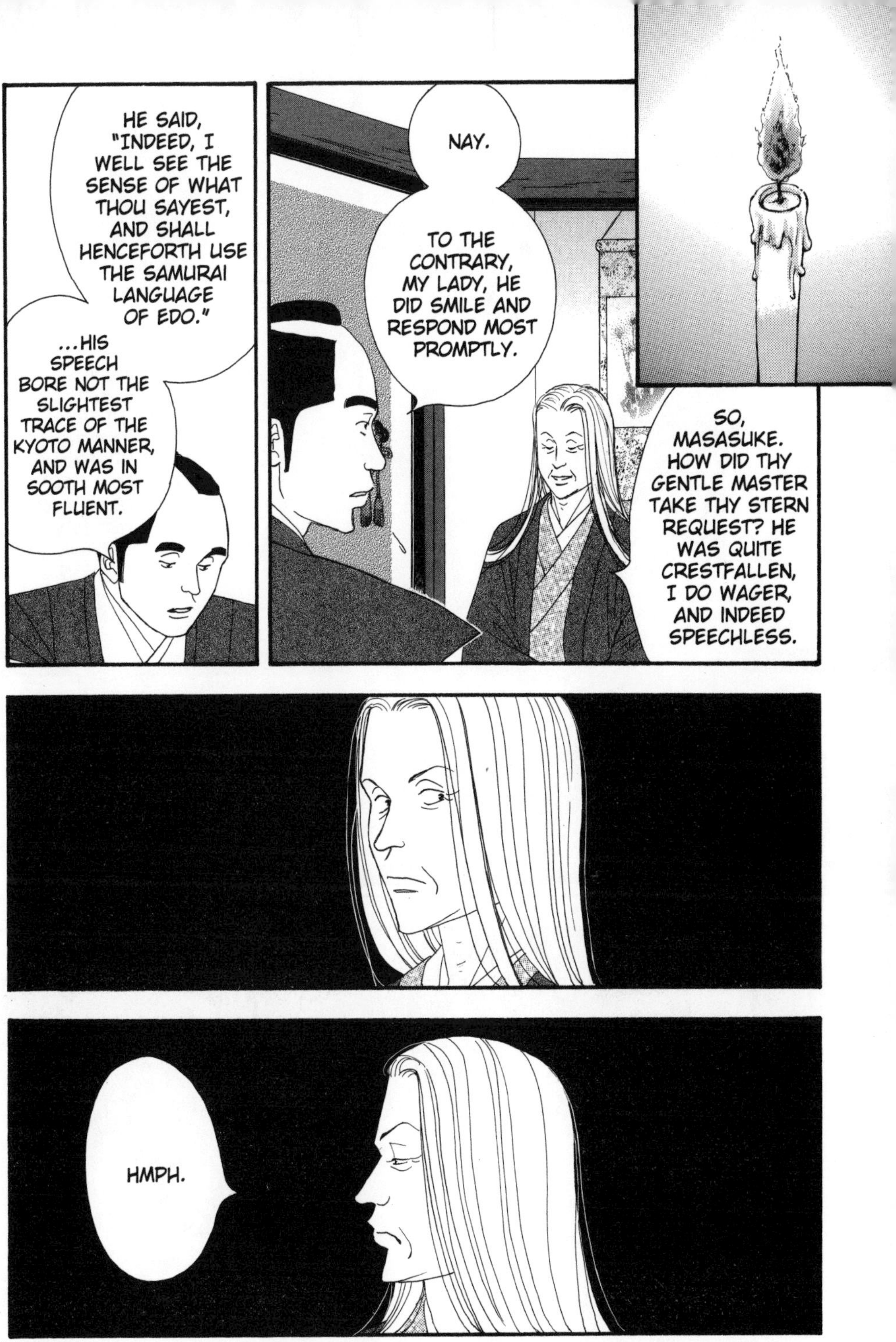
SO, MASASUKE. HOW DID THY GENTLE MASTER TAKE THY STERN REQUEST? HE WAS QUITE CRESTFALLEN, I DO WAGER, AND INDEED SPEECHLESS.
NAY.
TO THE CONTRARY, MY LADY, HE DID SMILE AND RESPOND MOST PROMPTLY.
HE SAID, "INDEED, I WELL SEE THE SENSE OF WHAT THOU SAYEST, AND SHALL HENCEFORTH USE THE SAMURAI LANGUAGE OF EDO."
...HIS SPEECH BORE NOT THE SLIGHTEST TRACE OF THE KYOTO MANNER, AND WAS IN SOOTH MOST FLUENT.
HMPH.

Ōoku
● THE INNER CHAMBERS

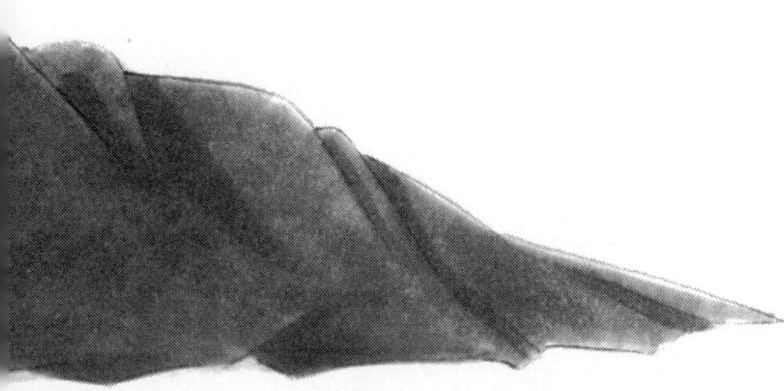

Ōoku

THE INNER CHAMBERS

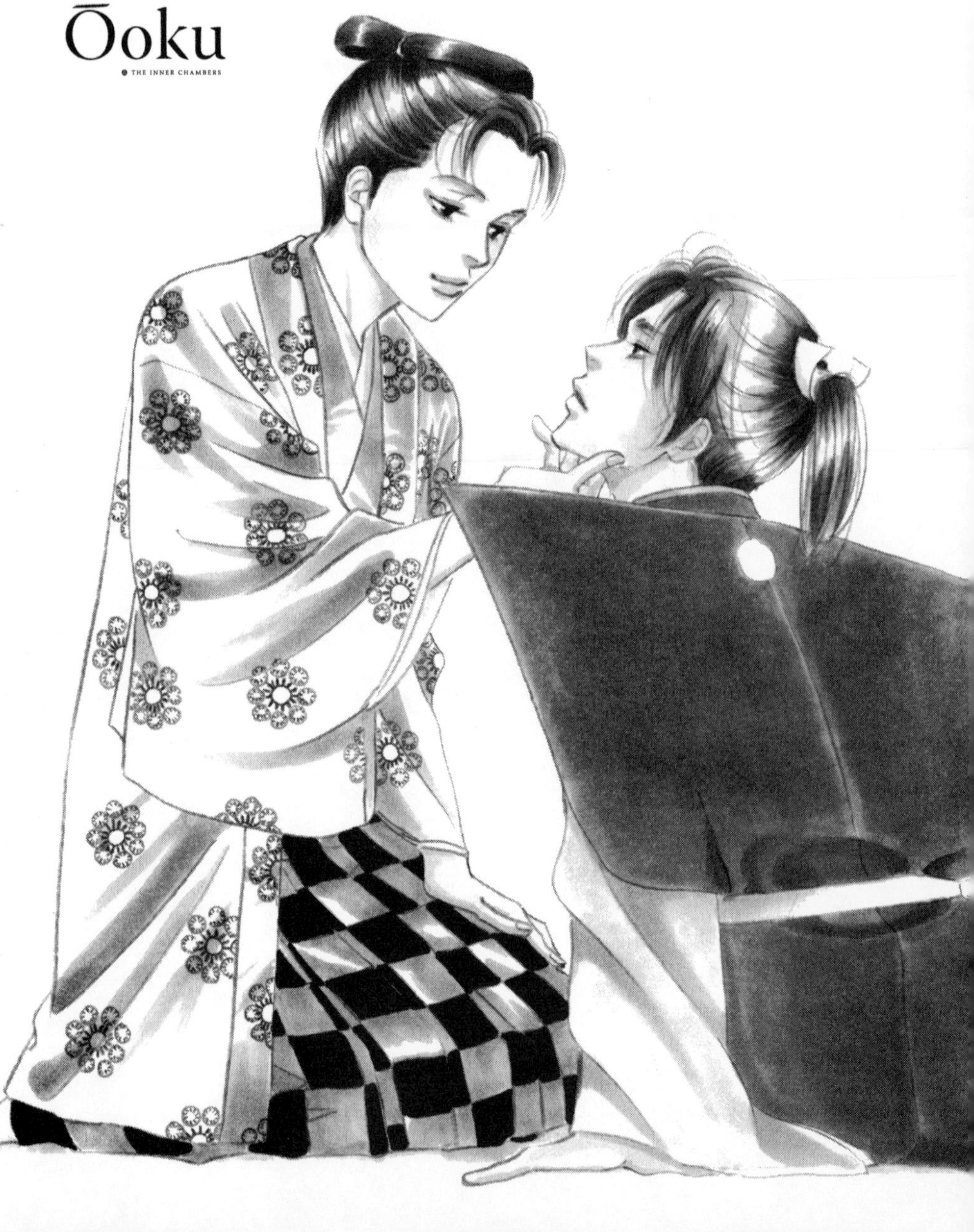

Ōoku
❀ THE INNER CHAMBERS

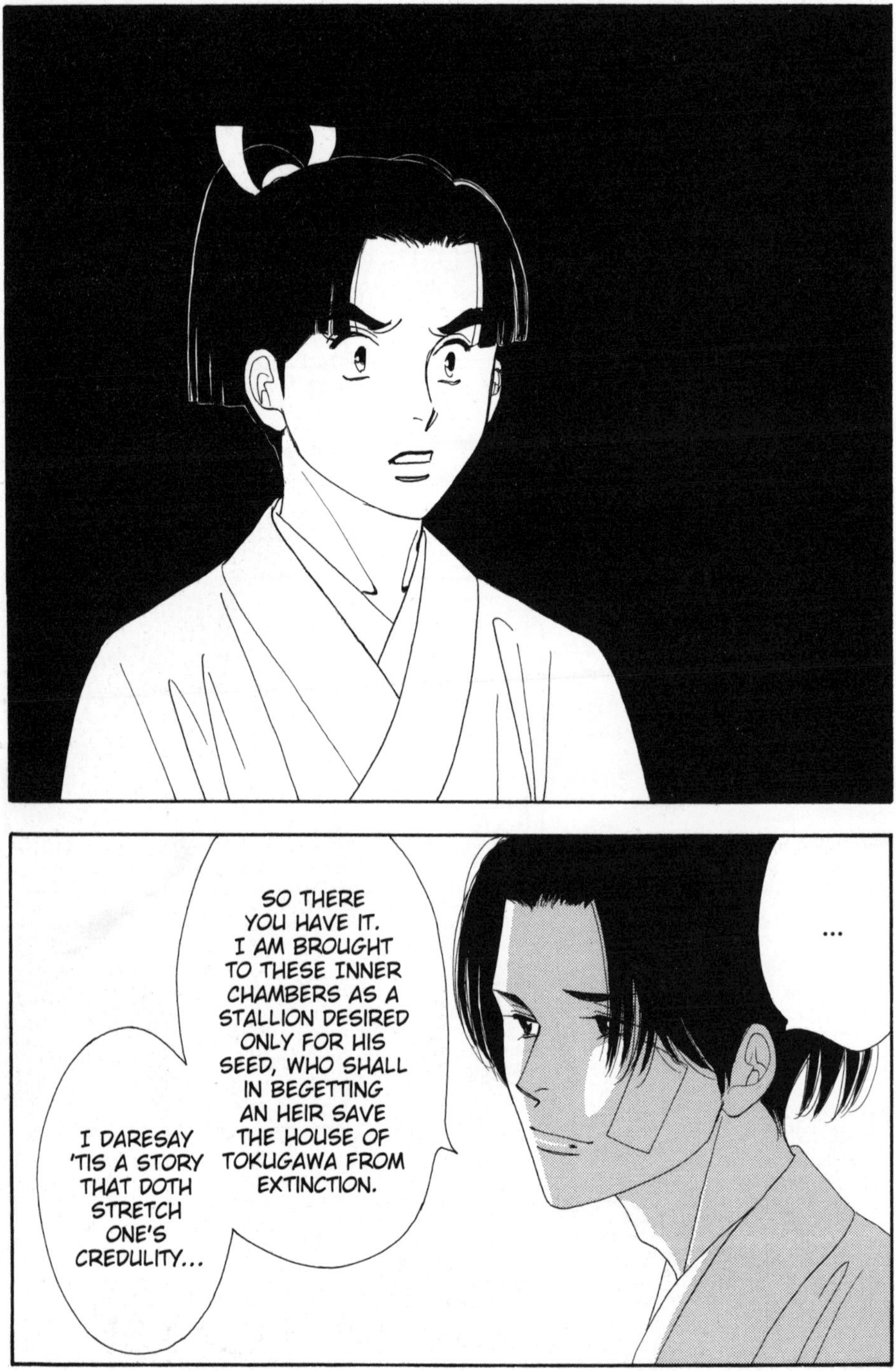
...
SO THERE YOU HAVE IT. I AM BROUGHT TO THESE INNER CHAMBERS AS A STALLION DESIRED ONLY FOR HIS SEED, WHO SHALL IN BEGETTING AN HEIR SAVE THE HOUSE OF TOKUGAWA FROM EXTINCTION.
I DARESAY 'TIS A STORY THAT DOTH STRETCH ONE'S CREDULITY...

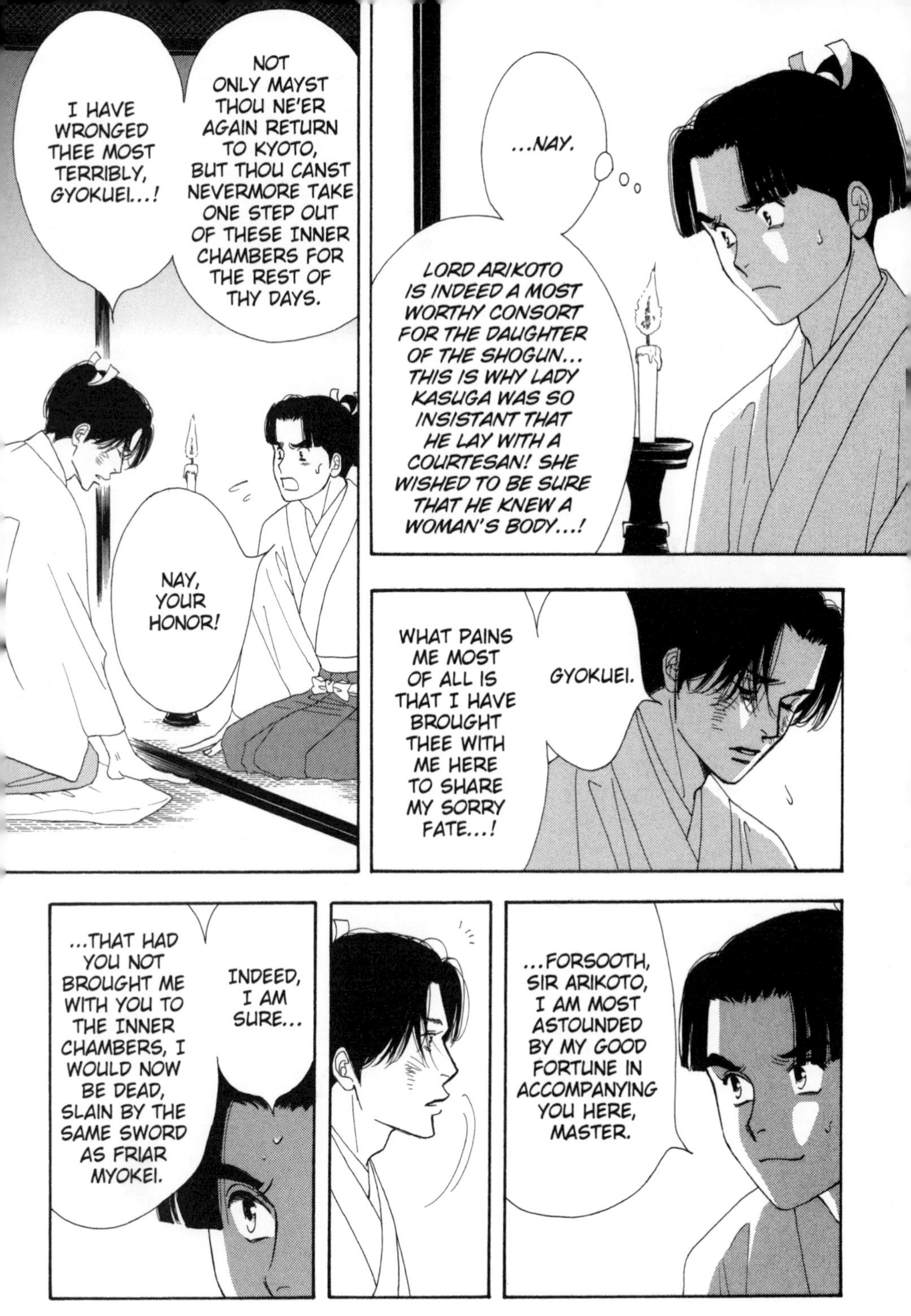
...NAY.
LORD ARIKOTO IS INDEED A MOST WORTHY CONSORT FOR THE DAUGHTER OF THE SHOGUN... THIS IS WHY LADY KASUGA WAS SO INSISTANT THAT HE LAY WITH A COURTESAN! SHE WISHED TO BE SURE THAT HE KNEW A WOMAN'S BODY...!
GYOKUEI.
WHAT PAINS ME MOST OF ALL IS THAT I HAVE BROUGHT THEE WITH ME HERE TO SHARE MY SORRY FATE...!
NOT ONLY MAYST THOU NE'ER AGAIN RETURN TO KYOTO, BUT THOU CANST NEVERMORE TAKE ONE STEP OUT OF THESE INNER CHAMBERS FOR THE REST OF THY DAYS.
I HAVE WRONGED THEE MOST TERRIBLY, GYOKUEI...!
NAY, YOUR HONOR!
...FORSOOTH, SIR ARIKOTO, I AM MOST ASTOUNDED BY MY GOOD FORTUNE IN ACCOMPANYING YOU HERE, MASTER.
INDEED, I AM SURE...
...THAT HAD YOU NOT BROUGHT ME WITH YOU TO THE INNER CHAMBERS, I WOULD NOW BE DEAD, SLAIN BY THE SAME SWORD AS FRIAR MYOKEI.

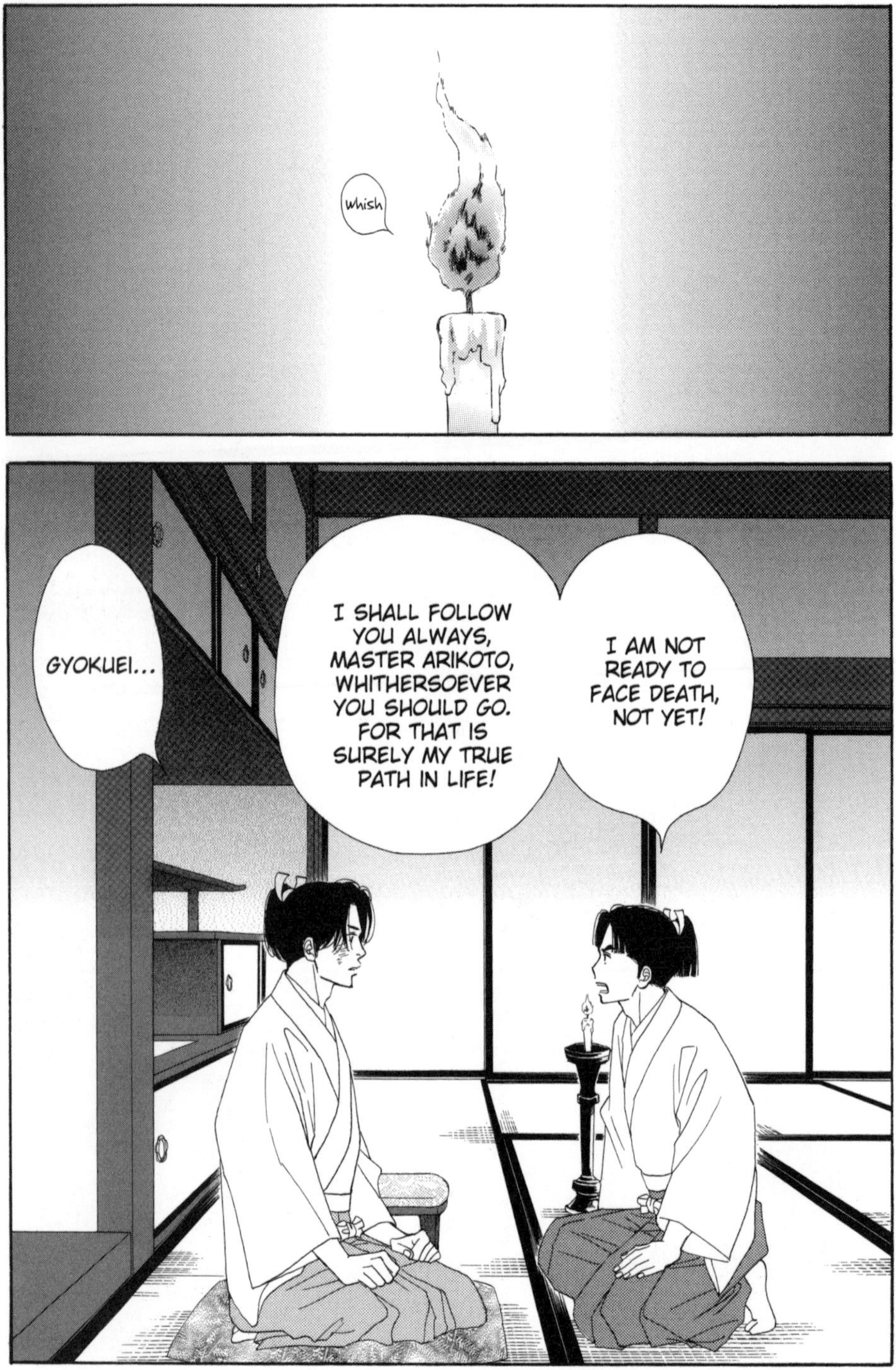
whish
I AM NOT READY TO FACE DEATH, NOT YET!
I SHALL FOLLOW YOU ALWAYS, MASTER ARIKOTO, WHITHERSOEVER YOU SHOULD GO. FOR THAT IS SURELY MY TRUE PATH IN LIFE!
GYOKUEI...

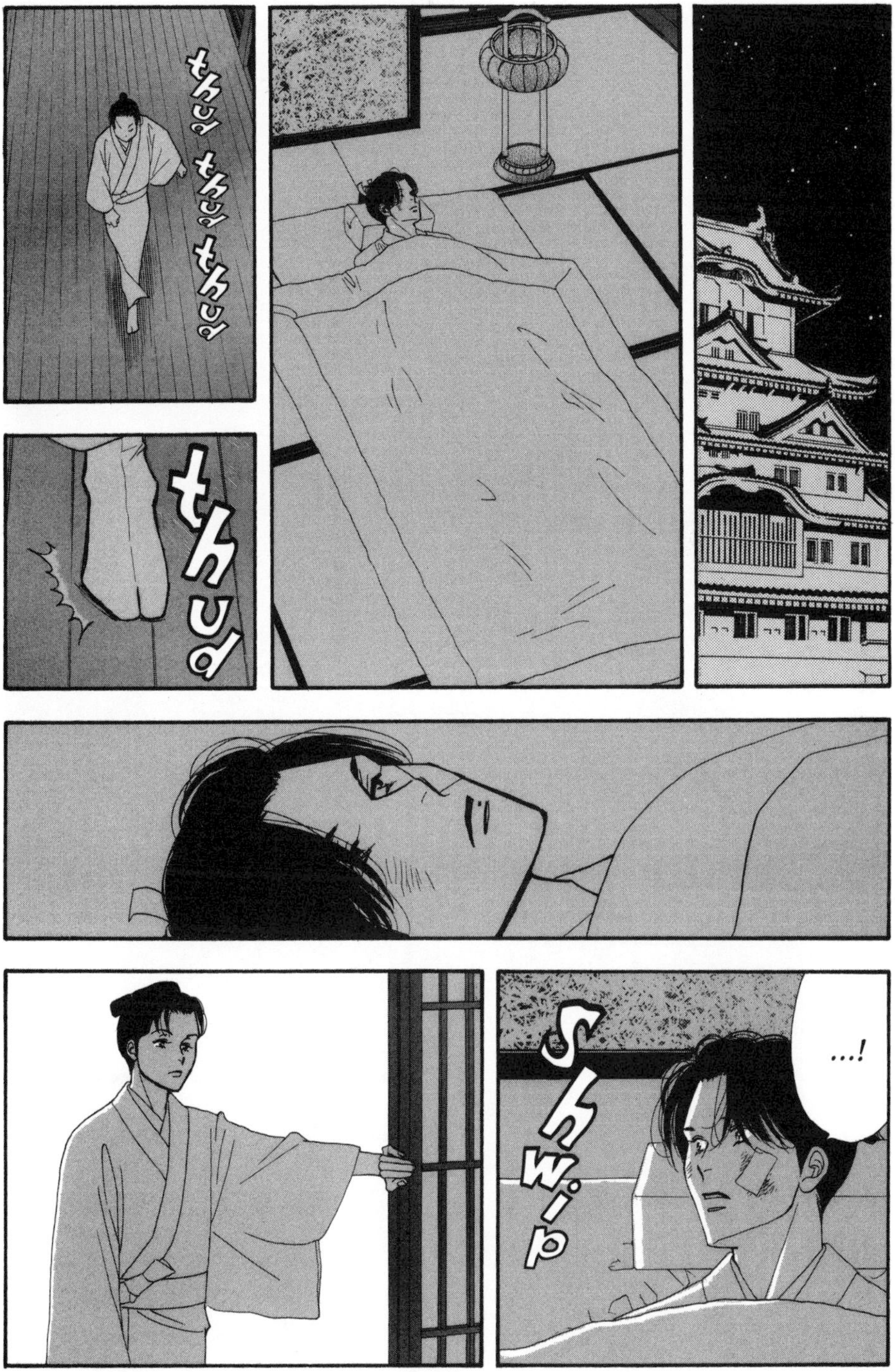
thud thud thud
thud
...!
shwip

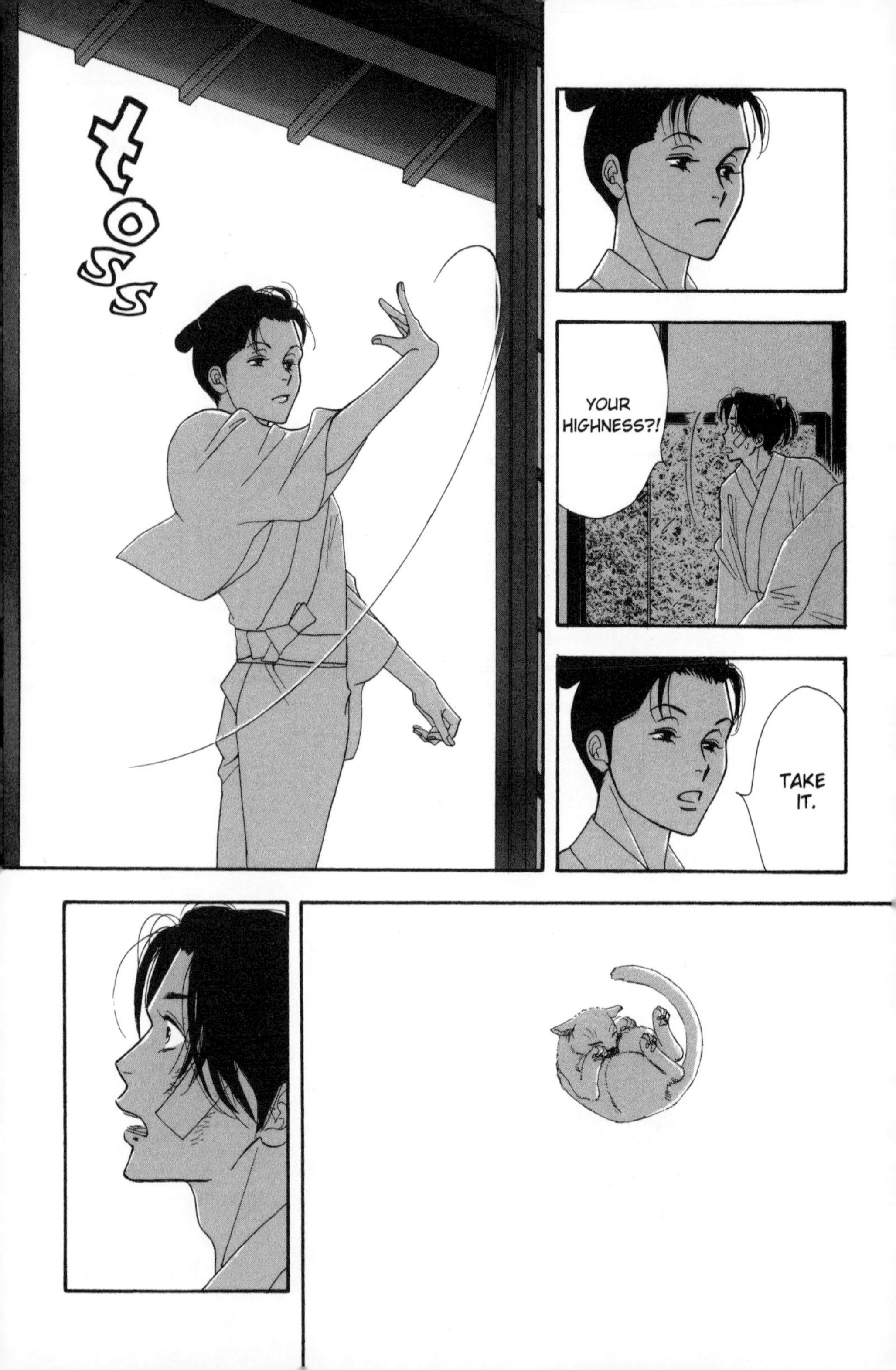
YOUR HIGHNESS?!
TAKE IT.
toss

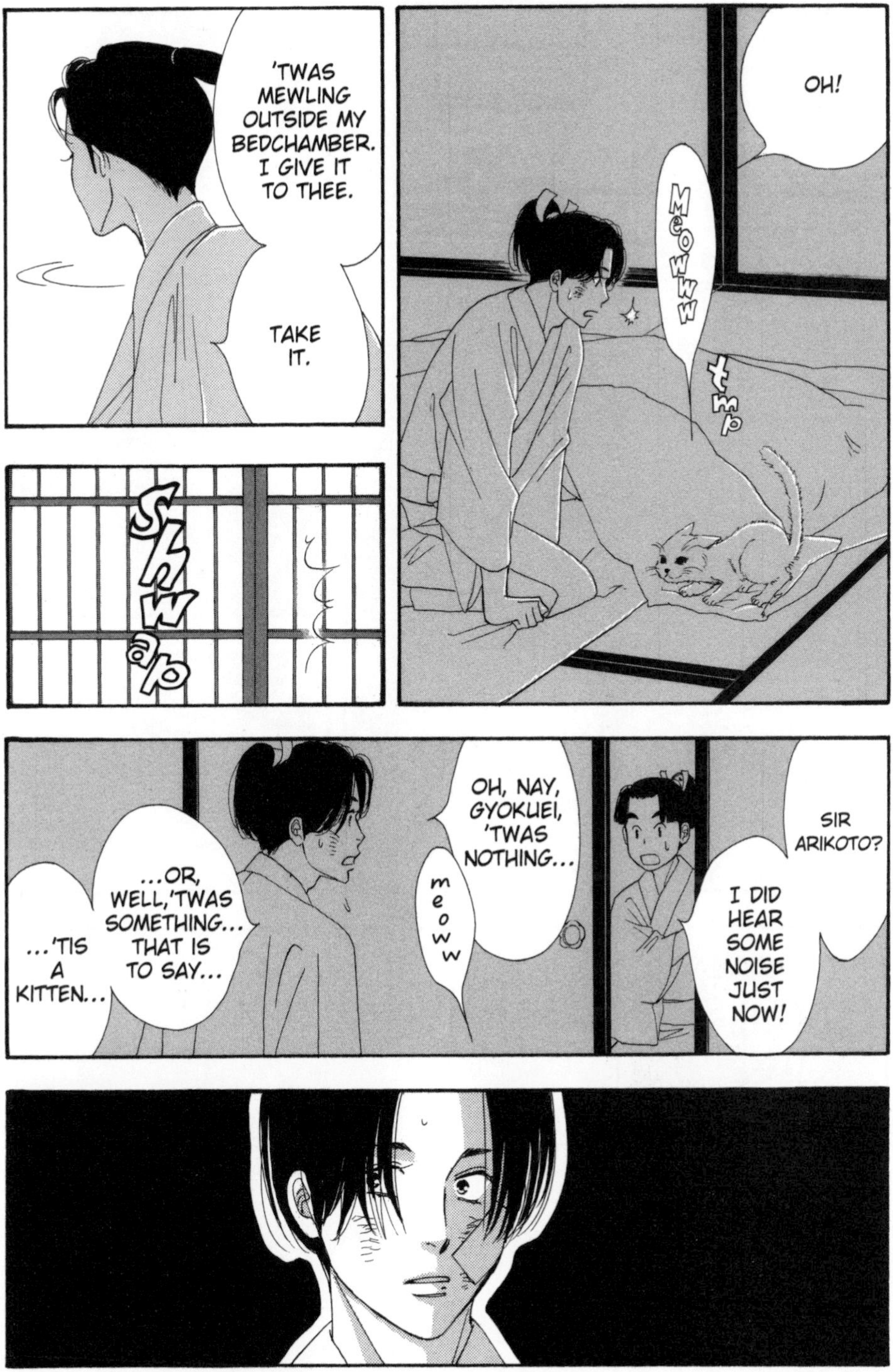
OH!
Meowww
tmp
'TWAS MEWLING OUTSIDE MY BEDCHAMBER. I GIVE IT TO THEE.
TAKE IT.
Shwap
SIR ARIKOTO?
I DID HEAR SOME NOISE JUST NOW!
OH, NAY, GYOKUEI, 'TWAS NOTHING…
meoww
…OR, WELL,'TWAS SOMETHING… THAT IS TO SAY…
…'TIS A KITTEN…

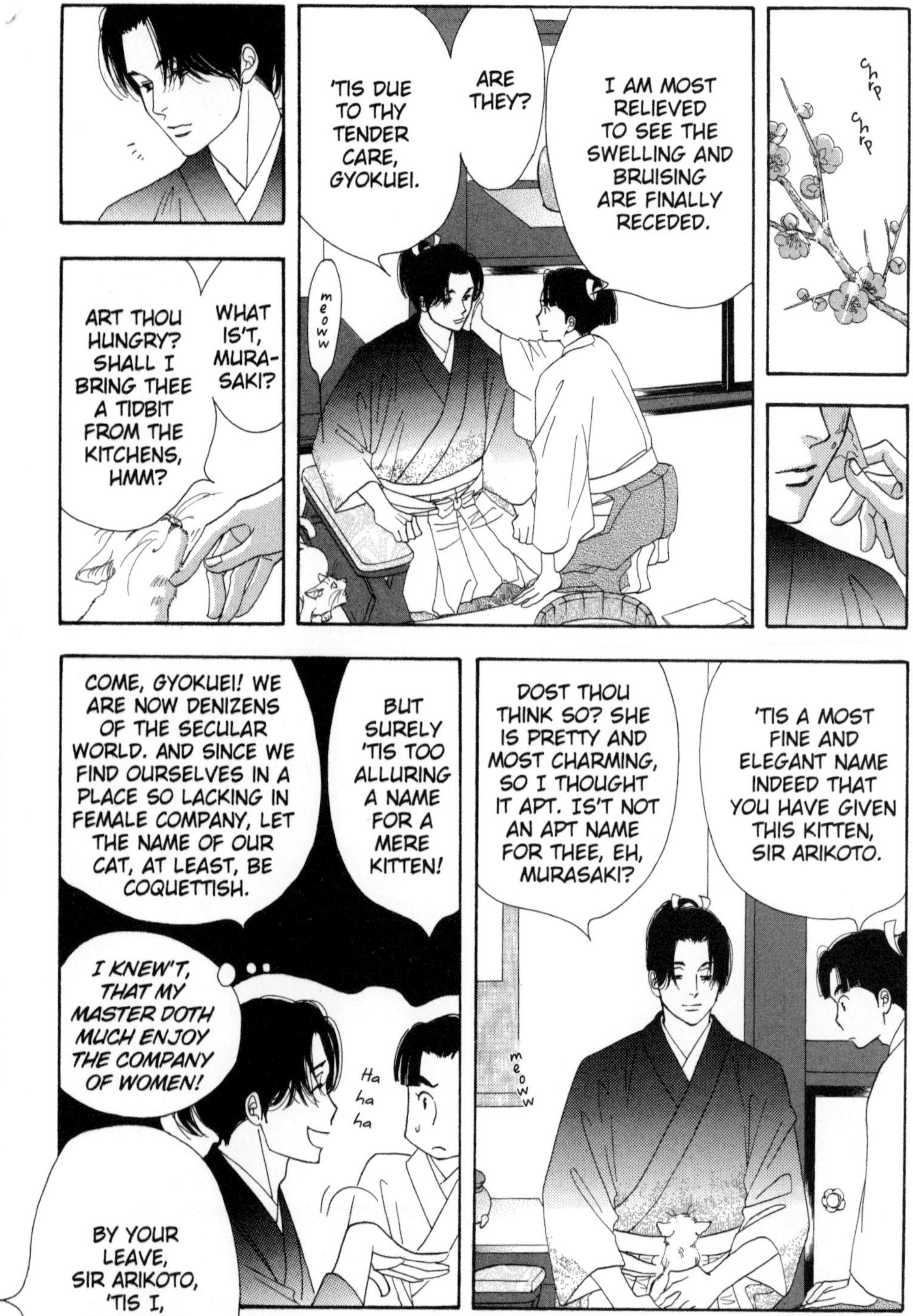
chrp
chrp
I AM MOST RELIEVED TO SEE THE SWELLING AND BRUISING ARE FINALLY RECEDED.
ARE THEY?
'TIS DUE TO THY TENDER CARE, GYOKUEI.
meoww
WHAT IS'T, MURA-SAKI?
ART THOU HUNGRY? SHALL I BRING THEE A TIDBIT FROM THE KITCHENS, HMM?
'TIS A MOST FINE AND ELEGANT NAME INDEED THAT YOU HAVE GIVEN THIS KITTEN, SIR ARIKOTO.
DOST THOU THINK SO? SHE IS PRETTY AND MOST CHARMING, SO I THOUGHT IT APT. IS'T NOT AN APT NAME FOR THEE, EH, MURASAKI?
meoww
BUT SURELY 'TIS TOO ALLURING A NAME FOR A MERE KITTEN!
COME, GYOKUEI! WE ARE NOW DENIZENS OF THE SECULAR WORLD. AND SINCE WE FIND OURSELVES IN A PLACE SO LACKING IN FEMALE COMPANY, LET THE NAME OF OUR CAT, AT LEAST, BE COQUETTISH.
I KNEW'T, THAT MY MASTER DOTH MUCH ENJOY THE COMPANY OF WOMEN!
Ha ha ha
BY YOUR LEAVE, SIR ARIKOTO, 'TIS I, MASASUKE.

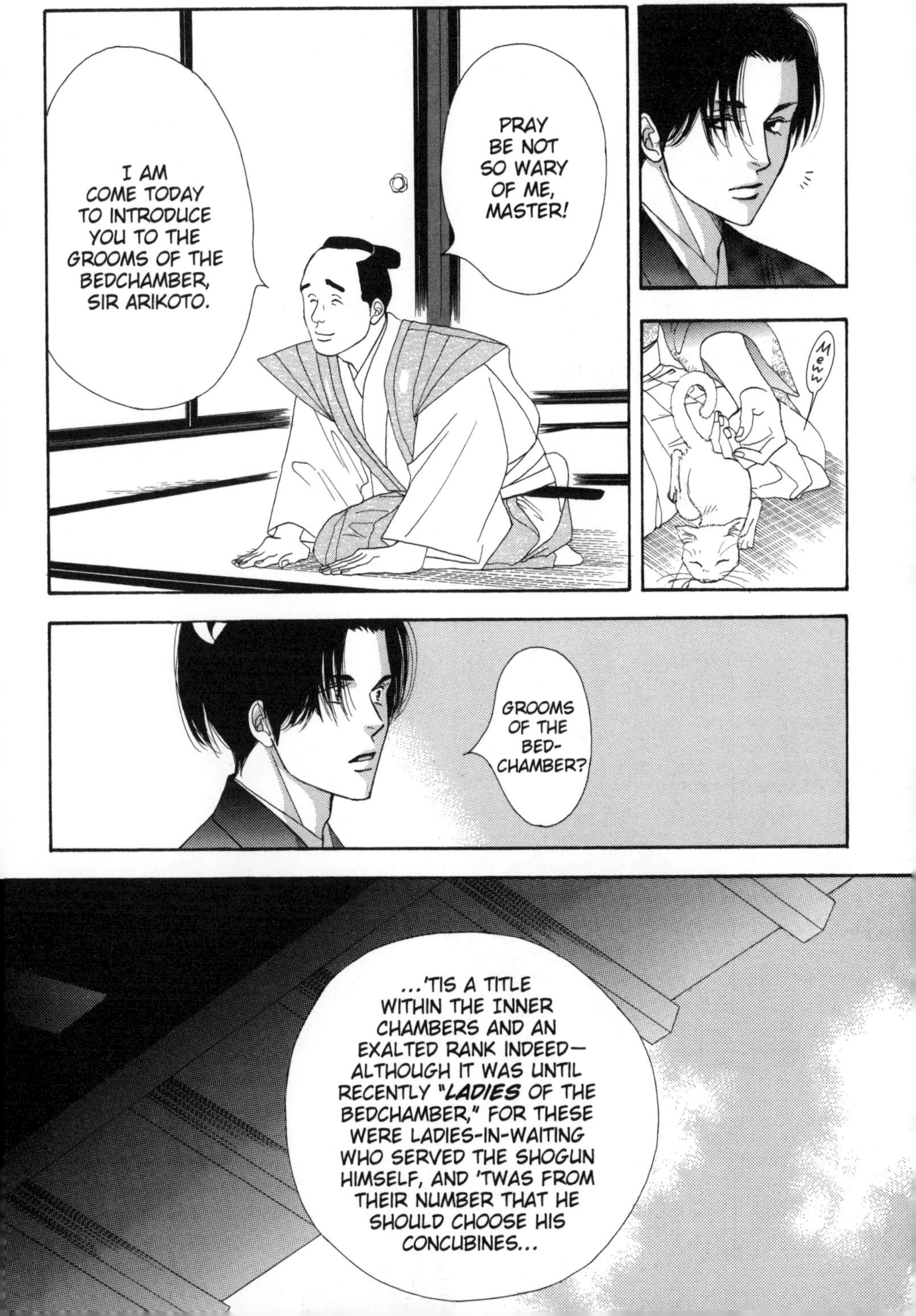
MEW
PRAY BE NOT SO WARY OF ME, MASTER!
I AM COME TODAY TO INTRODUCE YOU TO THE GROOMS OF THE BEDCHAMBER, SIR ARIKOTO.
GROOMS OF THE BED-CHAMBER?
...'TIS A TITLE WITHIN THE INNER CHAMBERS AND AN EXALTED RANK INDEED—ALTHOUGH IT WAS UNTIL RECENTLY "*LADIES* OF THE BEDCHAMBER," FOR THESE WERE LADIES-IN-WAITING WHO SERVED THE SHOGUN HIMSELF, AND 'TWAS FROM THEIR NUMBER THAT HE SHOULD CHOOSE HIS CONCUBINES...

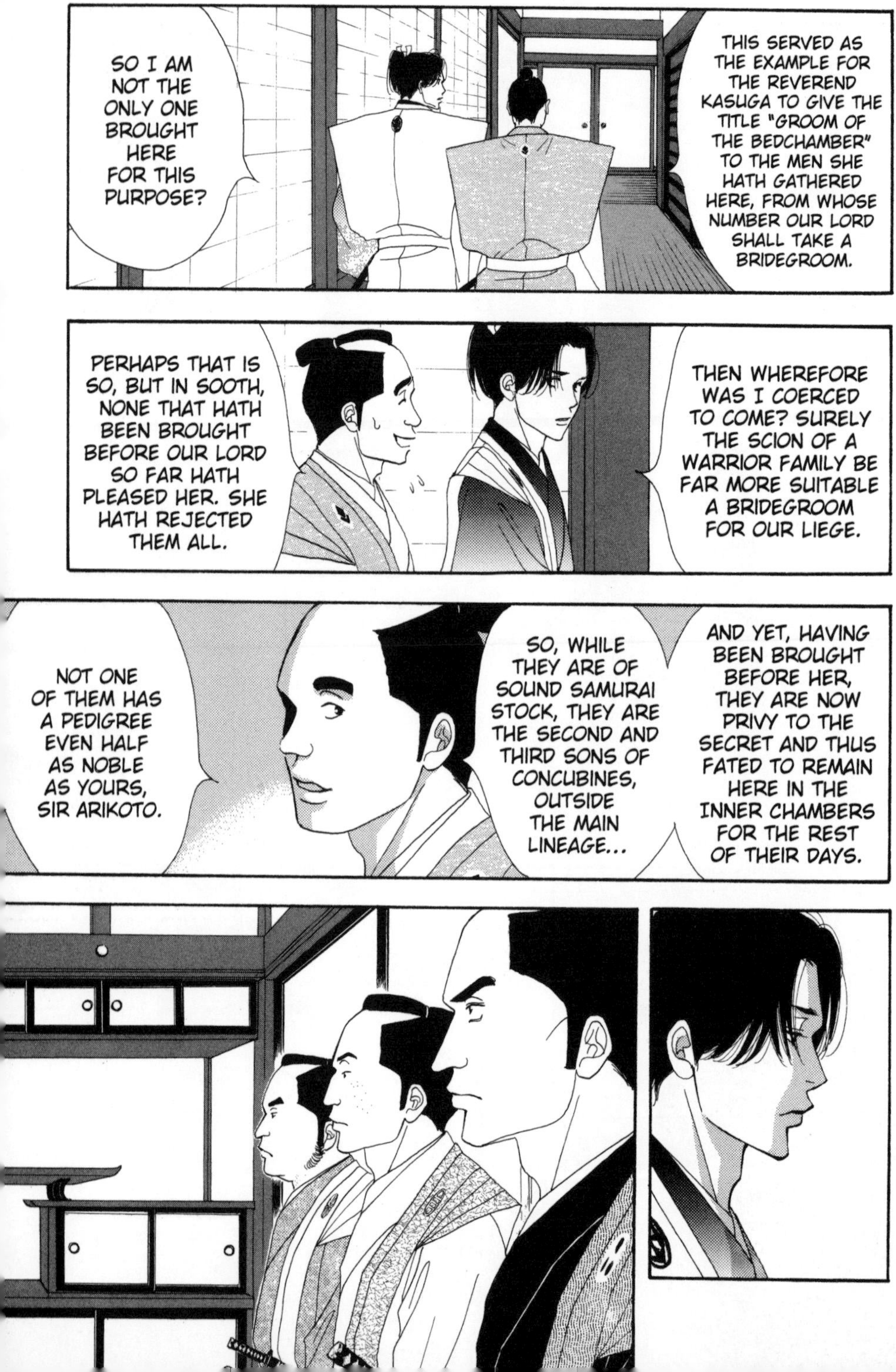
THIS SERVED AS THE EXAMPLE FOR THE REVEREND KASUGA TO GIVE THE TITLE "GROOM OF THE BEDCHAMBER" TO THE MEN SHE HATH GATHERED HERE, FROM WHOSE NUMBER OUR LORD SHALL TAKE A BRIDEGROOM.
SO I AM NOT THE ONLY ONE BROUGHT HERE FOR THIS PURPOSE?
THEN WHEREFORE WAS I COERCED TO COME? SURELY THE SCION OF A WARRIOR FAMILY BE FAR MORE SUITABLE A BRIDEGROOM FOR OUR LIEGE.
PERHAPS THAT IS SO, BUT IN SOOTH, NONE THAT HATH BEEN BROUGHT BEFORE OUR LORD SO FAR HATH PLEASED HER. SHE HATH REJECTED THEM ALL.
AND YET, HAVING BEEN BROUGHT BEFORE HER, THEY ARE NOW PRIVY TO THE SECRET AND THUS FATED TO REMAIN HERE IN THE INNER CHAMBERS FOR THE REST OF THEIR DAYS.
SO, WHILE THEY ARE OF SOUND SAMURAI STOCK, THEY ARE THE SECOND AND THIRD SONS OF CONCUBINES, OUTSIDE THE MAIN LINEAGE...
NOT ONE OF THEM HAS A PEDIGREE EVEN HALF AS NOBLE AS YOURS, SIR ARIKOTO.

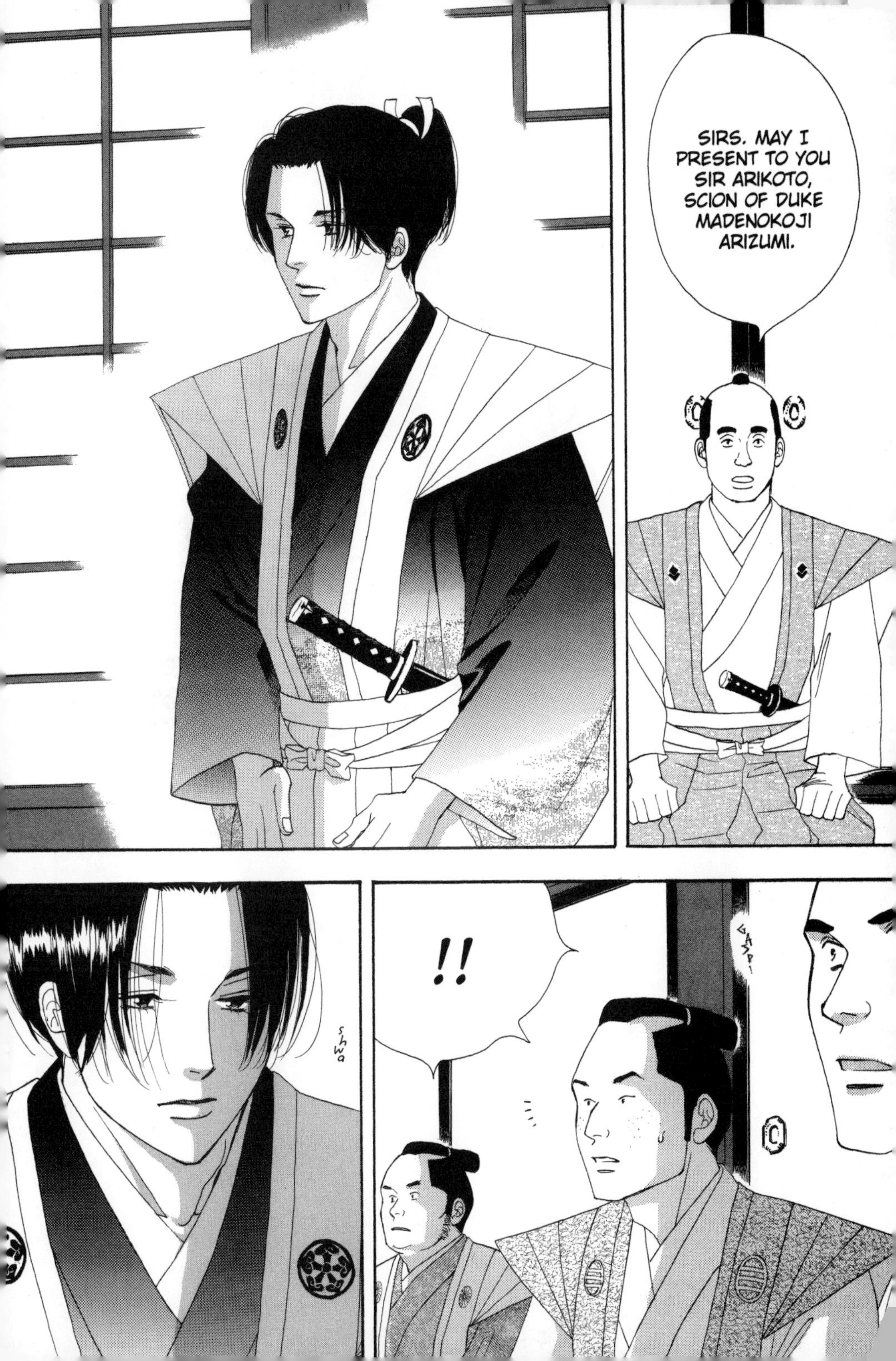
SIRS. MAY I PRESENT TO YOU SIR ARIKOTO, SCION OF DUKE MADENOKOJI ARIZUMI.
!!
GASP!
shwa

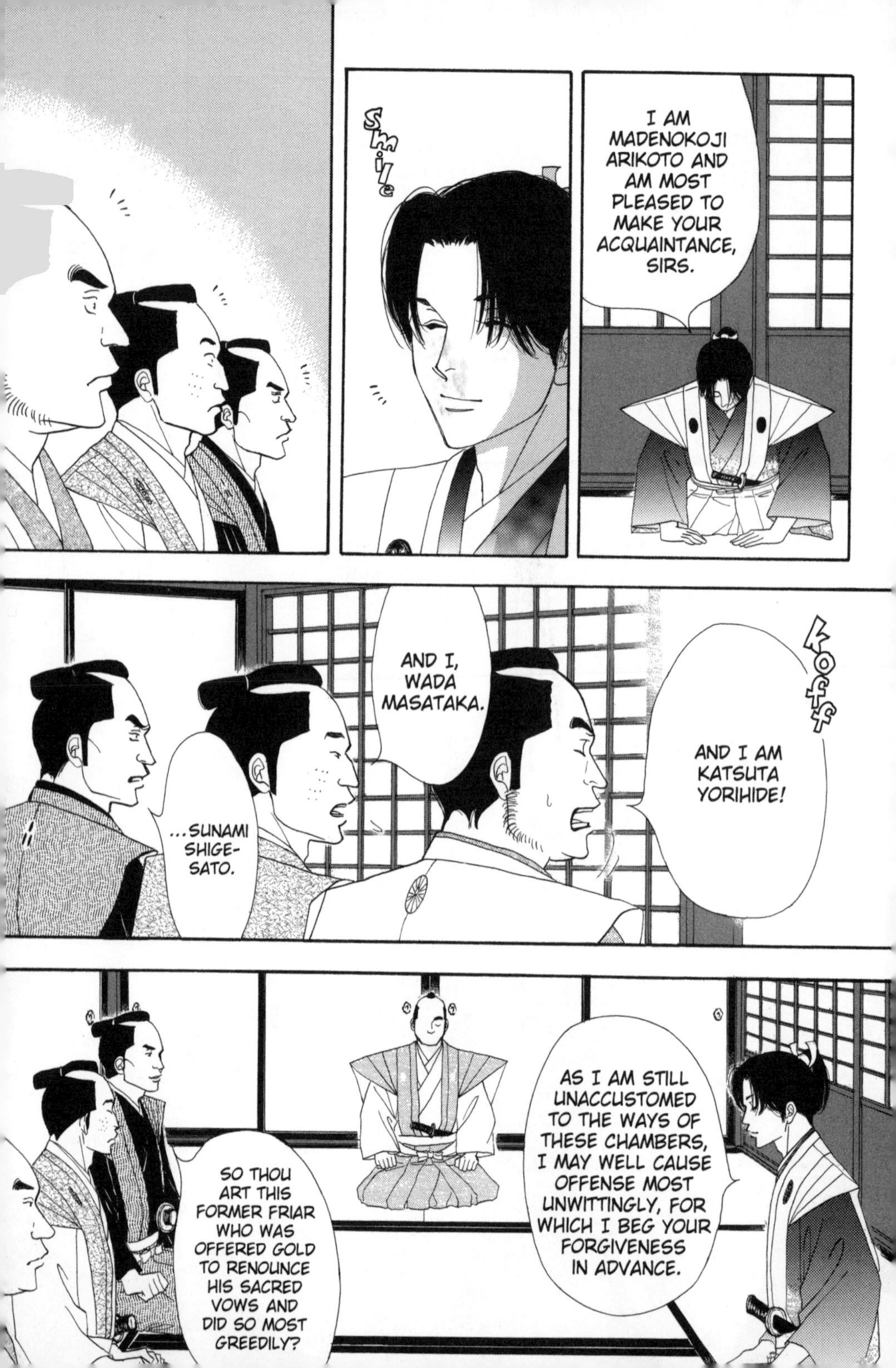
I AM MADENOKOJI ARIKOTO AND AM MOST PLEASED TO MAKE YOUR ACQUAINTANCE, SIRS.
Smile
koff
AND I AM KATSUTA YORIHIDE!
AND I, WADA MASATAKA.
...SUNAMI SHIGE-SATO.
AS I AM STILL UNACCUSTOMED TO THE WAYS OF THESE CHAMBERS, I MAY WELL CAUSE OFFENSE MOST UNWITTINGLY, FOR WHICH I BEG YOUR FORGIVENESS IN ADVANCE.
SO THOU ART THIS FORMER FRIAR WHO WAS OFFERED GOLD TO RENOUNCE HIS SACRED VOWS AND DID SO MOST GREEDILY?

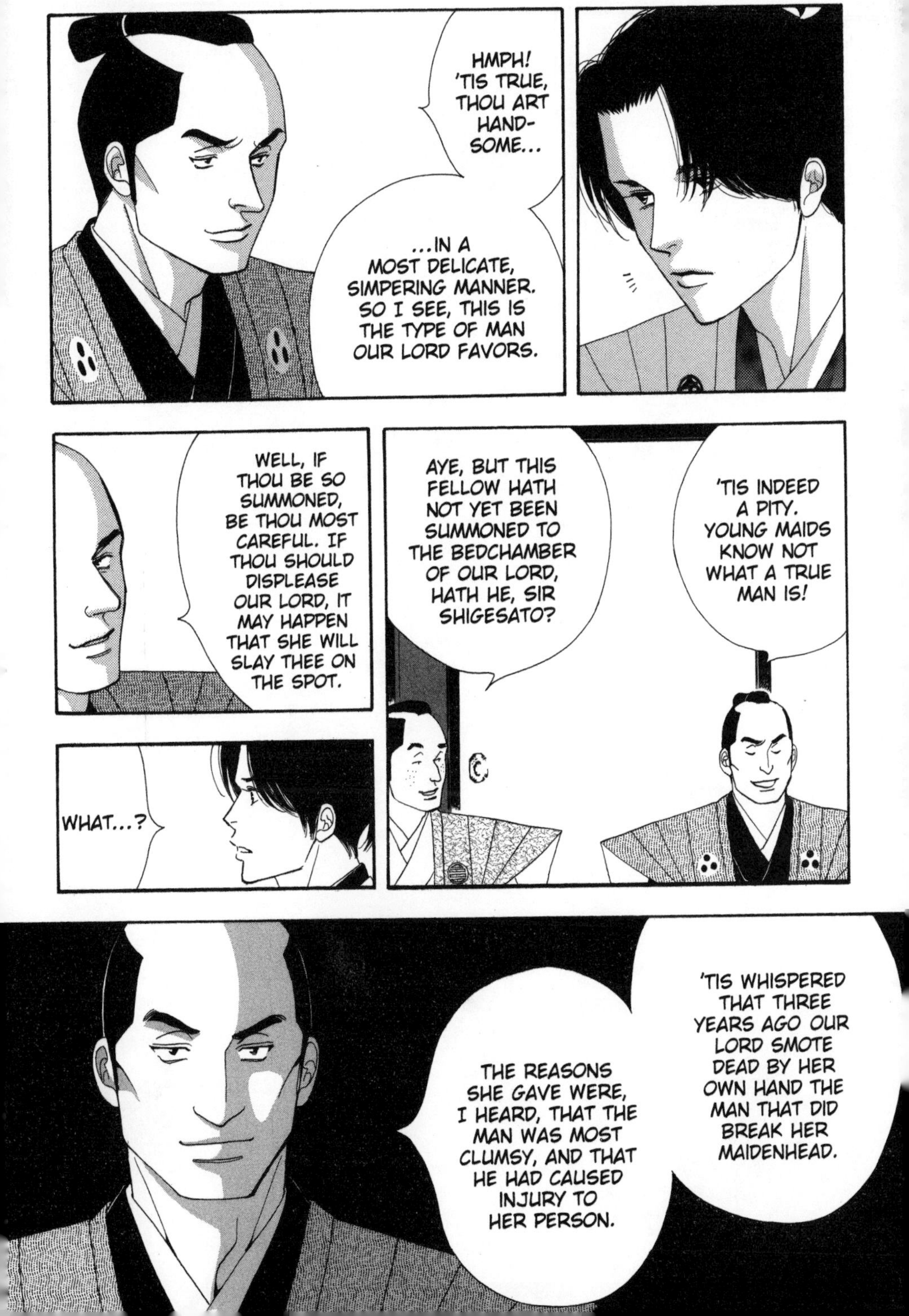
HMPH! 'TIS TRUE, THOU ART HAND-SOME...
...IN A MOST DELICATE, SIMPERING MANNER. SO I SEE, THIS IS THE TYPE OF MAN OUR LORD FAVORS.
'TIS INDEED A PITY. YOUNG MAIDS KNOW NOT WHAT A TRUE MAN IS!
AYE, BUT THIS FELLOW HATH NOT YET BEEN SUMMONED TO THE BEDCHAMBER OF OUR LORD, HATH HE, SIR SHIGESATO?
WELL, IF THOU BE SO SUMMONED, BE THOU MOST CAREFUL. IF THOU SHOULD DISPLEASE OUR LORD, IT MAY HAPPEN THAT SHE WILL SLAY THEE ON THE SPOT.
WHAT...?
'TIS WHISPERED THAT THREE YEARS AGO OUR LORD SMOTE DEAD BY HER OWN HAND THE MAN THAT DID BREAK HER MAIDENHEAD.
THE REASONS SHE GAVE WERE, I HEARD, THAT THE MAN WAS MOST CLUMSY, AND THAT HE HAD CAUSED INJURY TO HER PERSON.

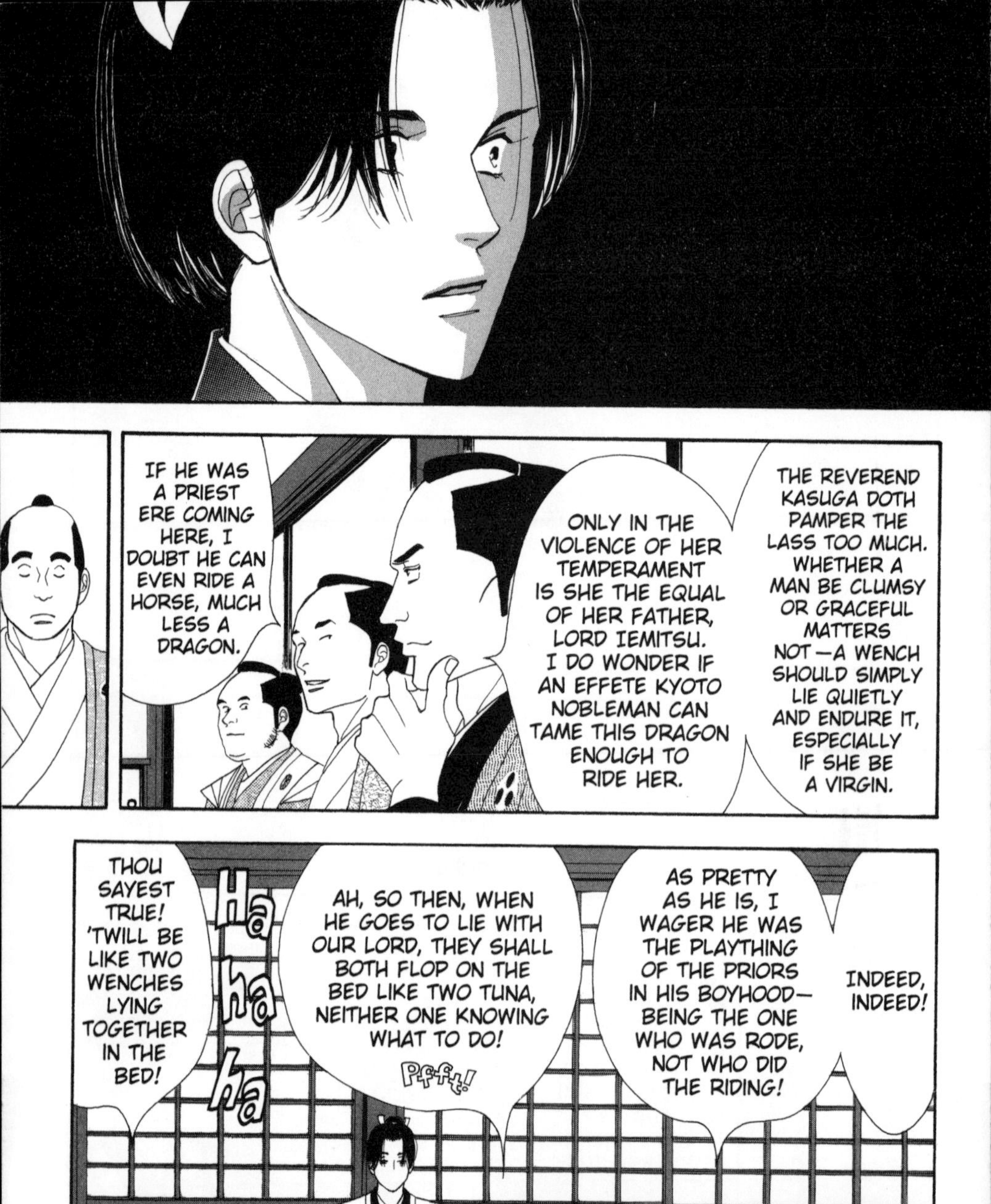
THE REVEREND KASUGA DOTH PAMPER THE LASS TOO MUCH. WHETHER A MAN BE CLUMSY OR GRACEFUL MATTERS NOT—A WENCH SHOULD SIMPLY LIE QUIETLY AND ENDURE IT, ESPECIALLY IF SHE BE A VIRGIN.
ONLY IN THE VIOLENCE OF HER TEMPERAMENT IS SHE THE EQUAL OF HER FATHER, LORD IEMITSU. I DO WONDER IF AN EFFETE KYOTO NOBLEMAN CAN TAME THIS DRAGON ENOUGH TO RIDE HER.
IF HE WAS A PRIEST ERE COMING HERE, I DOUBT HE CAN EVEN RIDE A HORSE, MUCH LESS A DRAGON.
INDEED, INDEED!
AS PRETTY AS HE IS, I WAGER HE WAS THE PLAYTHING OF THE PRIORS IN HIS BOYHOOD—BEING THE ONE WHO WAS RODE, NOT WHO DID THE RIDING!
AH, SO THEN, WHEN HE GOES TO LIE WITH OUR LORD, THEY SHALL BOTH FLOP ON THE BED LIKE TWO TUNA, NEITHER ONE KNOWING WHAT TO DO!
Pffft!
Ha ha ha
THOU SAYEST TRUE! 'TWILL BE LIKE TWO WENCHES LYING TOGETHER IN THE BED!

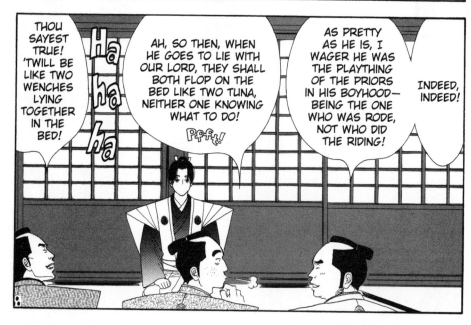

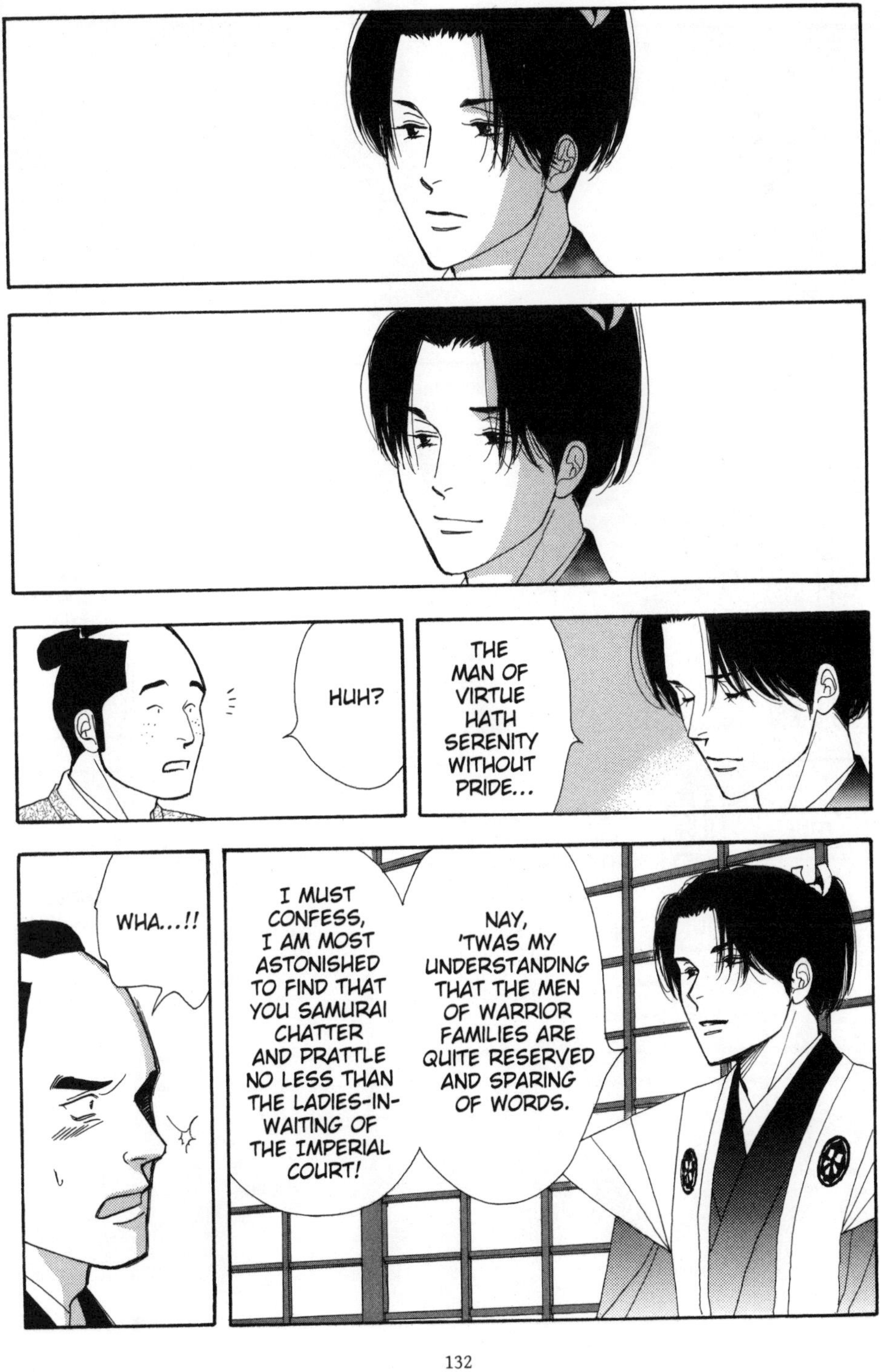
THE MAN OF VIRTUE HATH SERENITY WITHOUT PRIDE...
HUH?
NAY, 'TWAS MY UNDERSTANDING THAT THE MEN OF WARRIOR FAMILIES ARE QUITE RESERVED AND SPARING OF WORDS.
I MUST CONFESS, I AM MOST ASTONISHED TO FIND THAT YOU SAMURAI CHATTER AND PRATTLE NO LESS THAN THE LADIES-IN-WAITING OF THE IMPERIAL COURT!
WHA...!!

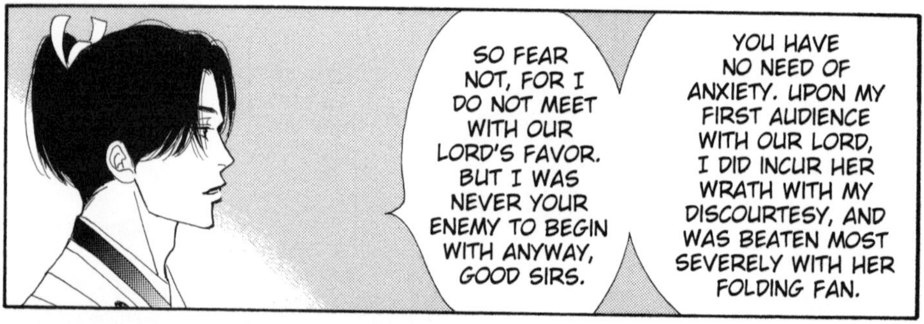
YOU HAVE NO NEED OF ANXIETY. UPON MY FIRST AUDIENCE WITH OUR LORD, I DID INCUR HER WRATH WITH MY DISCOURTESY, AND WAS BEATEN MOST SEVERELY WITH HER FOLDING FAN.
SO FEAR NOT, FOR I DO NOT MEET WITH OUR LORD'S FAVOR. BUT I WAS NEVER YOUR ENEMY TO BEGIN WITH ANYWAY, GOOD SIRS.

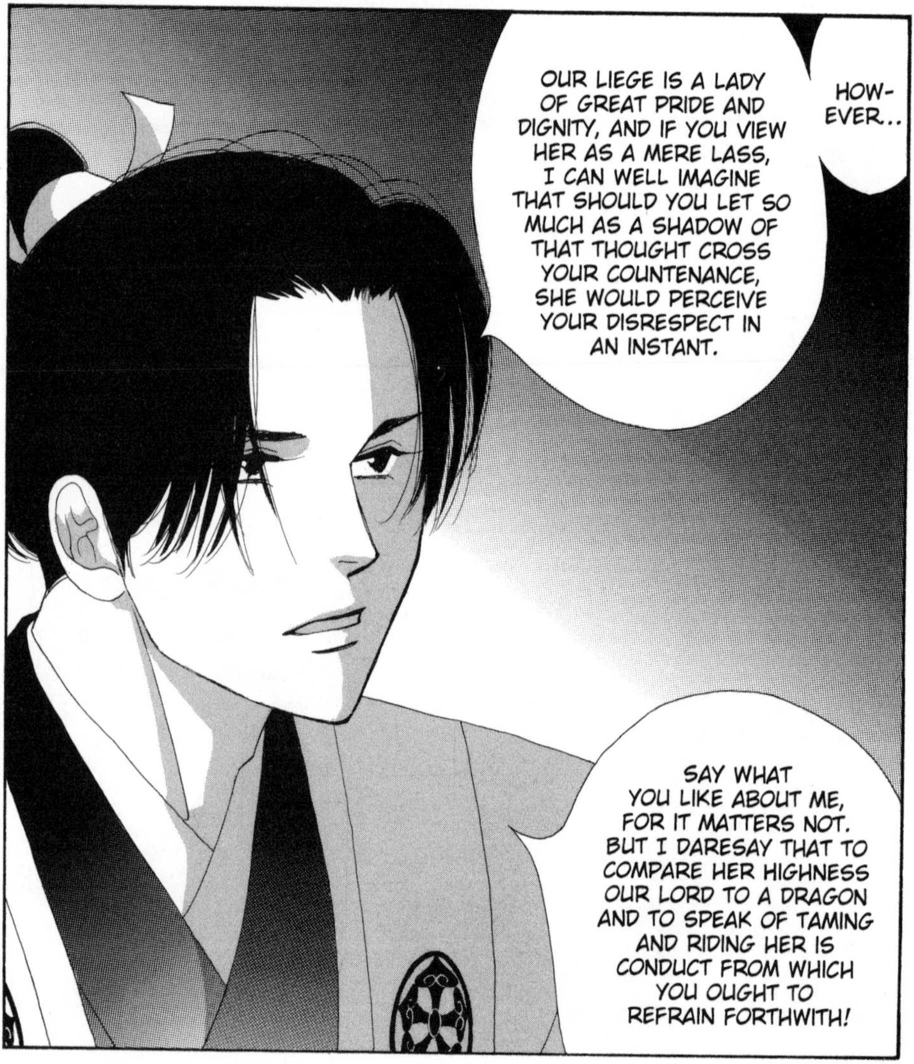
HOW-EVER...
OUR LIEGE IS A LADY OF GREAT PRIDE AND DIGNITY, AND IF YOU VIEW HER AS A MERE LASS, I CAN WELL IMAGINE THAT SHOULD YOU LET SO MUCH AS A SHADOW OF THAT THOUGHT CROSS YOUR COUNTENANCE, SHE WOULD PERCEIVE YOUR DISRESPECT IN AN INSTANT.
SAY WHAT YOU LIKE ABOUT ME, FOR IT MATTERS NOT. BUT I DARESAY THAT TO COMPARE HER HIGHNESS OUR LORD TO A DRAGON AND TO SPEAK OF TAMING AND RIDING HER IS CONDUCT FROM WHICH YOU OUGHT TO REFRAIN FORTHWITH!

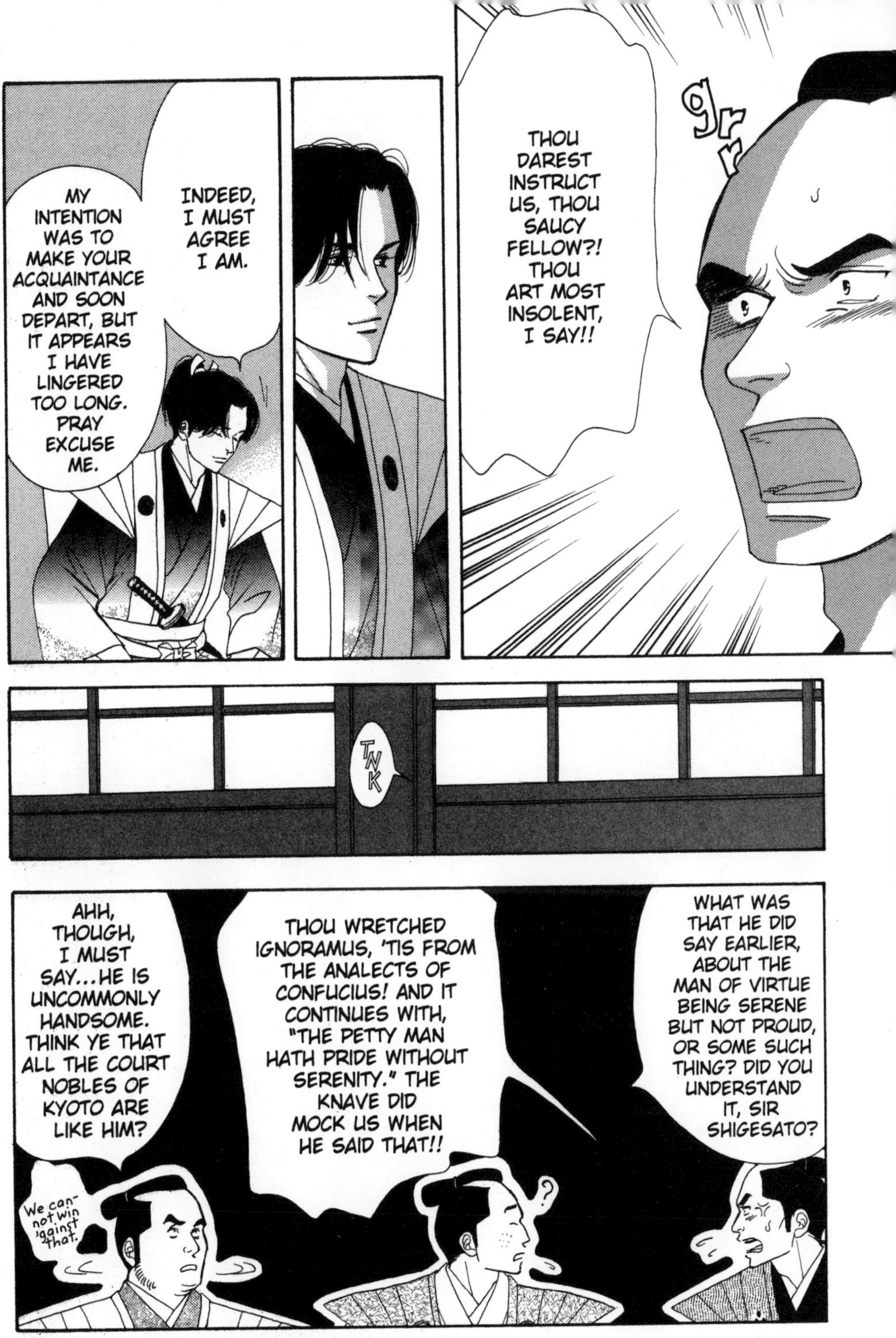
gr
THOU DAREST INSTRUCT US, THOU SAUCY FELLOW?! THOU ART MOST INSOLENT, I SAY!!
INDEED, I MUST AGREE I AM.
MY INTENTION WAS TO MAKE YOUR ACQUAINTANCE AND SOON DEPART, BUT IT APPEARS I HAVE LINGERED TOO LONG. PRAY EXCUSE ME.
TNK
WHAT WAS THAT HE DID SAY EARLIER, ABOUT THE MAN OF VIRTUE BEING SERENE BUT NOT PROUD, OR SOME SUCH THING? DID YOU UNDERSTAND IT, SIR SHIGESATO?
THOU WRETCHED IGNORAMUS, 'TIS FROM THE ANALECTS OF CONFUCIUS! AND IT CONTINUES WITH, "THE PETTY MAN HATH PRIDE WITHOUT SERENITY." THE KNAVE DID MOCK US WHEN HE SAID THAT!!
AHH, THOUGH, I MUST SAY...HE IS UNCOMMONLY HANDSOME. THINK YE THAT ALL THE COURT NOBLES OF KYOTO ARE LIKE HIM?
We cannot win 'gainst that.

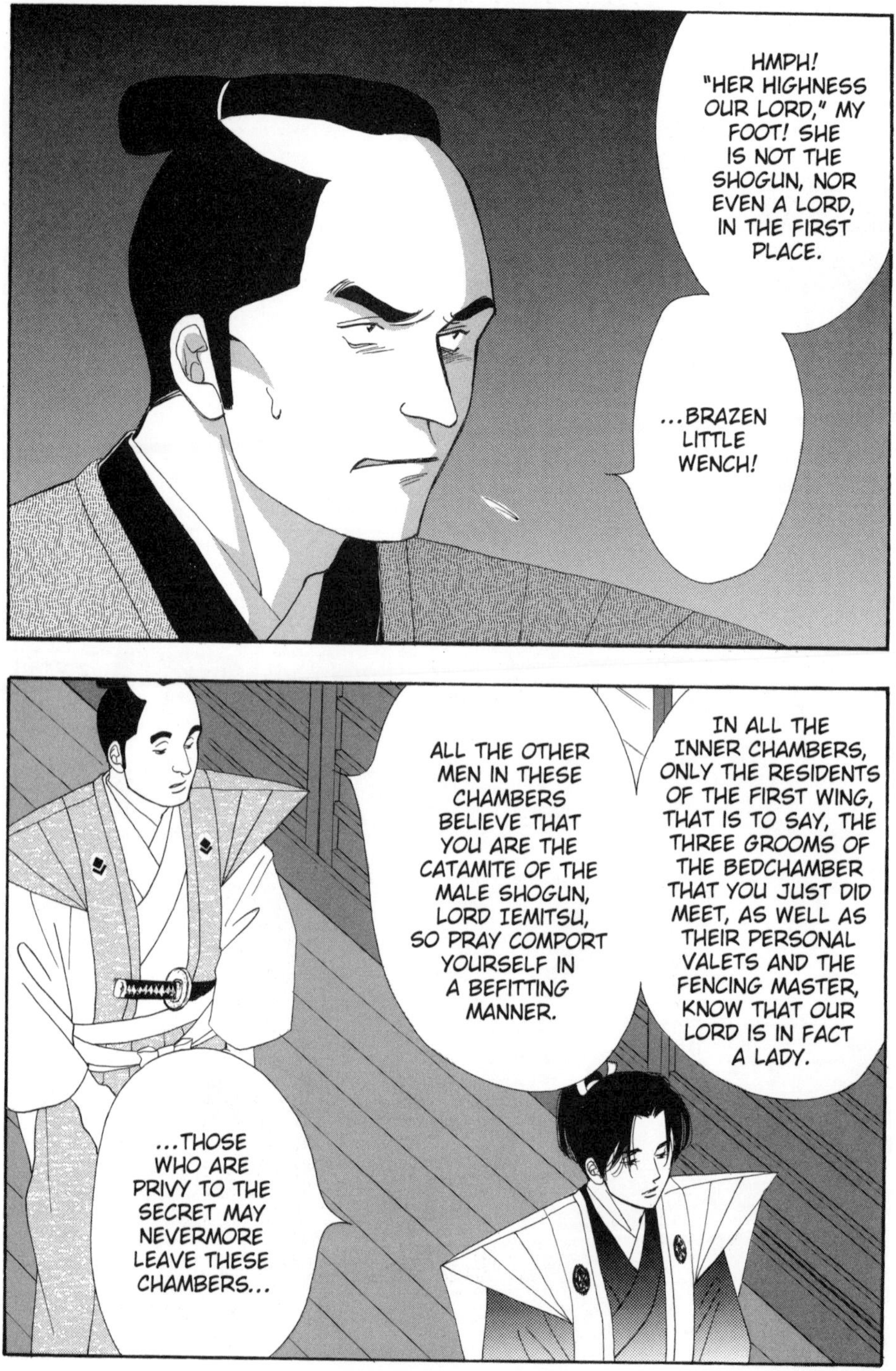
HMPH! "HER HIGHNESS OUR LORD," MY FOOT! SHE IS NOT THE SHOGUN, NOR EVEN A LORD, IN THE FIRST PLACE.
...BRAZEN LITTLE WENCH!
IN ALL THE INNER CHAMBERS, ONLY THE RESIDENTS OF THE FIRST WING, THAT IS TO SAY, THE THREE GROOMS OF THE BEDCHAMBER THAT YOU JUST DID MEET, AS WELL AS THEIR PERSONAL VALETS AND THE FENCING MASTER, KNOW THAT OUR LORD IS IN FACT A LADY.
ALL THE OTHER MEN IN THESE CHAMBERS BELIEVE THAT YOU ARE THE CATAMITE OF THE MALE SHOGUN, LORD IEMITSU, SO PRAY COMPORT YOURSELF IN A BEFITTING MANNER.
...THOSE WHO ARE PRIVY TO THE SECRET MAY NEVERMORE LEAVE THESE CHAMBERS...

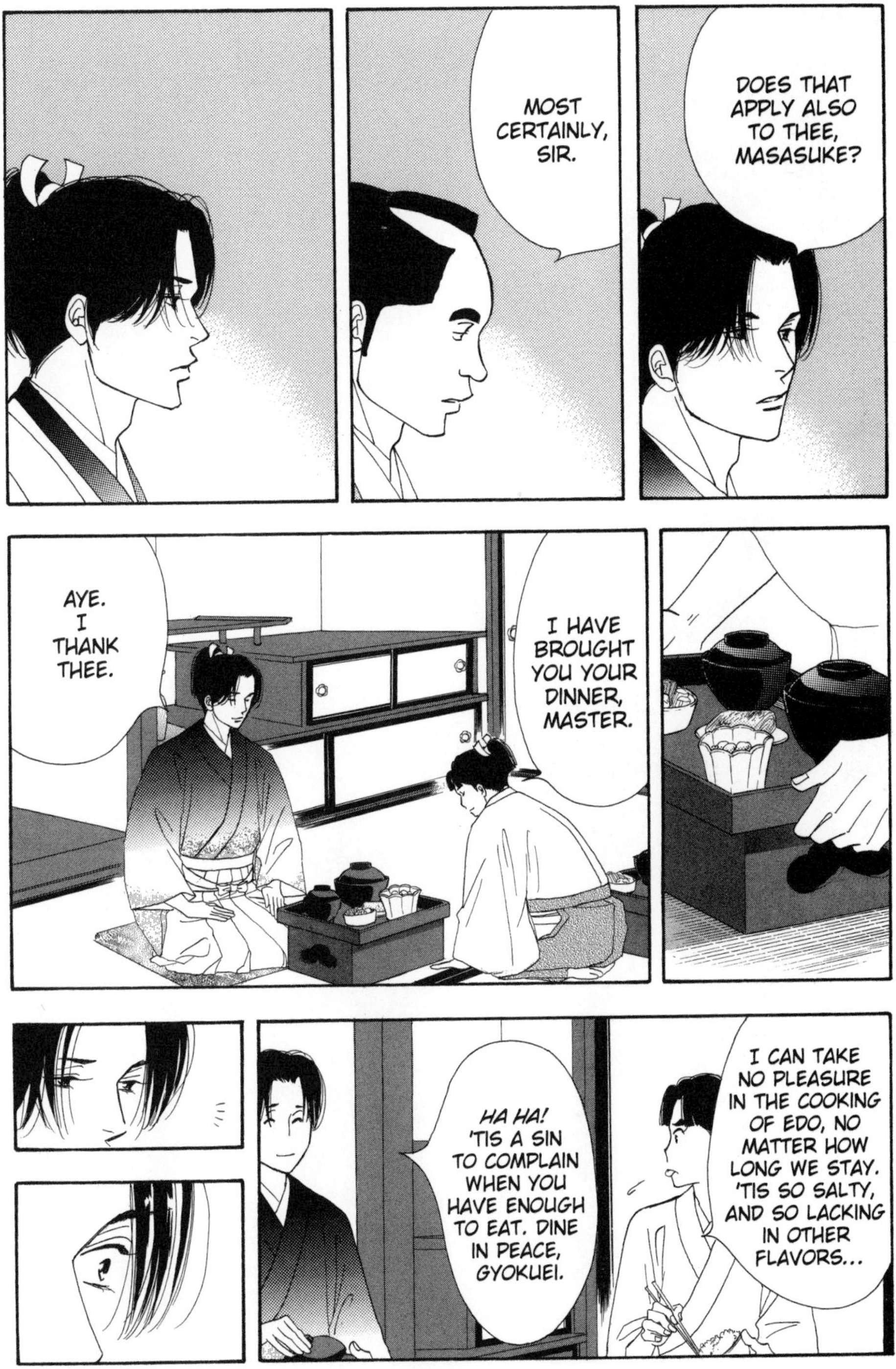
DOES THAT APPLY ALSO TO THEE, MASASUKE?
MOST CERTAINLY, SIR.
I HAVE BROUGHT YOU YOUR DINNER, MASTER.
AYE. I THANK THEE.
I CAN TAKE NO PLEASURE IN THE COOKING OF EDO, NO MATTER HOW LONG WE STAY. 'TIS SO SALTY, AND SO LACKING IN OTHER FLAVORS...
HA HA! 'TIS A SIN TO COMPLAIN WHEN YOU HAVE ENOUGH TO EAT. DINE IN PEACE, GYOKUEI.

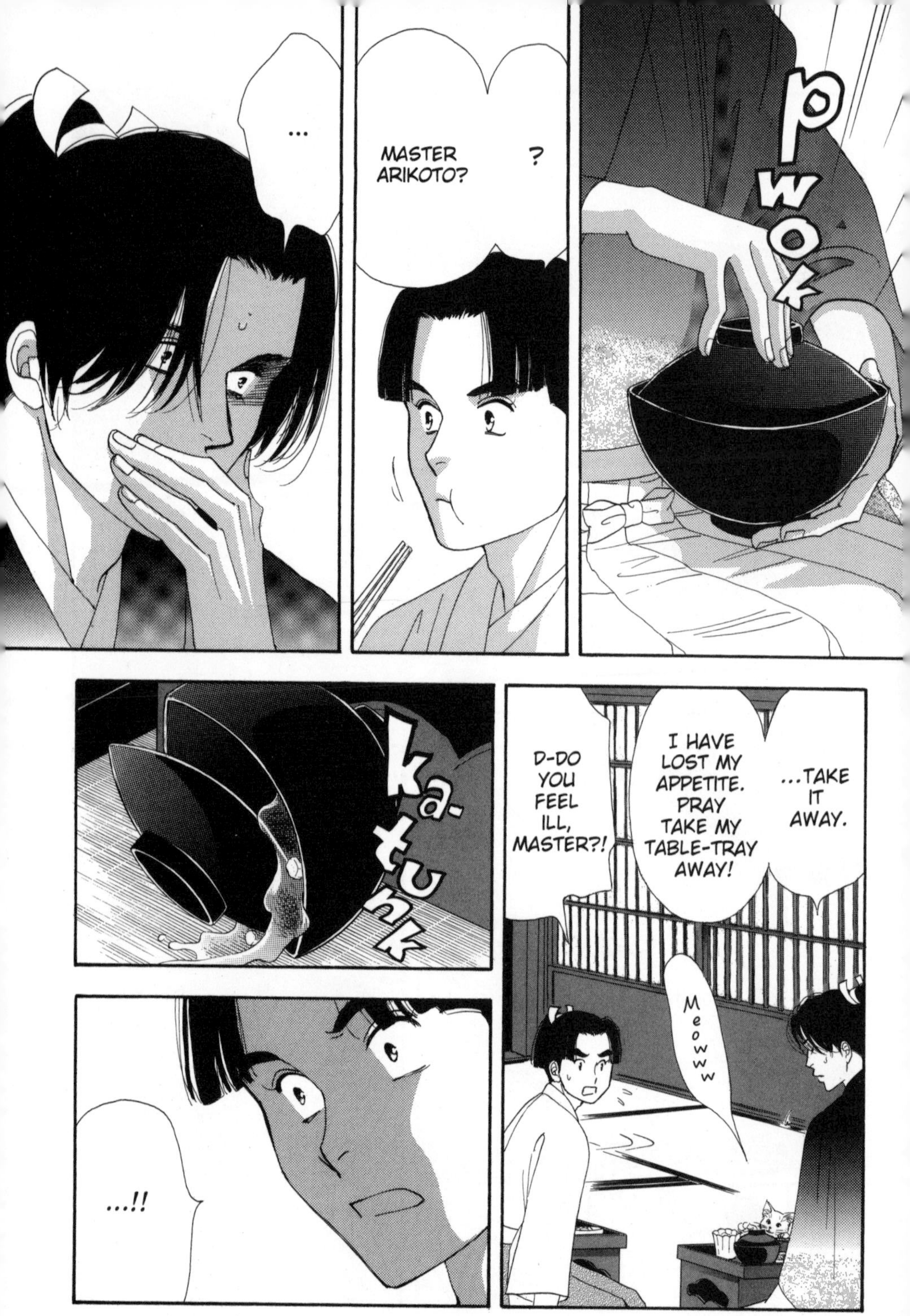
pwok
MASTER ARIKOTO?
?
...
...TAKE IT AWAY.
I HAVE LOST MY APPETITE. PRAY TAKE MY TABLE-TRAY AWAY!
D-DO YOU FEEL ILL, MASTER?!
Meowww
ka-tunk
...!!

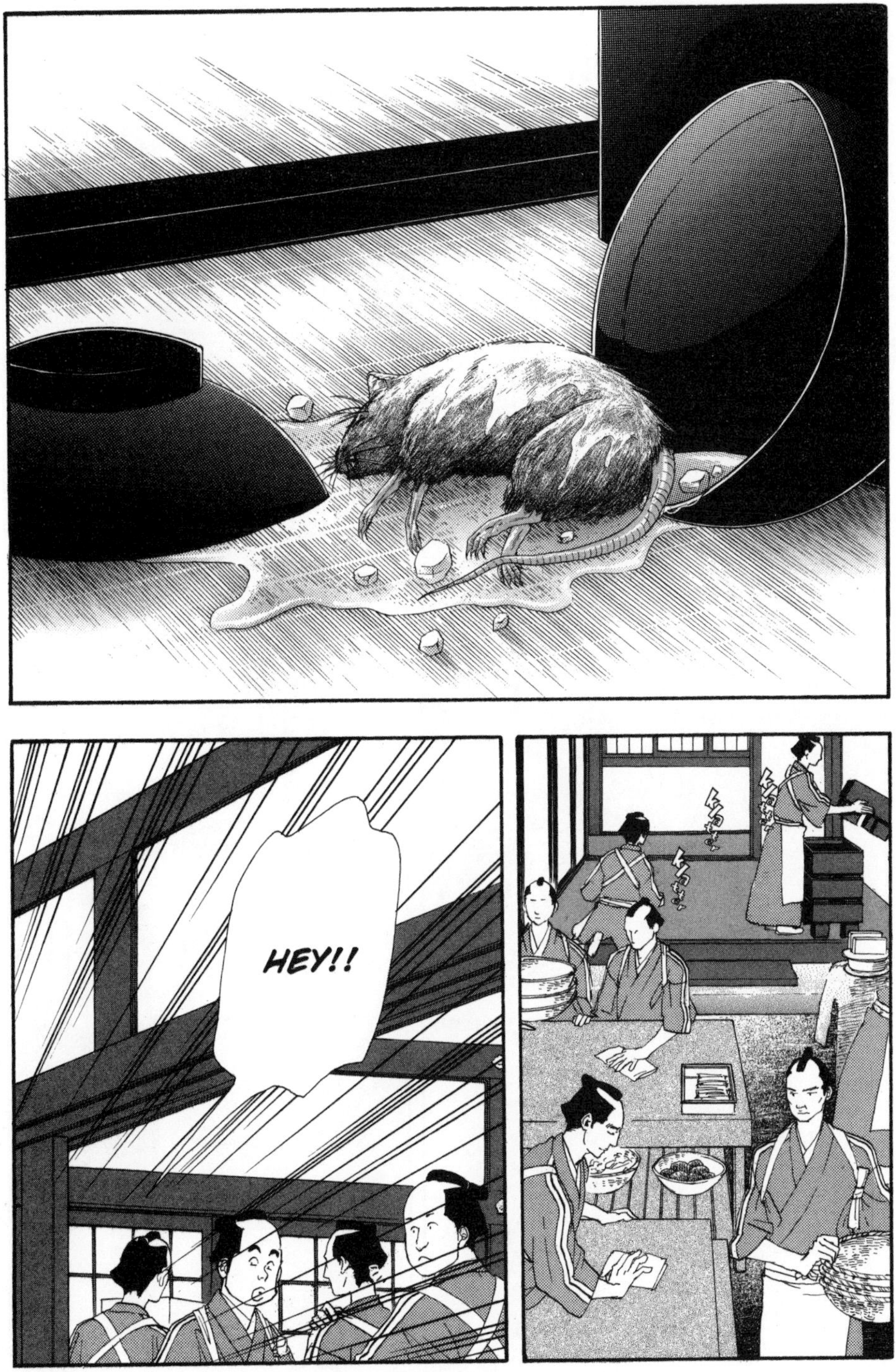
HEY!!

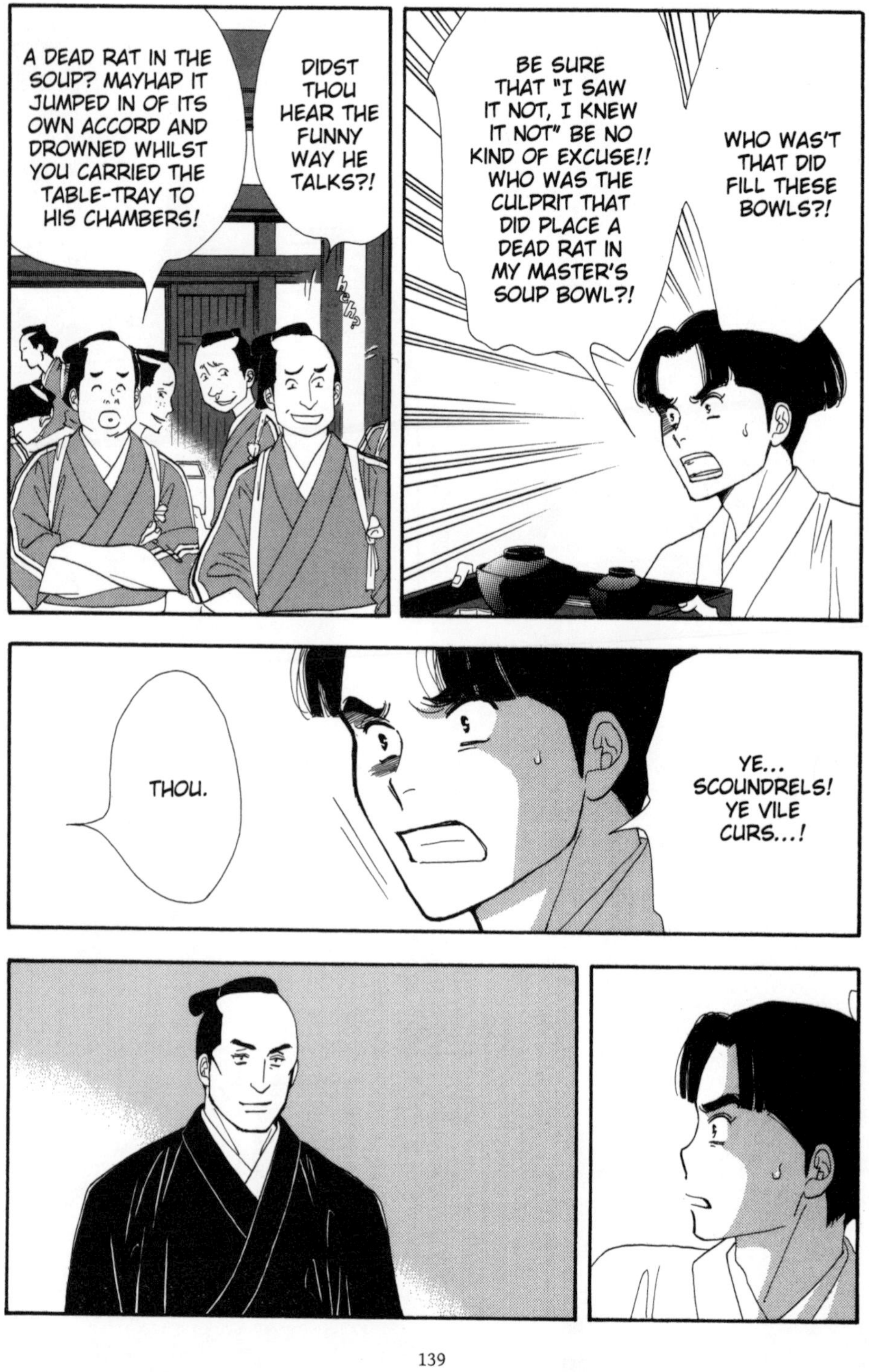
WHO WAS'T THAT DID FILL THESE BOWLS?!
BE SURE THAT "I SAW IT NOT, I KNEW IT NOT" BE NO KIND OF EXCUSE!! WHO WAS THE CULPRIT THAT DID PLACE A DEAD RAT IN MY MASTER'S SOUP BOWL?!
DIDST THOU HEAR THE FUNNY WAY HE TALKS?!
A DEAD RAT IN THE SOUP? MAYHAP IT JUMPED IN OF ITS OWN ACCORD AND DROWNED WHILST YOU CARRIED THE TABLE-TRAY TO HIS CHAMBERS!
YE... SCOUNDRELS! YE VILE CURS...!
THOU.

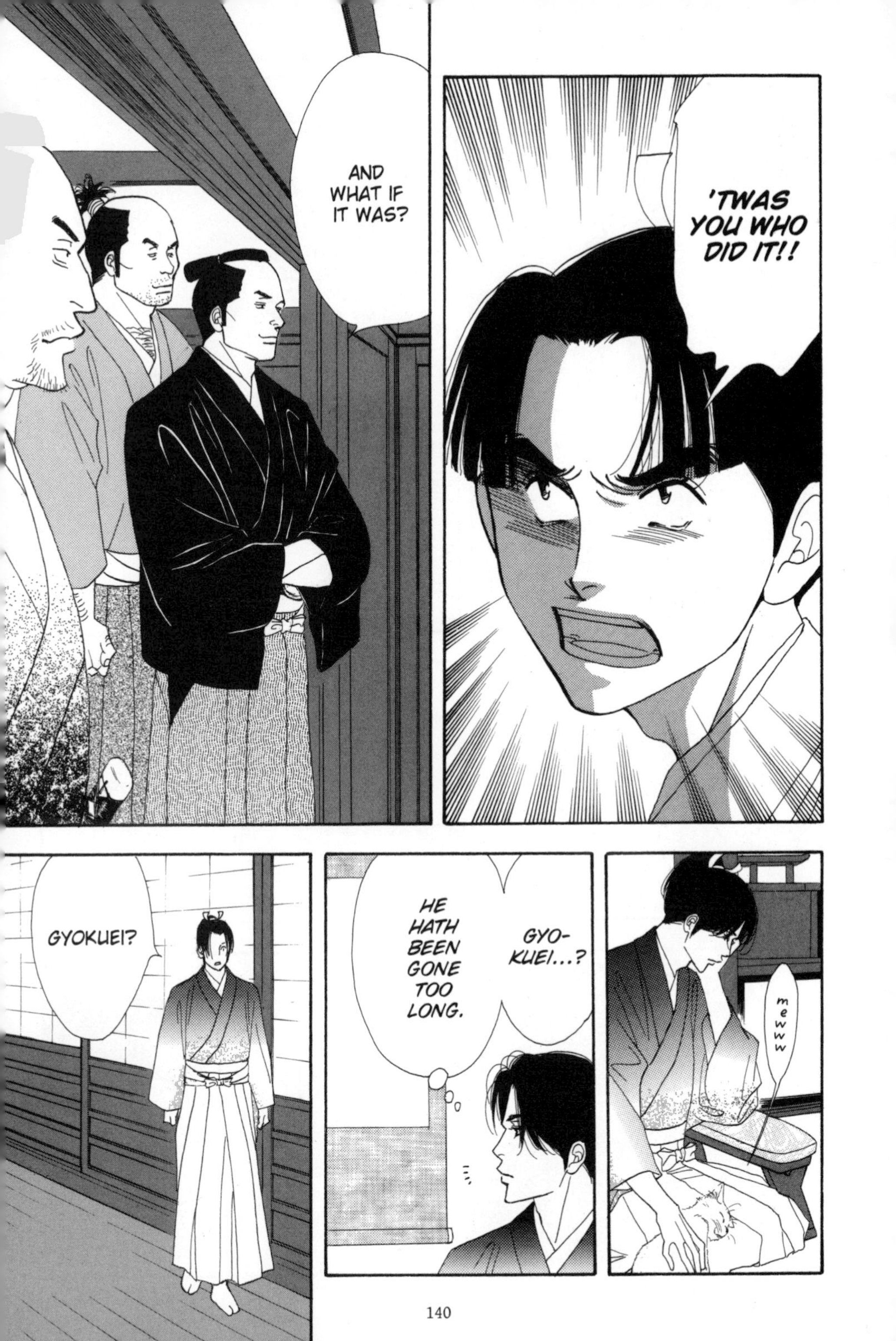
'TWAS YOU WHO DID IT!!
AND WHAT IF IT WAS?
mewww
GYO-KUEI...?
HE HATH BEEN GONE TOO LONG.
GYOKUEI?

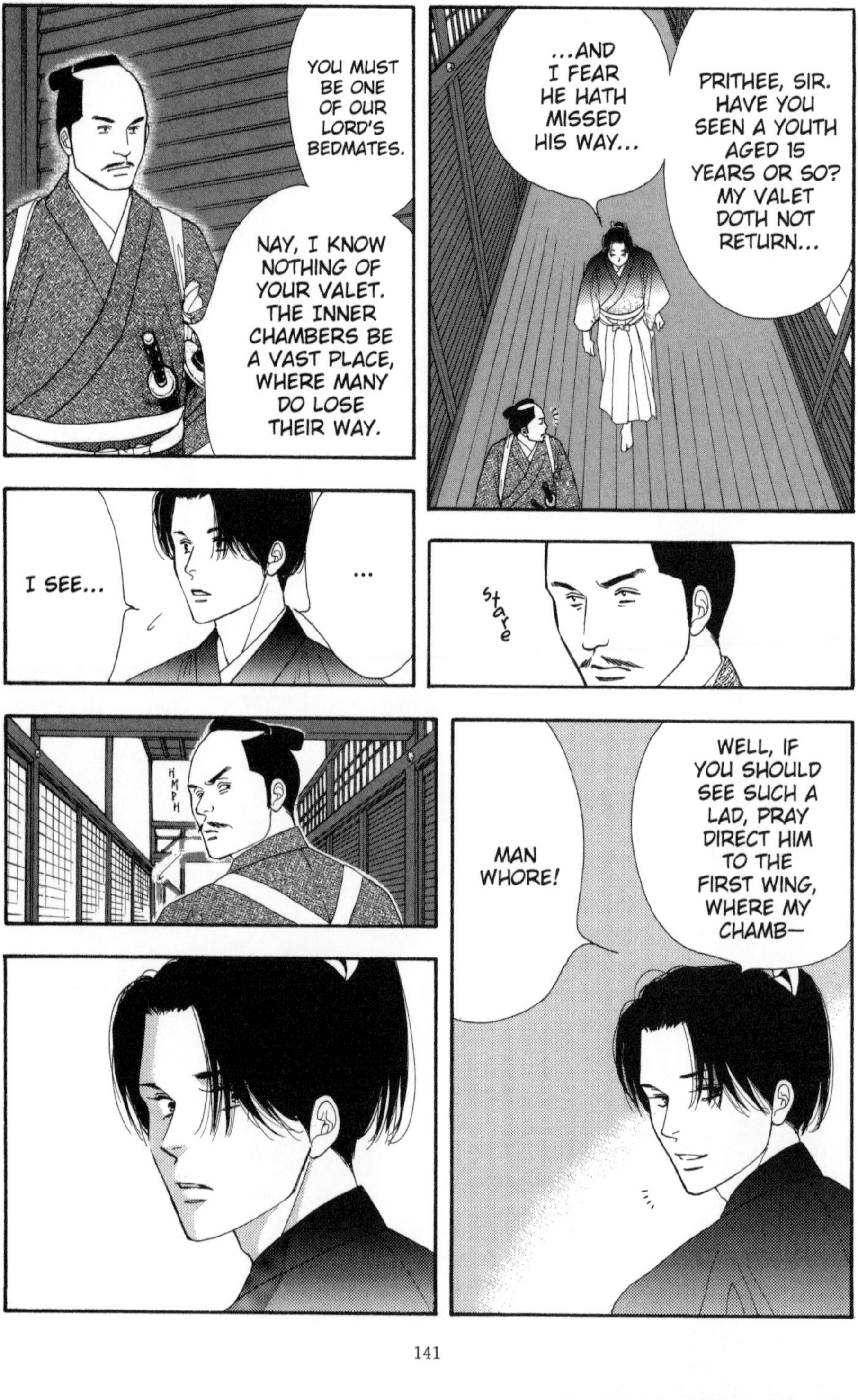
PRITHEE, SIR. HAVE YOU SEEN A YOUTH AGED 15 YEARS OR SO? MY VALET DOTH NOT RETURN...
...AND I FEAR HE HATH MISSED HIS WAY...
YOU MUST BE ONE OF OUR LORD'S BEDMATES.
NAY, I KNOW NOTHING OF YOUR VALET. THE INNER CHAMBERS BE A VAST PLACE, WHERE MANY DO LOSE THEIR WAY.
stare
...
I SEE...
WELL, IF YOU SHOULD SEE SUCH A LAD, PRAY DIRECT HIM TO THE FIRST WING, WHERE MY CHAMB—
MAN WHORE!
HMPH

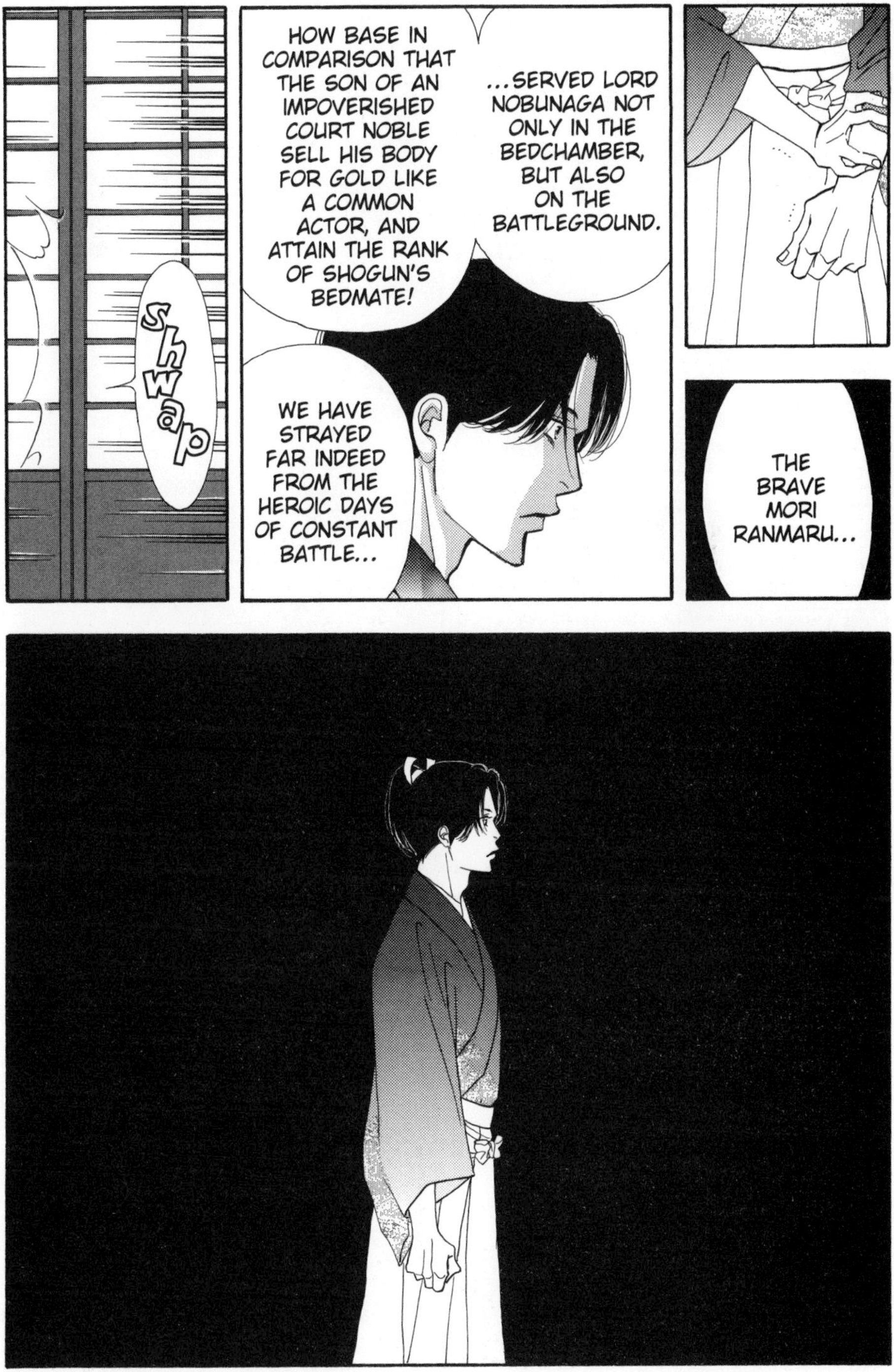
THE BRAVE MORI RANMARU...
...SERVED LORD NOBUNAGA NOT ONLY IN THE BEDCHAMBER, BUT ALSO ON THE BATTLEGROUND.
HOW BASE IN COMPARISON THAT THE SON OF AN IMPOVERISHED COURT NOBLE SELL HIS BODY FOR GOLD LIKE A COMMON ACTOR, AND ATTAIN THE RANK OF SHOGUN'S BEDMATE!
WE HAVE STRAYED FAR INDEED FROM THE HEROIC DAYS OF CONSTANT BATTLE...
Shwap

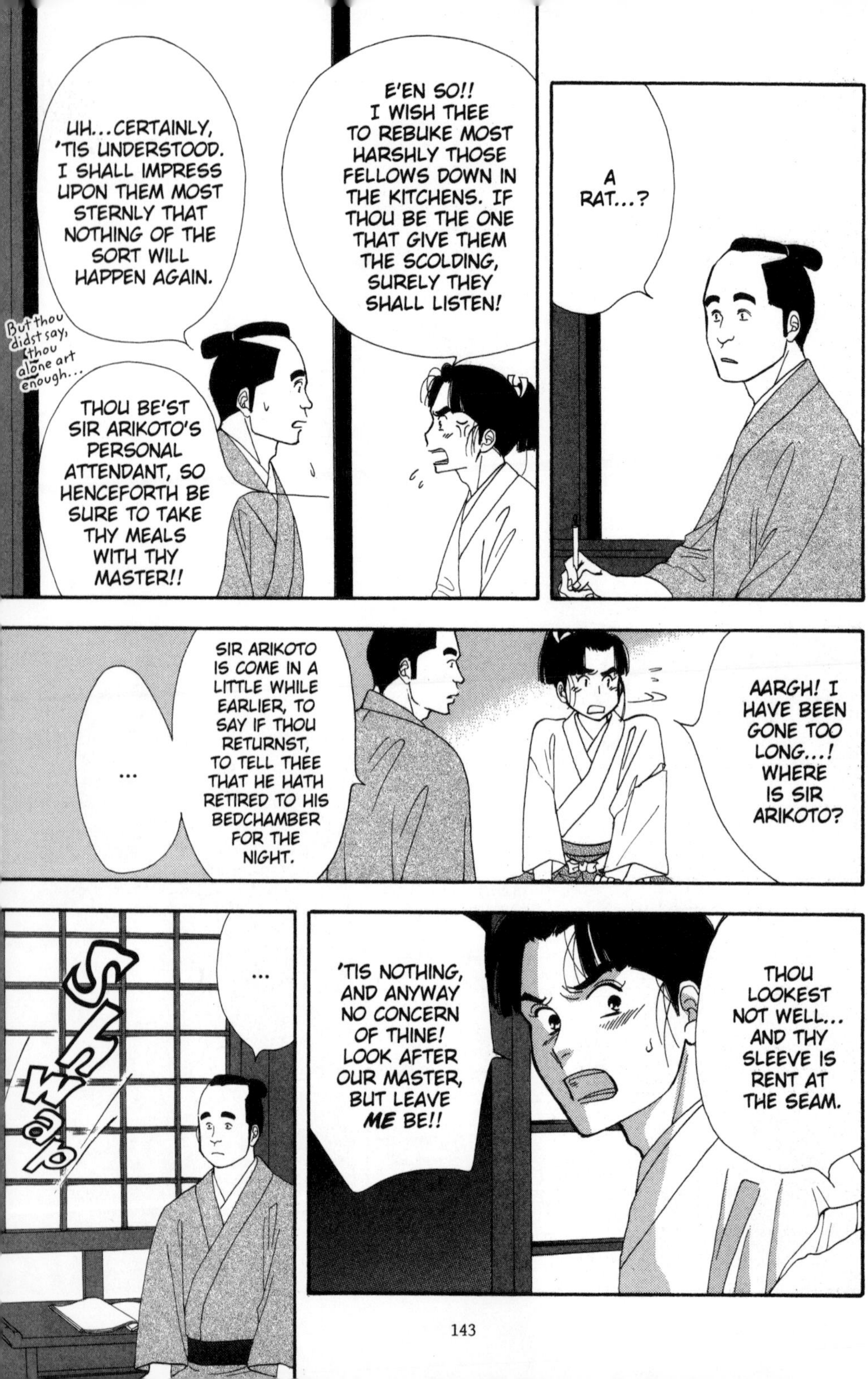
A RAT...?
E'EN SO!! I WISH THEE TO REBUKE MOST HARSHLY THOSE FELLOWS DOWN IN THE KITCHENS. IF THOU BE THE ONE THAT GIVE THEM THE SCOLDING, SURELY THEY SHALL LISTEN!
UH...CERTAINLY, 'TIS UNDERSTOOD. I SHALL IMPRESS UPON THEM MOST STERNLY THAT NOTHING OF THE SORT WILL HAPPEN AGAIN.
But thou didst say, thou alone art enough...
THOU BE'ST SIR ARIKOTO'S PERSONAL ATTENDANT, SO HENCEFORTH BE SURE TO TAKE THY MEALS WITH THY MASTER!!
AARGH! I HAVE BEEN GONE TOO LONG...! WHERE IS SIR ARIKOTO?
SIR ARIKOTO IS COME IN A LITTLE WHILE EARLIER, TO SAY IF THOU RETURNST, TO TELL THEE THAT HE HATH RETIRED TO HIS BEDCHAMBER FOR THE NIGHT.
...
THOU LOOKEST NOT WELL... AND THY SLEEVE IS RENT AT THE SEAM.
'TIS NOTHING, AND ANYWAY NO CONCERN OF THINE! LOOK AFTER OUR MASTER, BUT LEAVE ME BE!!
...
Shwap

NGH...!

AWWWGH!!

THOSE VILLAINS WERE CAREFUL THEIR TORTURE IS HIDDEN FROM SIGHT.

BRUTES...!!

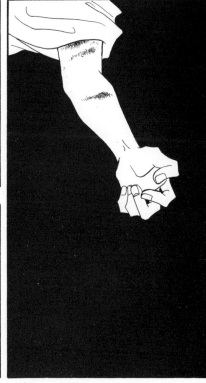

SIR SHIGESATO, PRITHEE GIVE US A TURN WITH HIM WHEN YOU ARE FINISHED...

BE MY GUEST. COOPED IN THE INNER CHAMBERS, YE CANNOT EVEN LIE WITH WHORES ANYMORE, I WAGER.

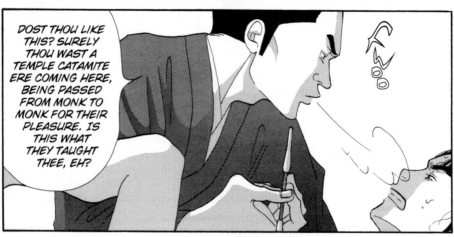

DOST THOU LIKE THIS? SURELY THOU WAST A TEMPLE CATAMITE ERE COMING HERE, BEING PASSED FROM MONK TO MONK FOR THEIR PLEASURE. IS THIS WHAT THEY TAUGHT THEE, EH?

VERILY SO—I AM WELL-ACCUSTOMED TO'T! BUT TO THE TEMPLE PRIORS I WAS MUCH BEHOLDEN, WHILE TO THEE, VILE CUR, NOT AT ALL.

...HEH!

REMEMBER THIS WELL, THAT I SHALL SURELY KILL THEE ONE DAY, THOU CLUMSY OAF!!

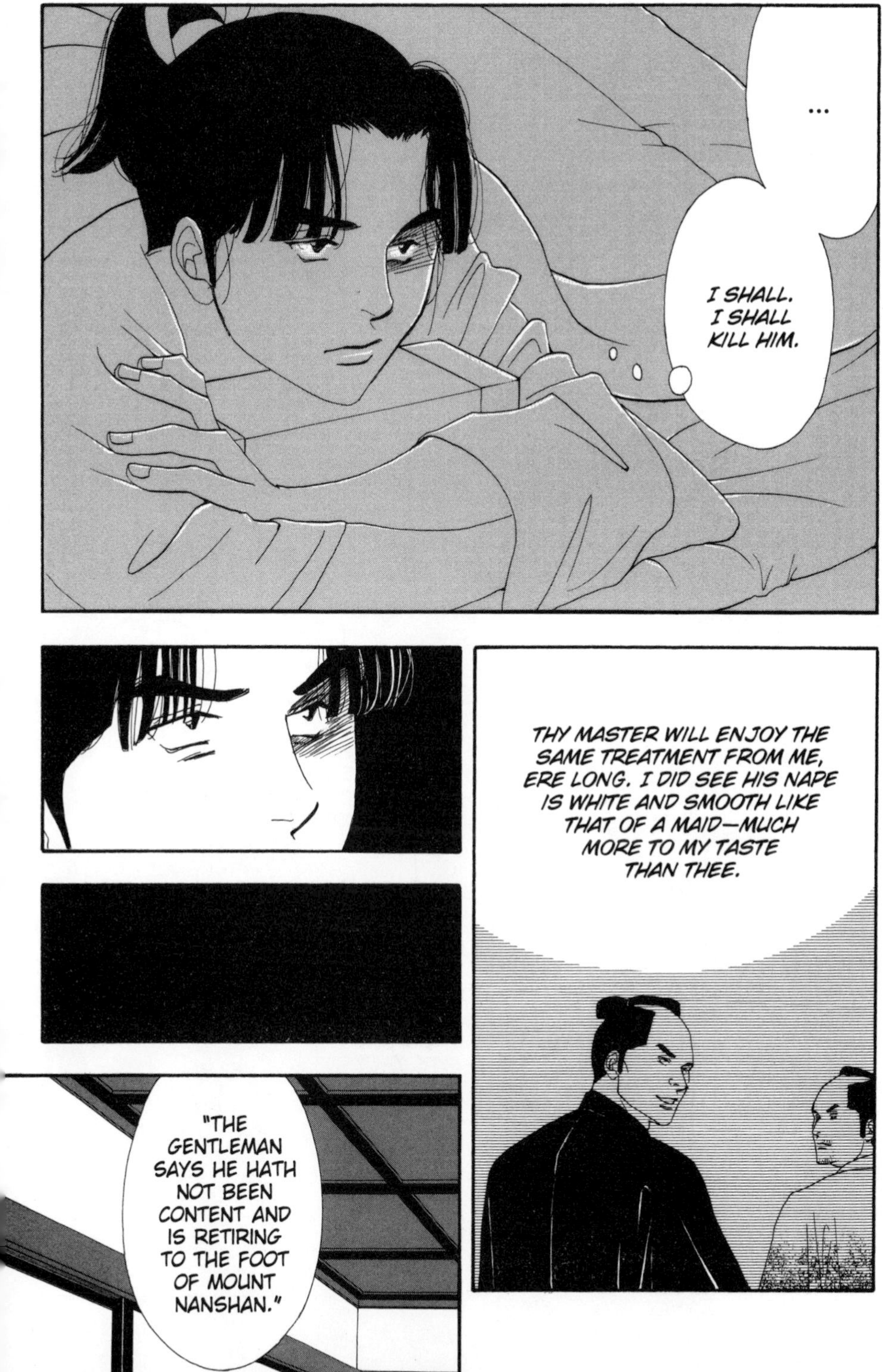
...
I SHALL. I SHALL KILL HIM.
THY MASTER WILL ENJOY THE SAME TREATMENT FROM ME, ERE LONG. I DID SEE HIS NAPE IS WHITE AND SMOOTH LIKE THAT OF A MAID—MUCH MORE TO MY TASTE THAN THEE.
"THE GENTLEMAN SAYS HE HATH NOT BEEN CONTENT AND IS RETIRING TO THE FOOT OF MOUNT NANSHAN."

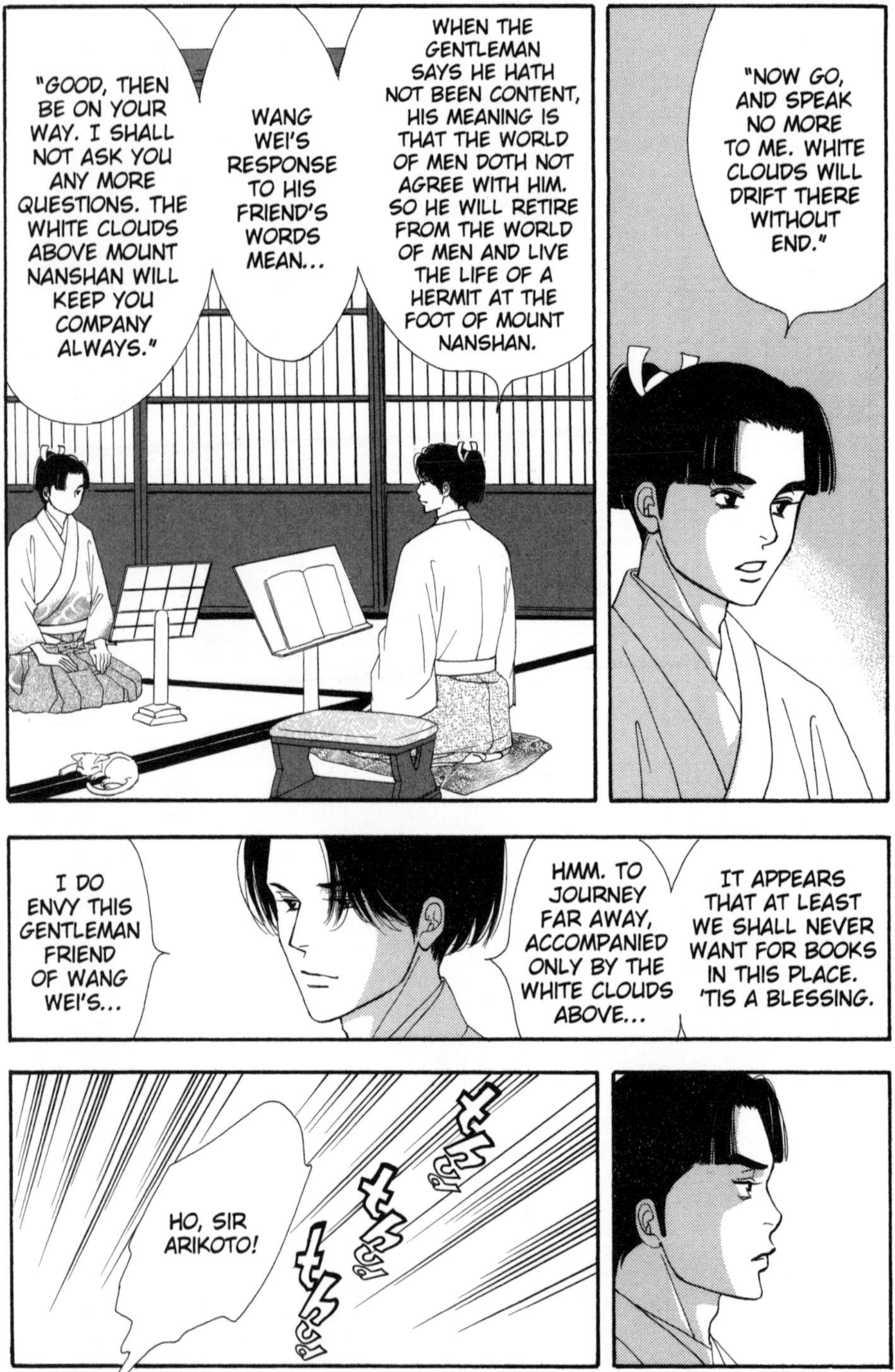

"NOW GO, AND SPEAK NO MORE TO ME. WHITE CLOUDS WILL DRIFT THERE WITHOUT END."
WHEN THE GENTLEMAN SAYS HE HATH NOT BEEN CONTENT, HIS MEANING IS THAT THE WORLD OF MEN DOTH NOT AGREE WITH HIM. SO HE WILL RETIRE FROM THE WORLD OF MEN AND LIVE THE LIFE OF A HERMIT AT THE FOOT OF MOUNT NANSHAN.
WANG WEI'S RESPONSE TO HIS FRIEND'S WORDS MEAN...
"GOOD, THEN BE ON YOUR WAY. I SHALL NOT ASK YOU ANY MORE QUESTIONS. THE WHITE CLOUDS ABOVE MOUNT NANSHAN WILL KEEP YOU COMPANY ALWAYS."
IT APPEARS THAT AT LEAST WE SHALL NEVER WANT FOR BOOKS IN THIS PLACE. 'TIS A BLESSING.
HMM. TO JOURNEY FAR AWAY, ACCOMPANIED ONLY BY THE WHITE CLOUDS ABOVE...
I DO ENVY THIS GENTLEMAN FRIEND OF WANG WEI'S...
HO, SIR ARIKOTO!

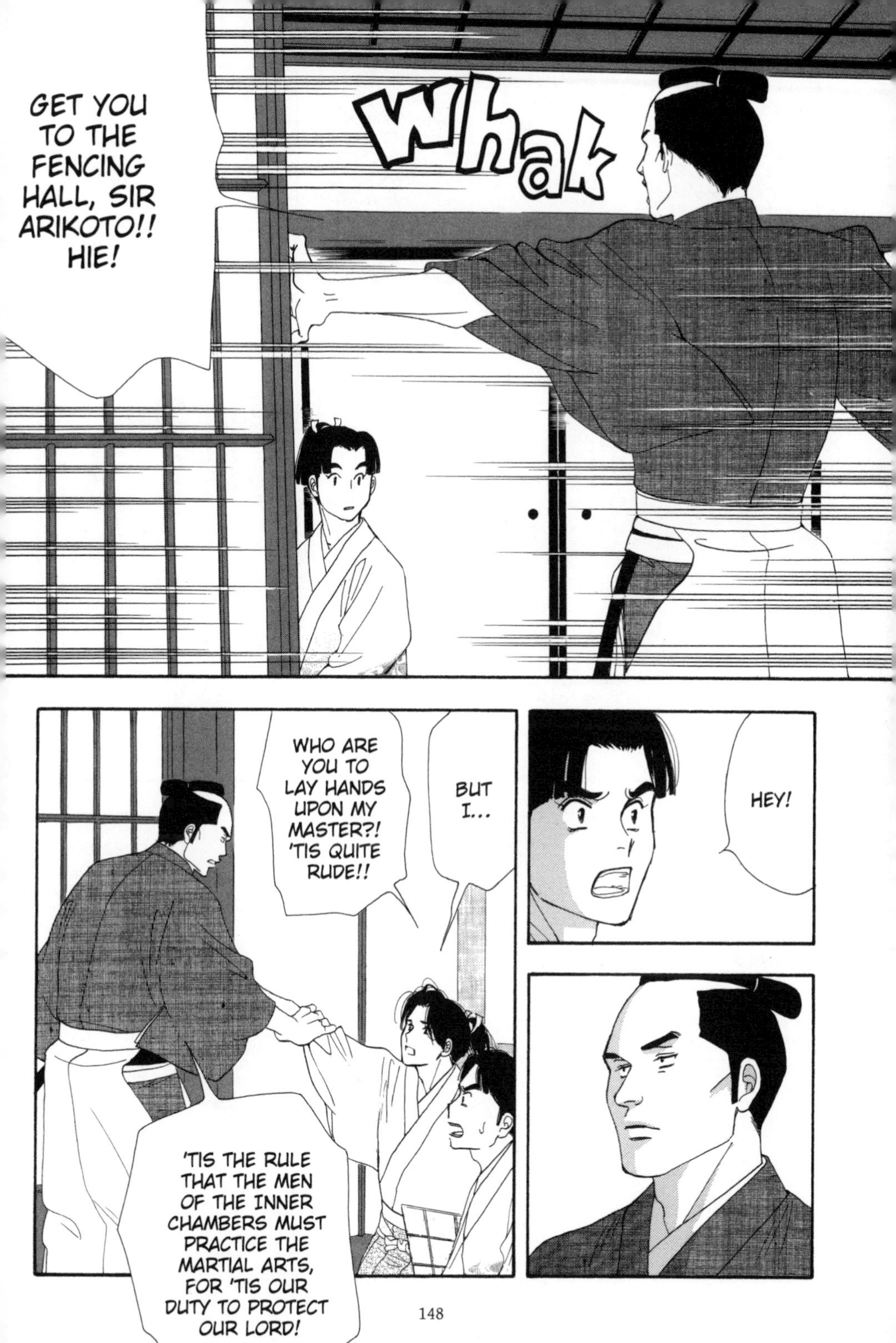
Whak
GET YOU TO THE FENCING HALL, SIR ARIKOTO!! HIE!
HEY!
BUT I...
WHO ARE YOU TO LAY HANDS UPON MY MASTER?! 'TIS QUITE RUDE!!
'TIS THE RULE THAT THE MEN OF THE INNER CHAMBERS MUST PRACTICE THE MARTIAL ARTS, FOR 'TIS OUR DUTY TO PROTECT OUR LORD!

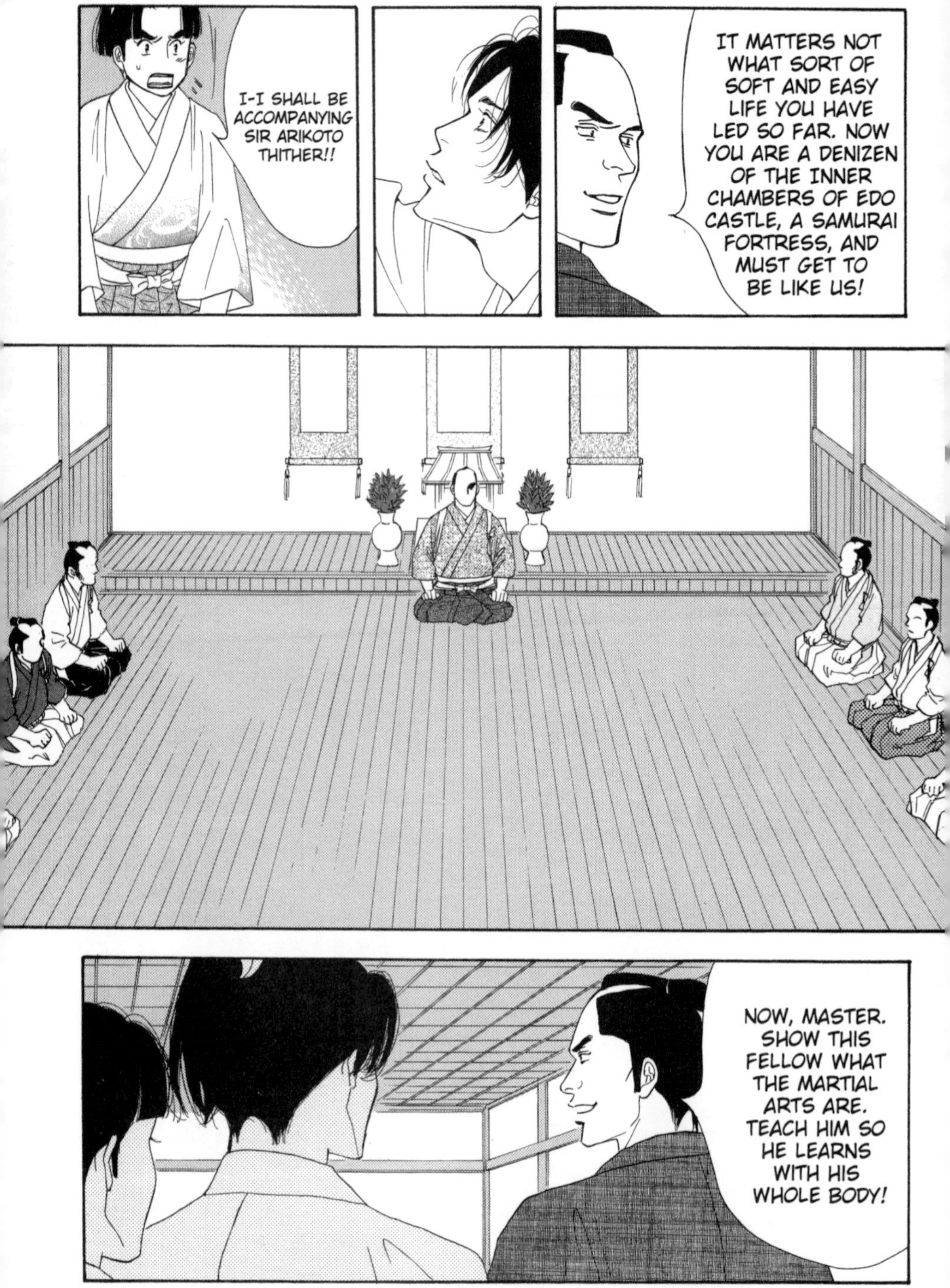
IT MATTERS NOT WHAT SORT OF SOFT AND EASY LIFE YOU HAVE LED SO FAR. NOW YOU ARE A DENIZEN OF THE INNER CHAMBERS OF EDO CASTLE, A SAMURAI FORTRESS, AND MUST GET TO BE LIKE US!
I-I SHALL BE ACCOMPANYING SIR ARIKOTO THITHER!!
NOW, MASTER. SHOW THIS FELLOW WHAT THE MARTIAL ARTS ARE. TEACH HIM SO HE LEARNS WITH HIS WHOLE BODY!

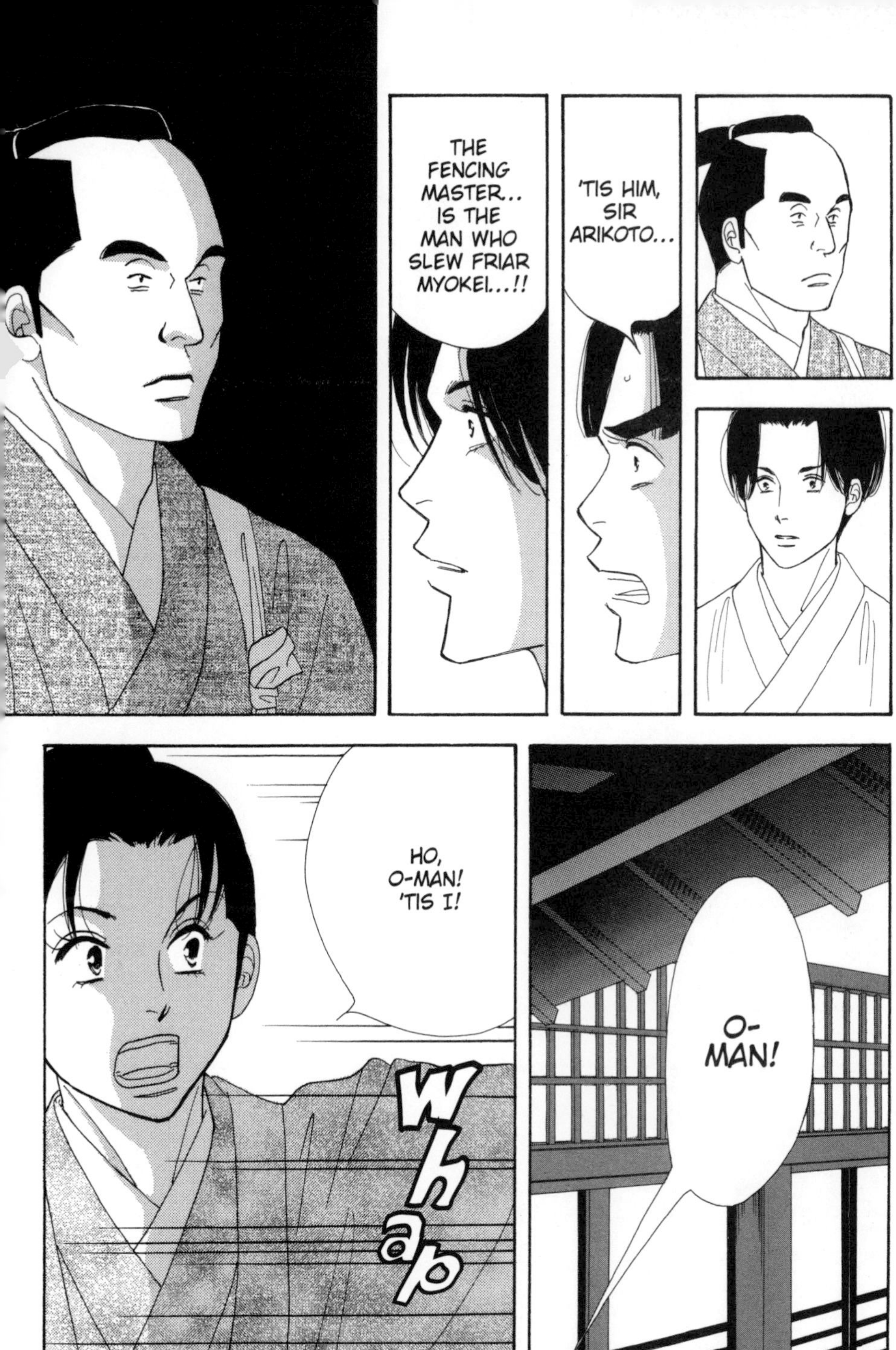
'TIS HIM, SIR ARIKOTO...
THE FENCING MASTER... IS THE MAN WHO SLEW FRIAR MYOKEI...!!
O-MAN!
HO, O-MAN! 'TIS I!
whap

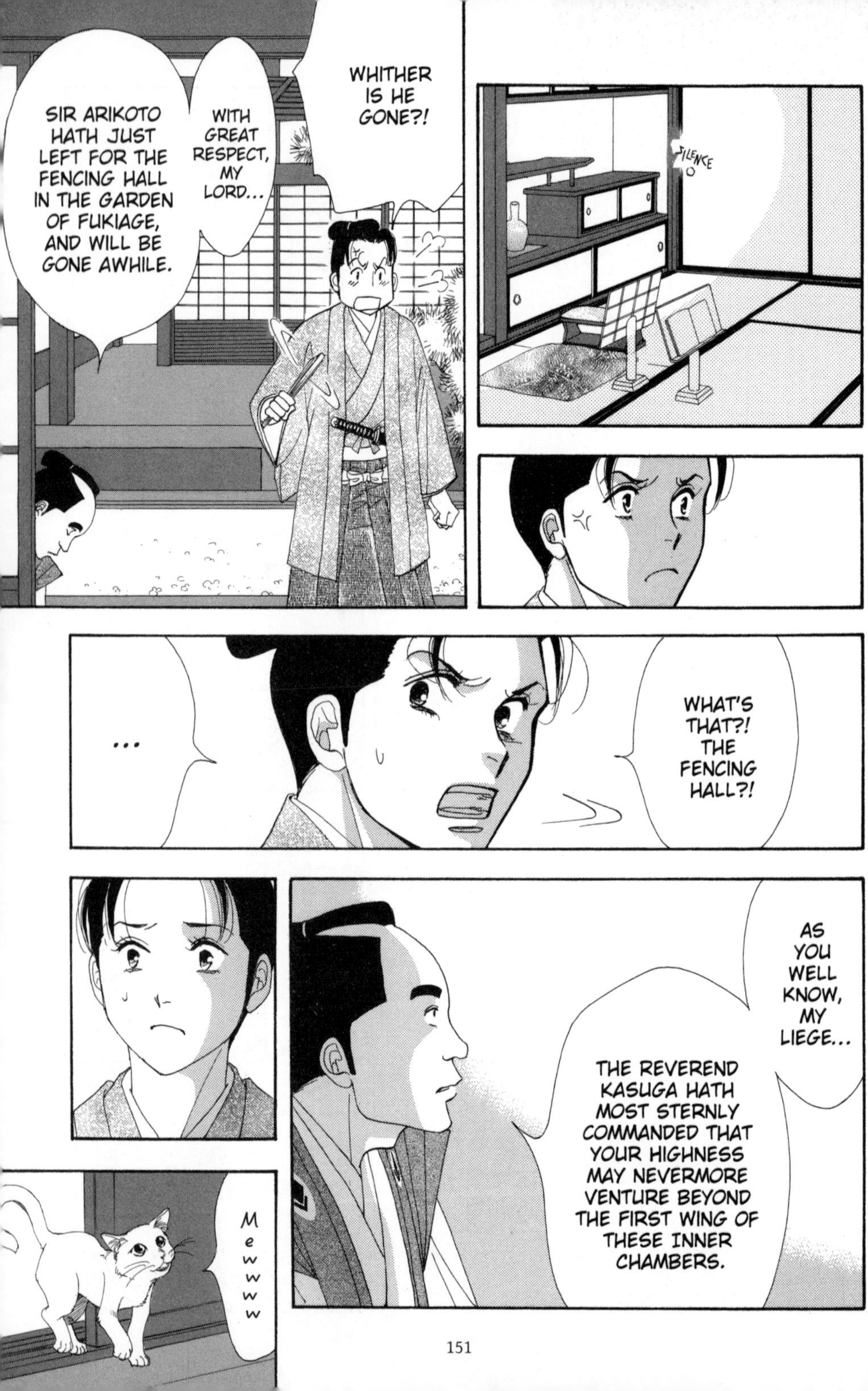
SILENCE
WHITHER IS HE GONE?!
WITH GREAT RESPECT, MY LORD...
SIR ARIKOTO HATH JUST LEFT FOR THE FENCING HALL IN THE GARDEN OF FUKIAGE, AND WILL BE GONE AWHILE.
WHAT'S THAT?! THE FENCING HALL?!
...
AS YOU WELL KNOW, MY LIEGE...
THE REVEREND KASUGA HATH MOST STERNLY COMMANDED THAT YOUR HIGHNESS MAY NEVERMORE VENTURE BEYOND THE FIRST WING OF THESE INNER CHAMBERS.
Mewwww

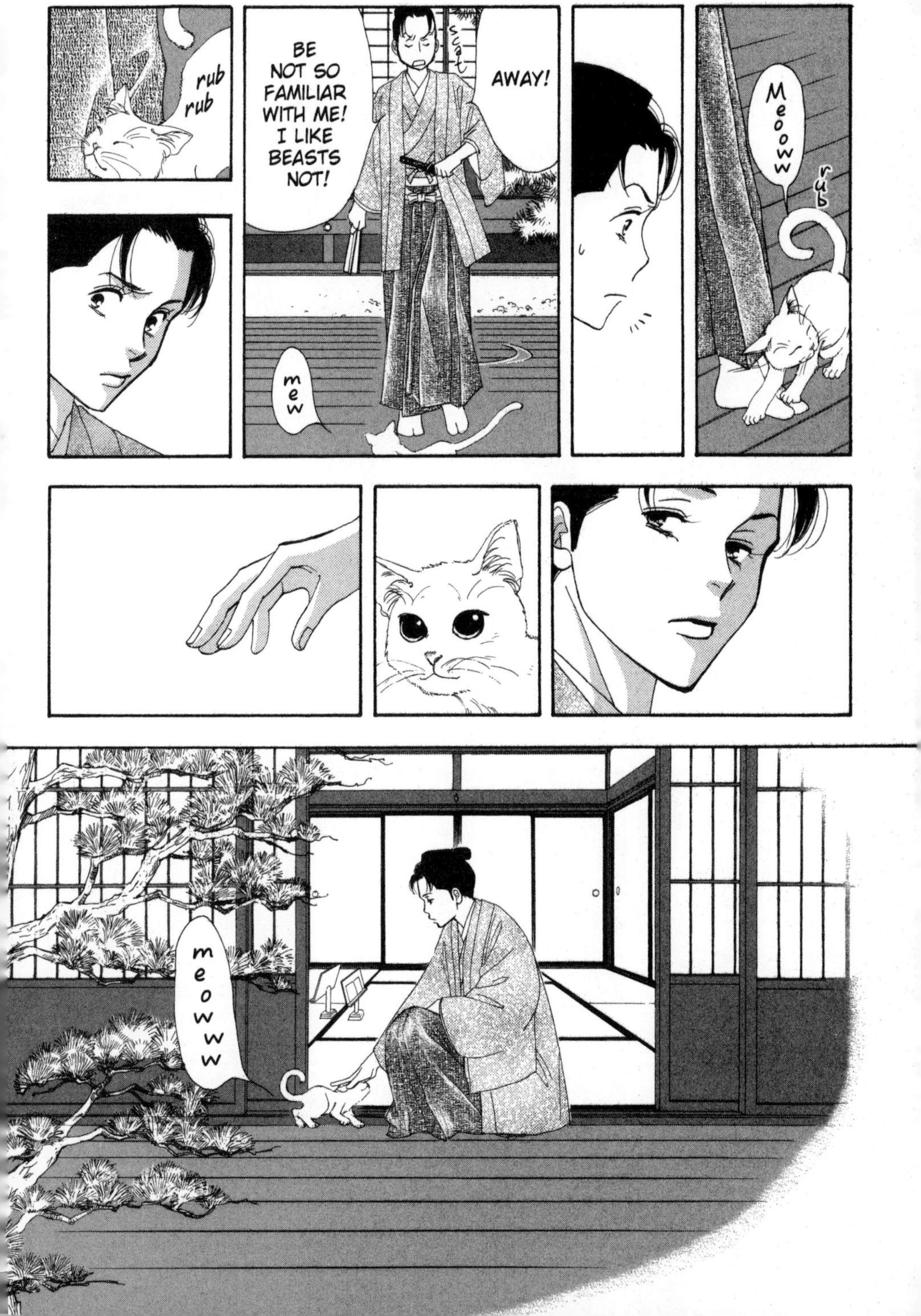
Meooww
rub
AWAY!
scat
BE NOT SO FAMILIAR WITH ME! I LIKE BEASTS NOT!
mew
rub rub
meowww

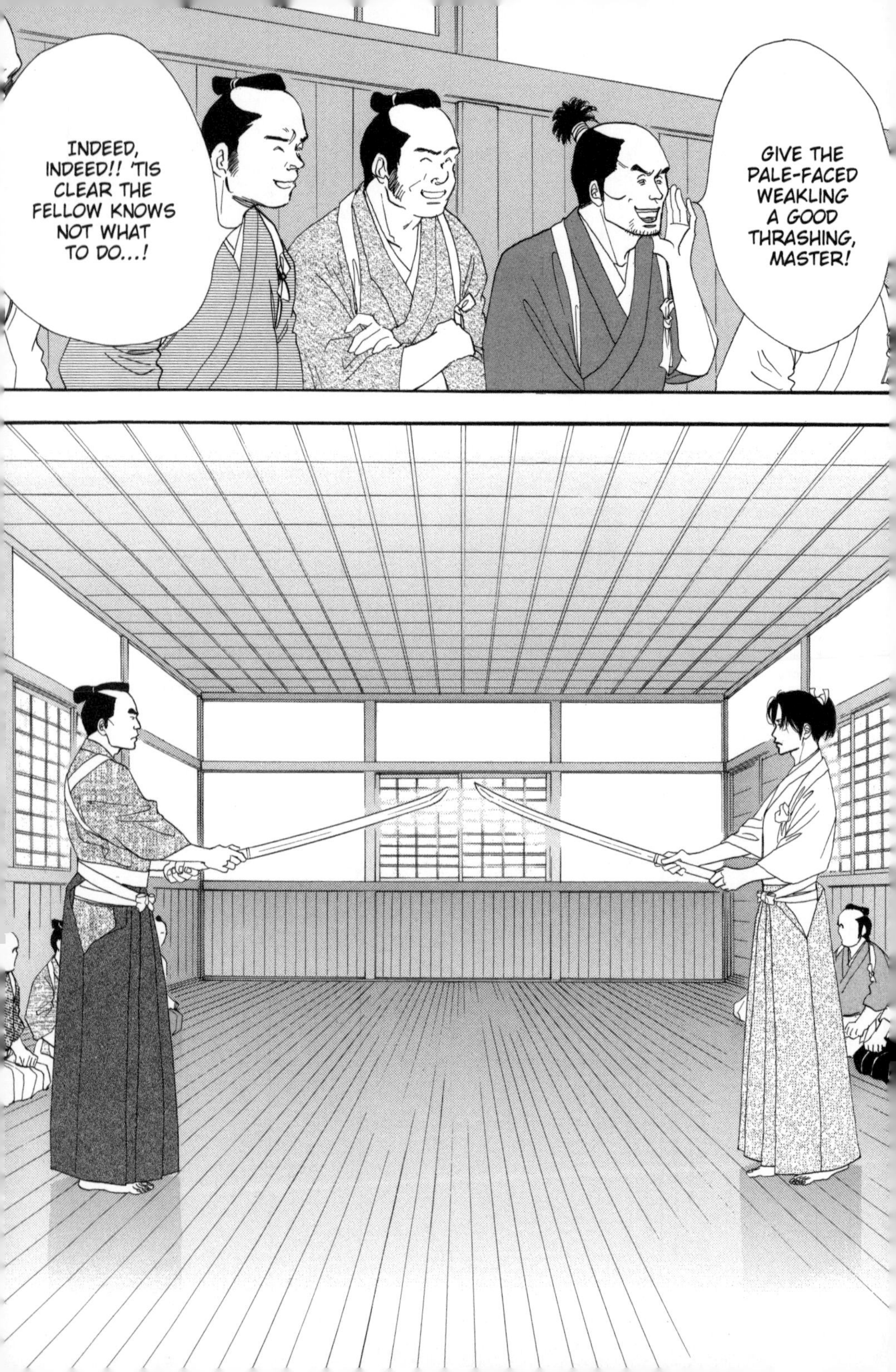
GIVE THE PALE-FACED WEAKLING A GOOD THRASHING, MASTER!
INDEED, INDEED!! 'TIS CLEAR THE FELLOW KNOWS NOT WHAT TO DO...!

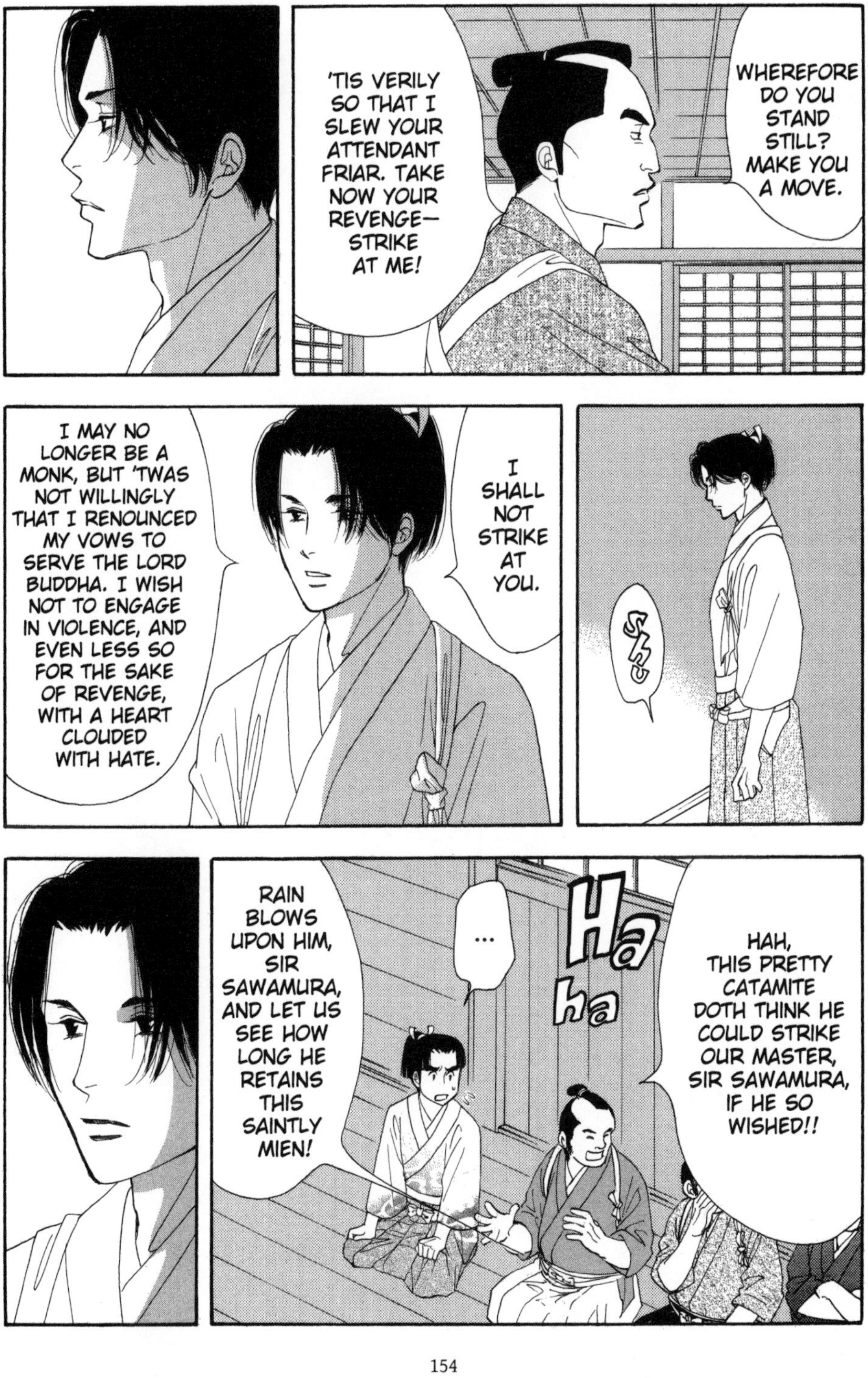
WHEREFORE DO YOU STAND STILL? MAKE YOU A MOVE.
'TIS VERILY SO THAT I SLEW YOUR ATTENDANT FRIAR. TAKE NOW YOUR REVENGE— STRIKE AT ME!
Shu
I SHALL NOT STRIKE AT YOU.
I MAY NO LONGER BE A MONK, BUT 'TWAS NOT WILLINGLY THAT I RENOUNCED MY VOWS TO SERVE THE LORD BUDDHA. I WISH NOT TO ENGAGE IN VIOLENCE, AND EVEN LESS SO FOR THE SAKE OF REVENGE, WITH A HEART CLOUDED WITH HATE.
HAH, THIS PRETTY CATAMITE DOTH THINK HE COULD STRIKE OUR MASTER, SIR SAWAMURA, IF HE SO WISHED!!
Ha ha
...
RAIN BLOWS UPON HIM, SIR SAWAMURA, AND LET US SEE HOW LONG HE RETAINS THIS SAINTLY MIEN!

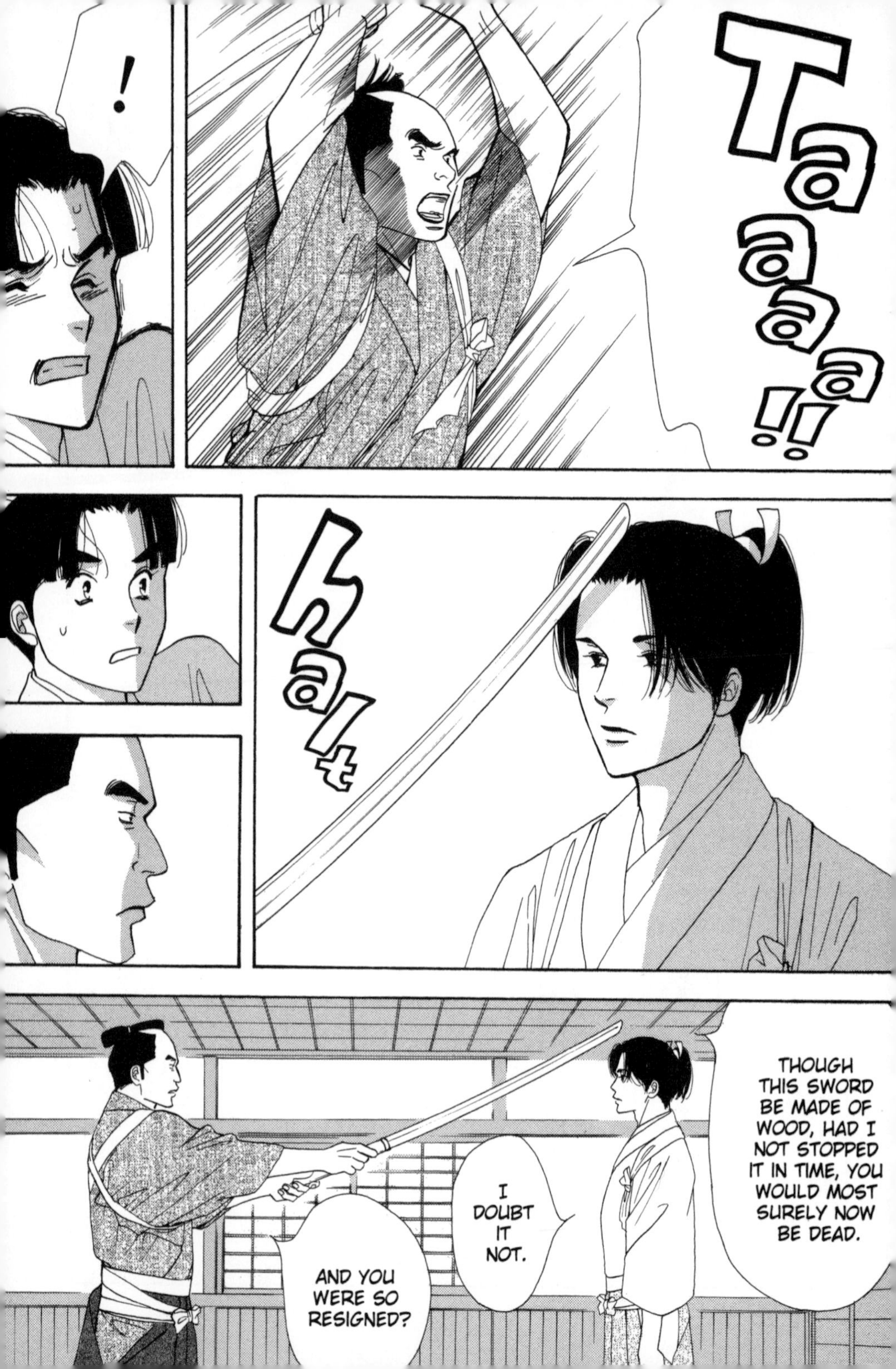
Taaaaa!!
!
halt
THOUGH THIS SWORD BE MADE OF WOOD, HAD I NOT STOPPED IT IN TIME, YOU WOULD MOST SURELY NOW BE DEAD.
I DOUBT IT NOT.
AND YOU WERE SO RESIGNED?

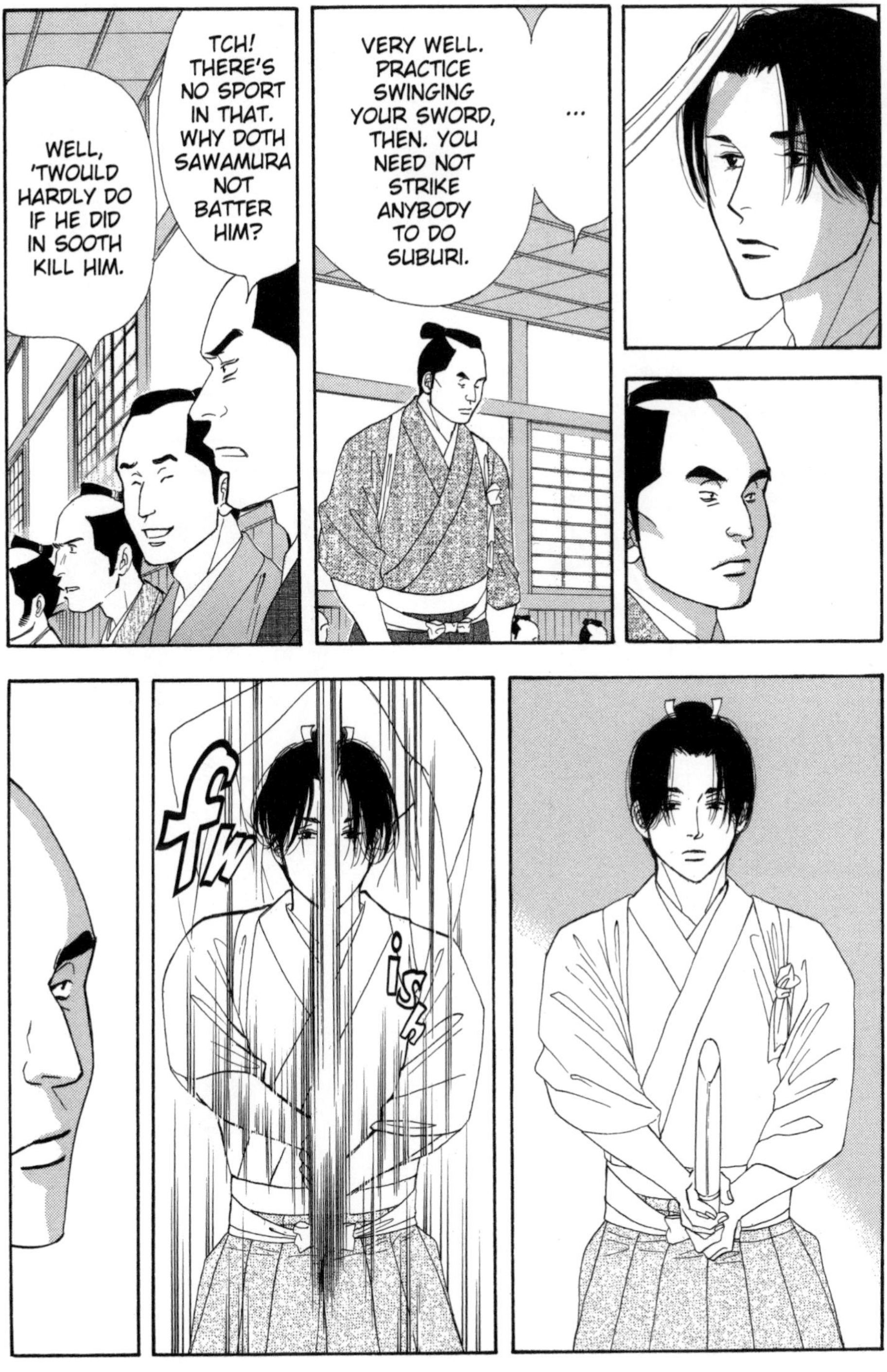
...
VERY WELL. PRACTICE SWINGING YOUR SWORD, THEN. YOU NEED NOT STRIKE ANYBODY TO DO SUBURI.
TCH! THERE'S NO SPORT IN THAT. WHY DOTH SAWAMURA NOT BATTER HIM?
WELL, 'TWOULD HARDLY DO IF HE DID IN SOOTH KILL HIM.
fw
ish

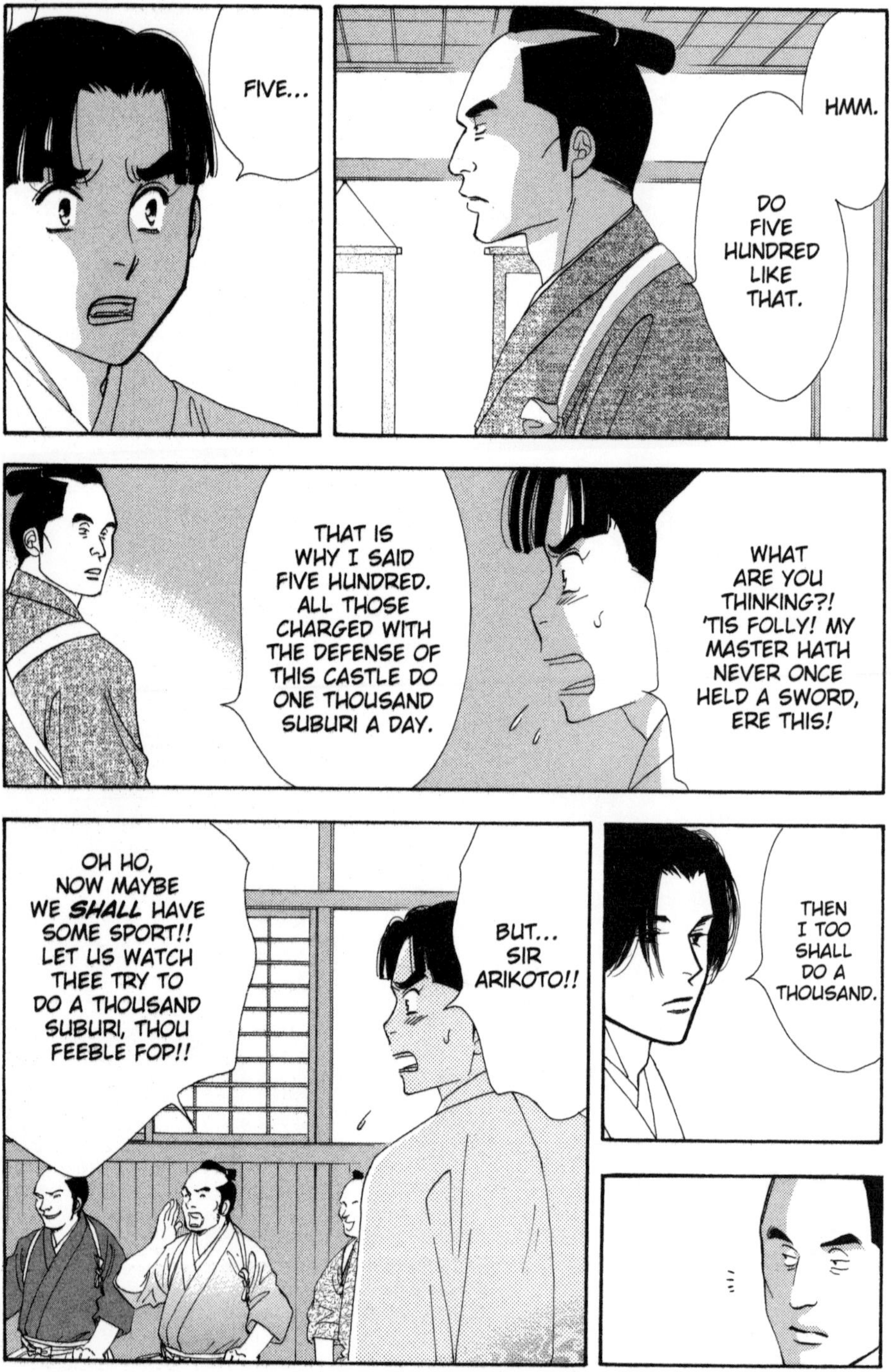
HMM.
DO FIVE HUNDRED LIKE THAT.
FIVE...
WHAT ARE YOU THINKING?! 'TIS FOLLY! MY MASTER HATH NEVER ONCE HELD A SWORD, ERE THIS!
THAT IS WHY I SAID FIVE HUNDRED. ALL THOSE CHARGED WITH THE DEFENSE OF THIS CASTLE DO ONE THOUSAND SUBURI A DAY.
THEN I TOO SHALL DO A THOUSAND.
...
BUT... SIR ARIKOTO!!
OH HO, NOW MAYBE WE *SHALL* HAVE SOME SPORT!! LET US WATCH THEE TRY TO DO A THOUSAND SUBURI, THOU FEEBLE FOP!!

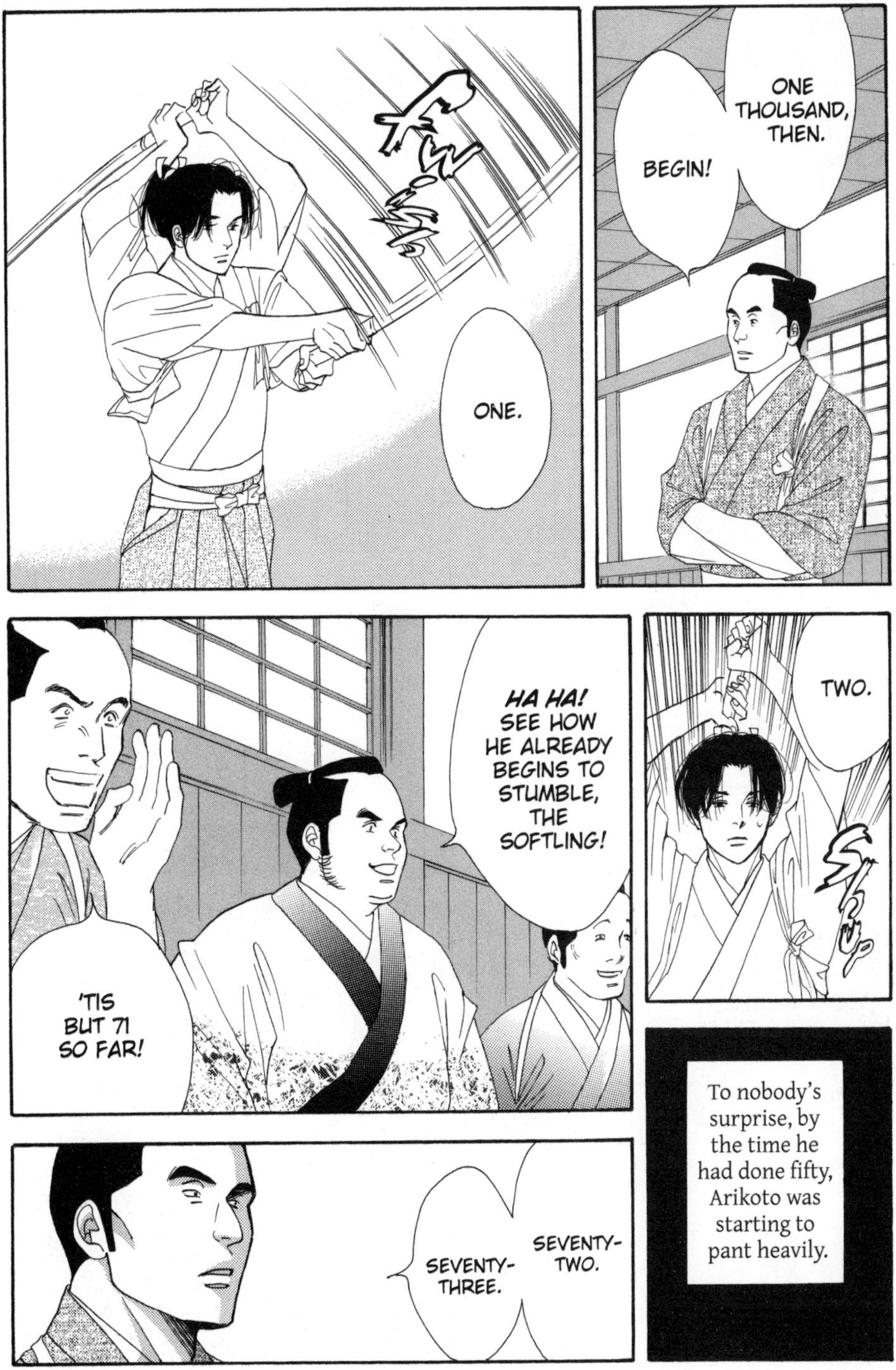
ONE THOUSAND, THEN.
BEGIN!
ONE.
TWO.
To nobody's surprise, by the time he had done fifty, Arikoto was starting to pant heavily.
HA HA! SEE HOW HE ALREADY BEGINS TO STUMBLE, THE SOFTLING!
'TIS BUT 71 SO FAR!
SEVENTY-TWO.
SEVENTY-THREE.

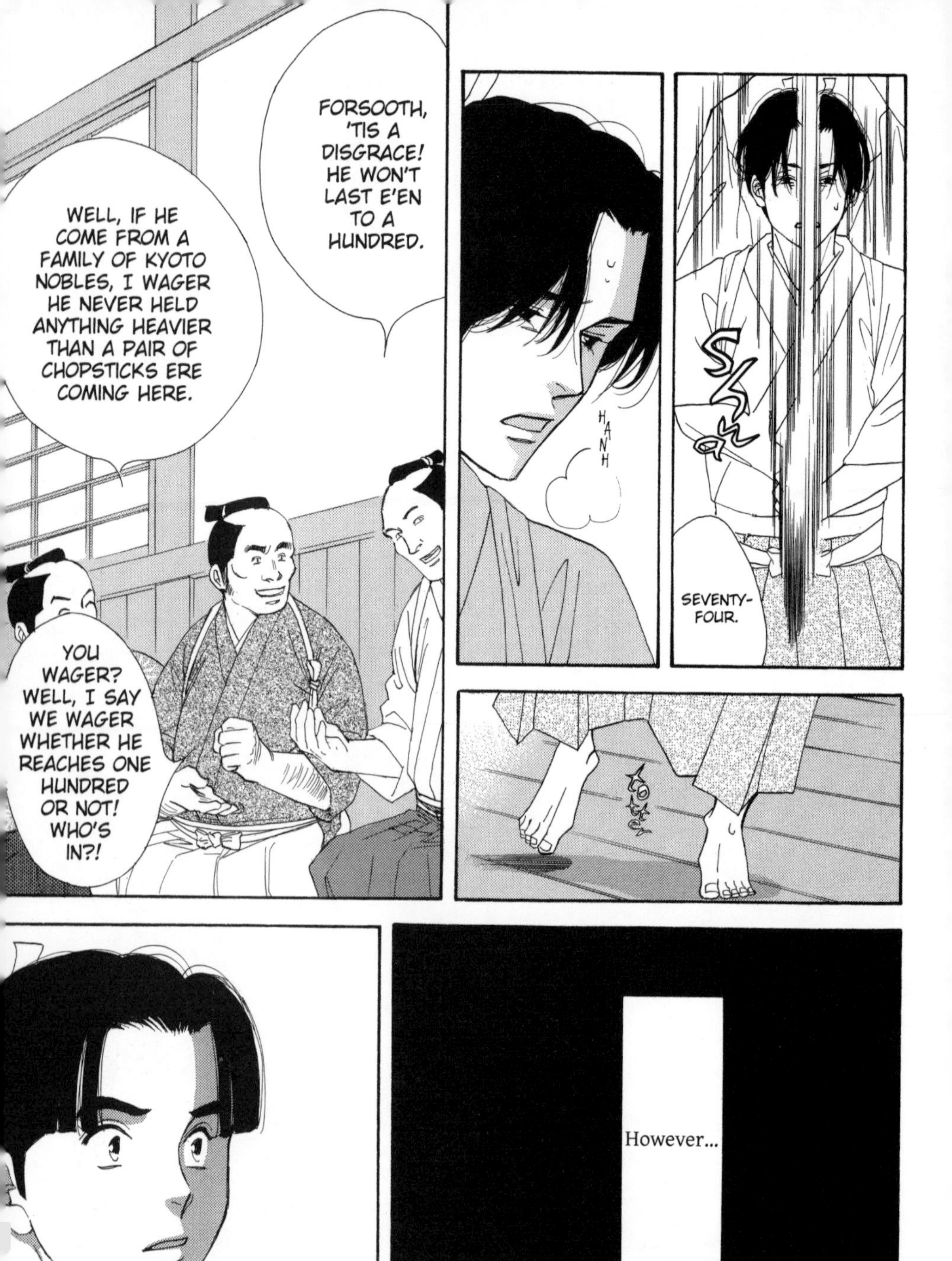

SHWA
SEVENTY-FOUR.
HANH
totter
FORSOOTH, 'TIS A DISGRACE! HE WON'T LAST E'EN TO A HUNDRED.
WELL, IF HE COME FROM A FAMILY OF KYOTO NOBLES, I WAGER HE NEVER HELD ANYTHING HEAVIER THAN A PAIR OF CHOPSTICKS ERE COMING HERE.
YOU WAGER? WELL, I SAY WE WAGER WHETHER HE REACHES ONE HUNDRED OR NOT! WHO'S IN?!
However...

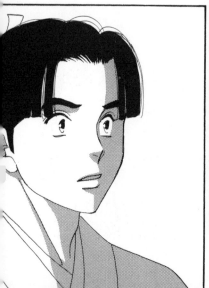

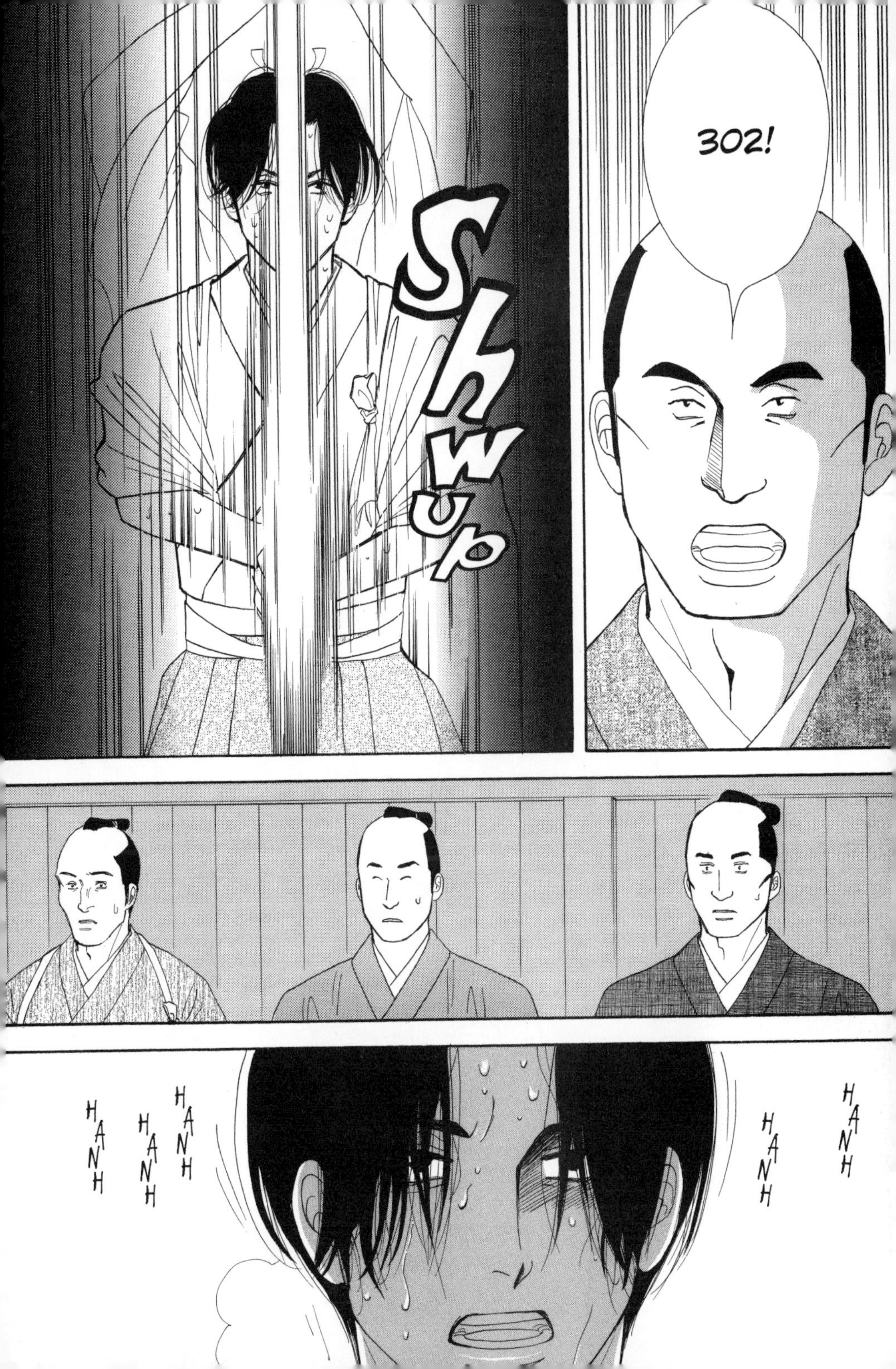
302!
Shwup
HANH
HANH
HANH
HANH
HANH

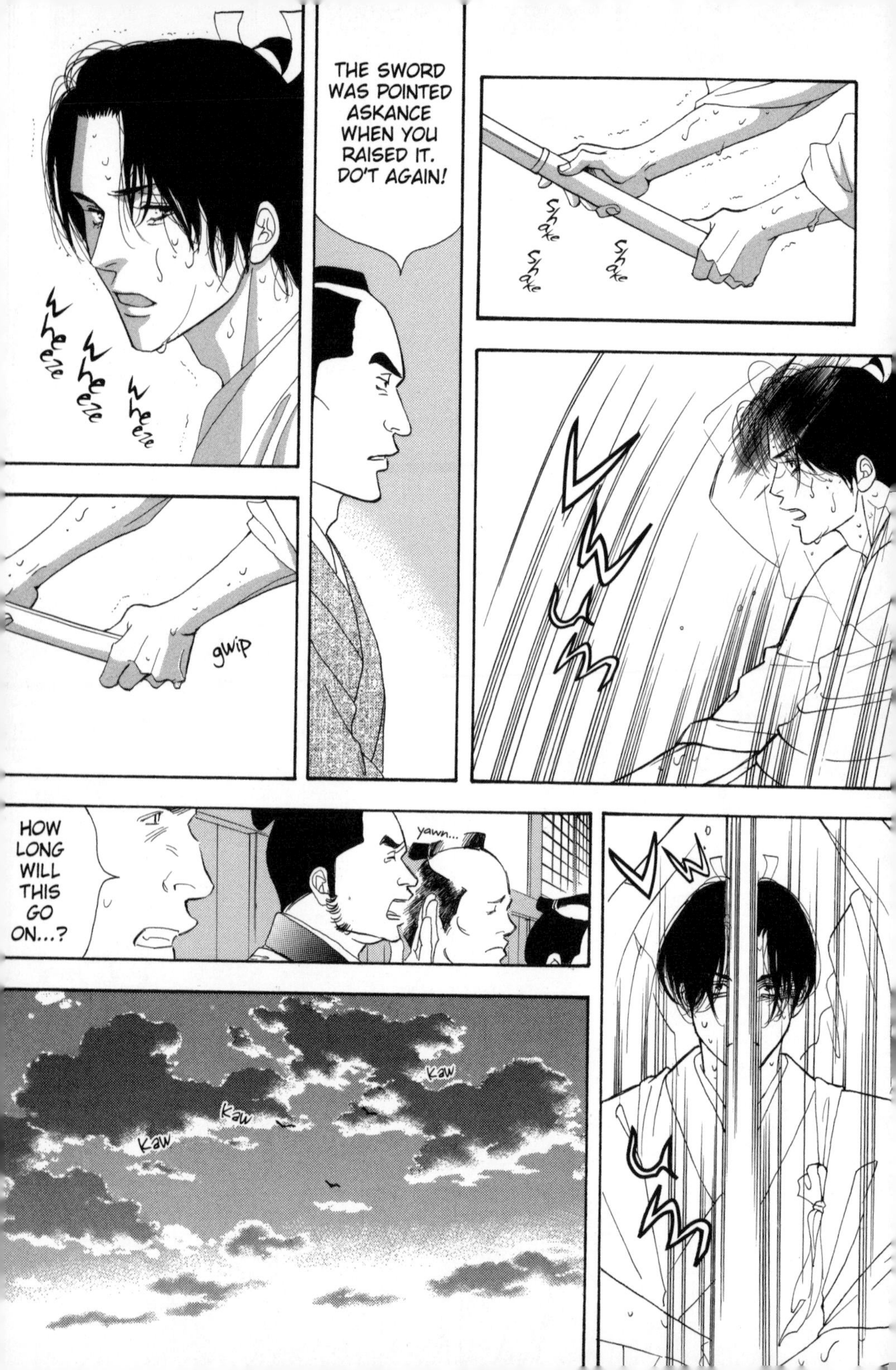
Shake
Shake
Shake
VWUM
THE SWORD WAS POINTED ASKANCE WHEN YOU RAISED IT. DO'T AGAIN!
wheeze
wheeze
wheeze
gwip
VW
UM
yawn...
HOW LONG WILL THIS GO ON...?
Kaw
Kaw
Kaw

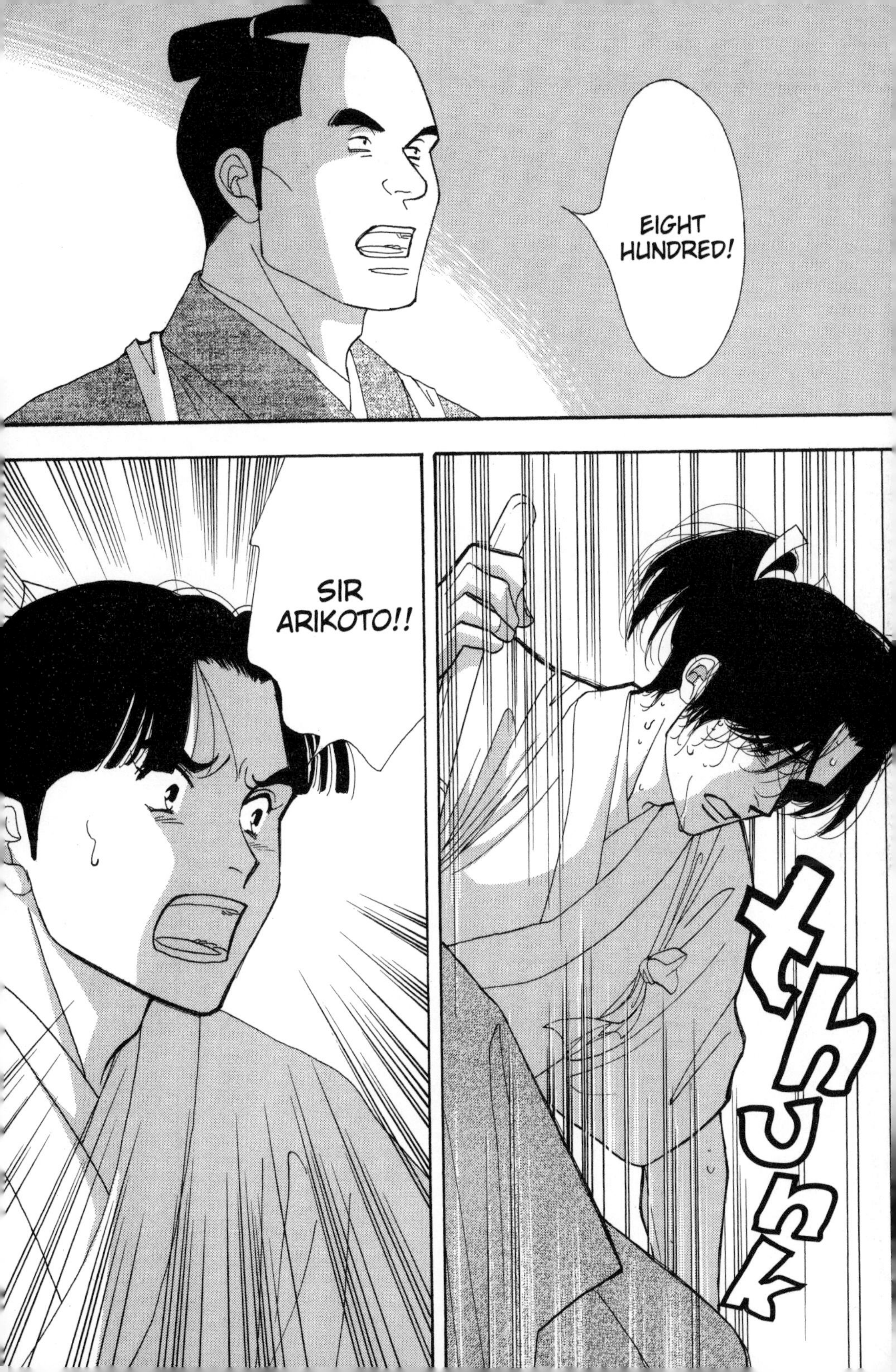
EIGHT HUNDRED!
SIR ARIKOTO!!
THHUNK

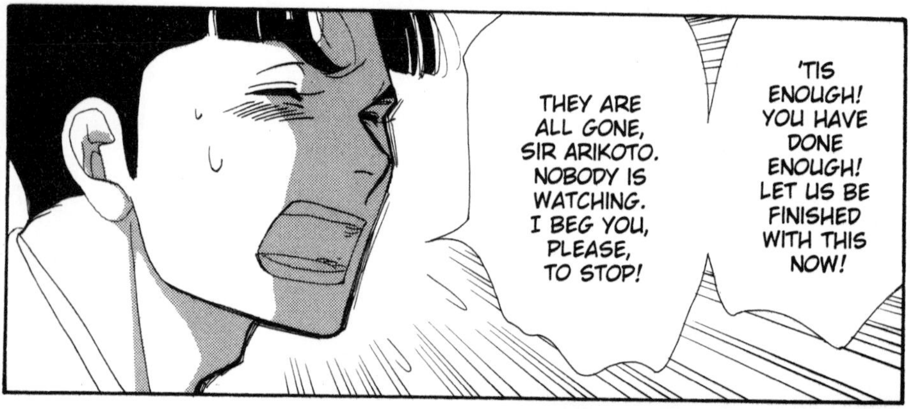
'TIS ENOUGH! YOU HAVE DONE ENOUGH! LET US BE FINISHED WITH THIS NOW!
THEY ARE ALL GONE, SIR ARIKOTO. NOBODY IS WATCHING. I BEG YOU, PLEASE, TO STOP!
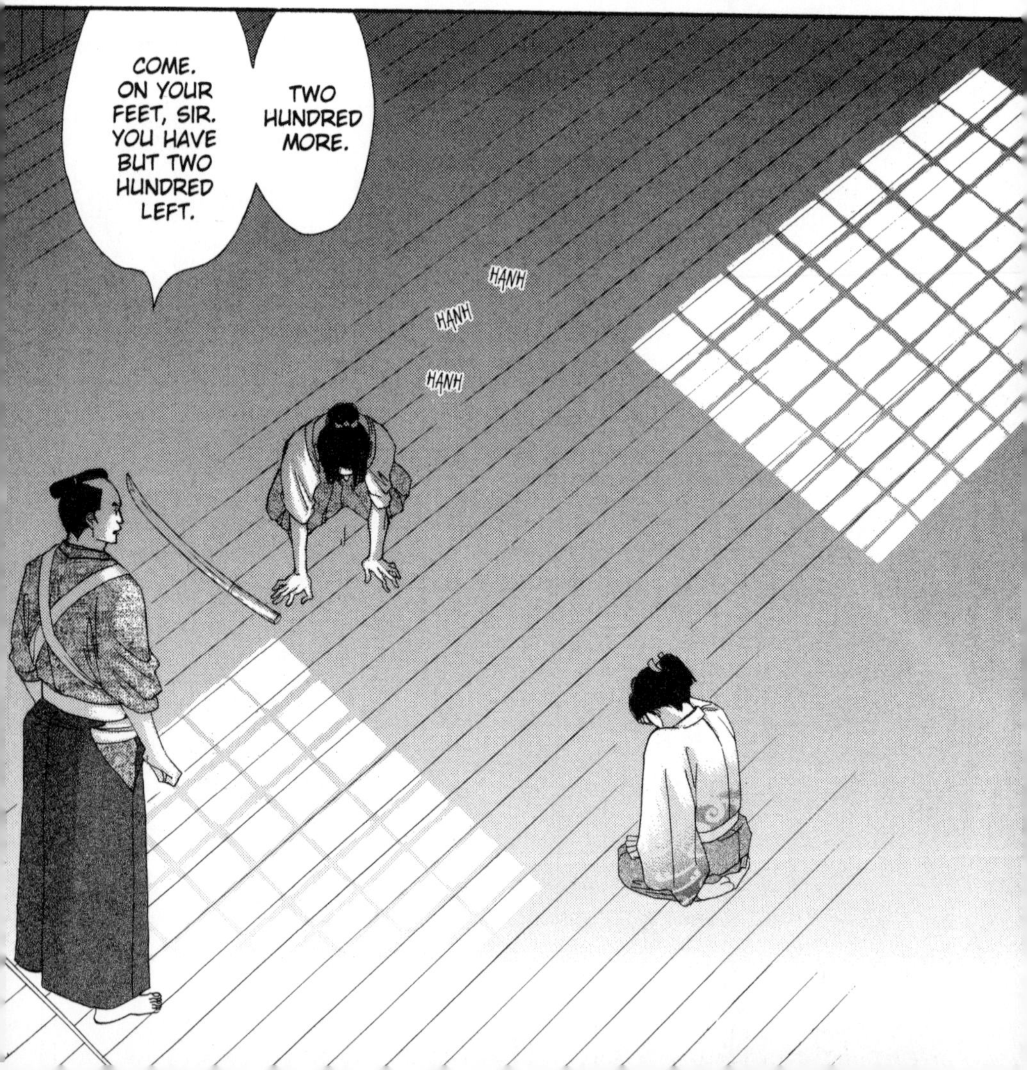
TWO HUNDRED MORE.
COME. ON YOUR FEET, SIR. YOU HAVE BUT TWO HUNDRED LEFT.
HANH
HANH
HANH

THERE IS NOBODY HERE, SO WHEREFORE CONTINUE? 'TIS FOR NAUGHT!

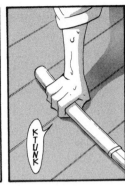

KTUNK

803.

804.

802.

801.

999!

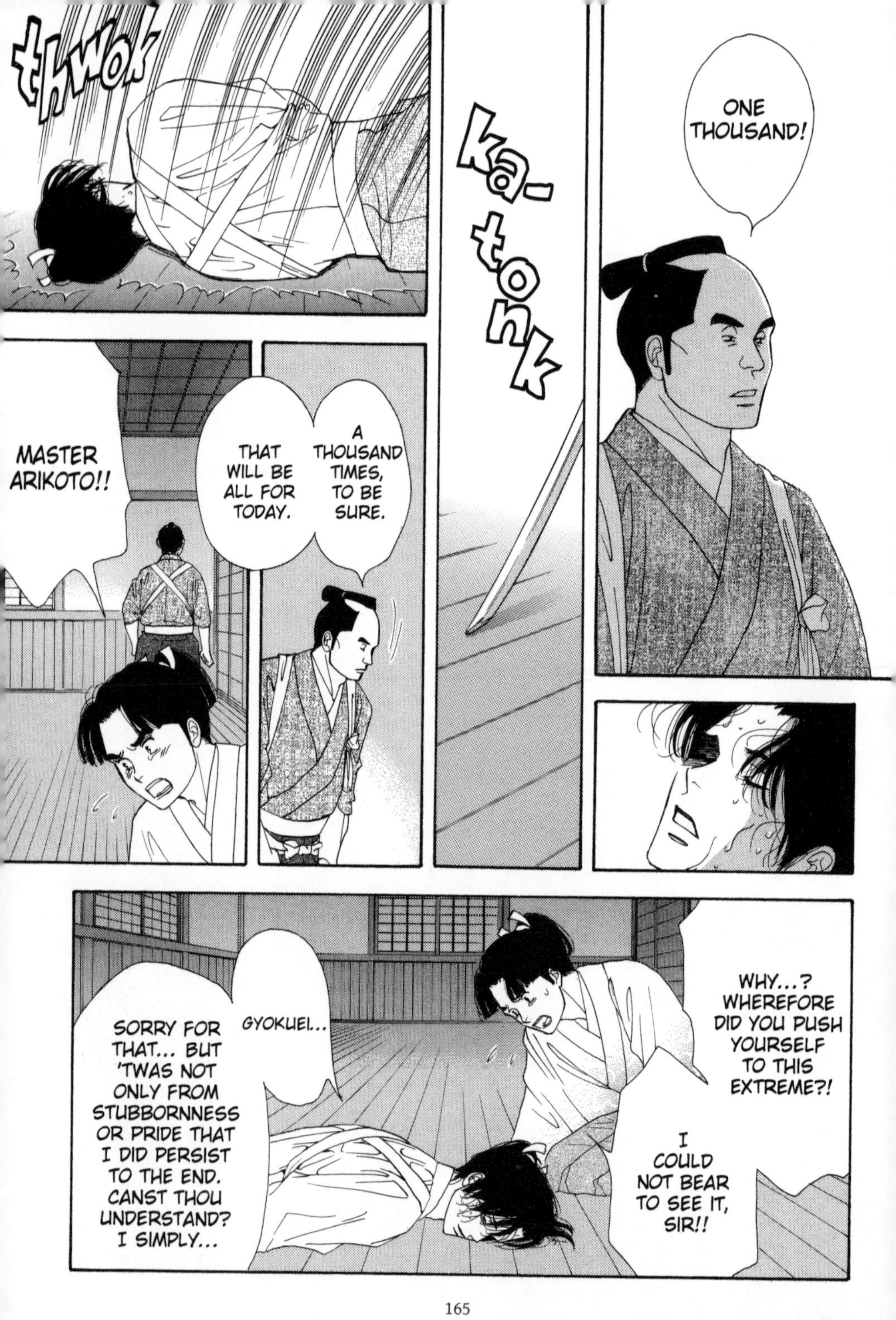
ONE THOUSAND!
ka-tonk
thwok
A THOUSAND TIMES, TO BE SURE.
THAT WILL BE ALL FOR TODAY.
MASTER ARIKOTO!!
WHY...? WHEREFORE DID YOU PUSH YOURSELF TO THIS EXTREME?!
I COULD NOT BEAR TO SEE IT, SIR!!
GYOKUEI...
SORRY FOR THAT... BUT 'TWAS NOT ONLY FROM STUBBORNNESS OR PRIDE THAT I DID PERSIST TO THE END. CANST THOU UNDERSTAND? I SIMPLY...

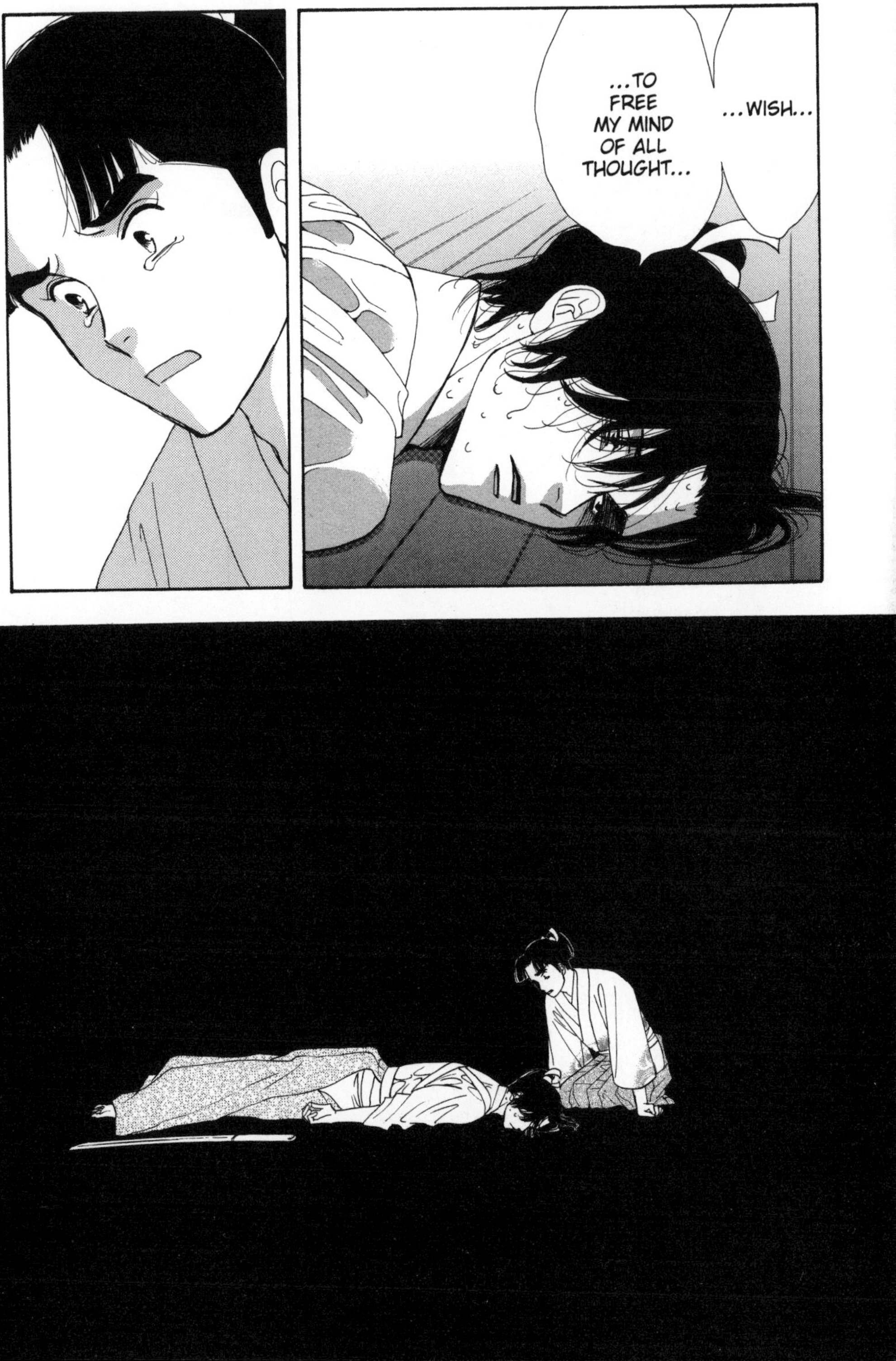
...WISH...
...TO FREE MY MIND OF ALL THOUGHT...

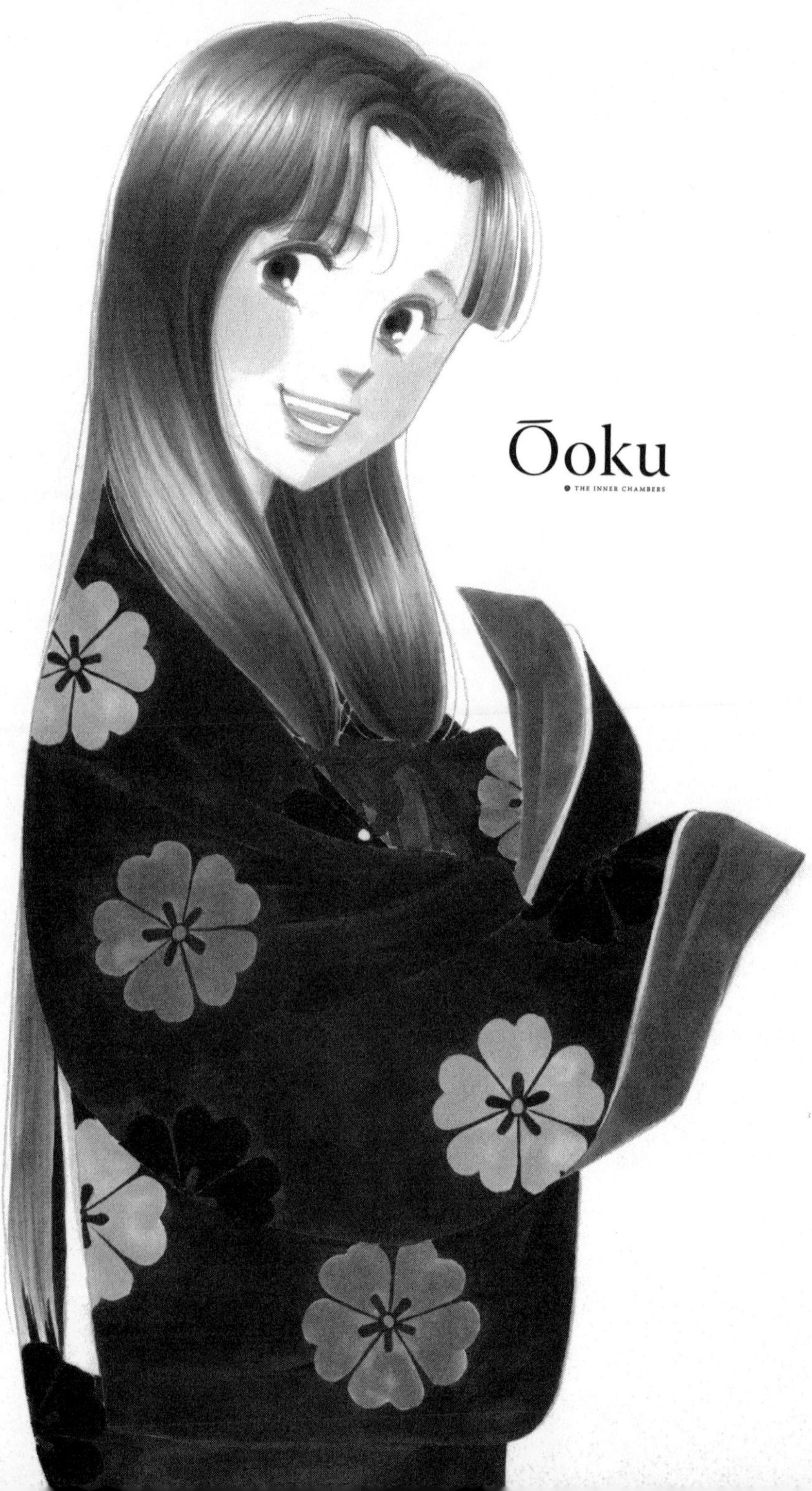
Ōoku
THE INNER CHAMBERS

Ōoku
THE INNER CHAMBERS

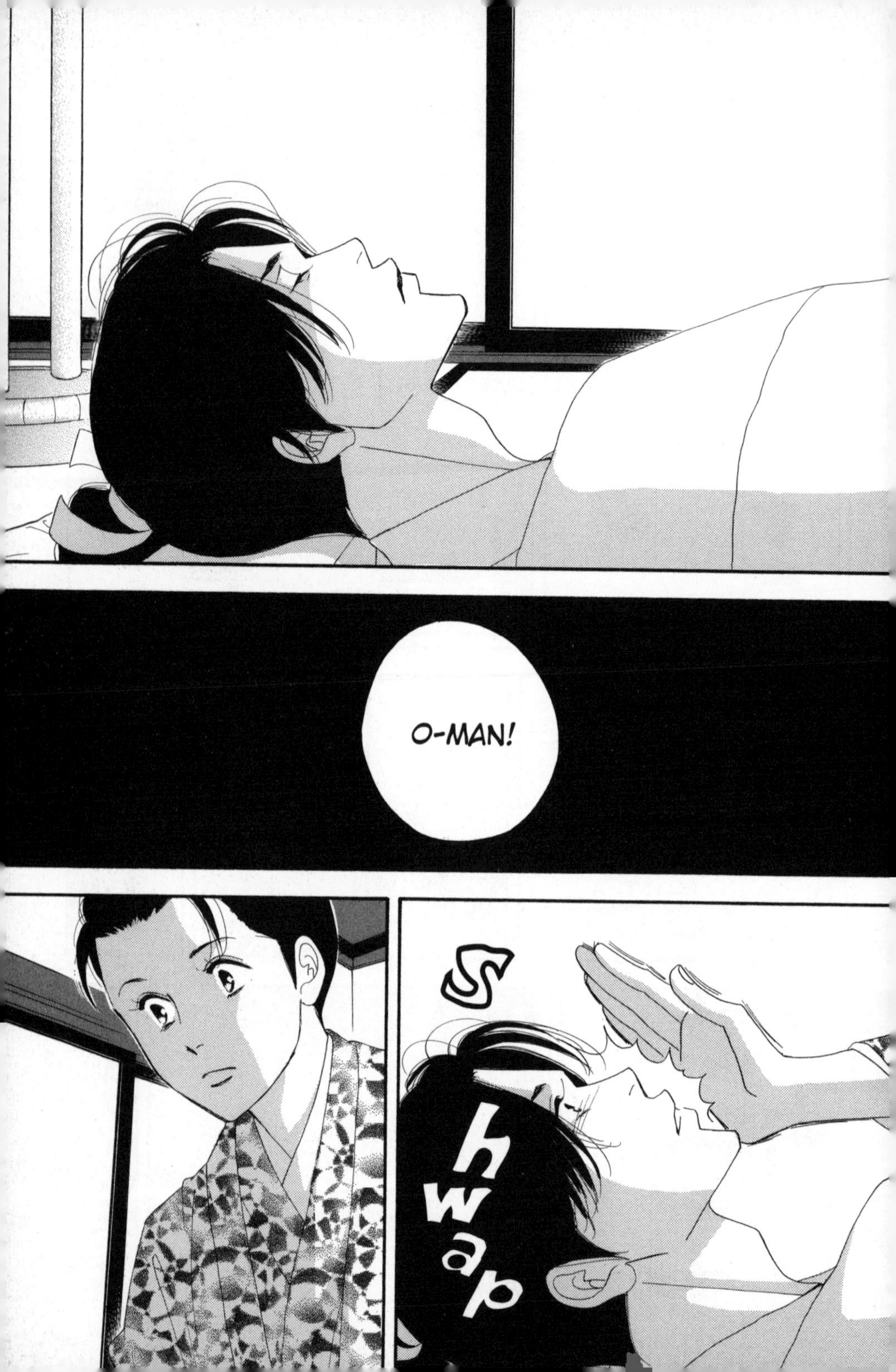
O-MAN!
Shwap

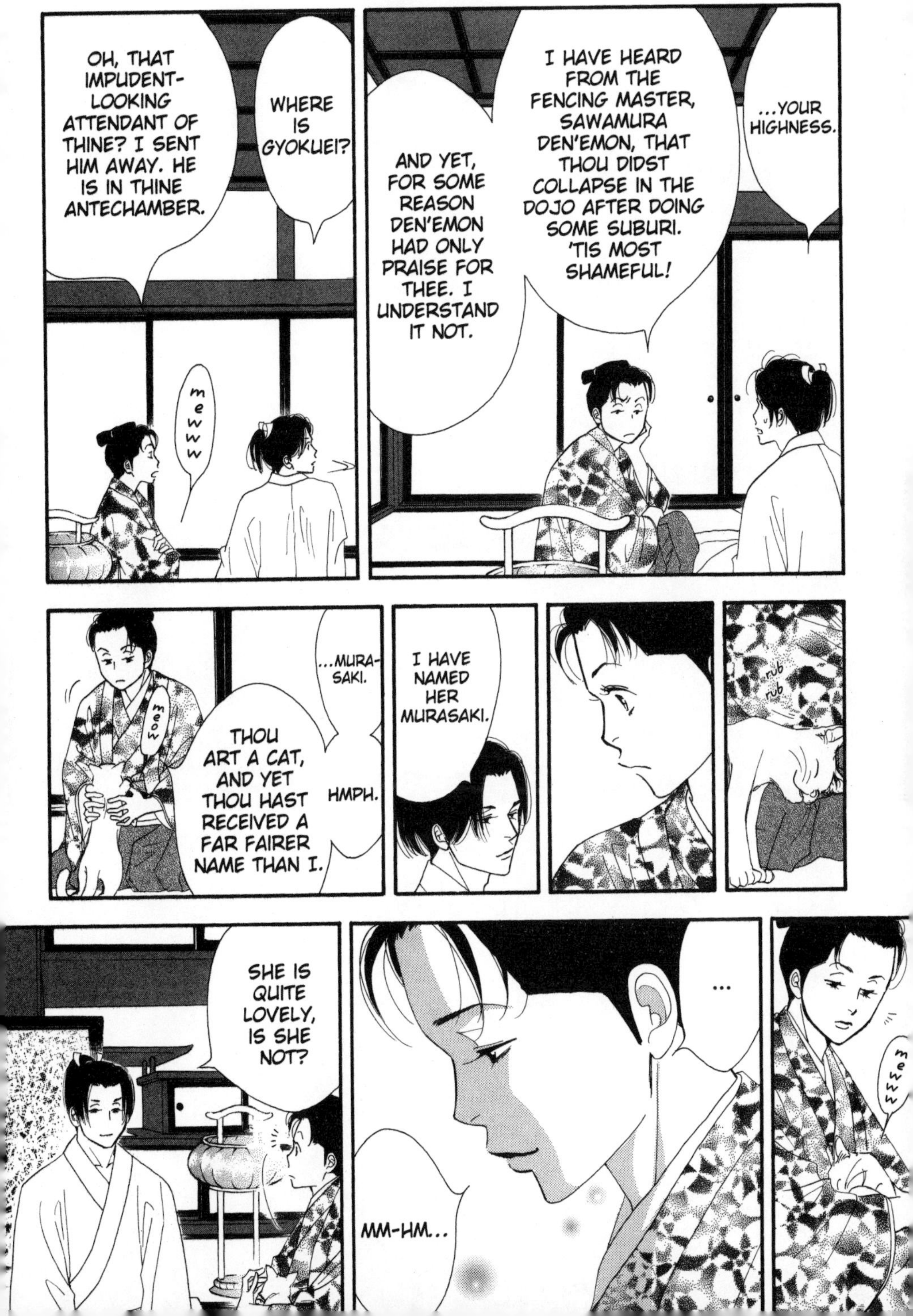
...YOUR HIGHNESS.
I HAVE HEARD FROM THE FENCING MASTER, SAWAMURA DEN'EMON, THAT THOU DIDST COLLAPSE IN THE DOJO AFTER DOING SOME SUBURI. 'TIS MOST SHAMEFUL!
AND YET, FOR SOME REASON DEN'EMON HAD ONLY PRAISE FOR THEE. I UNDERSTAND IT NOT.
WHERE IS GYOKUEI?
OH, THAT IMPUDENT-LOOKING ATTENDANT OF THINE? I SENT HIM AWAY. HE IS IN THINE ANTECHAMBER.
mewww
rub rub
I HAVE NAMED HER MURASAKI.
...MURA-SAKI.
HMPH.
THOU ART A CAT, AND YET THOU HAST RECEIVED A FAR FAIRER NAME THAN I.
meow
mewww
...
MM-HM...
SHE IS QUITE LOVELY, IS SHE NOT?

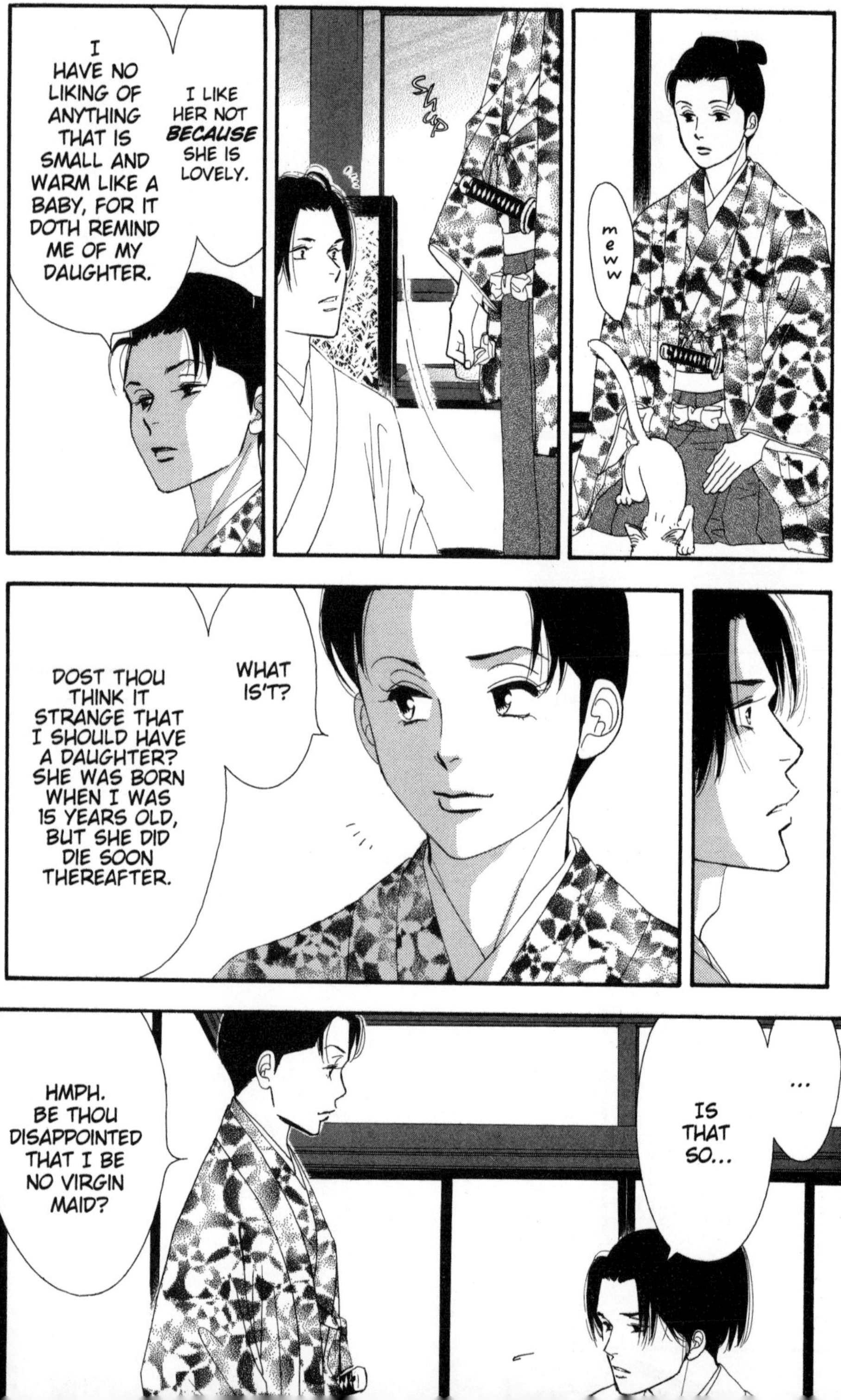
meww
SHUP
I LIKE HER NOT **BECAUSE** SHE IS LOVELY.
I HAVE NO LIKING OF ANYTHING THAT IS SMALL AND WARM LIKE A BABY, FOR IT DOTH REMIND ME OF MY DAUGHTER.
WHAT IS'T?
DOST THOU THINK IT STRANGE THAT I SHOULD HAVE A DAUGHTER? SHE WAS BORN WHEN I WAS 15 YEARS OLD, BUT SHE DID DIE SOON THEREAFTER.
...
IS THAT SO...
HMPH. BE THOU DISAPPOINTED THAT I BE NO VIRGIN MAID?

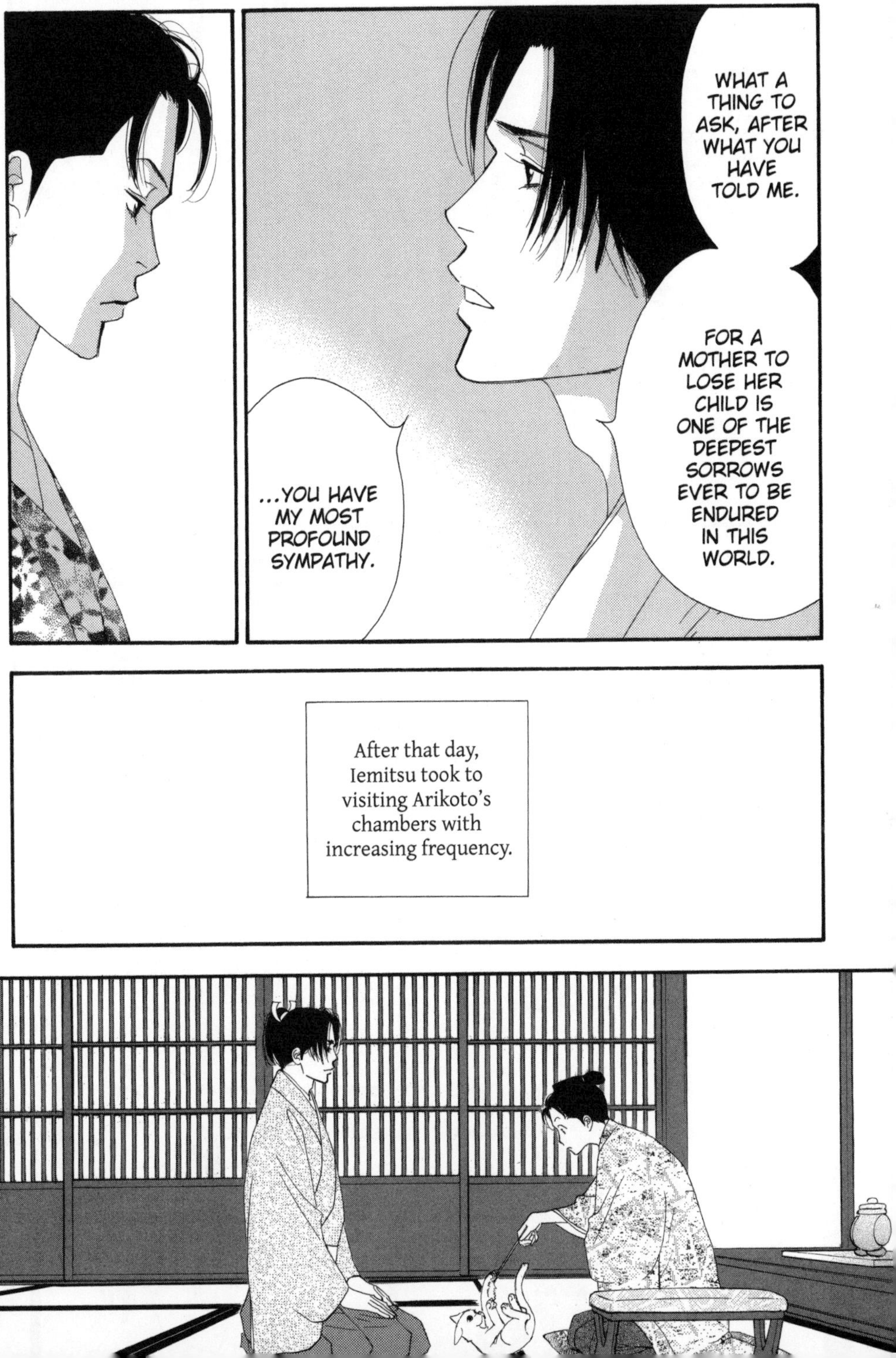
WHAT A THING TO ASK, AFTER WHAT YOU HAVE TOLD ME.
FOR A MOTHER TO LOSE HER CHILD IS ONE OF THE DEEPEST SORROWS EVER TO BE ENDURED IN THIS WORLD.
...YOU HAVE MY MOST PROFOUND SYMPATHY.
After that day, Iemitsu took to visiting Arikoto's chambers with increasing frequency.

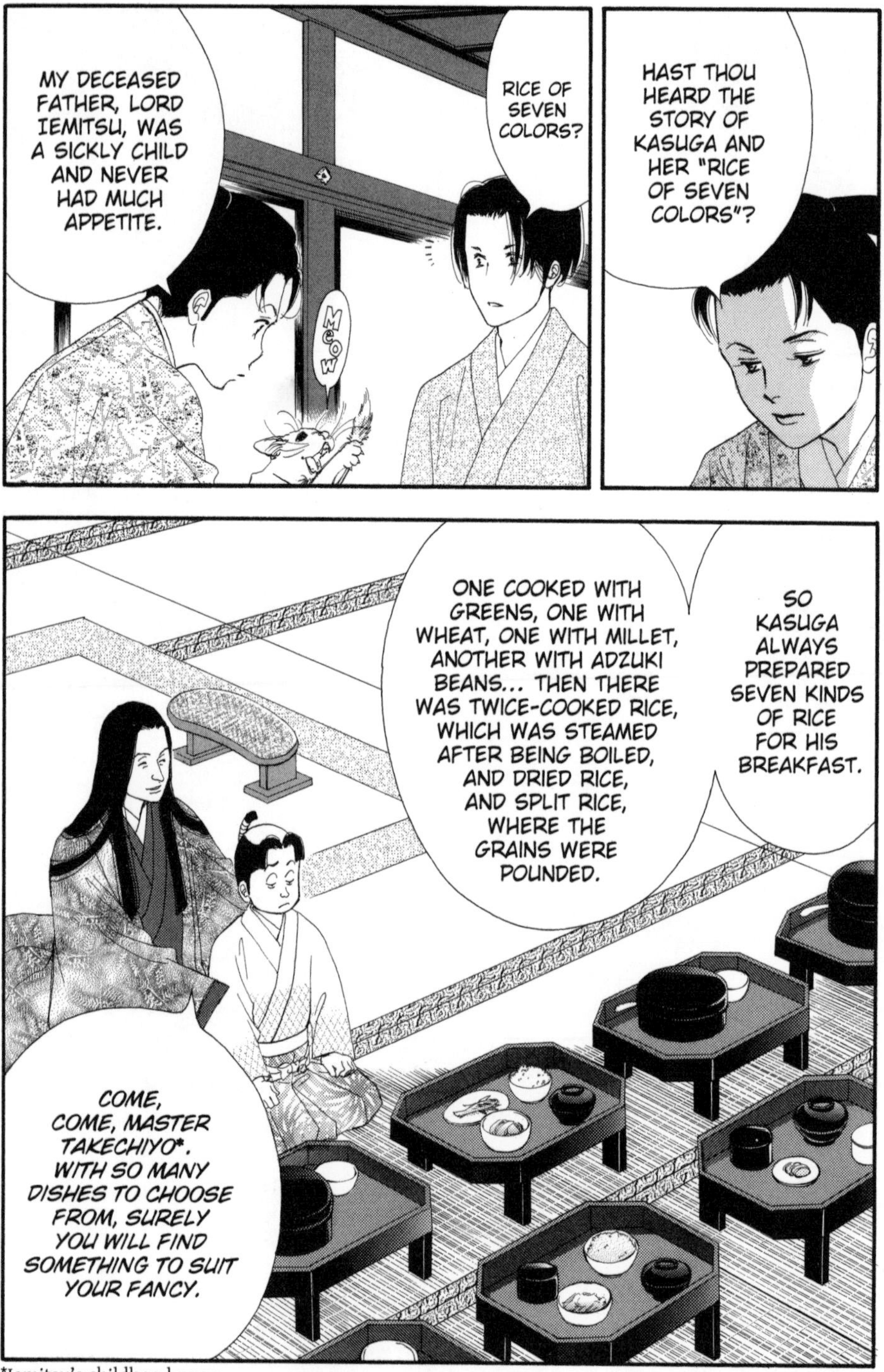
HAST THOU HEARD THE STORY OF KASUGA AND HER "RICE OF SEVEN COLORS"?
RICE OF SEVEN COLORS?
MY DECEASED FATHER, LORD IEMITSU, WAS A SICKLY CHILD AND NEVER HAD MUCH APPETITE.
MEOW
SO KASUGA ALWAYS PREPARED SEVEN KINDS OF RICE FOR HIS BREAKFAST.
ONE COOKED WITH GREENS, ONE WITH WHEAT, ONE WITH MILLET, ANOTHER WITH ADZUKI BEANS... THEN THERE WAS TWICE-COOKED RICE, WHICH WAS STEAMED AFTER BEING BOILED, AND DRIED RICE, AND SPLIT RICE, WHERE THE GRAINS WERE POUNDED.
COME, COME, MASTER TAKECHIYO*. WITH SO MANY DISHES TO CHOOSE FROM, SURELY YOU WILL FIND SOMETHING TO SUIT YOUR FANCY.

*Iemitsu's childhood name

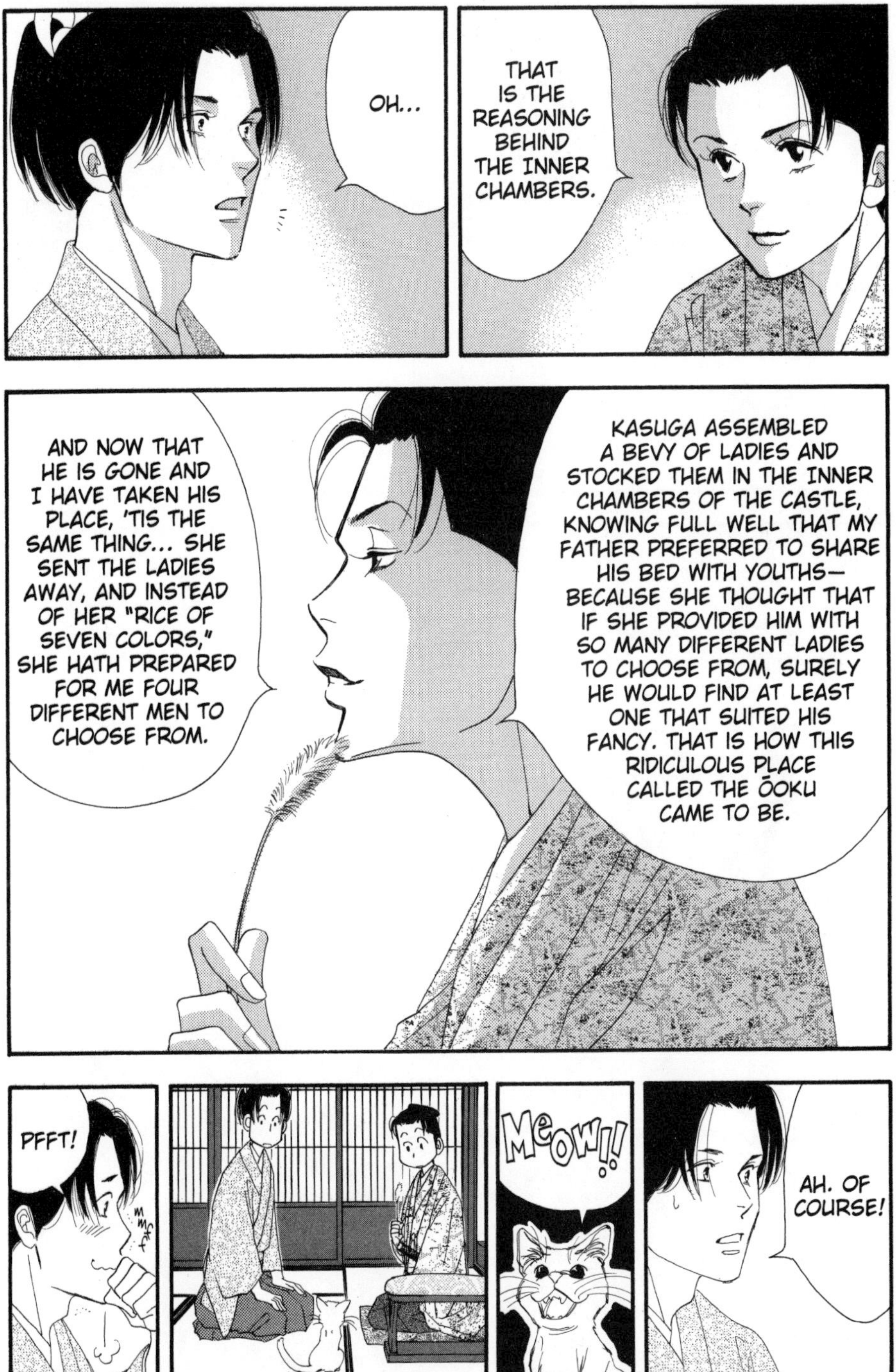
THAT IS THE REASONING BEHIND THE INNER CHAMBERS.
OH...
KASUGA ASSEMBLED A BEVY OF LADIES AND STOCKED THEM IN THE INNER CHAMBERS OF THE CASTLE, KNOWING FULL WELL THAT MY FATHER PREFERRED TO SHARE HIS BED WITH YOUTHS—BECAUSE SHE THOUGHT THAT IF SHE PROVIDED HIM WITH SO MANY DIFFERENT LADIES TO CHOOSE FROM, SURELY HE WOULD FIND AT LEAST ONE THAT SUITED HIS FANCY. THAT IS HOW THIS RIDICULOUS PLACE CALLED THE ŌOKU CAME TO BE.
AND NOW THAT HE IS GONE AND I HAVE TAKEN HIS PLACE, 'TIS THE SAME THING... SHE SENT THE LADIES AWAY, AND INSTEAD OF HER "RICE OF SEVEN COLORS," SHE HATH PREPARED FOR ME FOUR DIFFERENT MEN TO CHOOSE FROM.
AH. OF COURSE!
MEOW!!
PFFT!

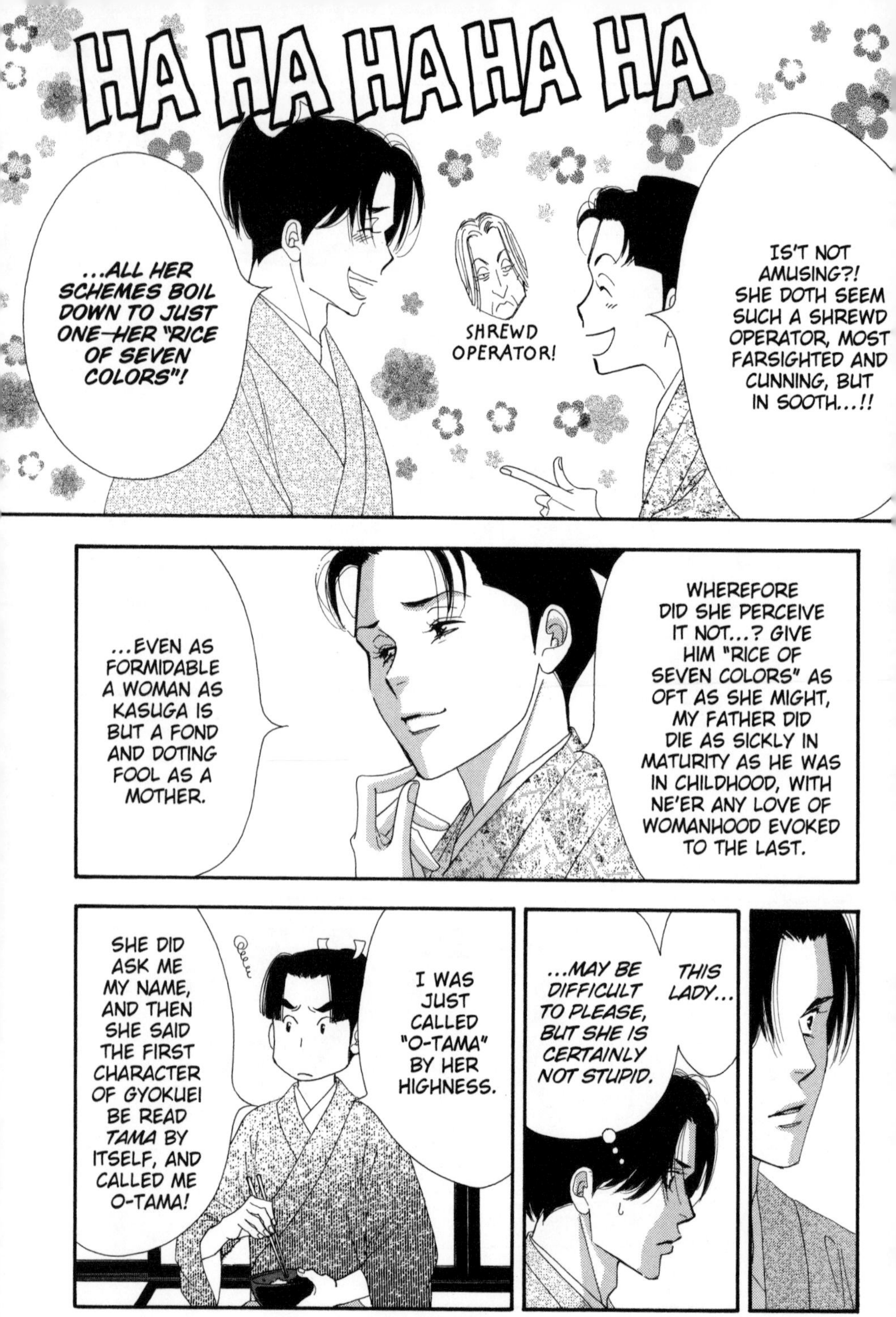
HA HA HA HA HA HA
IS'T NOT AMUSING?! SHE DOTH SEEM SUCH A SHREWD OPERATOR, MOST FARSIGHTED AND CUNNING, BUT IN SOOTH...!!
SHREWD OPERATOR!
...ALL HER SCHEMES BOIL DOWN TO JUST ONE—HER "RICE OF SEVEN COLORS"!
WHEREFORE DID SHE PERCEIVE IT NOT...? GIVE HIM "RICE OF SEVEN COLORS" AS OFT AS SHE MIGHT, MY FATHER DID DIE AS SICKLY IN MATURITY AS HE WAS IN CHILDHOOD, WITH NE'ER ANY LOVE OF WOMANHOOD EVOKED TO THE LAST.
...EVEN AS FORMIDABLE A WOMAN AS KASUGA IS BUT A FOND AND DOTING FOOL AS A MOTHER.
THIS LADY...
...MAY BE DIFFICULT TO PLEASE, BUT SHE IS CERTAINLY NOT STUPID.
I WAS JUST CALLED "O-TAMA" BY HER HIGHNESS.
SHE DID ASK ME MY NAME, AND THEN SHE SAID THE FIRST CHARACTER OF GYOKUEI BE READ TAMA BY ITSELF, AND CALLED ME O-TAMA!

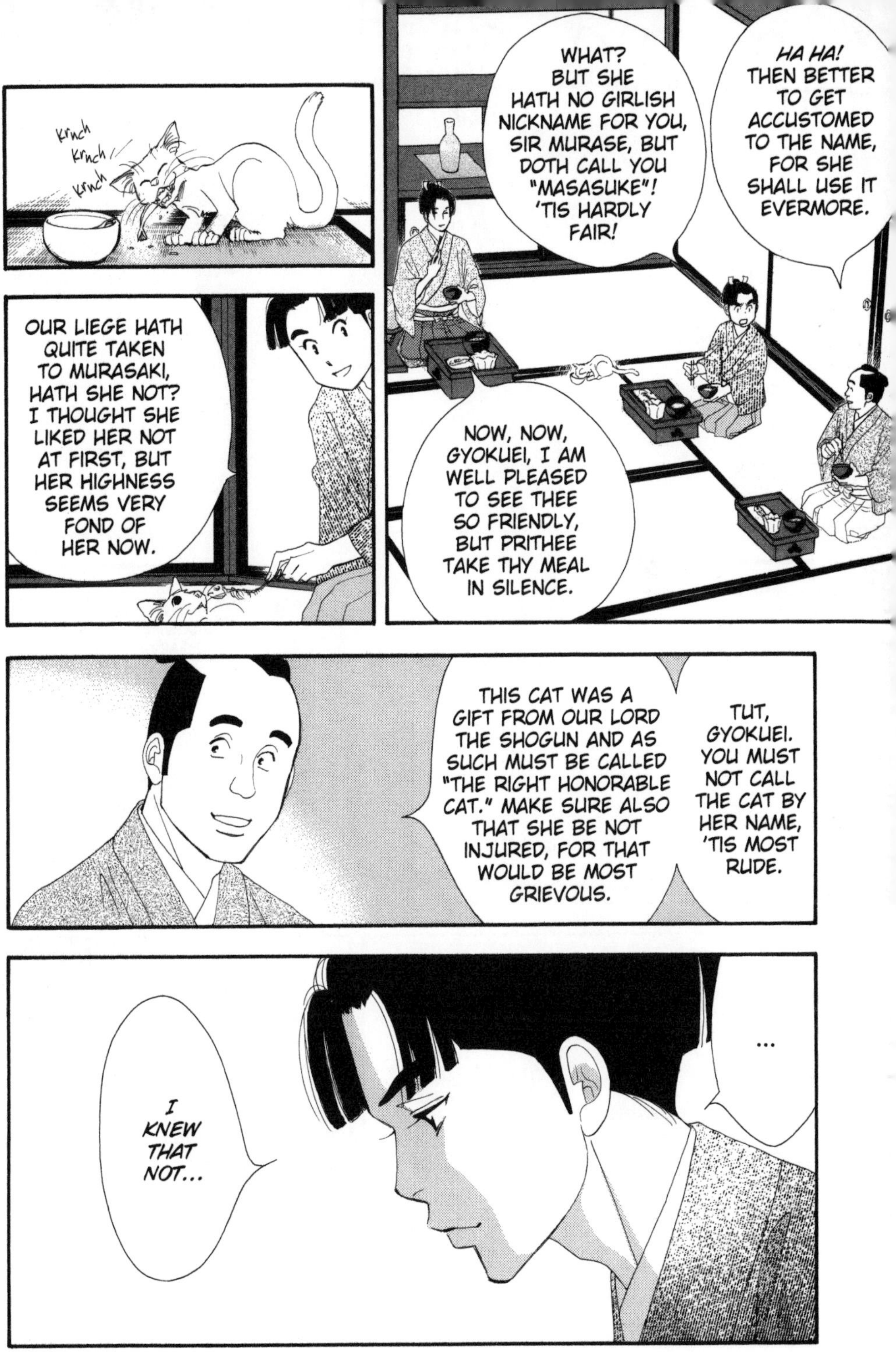
WHAT? BUT SHE HATH NO GIRLISH NICKNAME FOR YOU, SIR MURASE, BUT DOTH CALL YOU "MASASUKE"! 'TIS HARDLY FAIR!
HA HA! THEN BETTER TO GET ACCUSTOMED TO THE NAME, FOR SHE SHALL USE IT EVERMORE.
NOW, NOW, GYOKUEI, I AM WELL PLEASED TO SEE THEE SO FRIENDLY, BUT PRITHEE TAKE THY MEAL IN SILENCE.
Krnch
Krnch
Krnch
OUR LIEGE HATH QUITE TAKEN TO MURASAKI, HATH SHE NOT? I THOUGHT SHE LIKED HER NOT AT FIRST, BUT HER HIGHNESS SEEMS VERY FOND OF HER NOW.
TUT, GYOKUEI. YOU MUST NOT CALL THE CAT BY HER NAME, 'TIS MOST RUDE.
THIS CAT WAS A GIFT FROM OUR LORD THE SHOGUN AND AS SUCH MUST BE CALLED "THE RIGHT HONORABLE CAT." MAKE SURE ALSO THAT SHE BE NOT INJURED, FOR THAT WOULD BE MOST GRIEVOUS.
...
I KNEW THAT NOT...

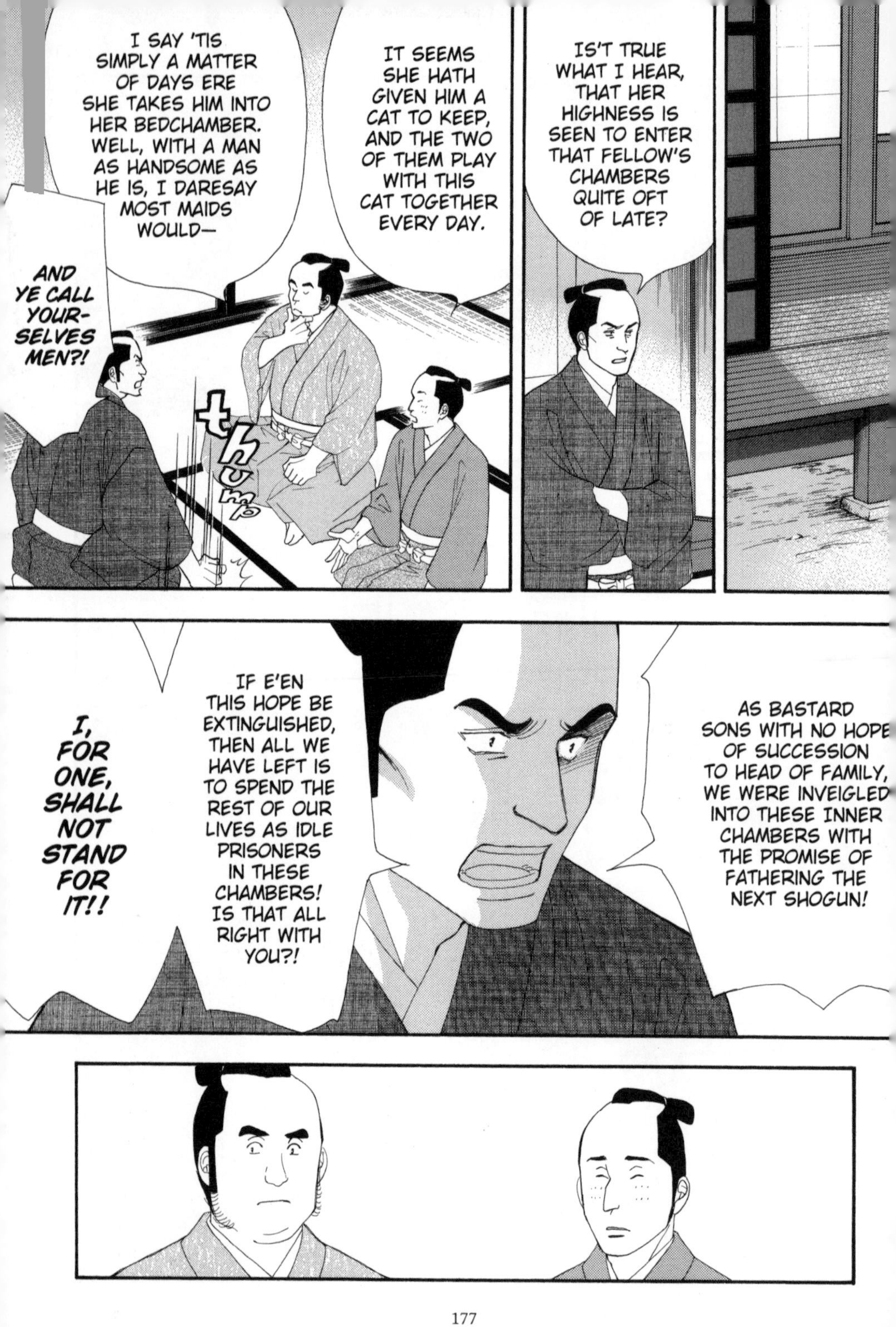
IS'T TRUE WHAT I HEAR, THAT HER HIGHNESS IS SEEN TO ENTER THAT FELLOW'S CHAMBERS QUITE OFT OF LATE?
IT SEEMS SHE HATH GIVEN HIM A CAT TO KEEP, AND THE TWO OF THEM PLAY WITH THIS CAT TOGETHER EVERY DAY.
I SAY 'TIS SIMPLY A MATTER OF DAYS ERE SHE TAKES HIM INTO HER BEDCHAMBER. WELL, WITH A MAN AS HANDSOME AS HE IS, I DARESAY MOST MAIDS WOULD—
AND YE CALL YOUR-SELVES MEN?!
thump
AS BASTARD SONS WITH NO HOPE OF SUCCESSION TO HEAD OF FAMILY, WE WERE INVEIGLED INTO THESE INNER CHAMBERS WITH THE PROMISE OF FATHERING THE NEXT SHOGUN!
IF E'EN THIS HOPE BE EXTINGUISHED, THEN ALL WE HAVE LEFT IS TO SPEND THE REST OF OUR LIVES AS IDLE PRISONERS IN THESE CHAMBERS! IS THAT ALL RIGHT WITH YOU?!
I, FOR ONE, SHALL NOT STAND FOR IT!!

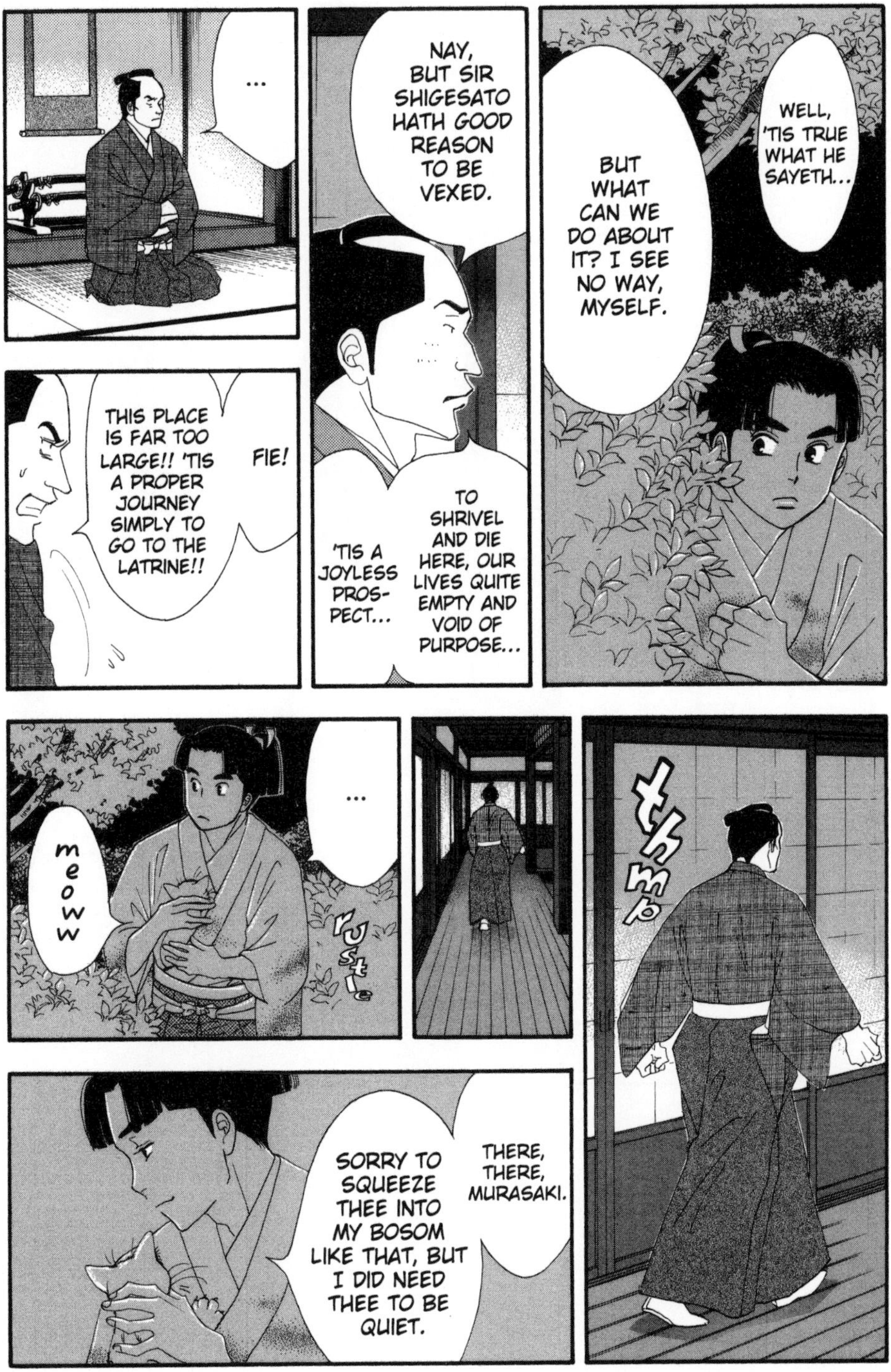
WELL, 'TIS TRUE WHAT HE SAYETH...
BUT WHAT CAN WE DO ABOUT IT? I SEE NO WAY, MYSELF.
NAY, BUT SIR SHIGESATO HATH GOOD REASON TO BE VEXED.
TO SHRIVEL AND DIE HERE, OUR LIVES QUITE EMPTY AND VOID OF PURPOSE...
'TIS A JOYLESS PROSPECT...
...
FIE!
THIS PLACE IS FAR TOO LARGE!! 'TIS A PROPER JOURNEY SIMPLY TO GO TO THE LATRINE!!
thmp
...
rustle
meoww
THERE, THERE, MURASAKI.
SORRY TO SQUEEZE THEE INTO MY BOSOM LIKE THAT, BUT I DID NEED THEE TO BE QUIET.

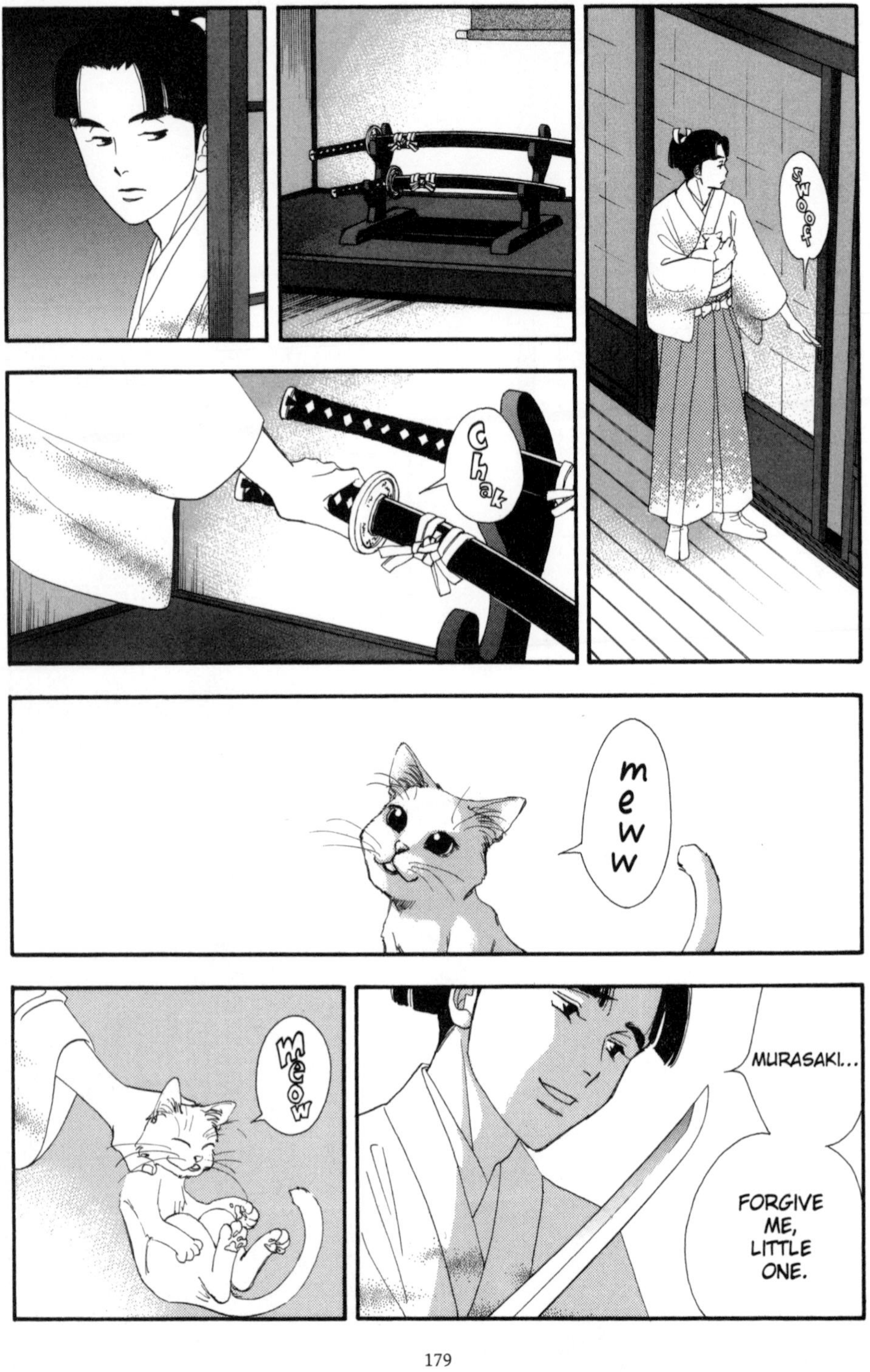
swoof
Chak
meww
MURASAKI...
FORGIVE ME, LITTLE ONE.
meow

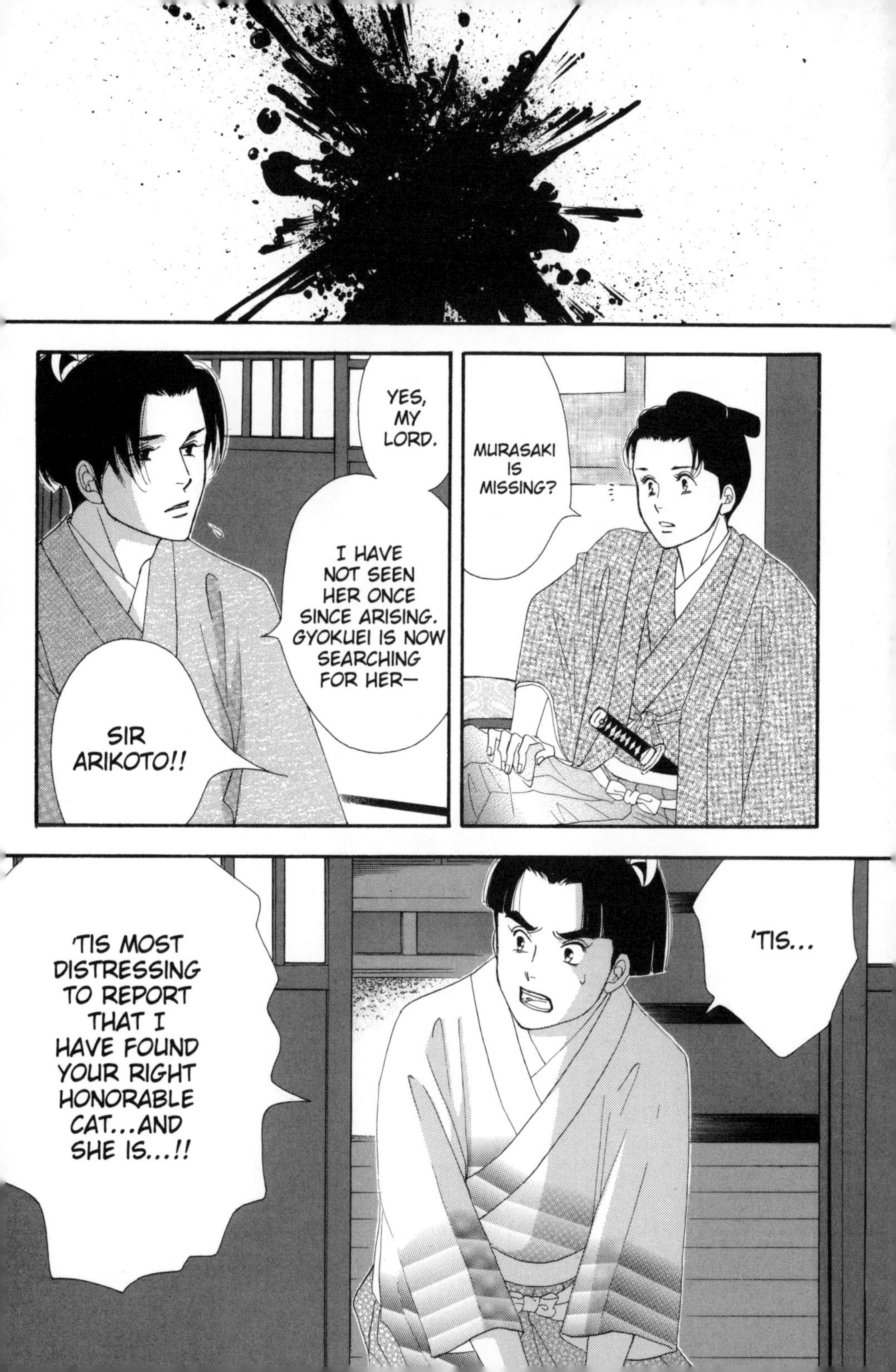
MURASAKI IS MISSING?
YES, MY LORD.
I HAVE NOT SEEN HER ONCE SINCE ARISING. GYOKUEI IS NOW SEARCHING FOR HER—
SIR ARIKOTO!!
'TIS...
'TIS MOST DISTRESSING TO REPORT THAT I HAVE FOUND YOUR RIGHT HONORABLE CAT...AND SHE IS...!!

AND YET, SHIGESATO... THE RIGHT HONORABLE CAT HATH BEEN FOUND IN THE GARDEN DIRECTLY OUTSIDE THY CHAMBERS, IN THIS MOST SORRY STATE.

I-I KNOW NOTHING OF THIS, I SWEAR IT MOST SOLEMNLY!

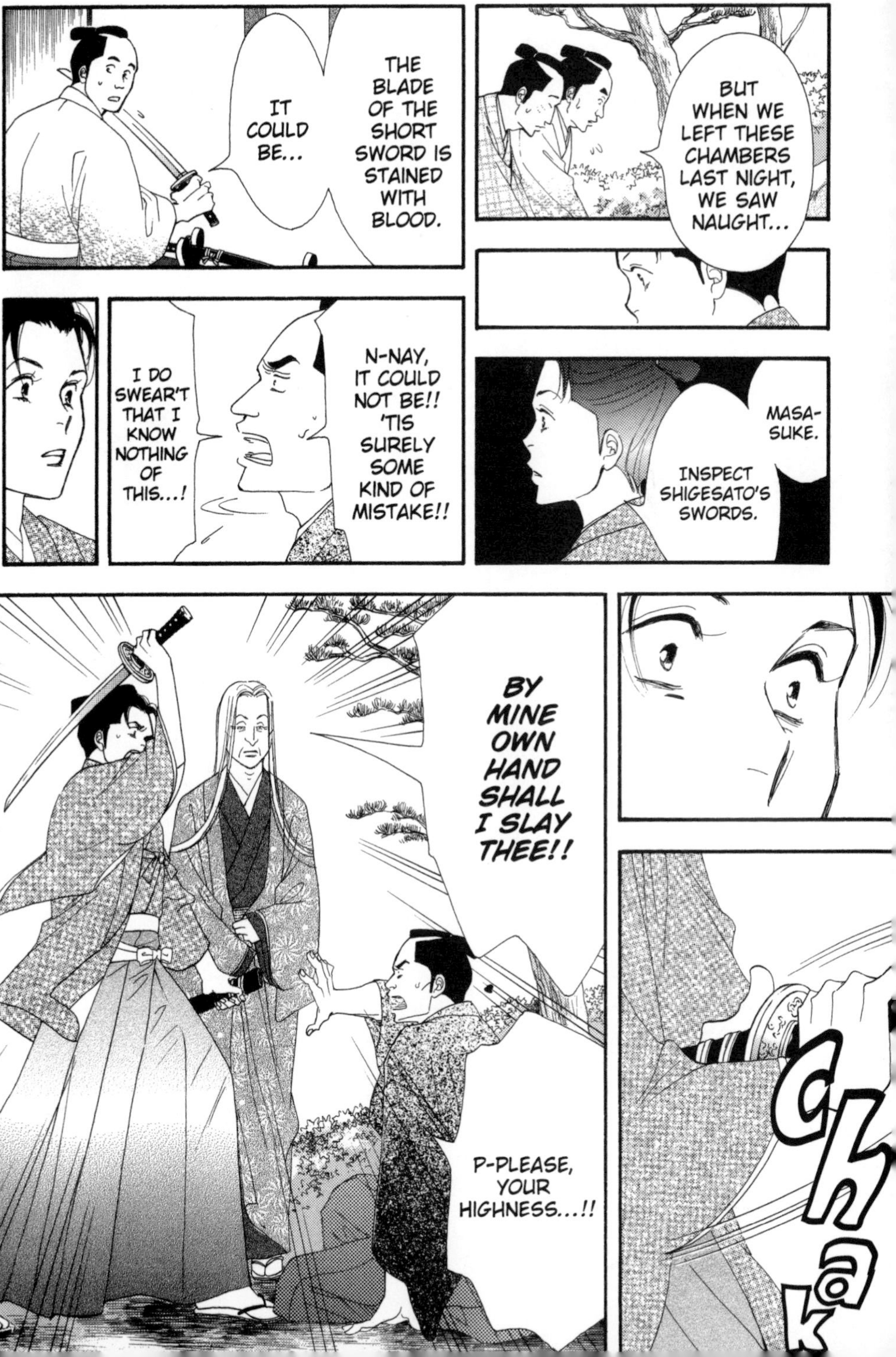
BUT WHEN WE LEFT THESE CHAMBERS LAST NIGHT, WE SAW NAUGHT...
THE BLADE OF THE SHORT SWORD IS STAINED WITH BLOOD.
IT COULD BE...
MASA-SUKE.
INSPECT SHIGESATO'S SWORDS.
N-NAY, IT COULD NOT BE!! 'TIS SURELY SOME KIND OF MISTAKE!!
I DO SWEAR'T THAT I KNOW NOTHING OF THIS...!
Chak
BY MINE OWN HAND SHALL I SLAY THEE!!
P-PLEASE, YOUR HIGHNESS...!!

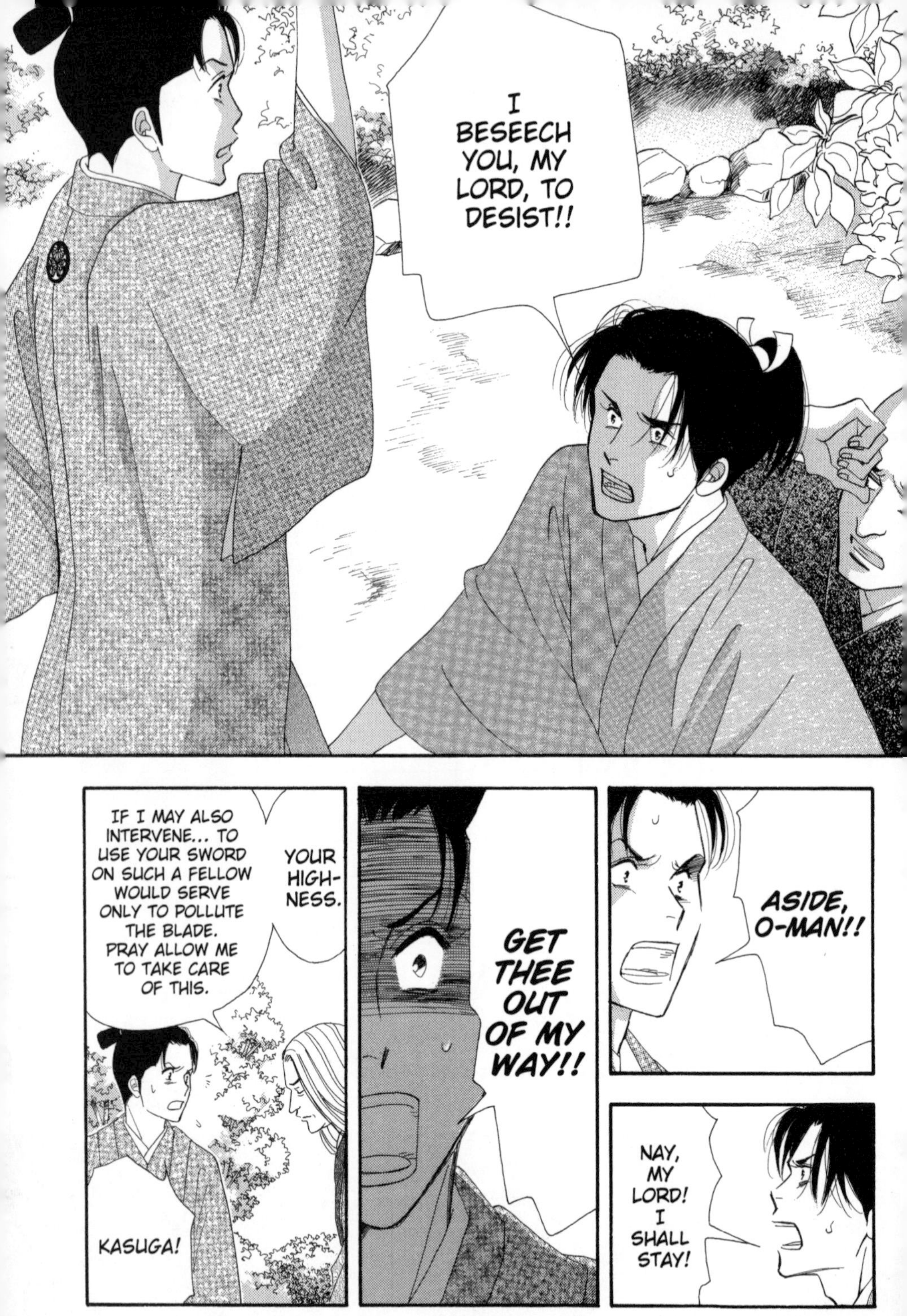
I BESEECH YOU, MY LORD, TO DESIST!!
ASIDE, O-MAN!!
NAY, MY LORD! I SHALL STAY!
GET THEE OUT OF MY WAY!!
YOUR HIGHNESS.
IF I MAY ALSO INTERVENE... TO USE YOUR SWORD ON SUCH A FELLOW WOULD SERVE ONLY TO POLLUTE THE BLADE. PRAY ALLOW ME TO TAKE CARE OF THIS.
KASUGA!

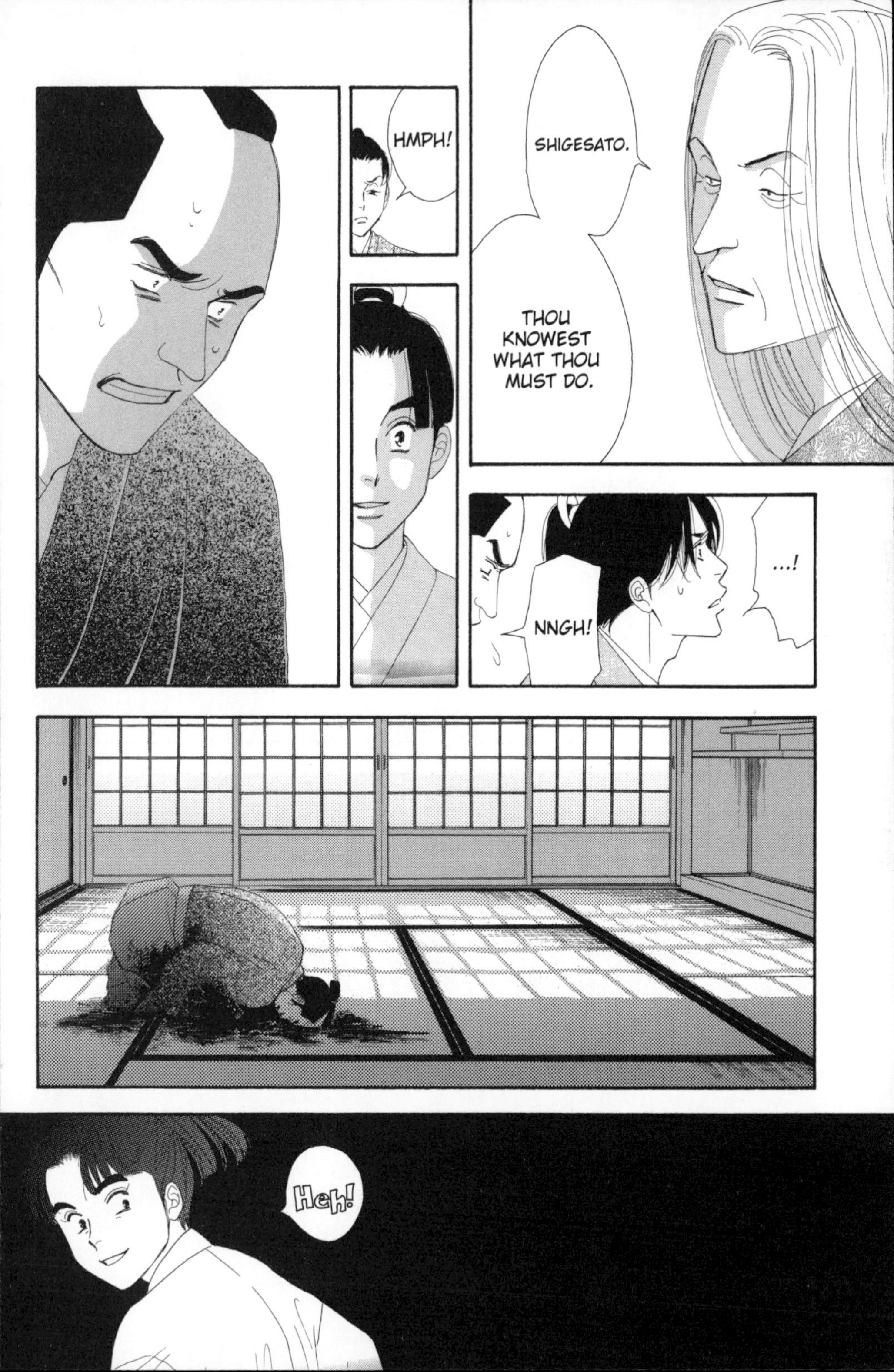
SHIGESATO.
THOU KNOWEST WHAT THOU MUST DO.
...!
NNGH!
HMPH!
Heh!

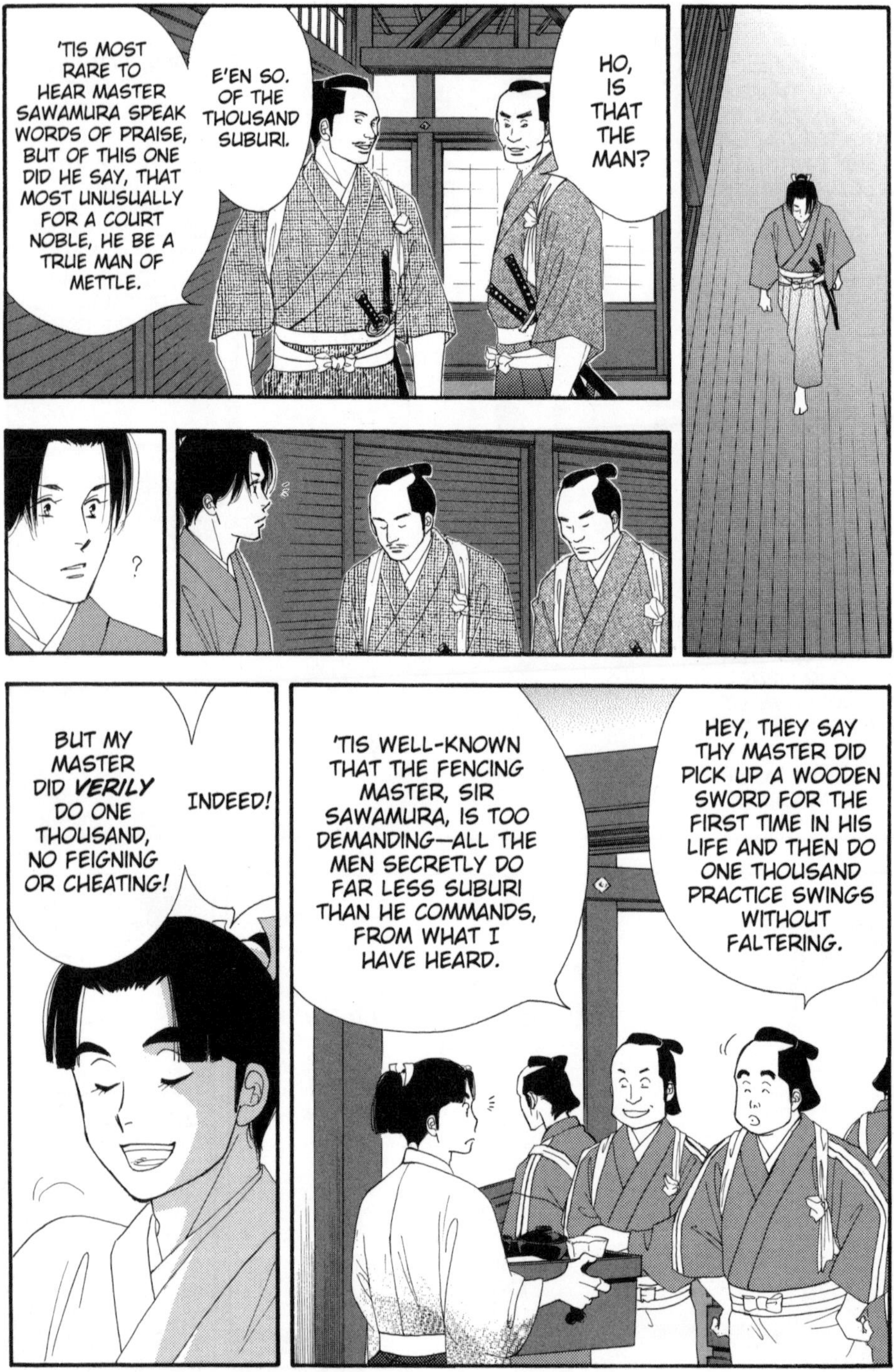
HO, IS THAT THE MAN?
E'EN SO. OF THE THOUSAND SUBURI.
'TIS MOST RARE TO HEAR MASTER SAWAMURA SPEAK WORDS OF PRAISE, BUT OF THIS ONE DID HE SAY, THAT MOST UNUSUALLY FOR A COURT NOBLE, HE BE A TRUE MAN OF METTLE.
?
HEY, THEY SAY THY MASTER DID PICK UP A WOODEN SWORD FOR THE FIRST TIME IN HIS LIFE AND THEN DO ONE THOUSAND PRACTICE SWINGS WITHOUT FALTERING.
'TIS WELL-KNOWN THAT THE FENCING MASTER, SIR SAWAMURA, IS TOO DEMANDING—ALL THE MEN SECRETLY DO FAR LESS SUBURI THAN HE COMMANDS, FROM WHAT I HAVE HEARD.
INDEED!
BUT MY MASTER DID *VERILY* DO ONE THOUSAND, NO FEIGNING OR CHEATING!

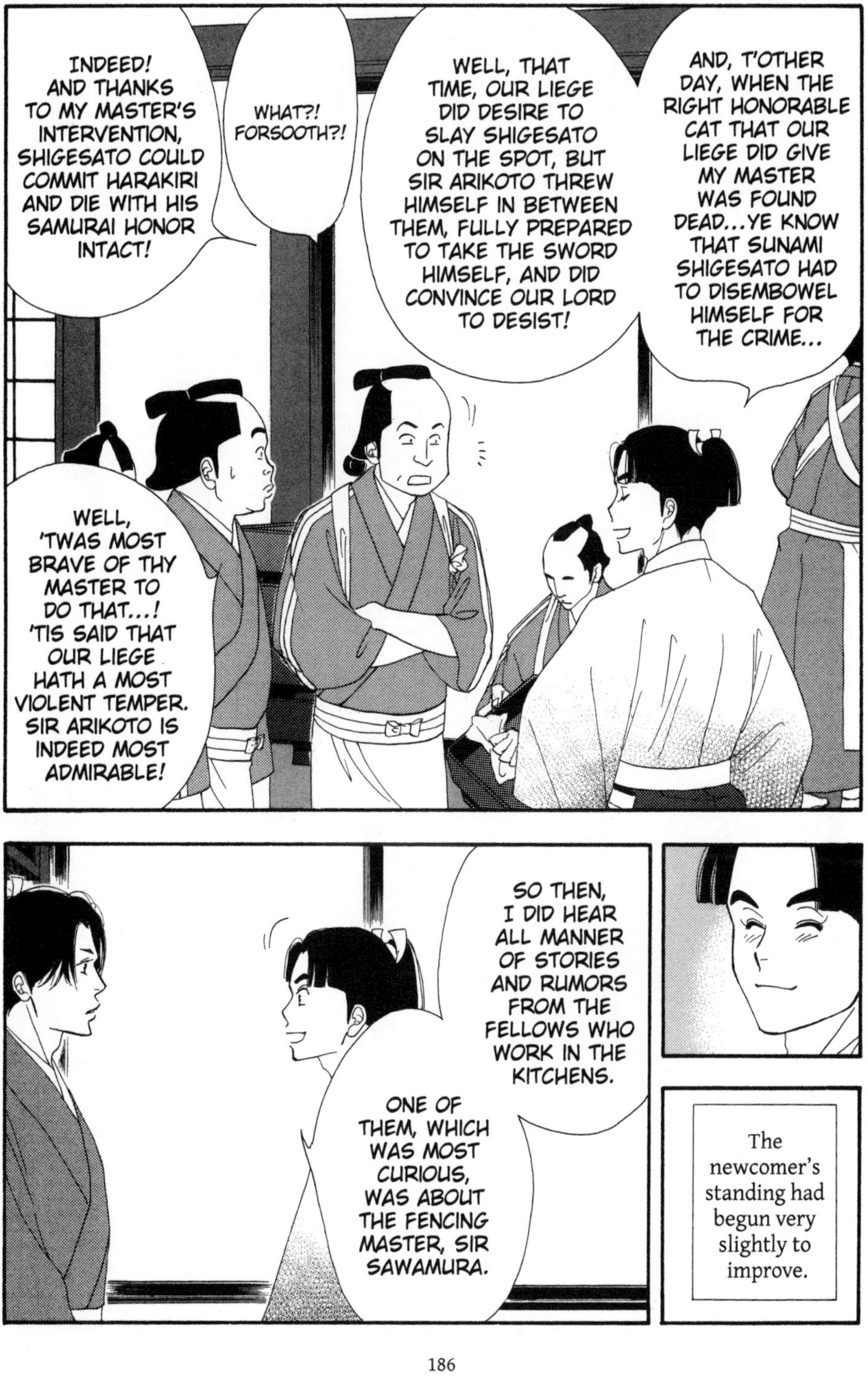
AND, T'OTHER DAY, WHEN THE RIGHT HONORABLE CAT THAT OUR LIEGE DID GIVE MY MASTER WAS FOUND DEAD...YE KNOW THAT SUNAMI SHIGESATO HAD TO DISEMBOWEL HIMSELF FOR THE CRIME...
WELL, THAT TIME, OUR LIEGE DID DESIRE TO SLAY SHIGESATO ON THE SPOT, BUT SIR ARIKOTO THREW HIMSELF IN BETWEEN THEM, FULLY PREPARED TO TAKE THE SWORD HIMSELF, AND DID CONVINCE OUR LORD TO DESIST!
WHAT?! FORSOOTH?!
INDEED! AND THANKS TO MY MASTER'S INTERVENTION, SHIGESATO COULD COMMIT HARAKIRI AND DIE WITH HIS SAMURAI HONOR INTACT!
WELL, 'TWAS MOST BRAVE OF THY MASTER TO DO THAT...! 'TIS SAID THAT OUR LIEGE HATH A MOST VIOLENT TEMPER. SIR ARIKOTO IS INDEED MOST ADMIRABLE!
The newcomer's standing had begun very slightly to improve.
SO THEN, I DID HEAR ALL MANNER OF STORIES AND RUMORS FROM THE FELLOWS WHO WORK IN THE KITCHENS.
ONE OF THEM, WHICH WAS MOST CURIOUS, WAS ABOUT THE FENCING MASTER, SIR SAWAMURA.

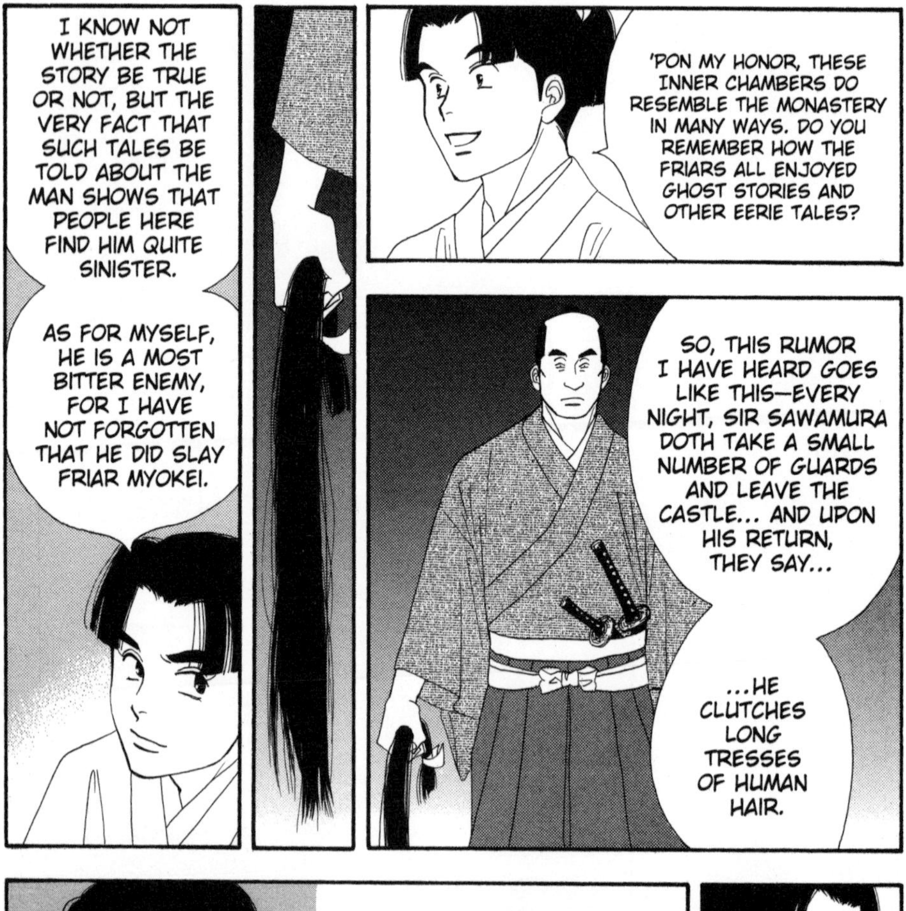
'PON MY HONOR, THESE INNER CHAMBERS DO RESEMBLE THE MONASTERY IN MANY WAYS. DO YOU REMEMBER HOW THE FRIARS ALL ENJOYED GHOST STORIES AND OTHER EERIE TALES?
SO, THIS RUMOR I HAVE HEARD GOES LIKE THIS—EVERY NIGHT, SIR SAWAMURA DOTH TAKE A SMALL NUMBER OF GUARDS AND LEAVE THE CASTLE... AND UPON HIS RETURN, THEY SAY...
...HE CLUTCHES LONG TRESSES OF HUMAN HAIR.
I KNOW NOT WHETHER THE STORY BE TRUE OR NOT, BUT THE VERY FACT THAT SUCH TALES BE TOLD ABOUT THE MAN SHOWS THAT PEOPLE HERE FIND HIM QUITE SINISTER.
AS FOR MYSELF, HE IS A MOST BITTER ENEMY, FOR I HAVE NOT FORGOTTEN THAT HE DID SLAY FRIAR MYOKEI.
'TIS A SWORD-BEARING MAN OF THE WARRIOR CLASS, WHO STRIDES THE STREETS AT NIGHT AND HACKS OFF THE HAIR OF PASSING MAIDENS, AS IF TESTING THE SHARPNESS OF HIS BLADE.

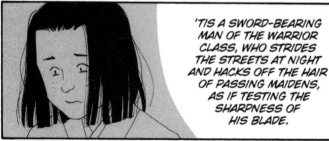

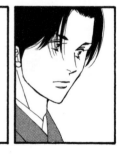

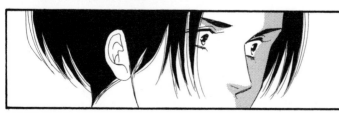

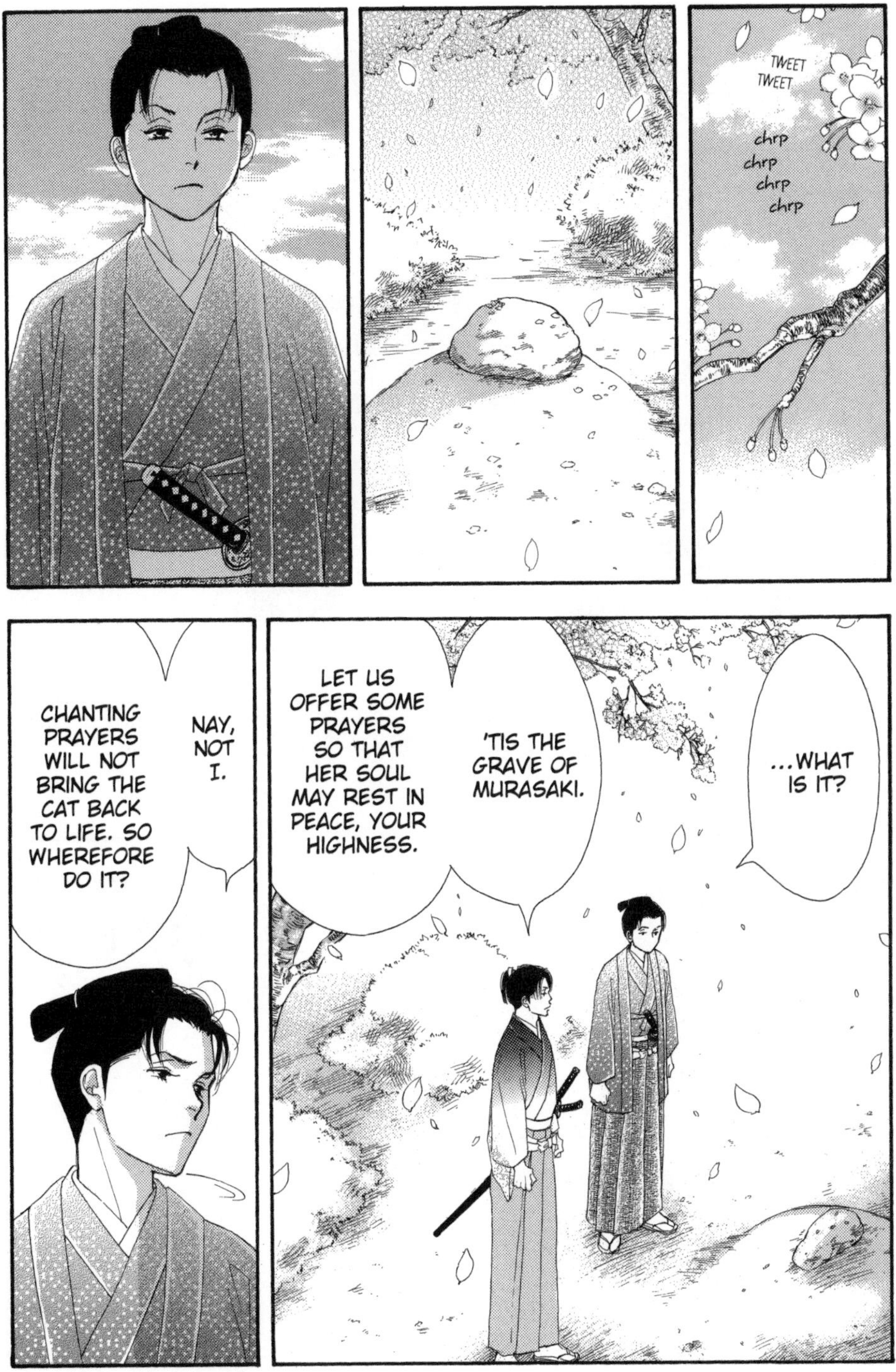
TWEET TWEET
chrp chrp chrp chrp
...WHAT IS IT?
'TIS THE GRAVE OF MURASAKI.
LET US OFFER SOME PRAYERS SO THAT HER SOUL MAY REST IN PEACE, YOUR HIGHNESS.
NAY, NOT I.
CHANTING PRAYERS WILL NOT BRING THE CAT BACK TO LIFE. SO WHEREFORE DO IT?

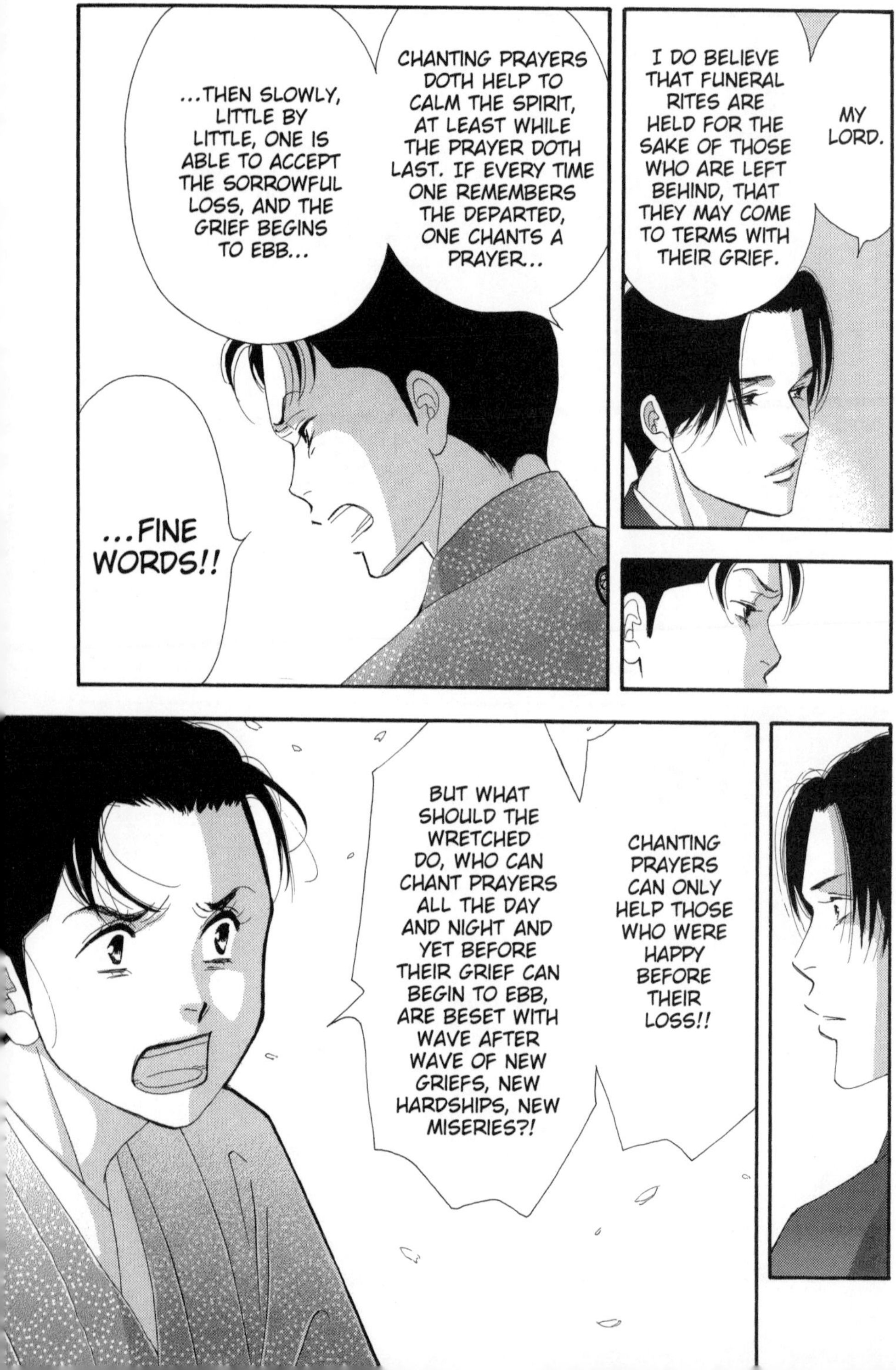
MY LORD.
I DO BELIEVE THAT FUNERAL RITES ARE HELD FOR THE SAKE OF THOSE WHO ARE LEFT BEHIND, THAT THEY MAY COME TO TERMS WITH THEIR GRIEF.
CHANTING PRAYERS DOTH HELP TO CALM THE SPIRIT, AT LEAST WHILE THE PRAYER DOTH LAST. IF EVERY TIME ONE REMEMBERS THE DEPARTED, ONE CHANTS A PRAYER...
...THEN SLOWLY, LITTLE BY LITTLE, ONE IS ABLE TO ACCEPT THE SORROWFUL LOSS, AND THE GRIEF BEGINS TO EBB...
...FINE WORDS!!
CHANTING PRAYERS CAN ONLY HELP THOSE WHO WERE HAPPY BEFORE THEIR LOSS!!
BUT WHAT SHOULD THE WRETCHED DO, WHO CAN CHANT PRAYERS ALL THE DAY AND NIGHT AND YET BEFORE THEIR GRIEF CAN BEGIN TO EBB, ARE BESET WITH WAVE AFTER WAVE OF NEW GRIEFS, NEW HARDSHIPS, NEW MISERIES?!

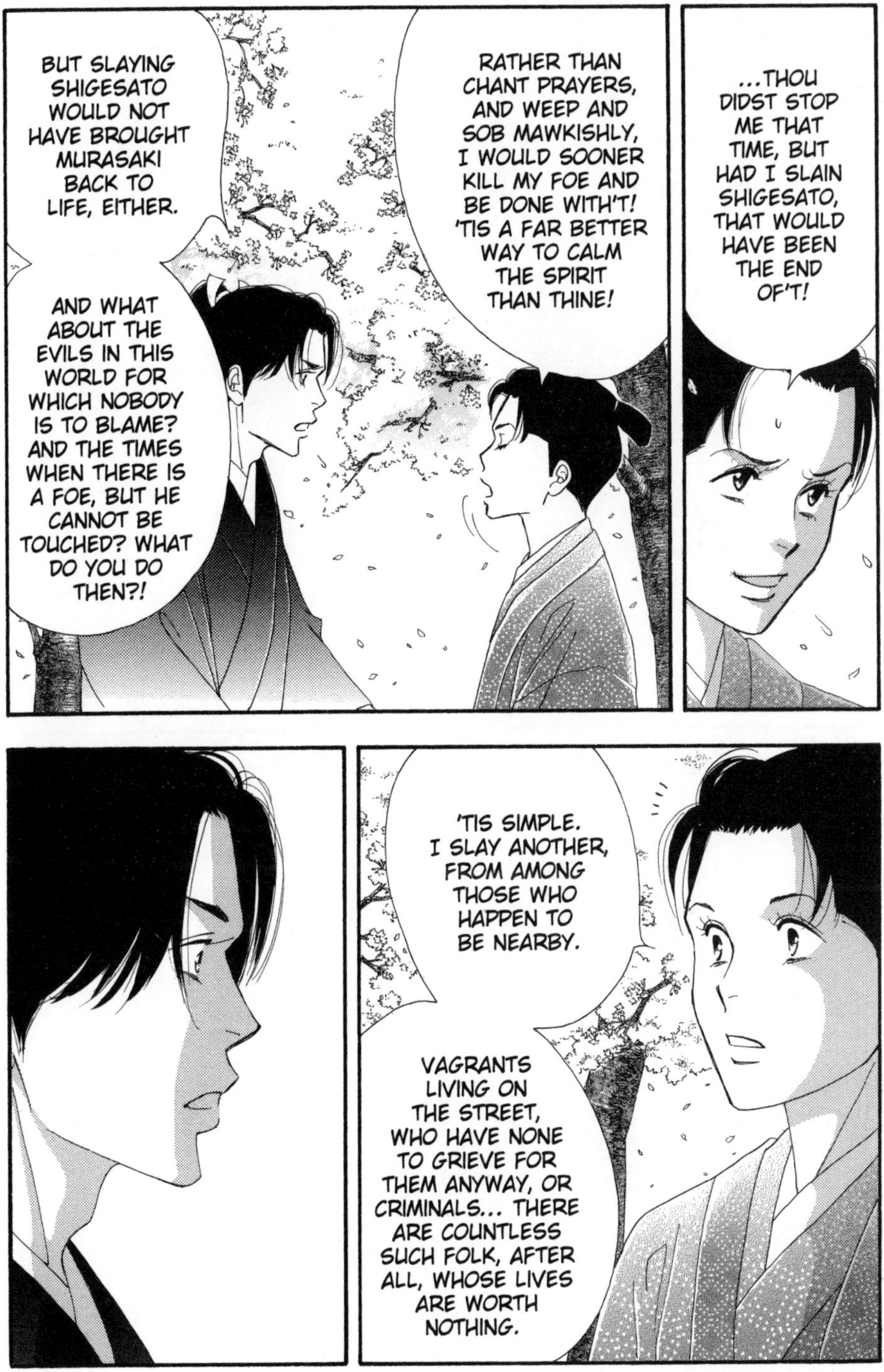
...THOU DIDST STOP ME THAT TIME, BUT HAD I SLAIN SHIGESATO, THAT WOULD HAVE BEEN THE END OF'T!
RATHER THAN CHANT PRAYERS, AND WEEP AND SOB MAWKISHLY, I WOULD SOONER KILL MY FOE AND BE DONE WITH'T! 'TIS A FAR BETTER WAY TO CALM THE SPIRIT THAN THINE!
BUT SLAYING SHIGESATO WOULD NOT HAVE BROUGHT MURASAKI BACK TO LIFE, EITHER.
AND WHAT ABOUT THE EVILS IN THIS WORLD FOR WHICH NOBODY IS TO BLAME? AND THE TIMES WHEN THERE IS A FOE, BUT HE CANNOT BE TOUCHED? WHAT DO YOU DO THEN?!
'TIS SIMPLE. I SLAY ANOTHER, FROM AMONG THOSE WHO HAPPEN TO BE NEARBY.
VAGRANTS LIVING ON THE STREET, WHO HAVE NONE TO GRIEVE FOR THEM ANYWAY, OR CRIMINALS... THERE ARE COUNTLESS SUCH FOLK, AFTER ALL, WHOSE LIVES ARE WORTH NOTHING.

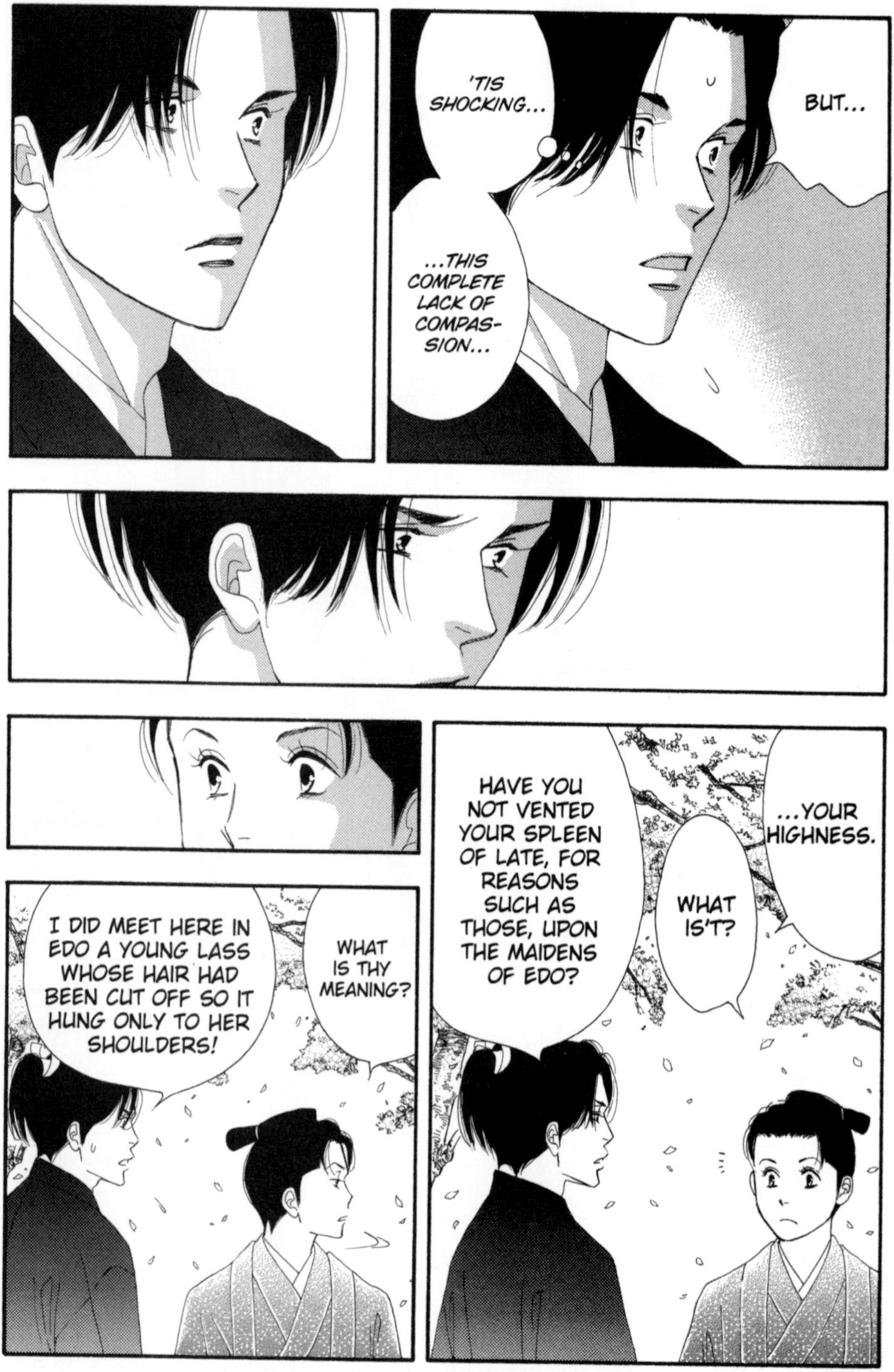
'TIS SHOCKING...
...THIS COMPLETE LACK OF COMPASSION...
BUT...
...YOUR HIGHNESS.
WHAT IS'T?
HAVE YOU NOT VENTED YOUR SPLEEN OF LATE, FOR REASONS SUCH AS THOSE, UPON THE MAIDENS OF EDO?
WHAT IS THY MEANING?
I DID MEET HERE IN EDO A YOUNG LASS WHOSE HAIR HAD BEEN CUT OFF SO IT HUNG ONLY TO HER SHOULDERS!

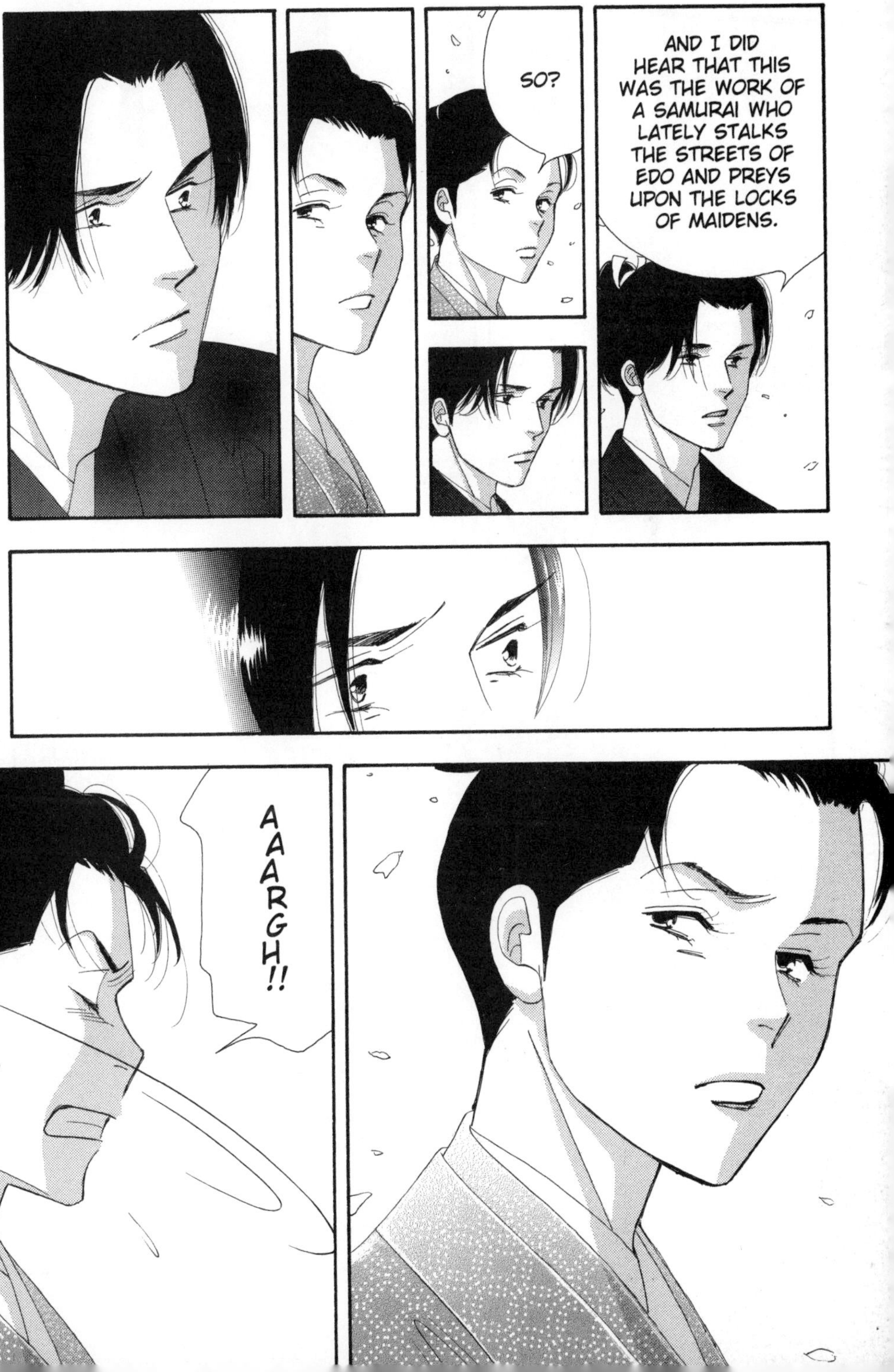
AND I DID HEAR THAT THIS WAS THE WORK OF A SAMURAI WHO LATELY STALKS THE STREETS OF EDO AND PREYS UPON THE LOCKS OF MAIDENS.
SO?
AAARGH!!

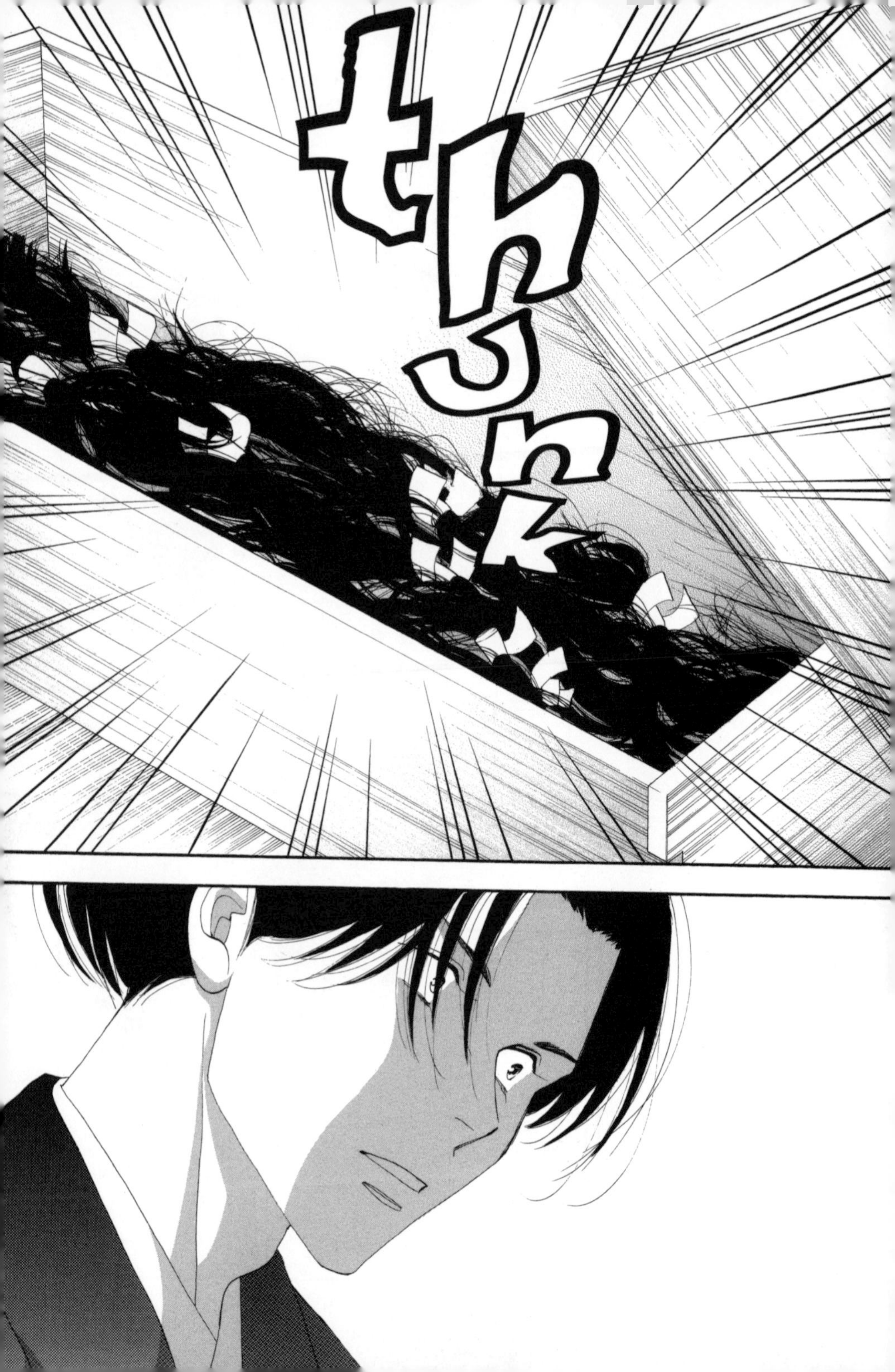
thunk

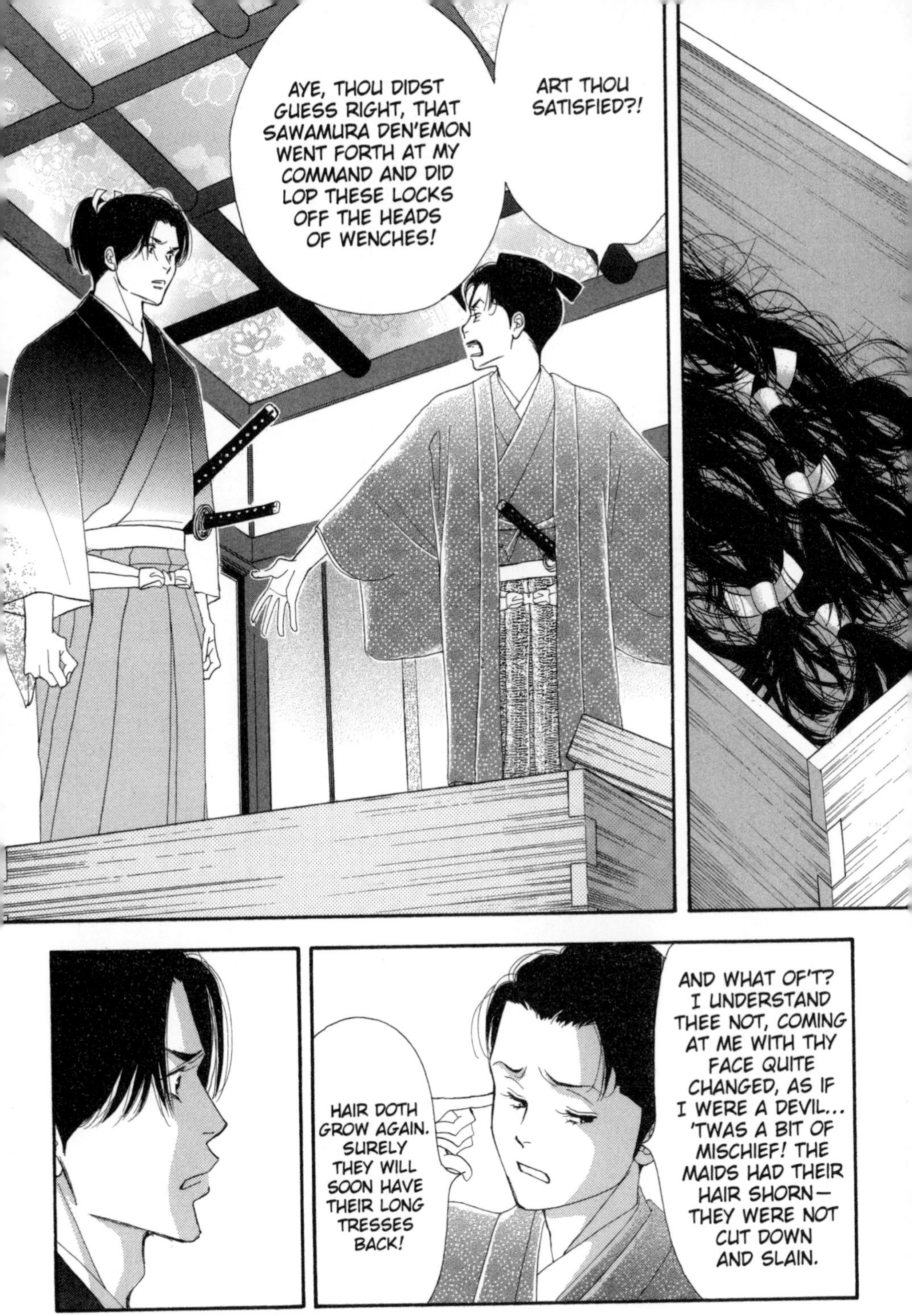
ART THOU SATISFIED?!
AYE, THOU DIDST GUESS RIGHT, THAT SAWAMURA DEN'EMON WENT FORTH AT MY COMMAND AND DID LOP THESE LOCKS OFF THE HEADS OF WENCHES!
AND WHAT OF'T? I UNDERSTAND THEE NOT, COMING AT ME WITH THY FACE QUITE CHANGED, AS IF I WERE A DEVIL... 'TWAS A BIT OF MISCHIEF! THE MAIDS HAD THEIR HAIR SHORN— THEY WERE NOT CUT DOWN AND SLAIN.
HAIR DOTH GROW AGAIN. SURELY THEY WILL SOON HAVE THEIR LONG TRESSES BACK!

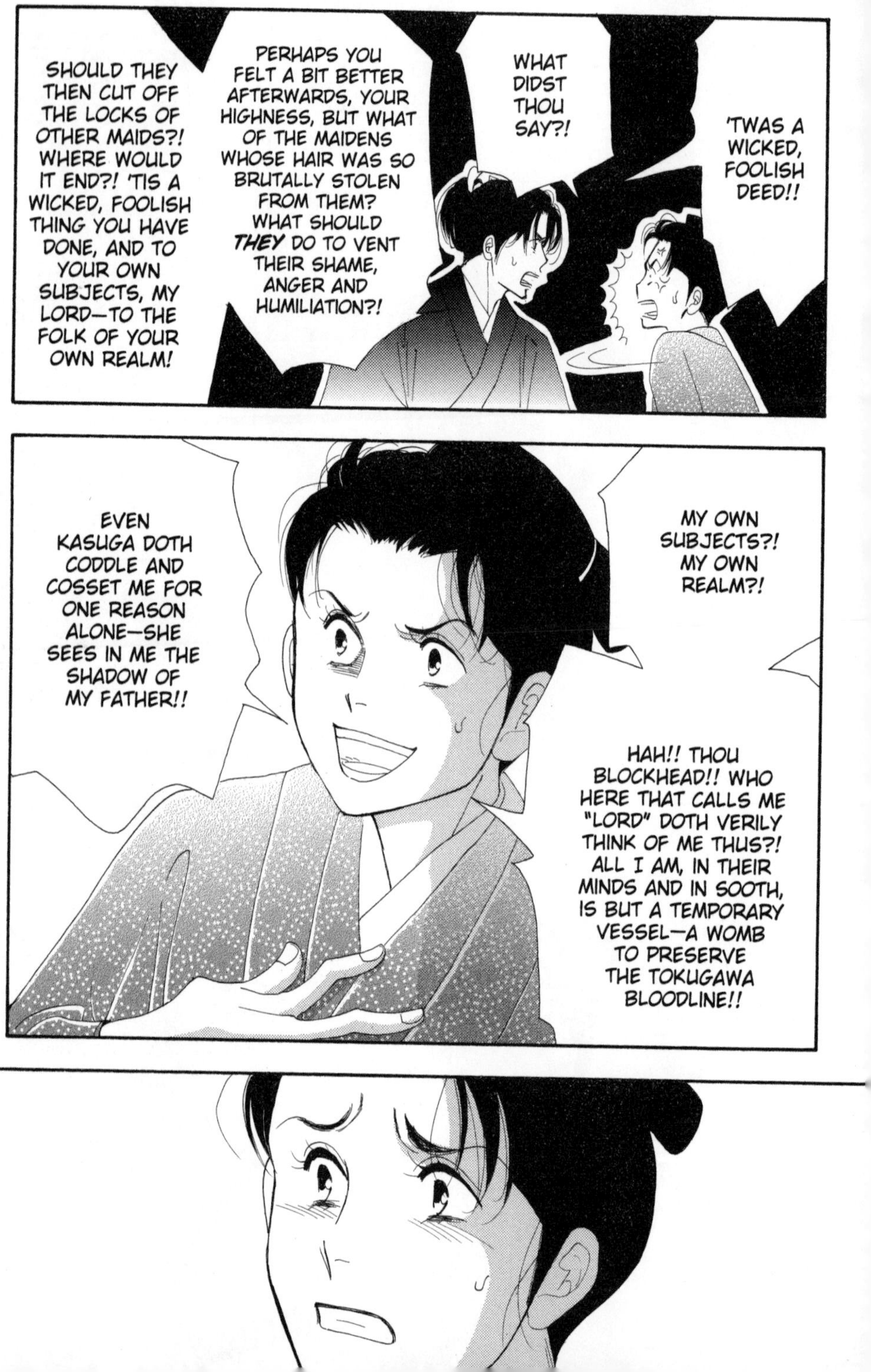
'TWAS A WICKED, FOOLISH DEED!!
WHAT DIDST THOU SAY?!
PERHAPS YOU FELT A BIT BETTER AFTERWARDS, YOUR HIGHNESS, BUT WHAT OF THE MAIDENS WHOSE HAIR WAS SO BRUTALLY STOLEN FROM THEM? WHAT SHOULD *THEY* DO TO VENT THEIR SHAME, ANGER AND HUMILIATION?!
SHOULD THEY THEN CUT OFF THE LOCKS OF OTHER MAIDS?! WHERE WOULD IT END?! 'TIS A WICKED, FOOLISH THING YOU HAVE DONE, AND TO YOUR OWN SUBJECTS, MY LORD—TO THE FOLK OF YOUR OWN REALM!
MY OWN SUBJECTS?! MY OWN REALM?!
HAH!! THOU BLOCKHEAD!! WHO HERE THAT CALLS ME "LORD" DOTH VERILY THINK OF ME THUS?! ALL I AM, IN THEIR MINDS AND IN SOOTH, IS BUT A TEMPORARY VESSEL—A WOMB TO PRESERVE THE TOKUGAWA BLOODLINE!!
EVEN KASUGA DOTH CODDLE AND COSSET ME FOR ONE REASON ALONE—SHE SEES IN ME THE SHADOW OF MY FATHER!!

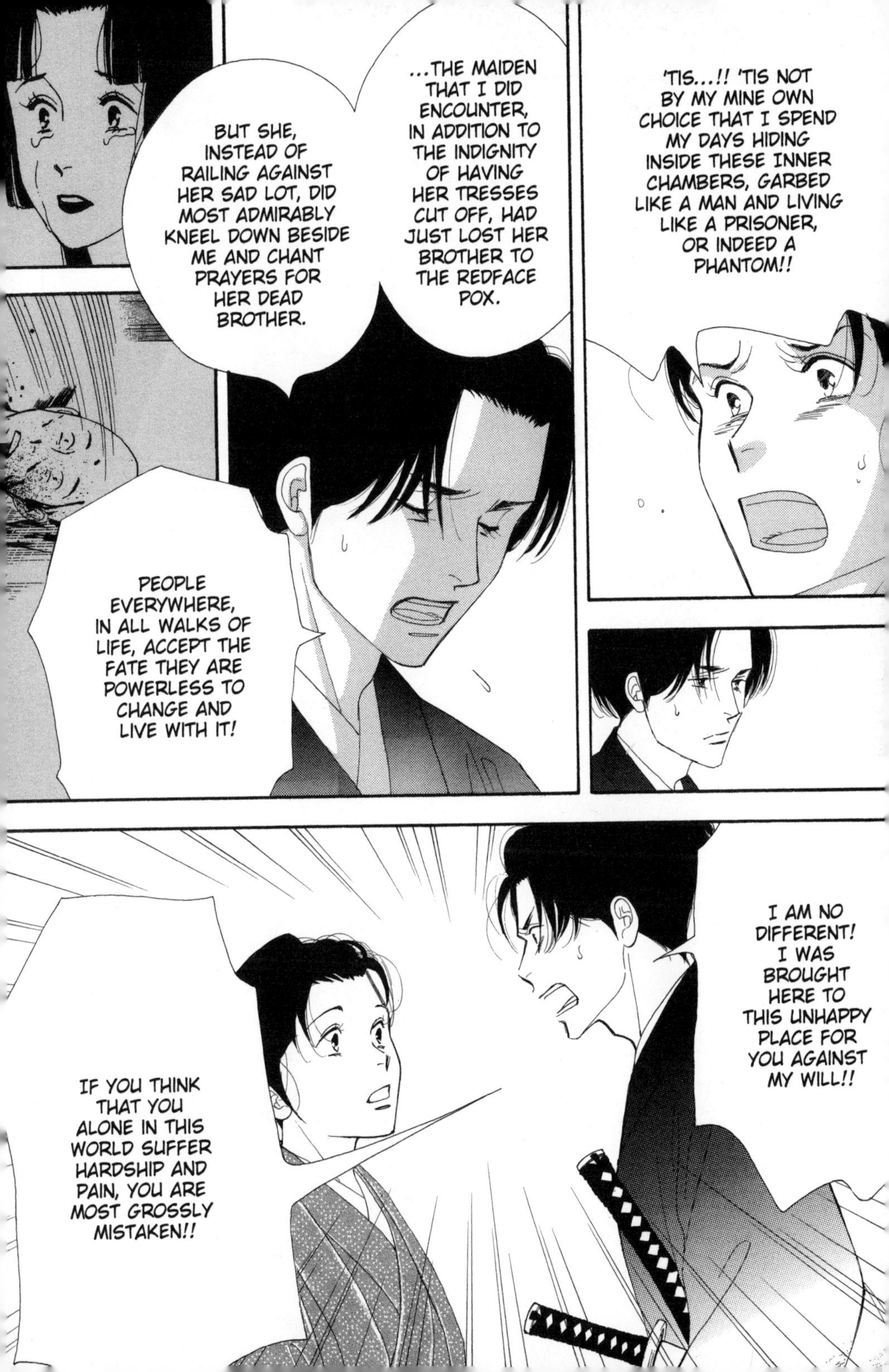
'TIS...!! 'TIS NOT BY MY MINE OWN CHOICE THAT I SPEND MY DAYS HIDING INSIDE THESE INNER CHAMBERS, GARBED LIKE A MAN AND LIVING LIKE A PRISONER, OR INDEED A PHANTOM!!
...THE MAIDEN THAT I DID ENCOUNTER, IN ADDITION TO THE INDIGNITY OF HAVING HER TRESSES CUT OFF, HAD JUST LOST HER BROTHER TO THE REDFACE POX.
BUT SHE, INSTEAD OF RAILING AGAINST HER SAD LOT, DID MOST ADMIRABLY KNEEL DOWN BESIDE ME AND CHANT PRAYERS FOR HER DEAD BROTHER.
PEOPLE EVERYWHERE, IN ALL WALKS OF LIFE, ACCEPT THE FATE THEY ARE POWERLESS TO CHANGE AND LIVE WITH IT!
I AM NO DIFFERENT! I WAS BROUGHT HERE TO THIS UNHAPPY PLACE FOR YOU AGAINST MY WILL!!
IF YOU THINK THAT YOU ALONE IN THIS WORLD SUFFER HARDSHIP AND PAIN, YOU ARE MOST GROSSLY MISTAKEN!!

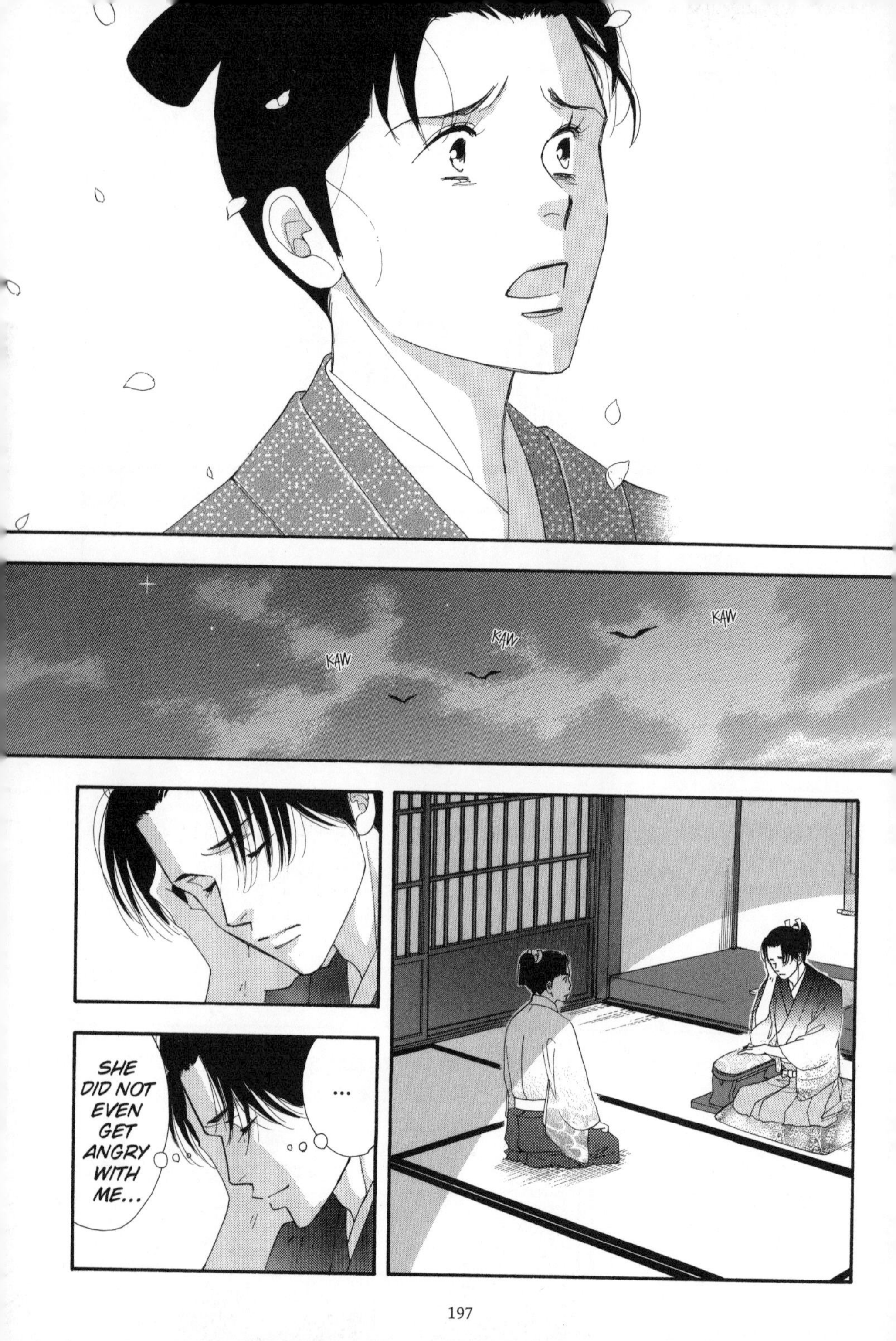
KAW
KAW
KAW
...
SHE DID NOT EVEN GET ANGRY WITH ME...

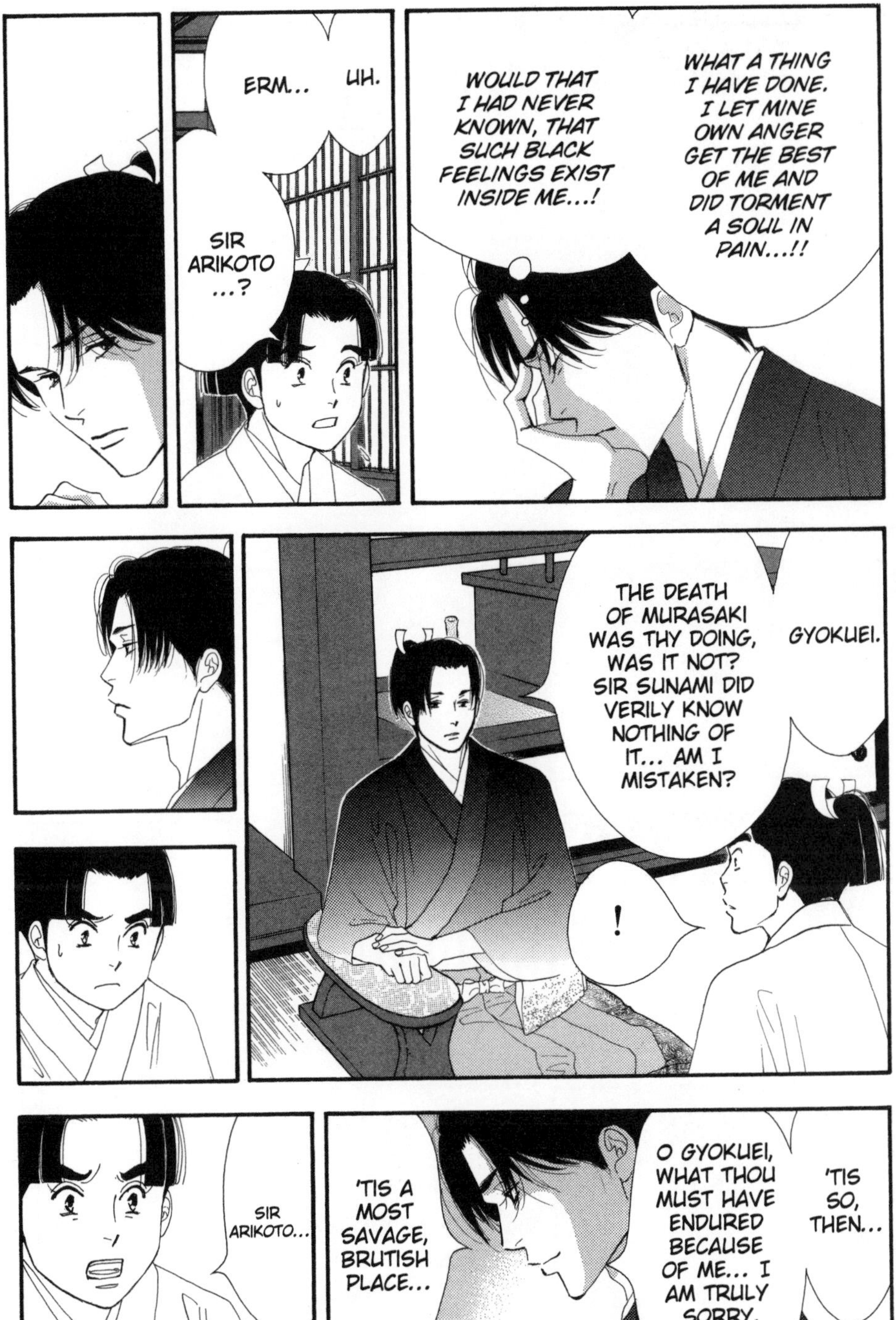

WHAT A THING I HAVE DONE. I LET MINE OWN ANGER GET THE BEST OF ME AND DID TORMENT A SOUL IN PAIN...!!
WOULD THAT I HAD NEVER KNOWN, THAT SUCH BLACK FEELINGS EXIST INSIDE ME...!
UH.
ERM...
SIR ARIKOTO ...?
GYOKUEI.
THE DEATH OF MURASAKI WAS THY DOING, WAS IT NOT? SIR SUNAMI DID VERILY KNOW NOTHING OF IT... AM I MISTAKEN?
!
'TIS SO, THEN...
O GYOKUEI, WHAT THOU MUST HAVE ENDURED BECAUSE OF ME... I AM TRULY SORRY.
'TIS A MOST SAVAGE, BRUTISH PLACE...
SIR ARIKOTO...

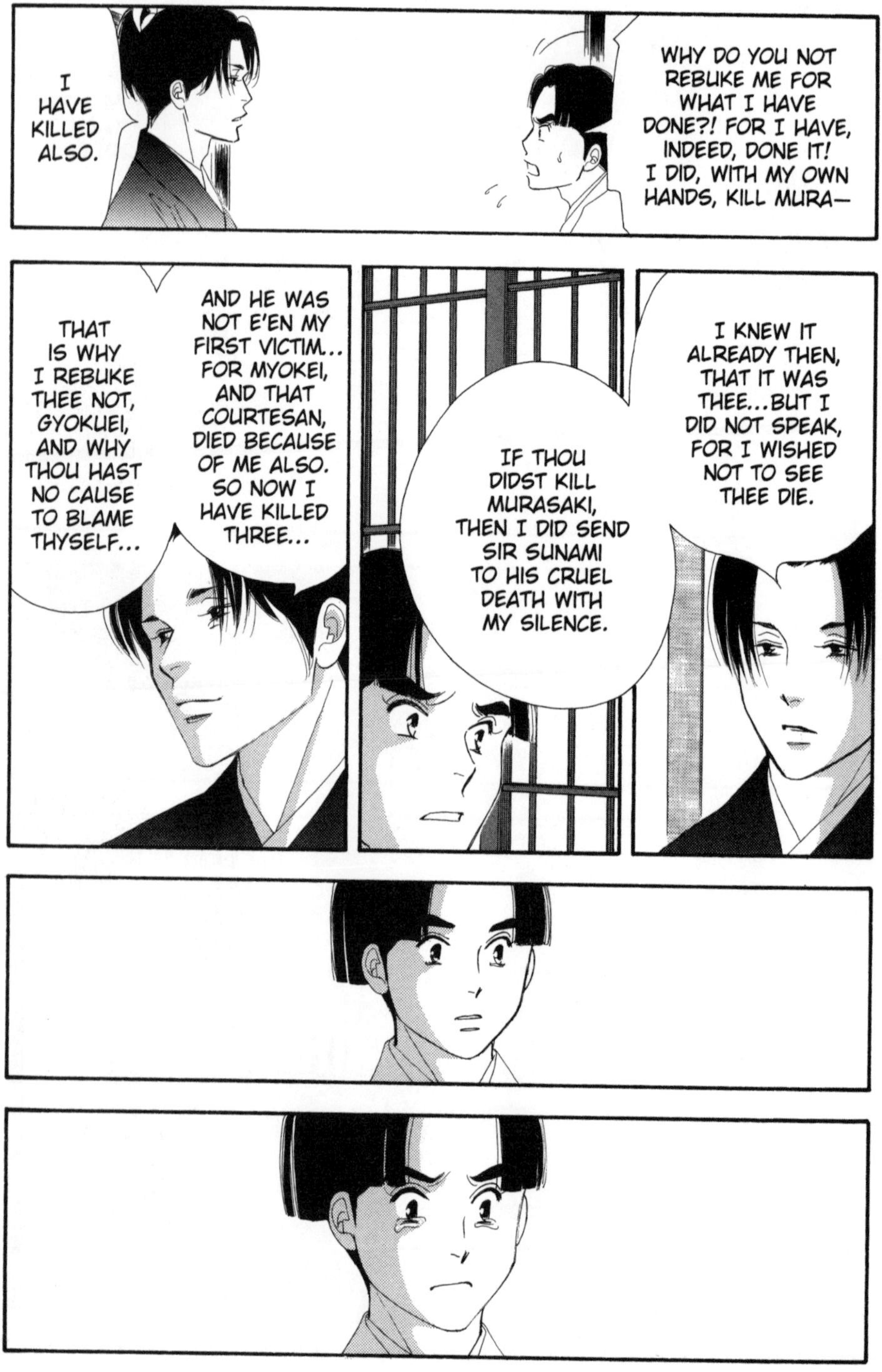
WHY DO YOU NOT REBUKE ME FOR WHAT I HAVE DONE?! FOR I HAVE, INDEED, DONE IT! I DID, WITH MY OWN HANDS, KILL MURA—
I HAVE KILLED ALSO.
I KNEW IT ALREADY THEN, THAT IT WAS THEE...BUT I DID NOT SPEAK, FOR I WISHED NOT TO SEE THEE DIE.
IF THOU DIDST KILL MURASAKI, THEN I DID SEND SIR SUNAMI TO HIS CRUEL DEATH WITH MY SILENCE.
AND HE WAS NOT E'EN MY FIRST VICTIM... FOR MYOKEI, AND THAT COURTESAN, DIED BECAUSE OF ME ALSO. SO NOW I HAVE KILLED THREE...
THAT IS WHY I REBUKE THEE NOT, GYOKUEI, AND WHY THOU HAST NO CAUSE TO BLAME THYSELF...

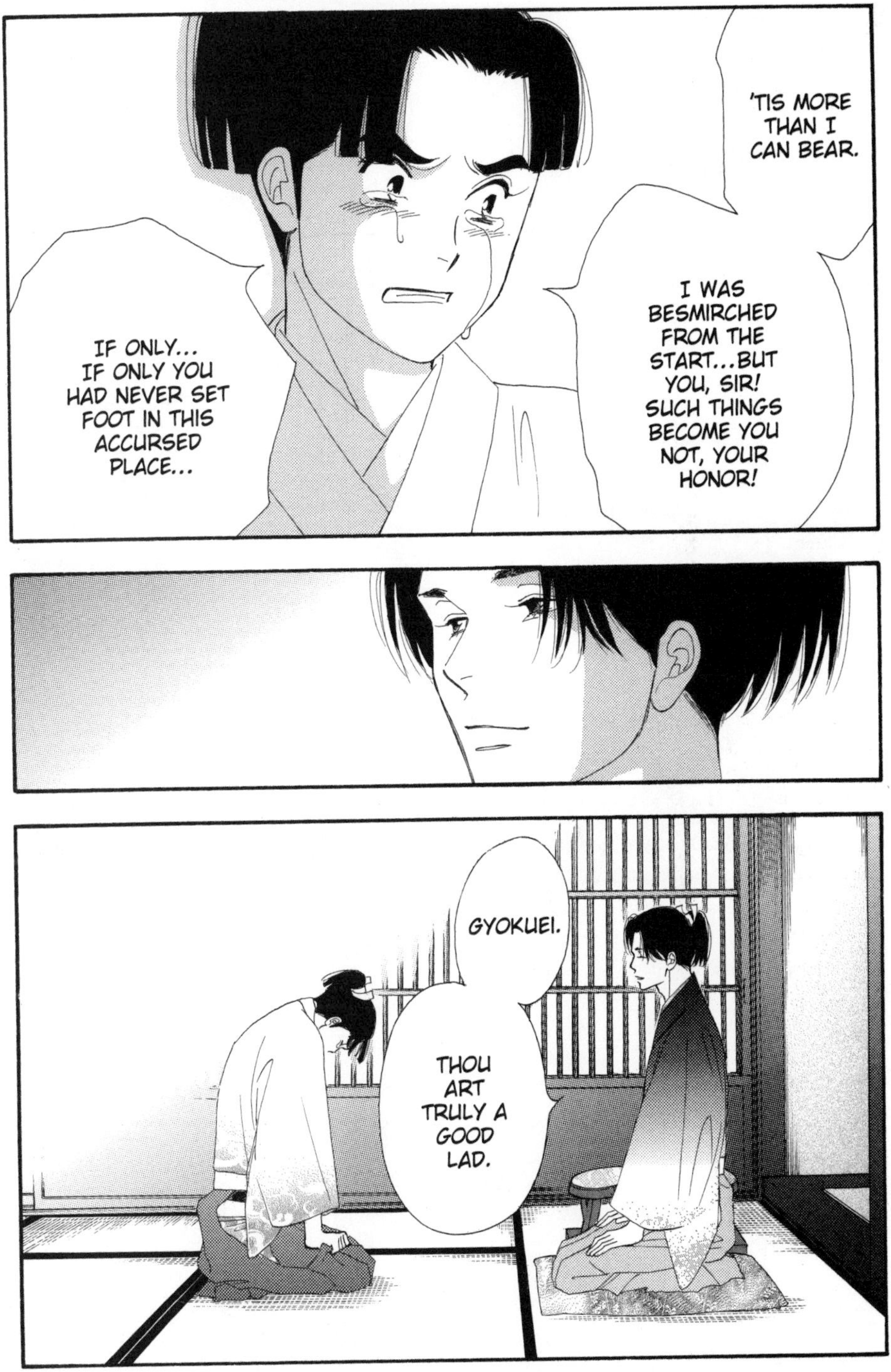
'TIS MORE THAN I CAN BEAR.
I WAS BESMIRCHED FROM THE START...BUT YOU, SIR! SUCH THINGS BECOME YOU NOT, YOUR HONOR!
IF ONLY... IF ONLY YOU HAD NEVER SET FOOT IN THIS ACCURSED PLACE...
GYOKUEI.
THOU ART TRULY A GOOD LAD.

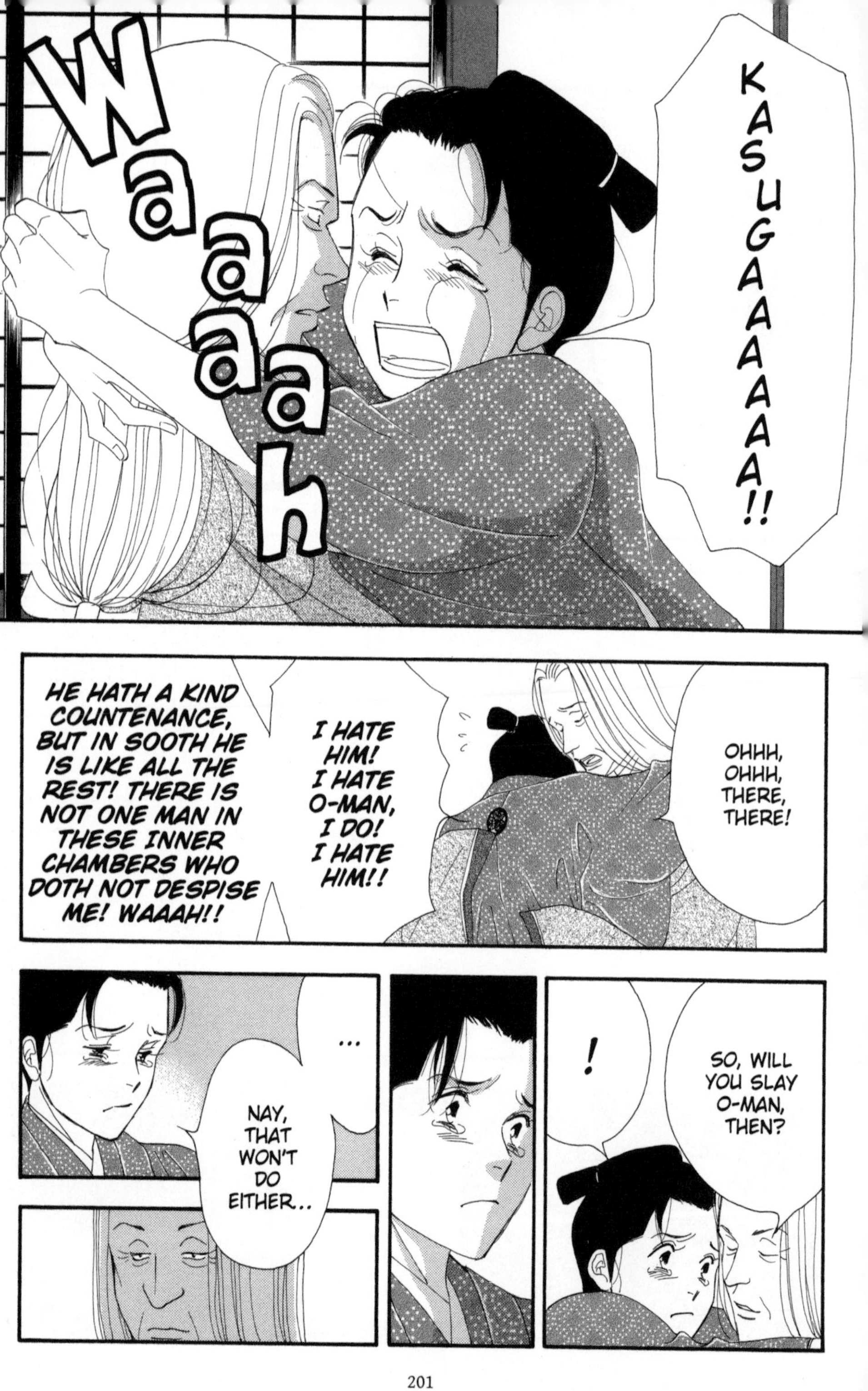
KASUGAAAAAAAA!!
Waaaaah
OHHH, OHHH, THERE, THERE!
I HATE HIM! I HATE O-MAN, I DO! I HATE HIM!!
HE HATH A KIND COUNTENANCE, BUT IN SOOTH HE IS LIKE ALL THE REST! THERE IS NOT ONE MAN IN THESE INNER CHAMBERS WHO DOTH NOT DESPISE ME! WAAAH!!
SO, WILL YOU SLAY O-MAN, THEN?
!
...
NAY, THAT WON'T DO EITHER...

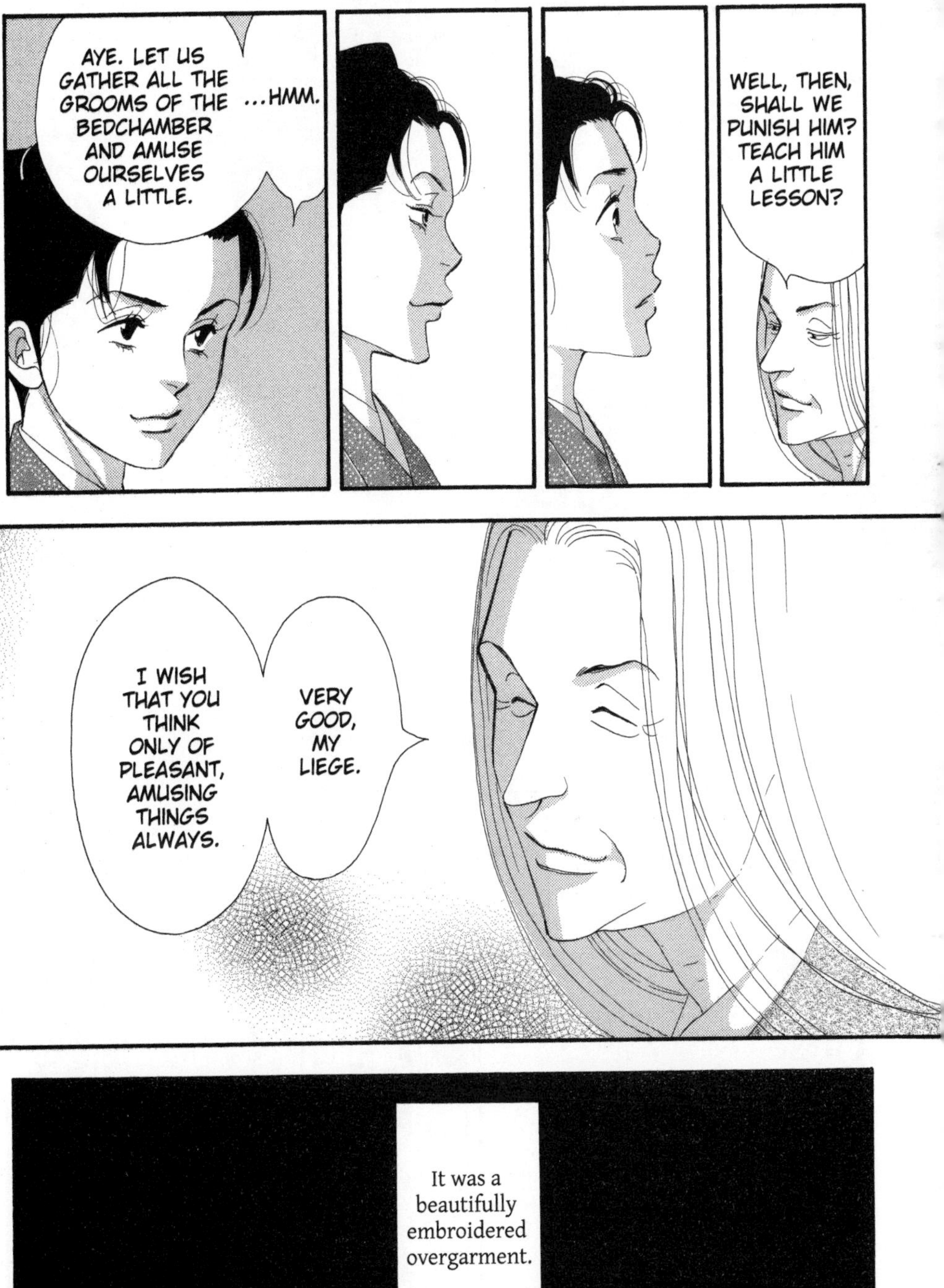
WELL, THEN, SHALL WE PUNISH HIM? TEACH HIM A LITTLE LESSON?
...HMM.
AYE. LET US GATHER ALL THE GROOMS OF THE BEDCHAMBER AND AMUSE OURSELVES A LITTLE.
VERY GOOD, MY LIEGE.
I WISH THAT YOU THINK ONLY OF PLEASANT, AMUSING THINGS ALWAYS.
It was a beautifully embroidered overgarment.

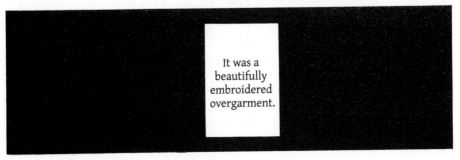

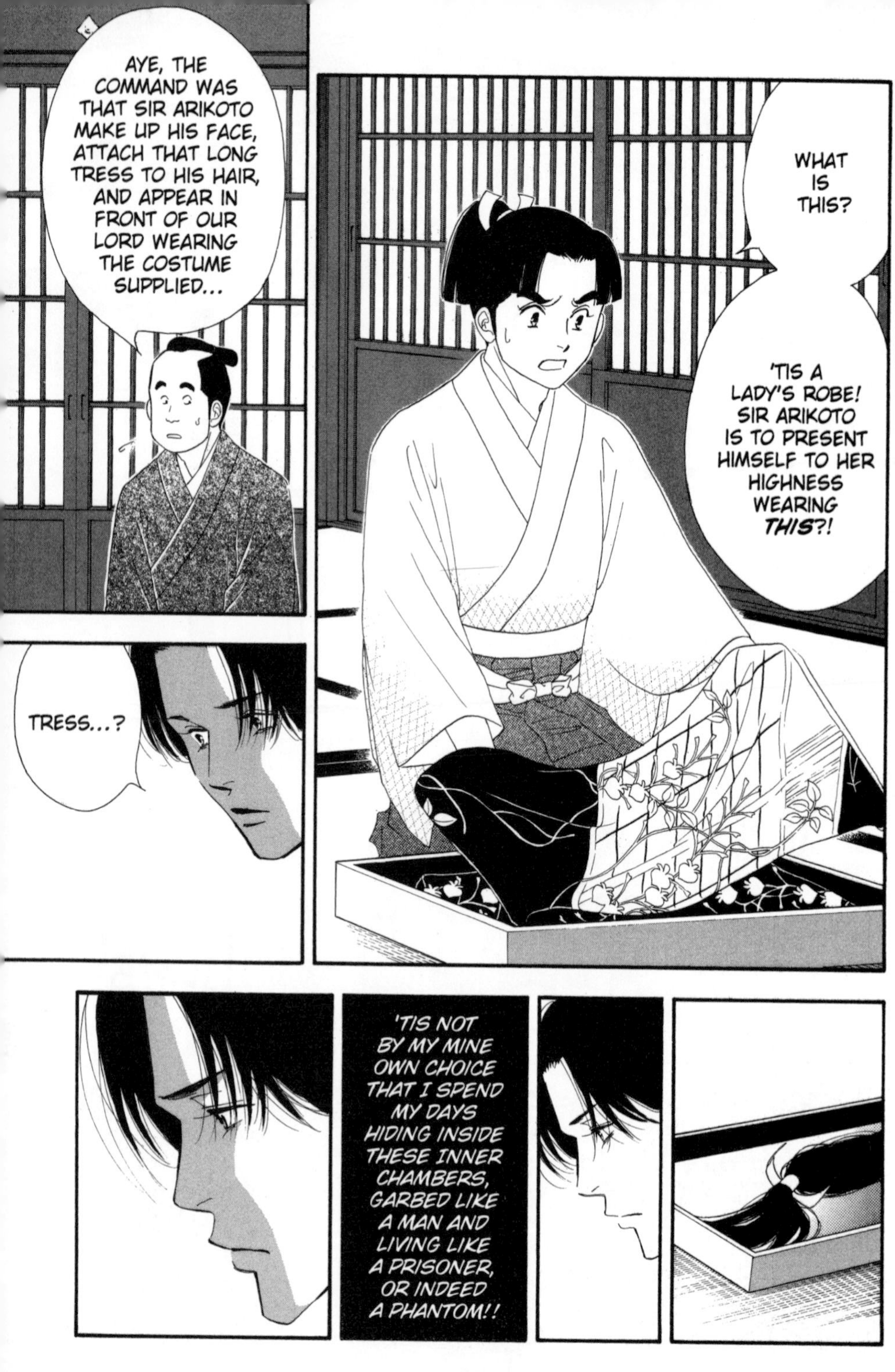
WHAT IS THIS?
'TIS A LADY'S ROBE! SIR ARIKOTO IS TO PRESENT HIMSELF TO HER HIGHNESS WEARING *THIS*?!
AYE, THE COMMAND WAS THAT SIR ARIKOTO MAKE UP HIS FACE, ATTACH THAT LONG TRESS TO HIS HAIR, AND APPEAR IN FRONT OF OUR LORD WEARING THE COSTUME SUPPLIED...
TRESS...?
'TIS NOT BY MY MINE OWN CHOICE THAT I SPEND MY DAYS HIDING INSIDE THESE INNER CHAMBERS, GARBED LIKE A MAN AND LIVING LIKE A PRISONER, OR INDEED A PHANTOM!!

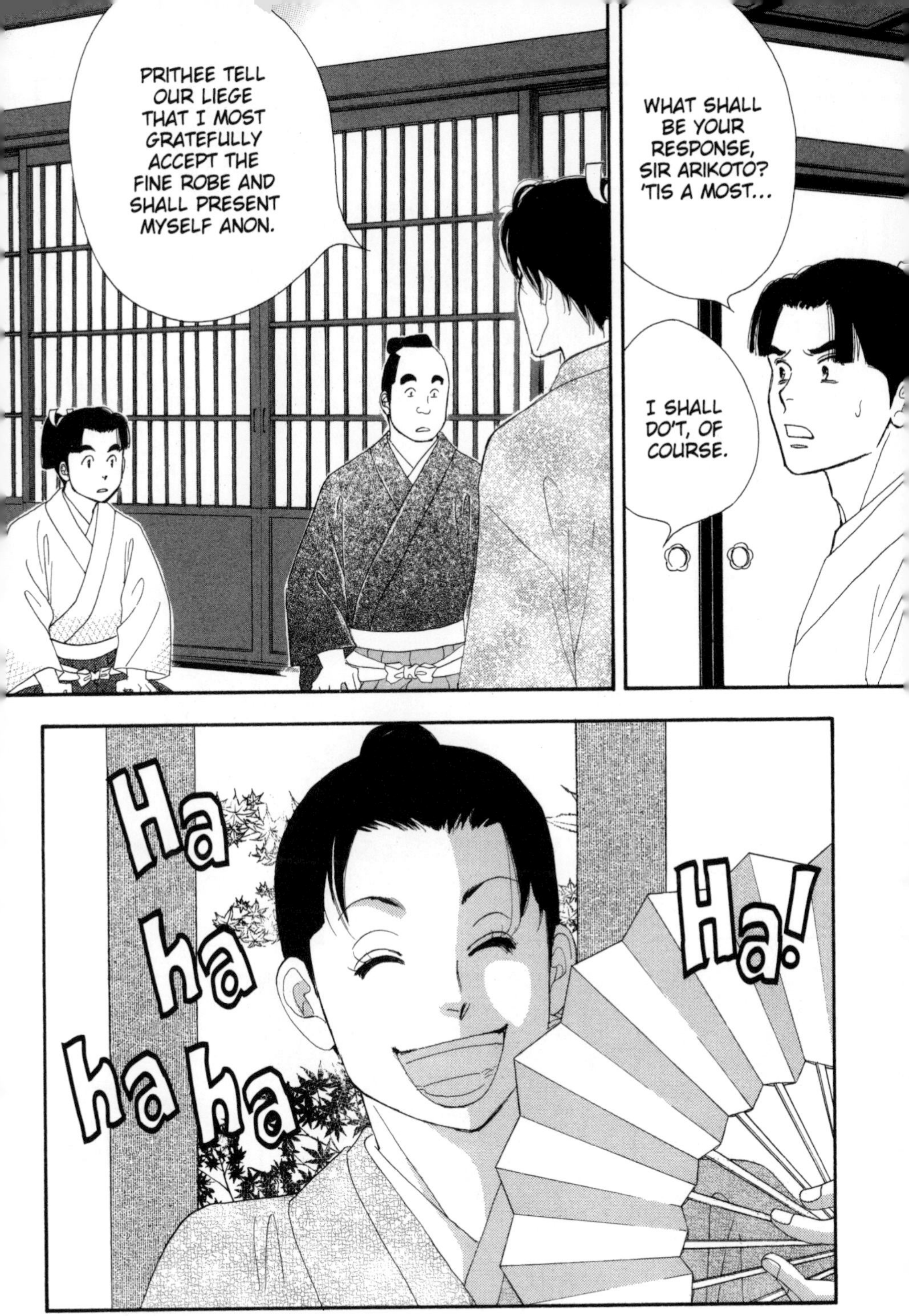
WHAT SHALL BE YOUR RESPONSE, SIR ARIKOTO? 'TIS A MOST...
I SHALL DO'T, OF COURSE.
PRITHEE TELL OUR LIEGE THAT I MOST GRATEFULLY ACCEPT THE FINE ROBE AND SHALL PRESENT MYSELF ANON.
Ha ha ha ha ha
Ha!

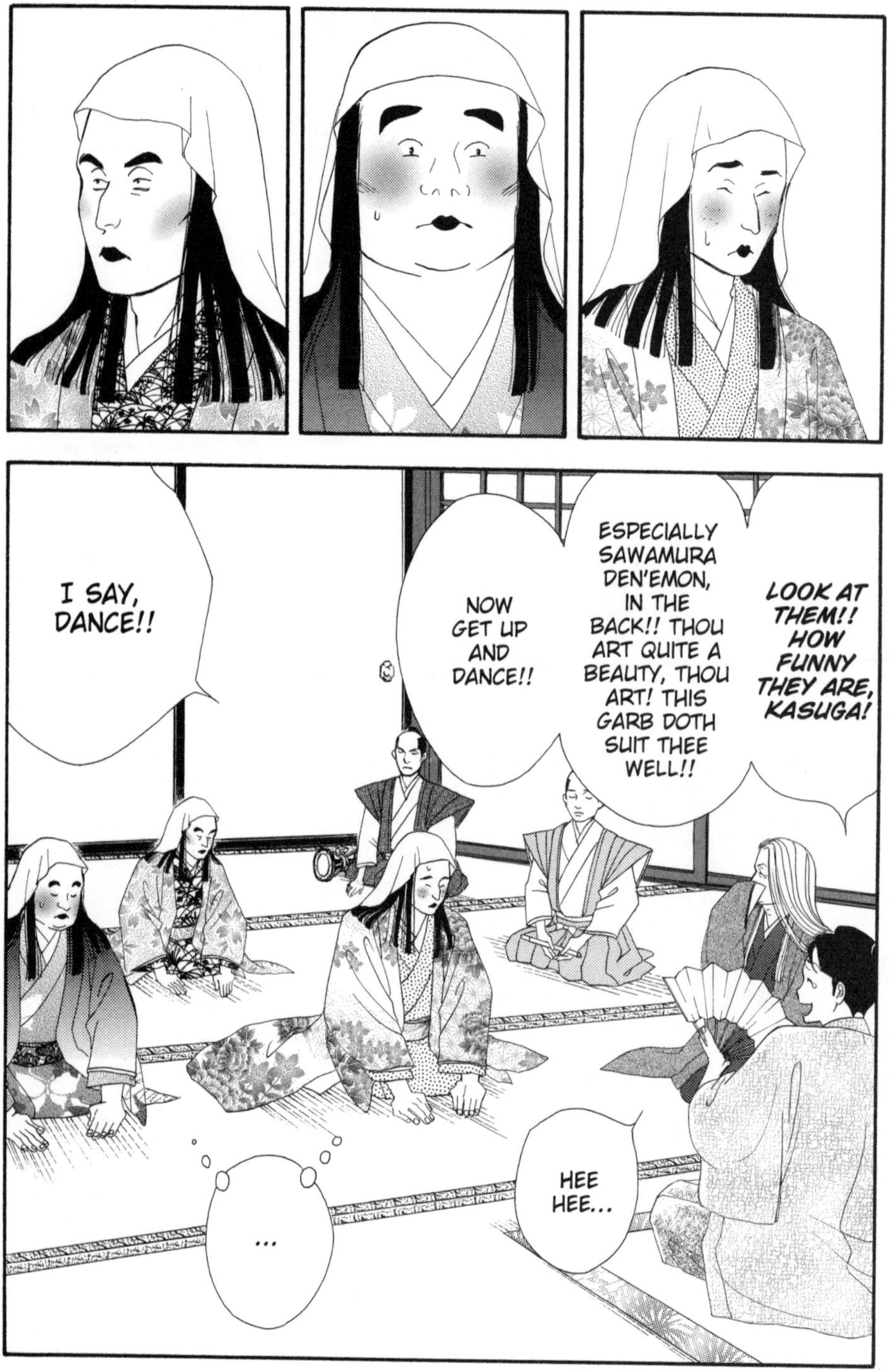
LOOK AT THEM!! HOW FUNNY THEY ARE, KASUGA!
ESPECIALLY SAWAMURA DEN'EMON, IN THE BACK!! THOU ART QUITE A BEAUTY, THOU ART! THIS GARB DOTH SUIT THEE WELL!!
NOW GET UP AND DANCE!!
I SAY, DANCE!!
HEE HEE...
...

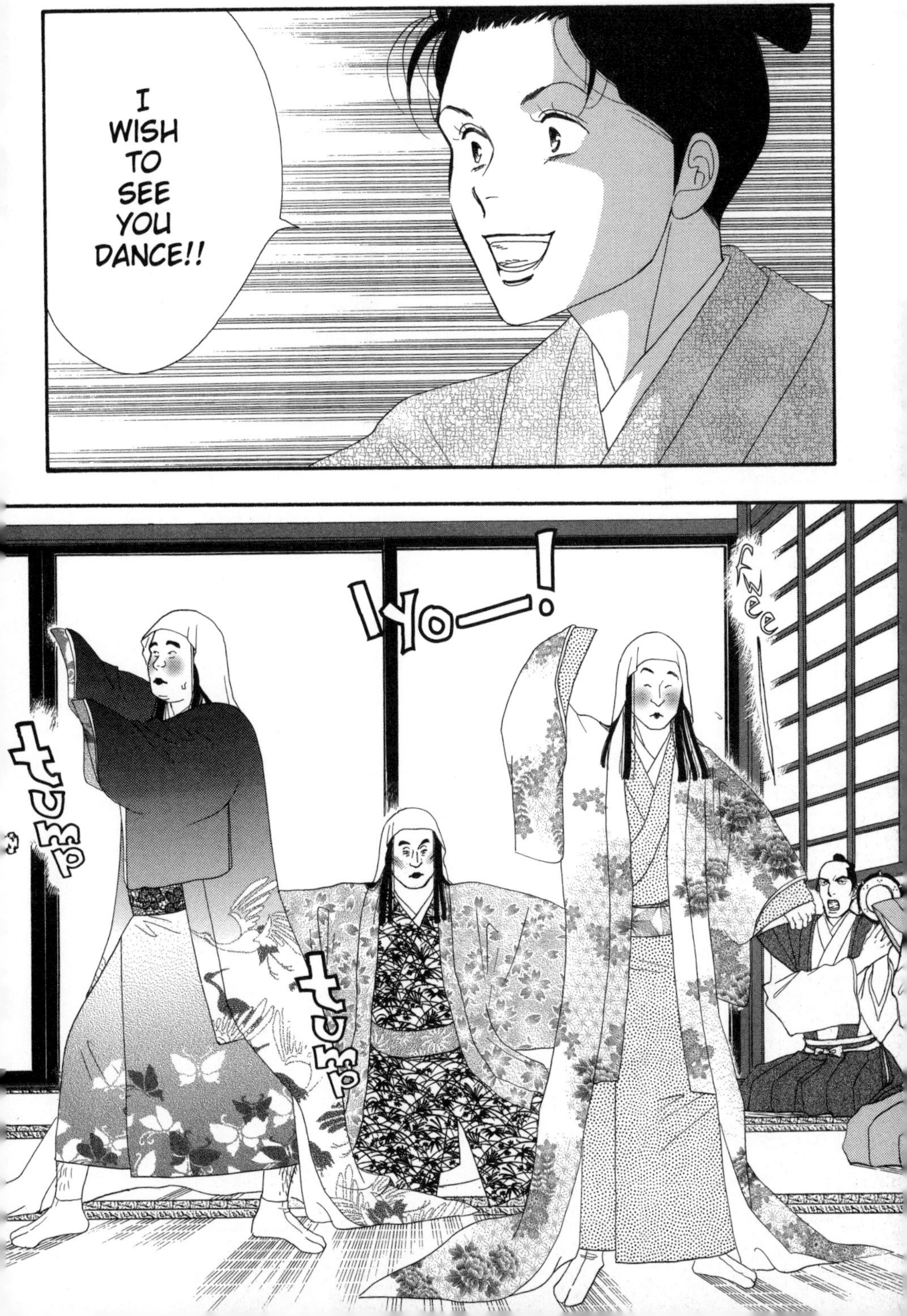
I WISH TO SEE YOU DANCE!!
fwee
IYO—!

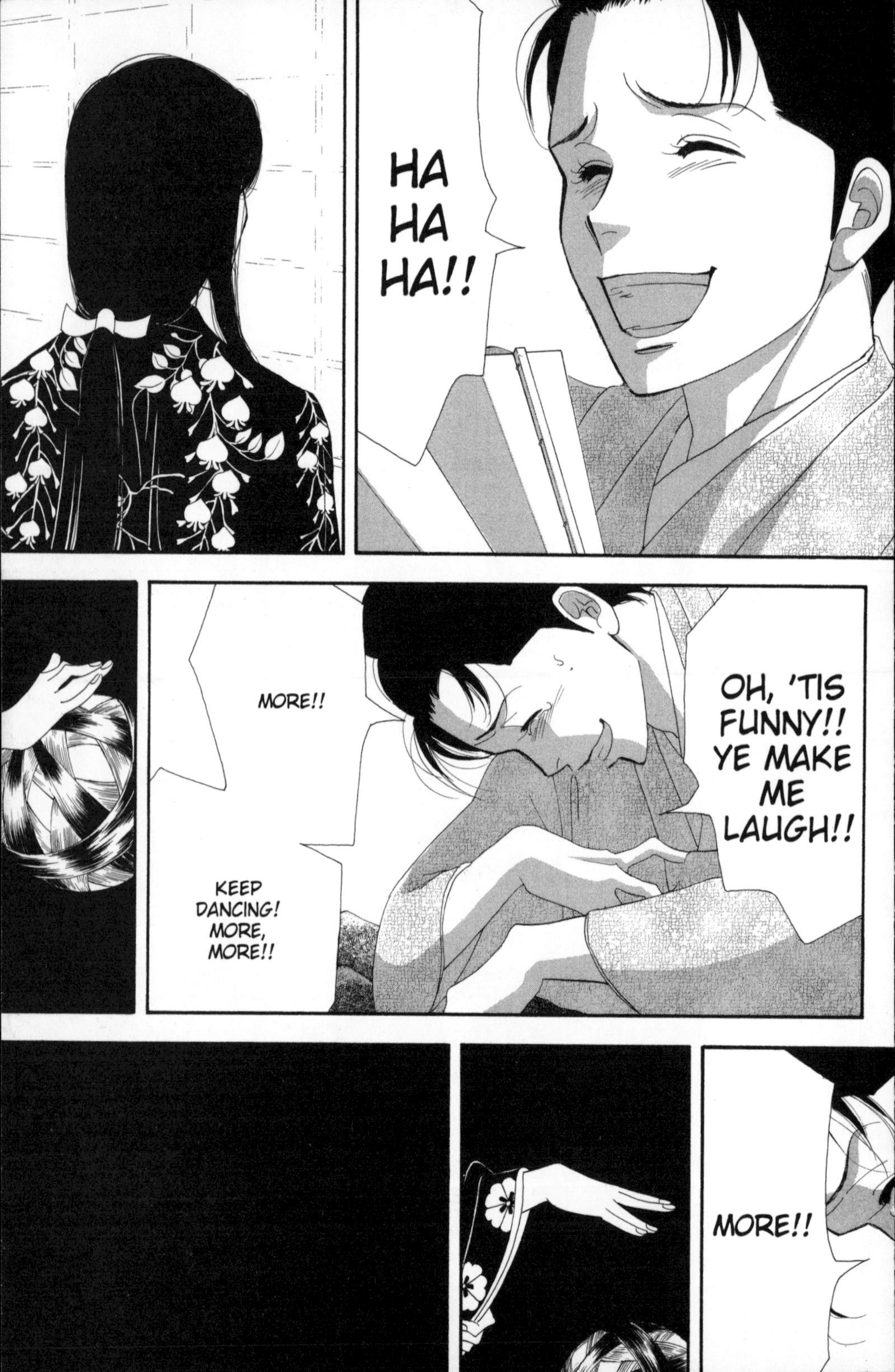
HA HA HA!!
OH, 'TIS FUNNY!! YE MAKE ME LAUGH!!
MORE!!
KEEP DANCING! MORE, MORE!!
MORE!!

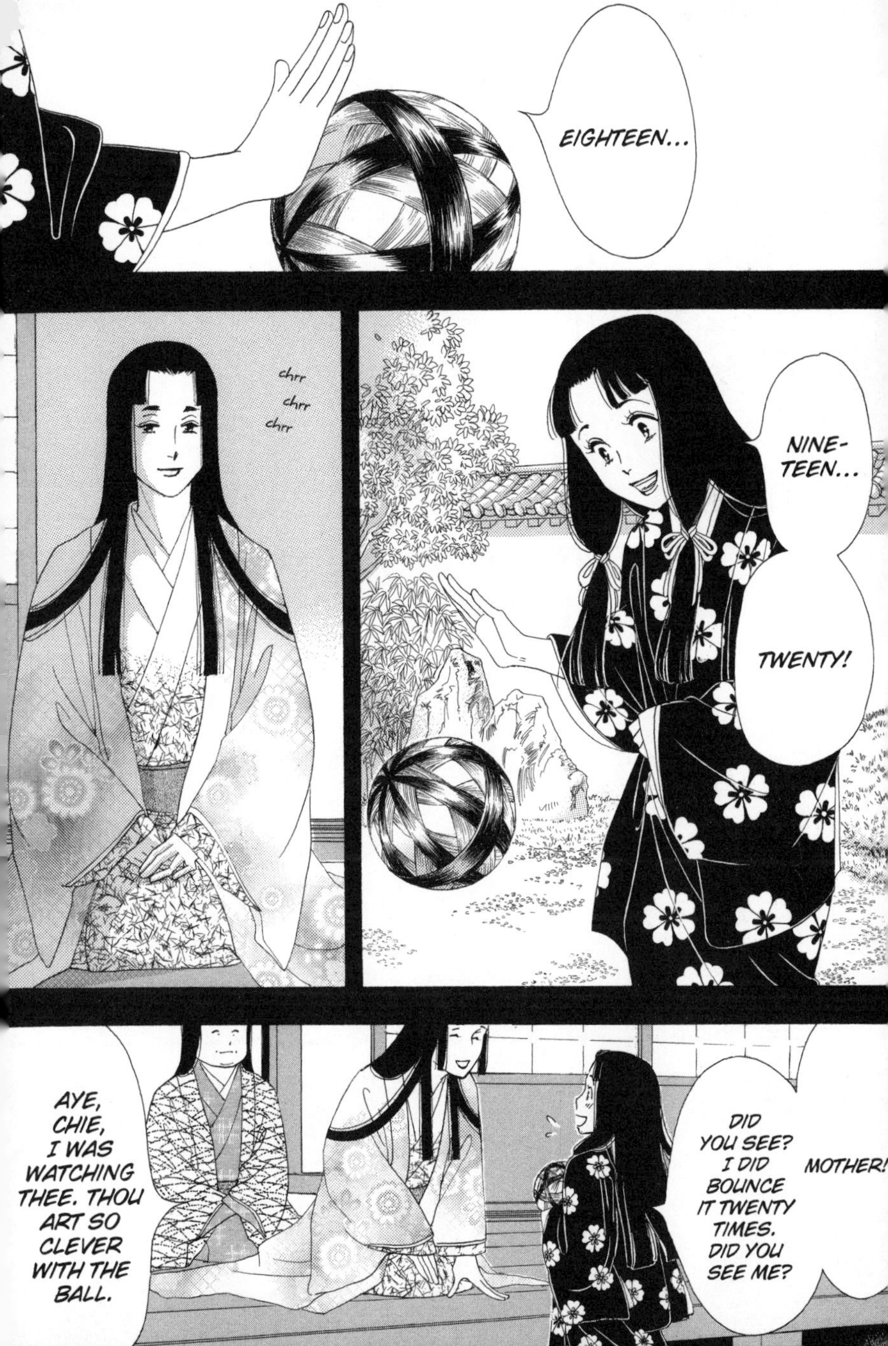
EIGHTEEN...
NINE-TEEN...
TWENTY!
chrr chrr chrr
MOTHER!
DID YOU SEE? I DID BOUNCE IT TWENTY TIMES. DID YOU SEE ME?
AYE, CHIE, I WAS WATCHING THEE. THOU ART SO CLEVER WITH THE BALL.

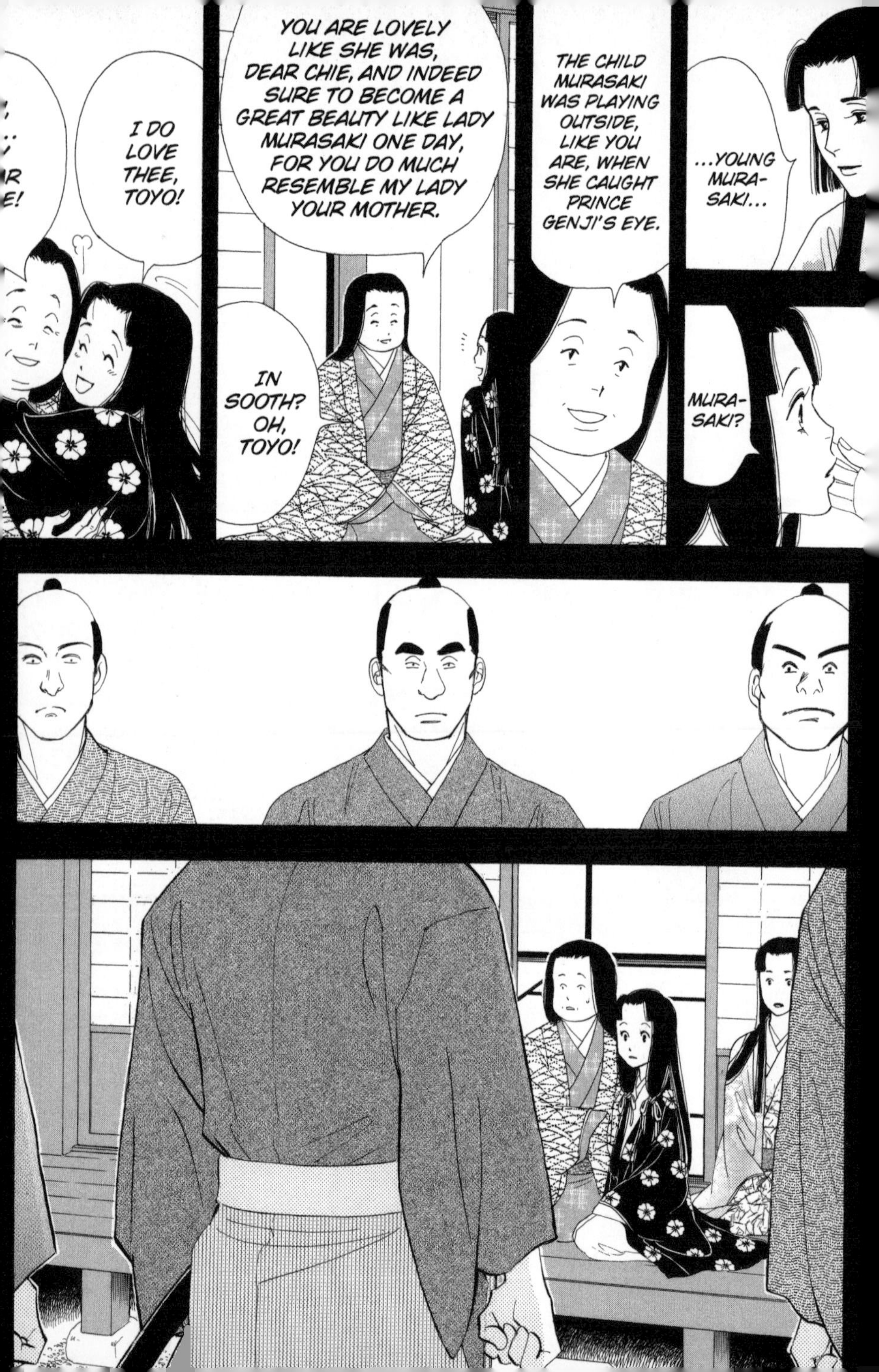
...YOUNG MURA-SAKI...
MURA-SAKI?
THE CHILD MURASAKI WAS PLAYING OUTSIDE, LIKE YOU ARE, WHEN SHE CAUGHT PRINCE GENJI'S EYE.
YOU ARE LOVELY LIKE SHE WAS, DEAR CHIE, AND INDEED SURE TO BECOME A GREAT BEAUTY LIKE LADY MURASAKI ONE DAY, FOR YOU DO MUCH RESEMBLE MY LADY YOUR MOTHER.
IN SOOTH? OH, TOYO!
I DO LOVE THEE, TOYO!

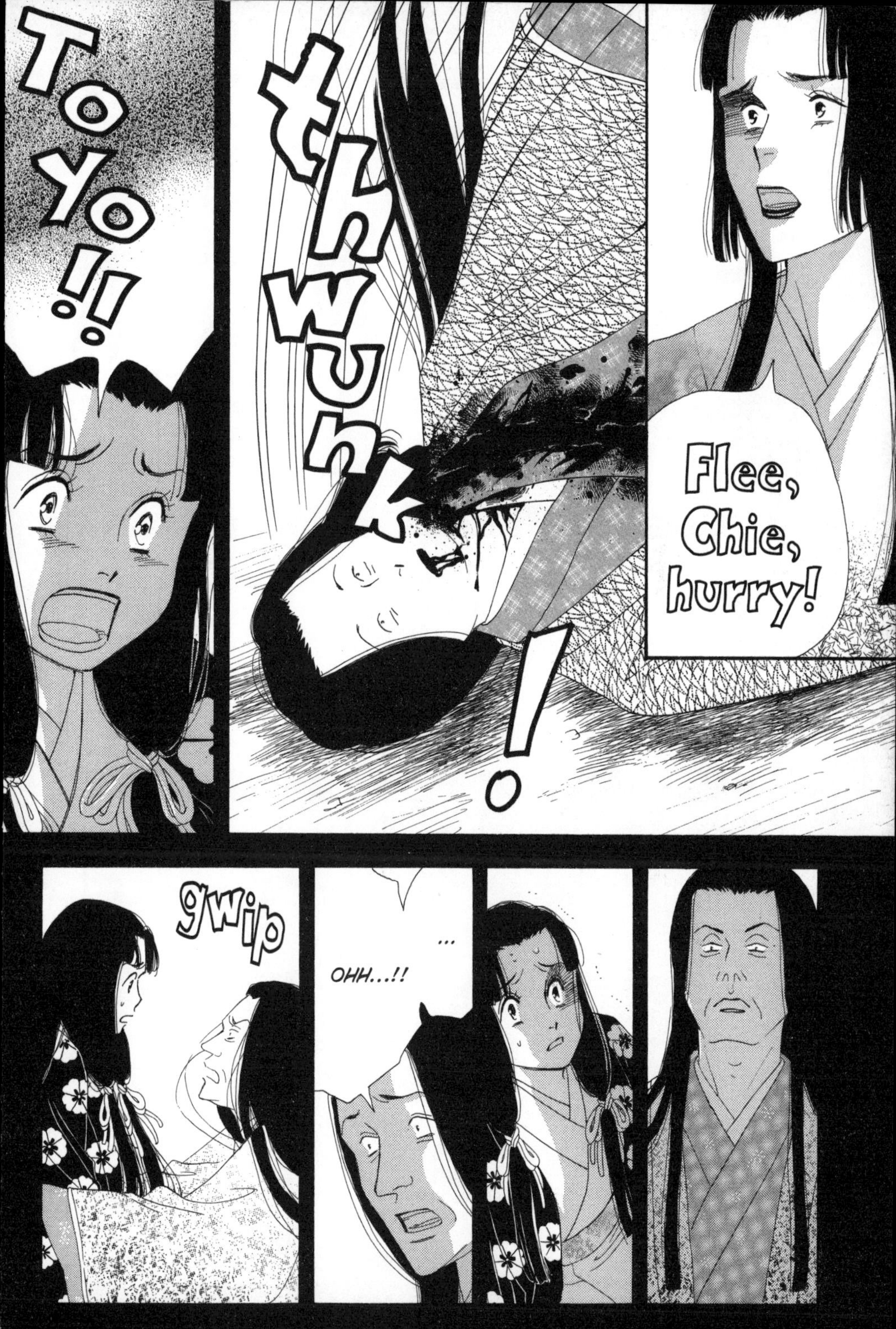
Flee, Chie, hurry!
thwunk!
Toyo!!
...
OHH...!!
gwip

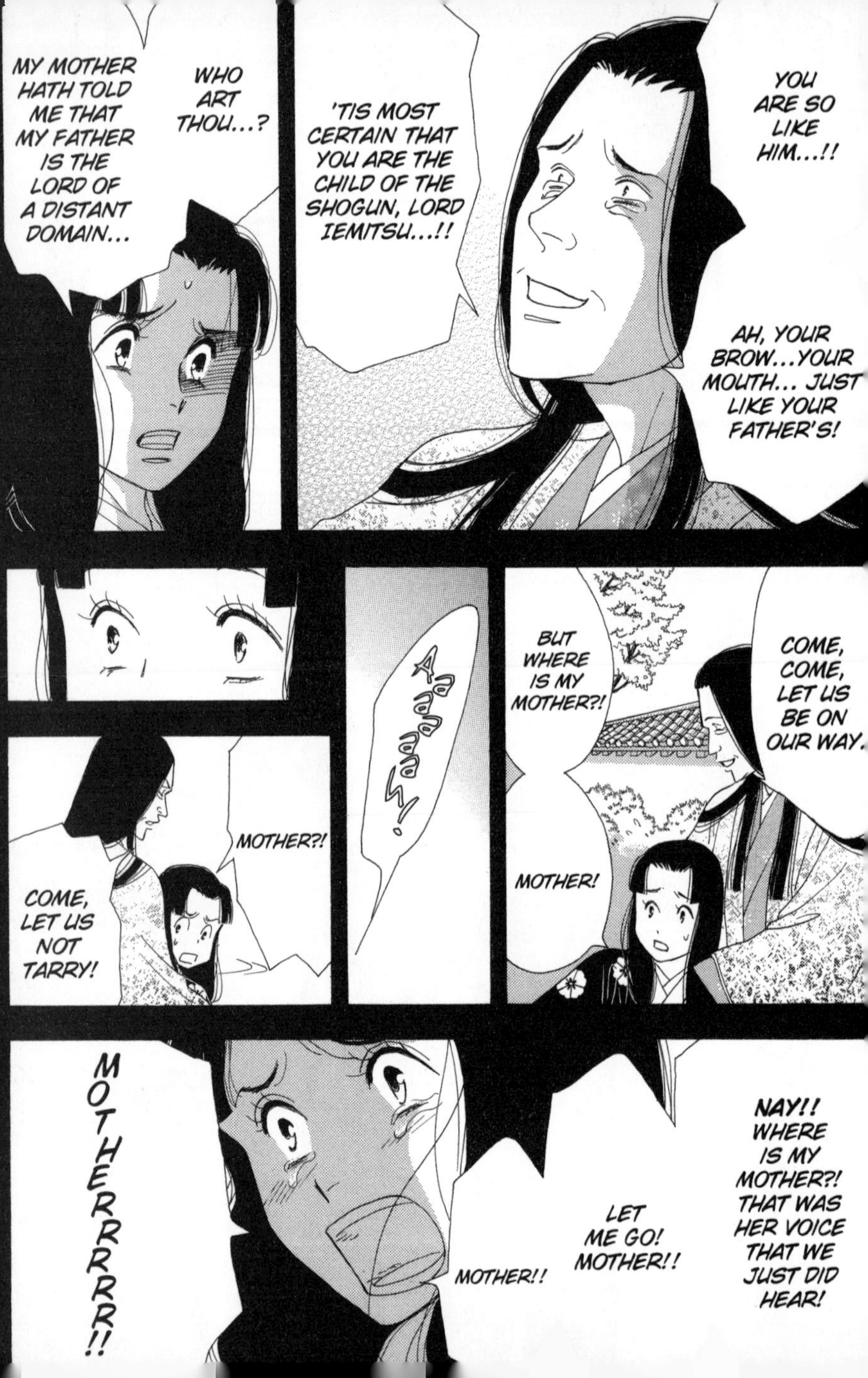
YOU ARE SO LIKE HIM...!!
'TIS MOST CERTAIN THAT YOU ARE THE CHILD OF THE SHOGUN, LORD IEMITSU...!!
AH, YOUR BROW...YOUR MOUTH... JUST LIKE YOUR FATHER'S!
WHO ART THOU...?
MY MOTHER HATH TOLD ME THAT MY FATHER IS THE LORD OF A DISTANT DOMAIN...
COME, COME, LET US BE ON OUR WAY.
BUT WHERE IS MY MOTHER?!
MOTHER!
Aaaaaah!
MOTHER?!
COME, LET US NOT TARRY!
NAY!! WHERE IS MY MOTHER?! THAT WAS HER VOICE THAT WE JUST DID HEAR!
LET ME GO! MOTHER!!
MOTHER!!
MOTHERRRRR!!

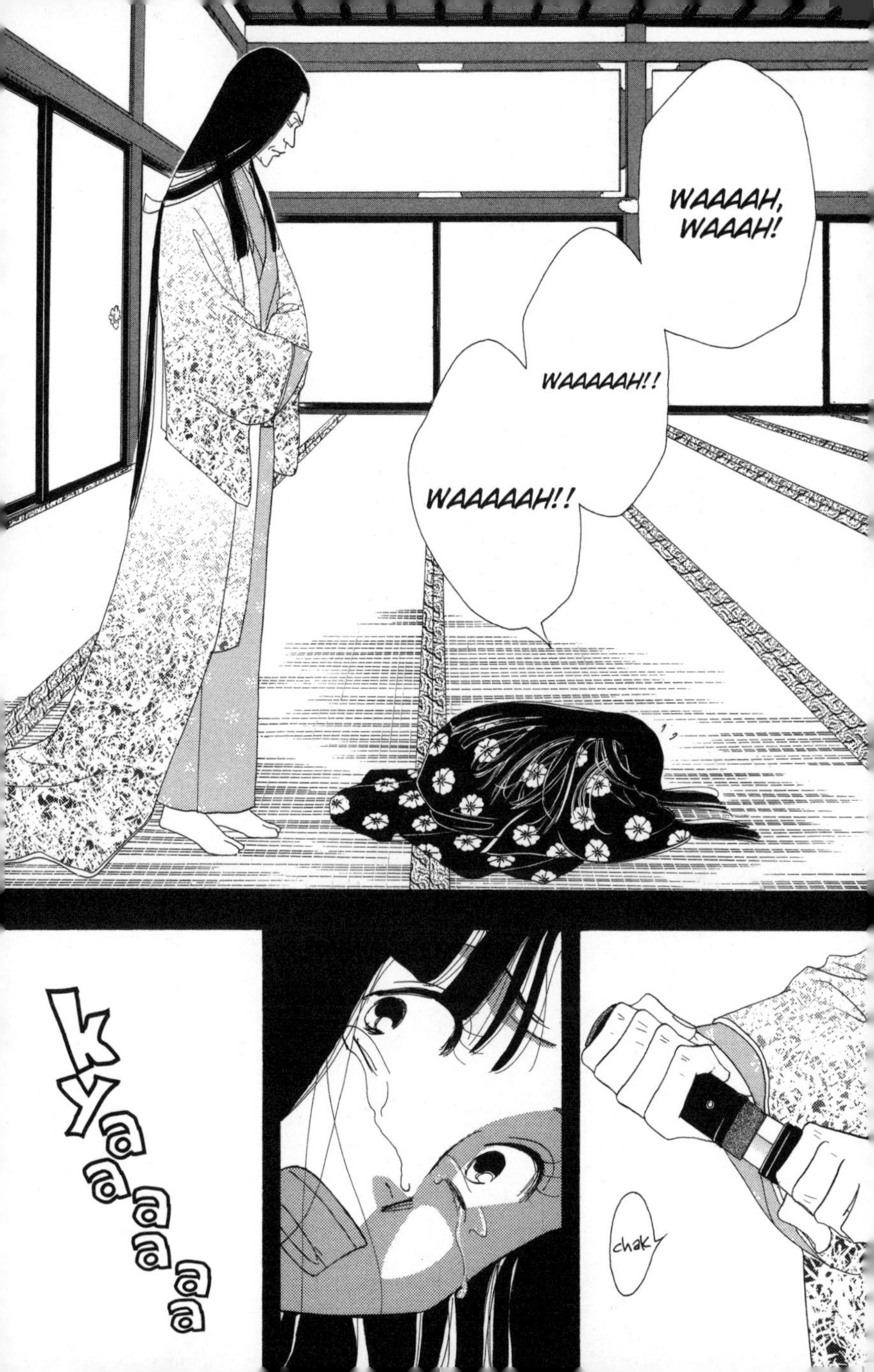
WAAAAH, WAAAH!
WAAAAAH!!
WAAAAAH!!
chak
kyaaaaaa

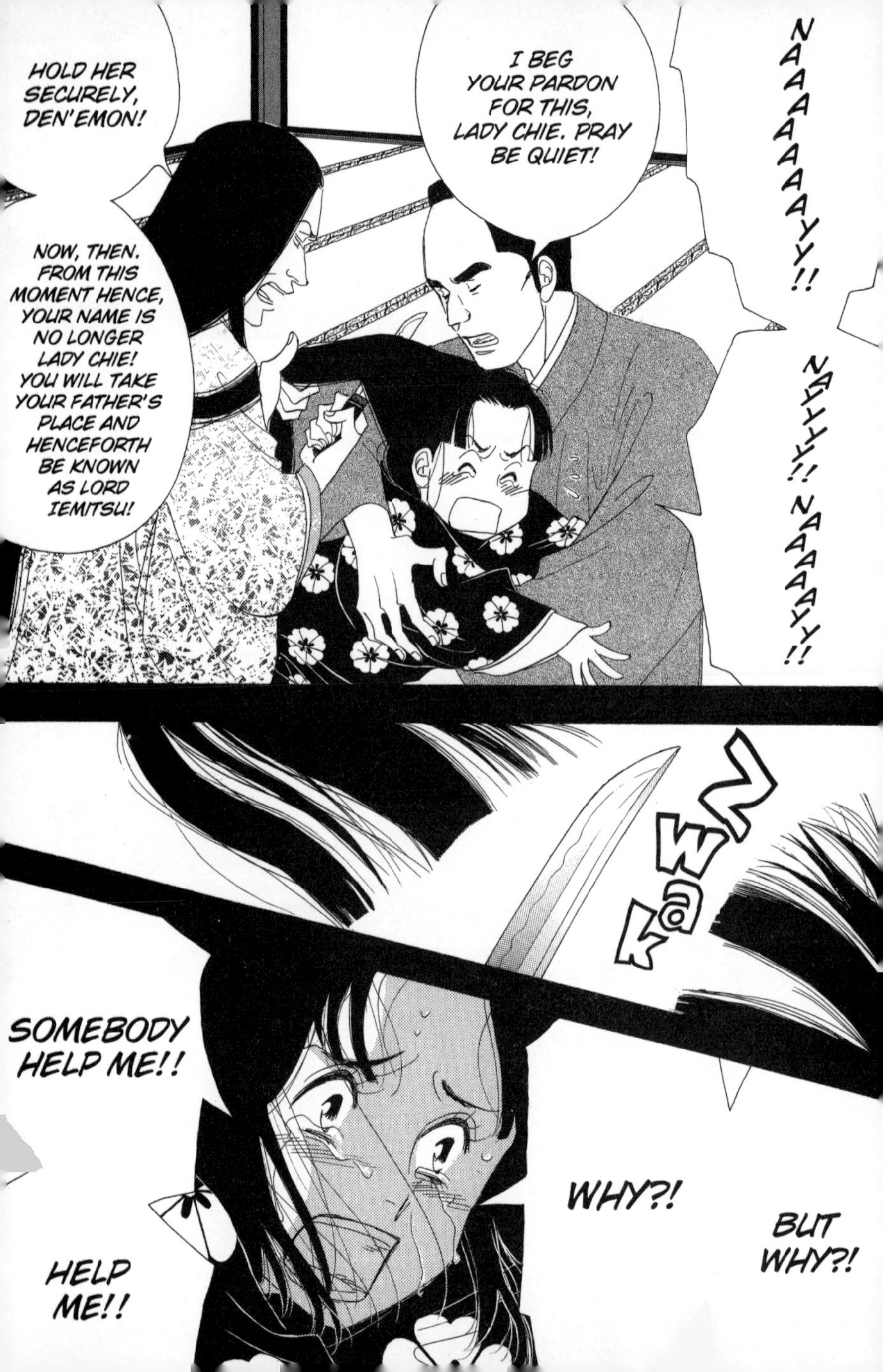
NAAAAAAAAYY!!
I BEG YOUR PARDON FOR THIS, LADY CHIE. PRAY BE QUIET!
HOLD HER SECURELY, DEN'EMON!
NOW, THEN. FROM THIS MOMENT HENCE, YOUR NAME IS NO LONGER LADY CHIE! YOU WILL TAKE YOUR FATHER'S PLACE AND HENCEFORTH BE KNOWN AS LORD IEMITSU!
NAYYYY!! NAAAAAYY!!
ZWAK
BUT WHY?!
WHY?!
SOMEBODY HELP ME!!
HELP ME!!

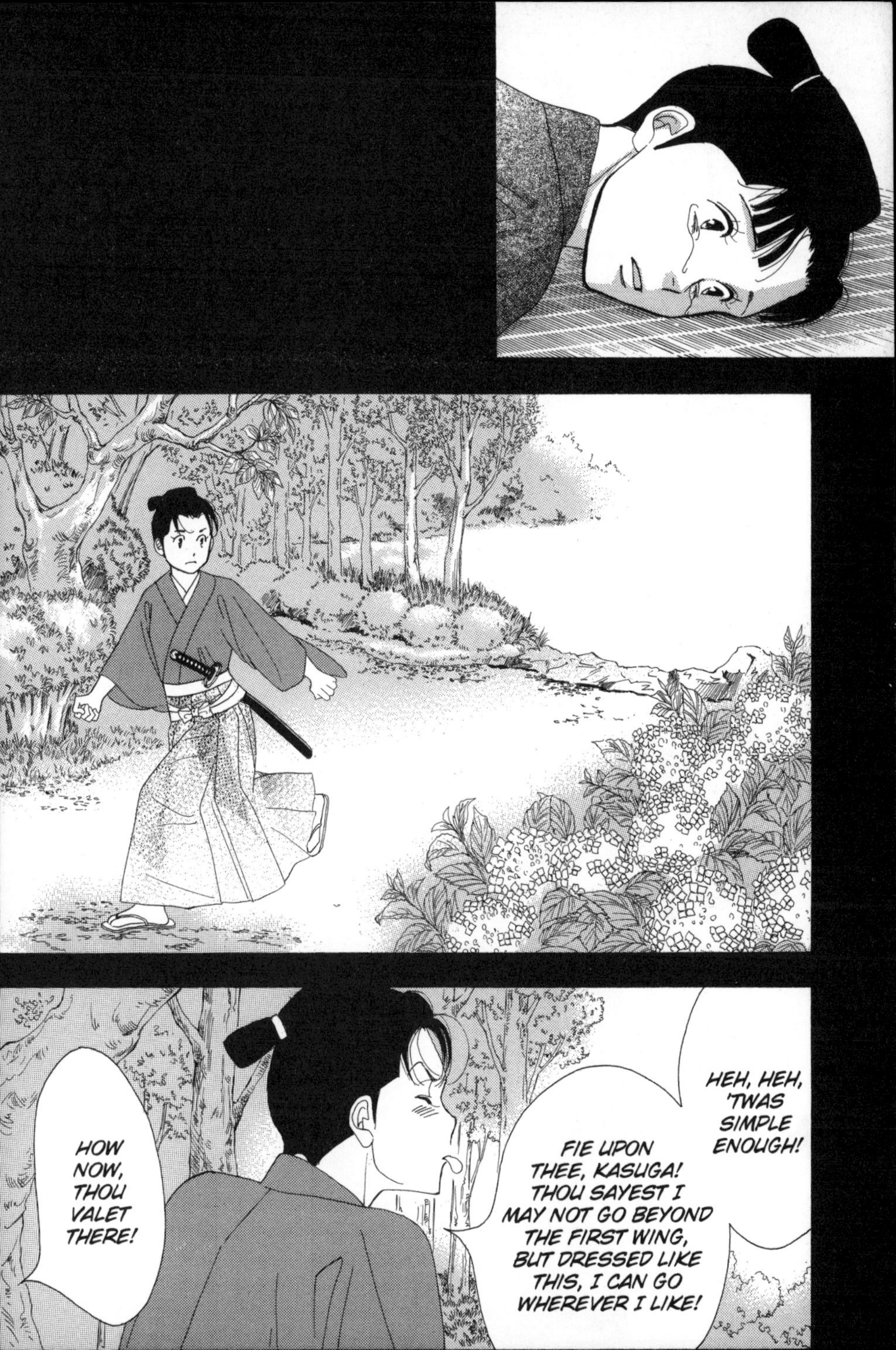
HEH, HEH, 'TWAS SIMPLE ENOUGH!
FIE UPON THEE, KASUGA! THOU SAYEST I MAY NOT GO BEYOND THE FIRST WING, BUT DRESSED LIKE THIS, I CAN GO WHEREVER I LIKE!
HOW NOW, THOU VALET THERE!

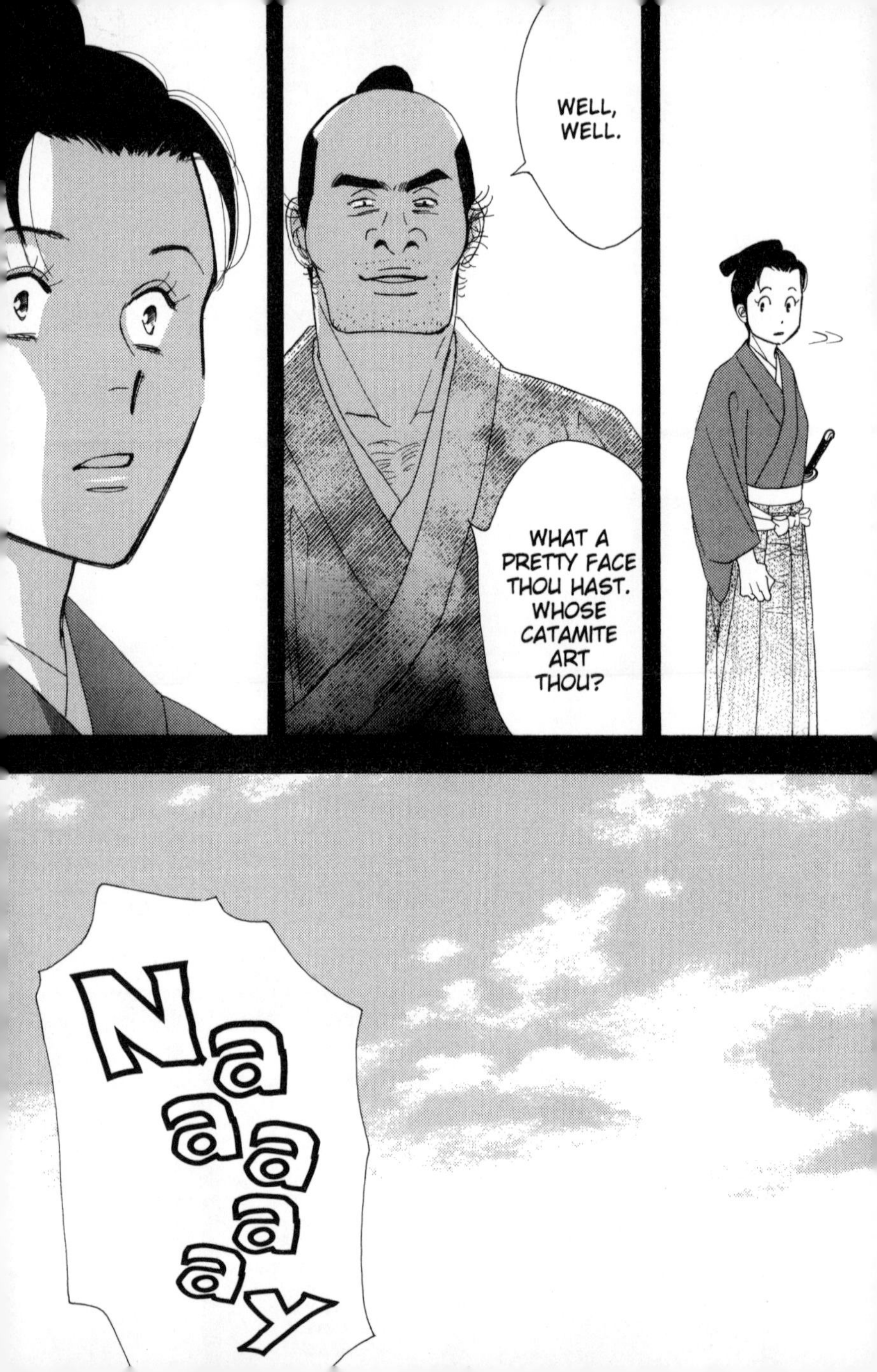
WELL, WELL.
WHAT A PRETTY FACE THOU HAST. WHOSE CATAMITE ART THOU?
Naaaaaay

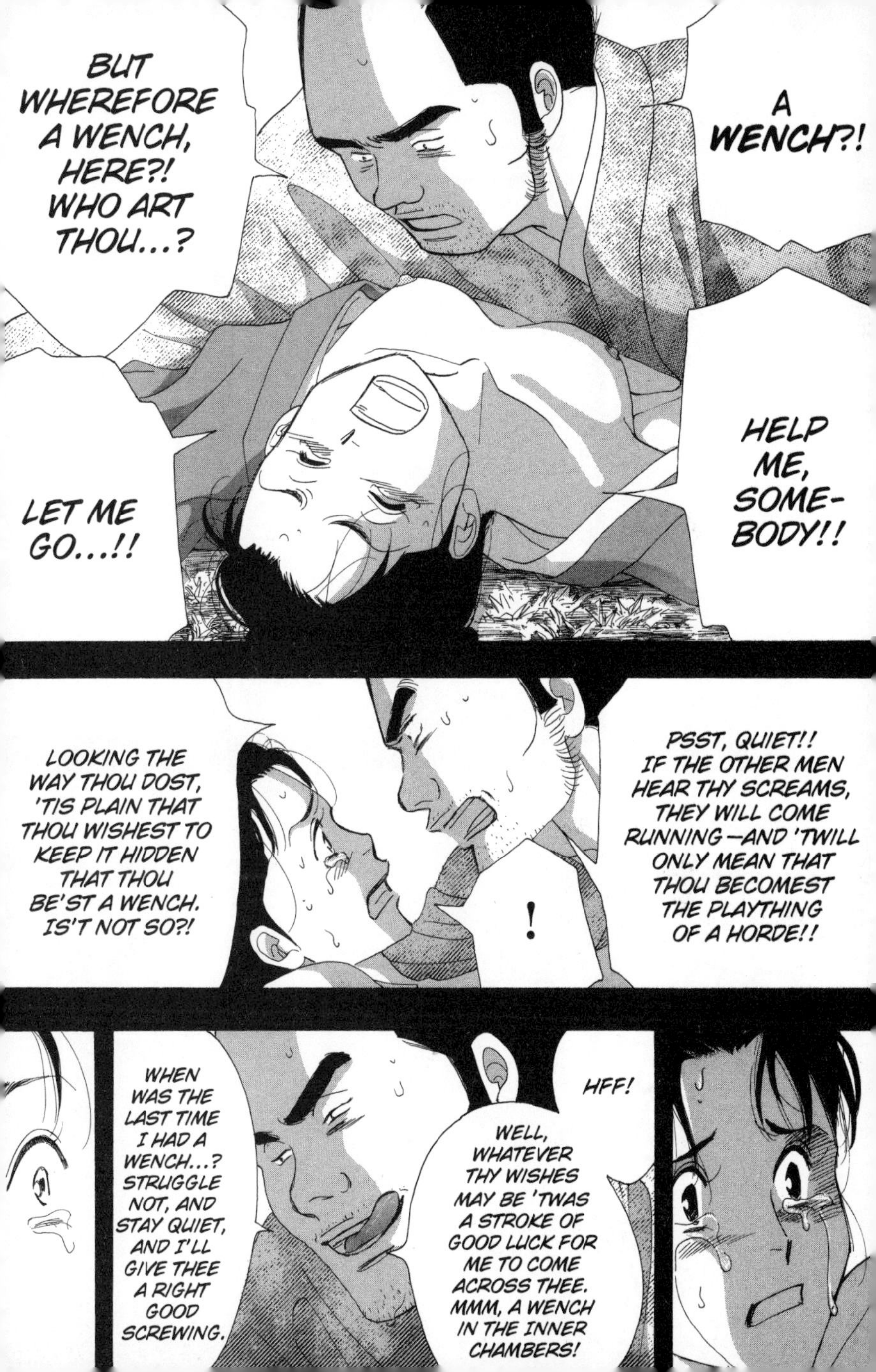
A WENCH?!
BUT WHEREFORE A WENCH, HERE?! WHO ART THOU...?
HELP ME, SOME-BODY!!
LET ME GO...!!
PSST, QUIET!! IF THE OTHER MEN HEAR THY SCREAMS, THEY WILL COME RUNNING—AND 'TWILL ONLY MEAN THAT THOU BECOMEST THE PLAYTHING OF A HORDE!!
!
LOOKING THE WAY THOU DOST, 'TIS PLAIN THAT THOU WISHEST TO KEEP IT HIDDEN THAT THOU BE'ST A WENCH. IS'T NOT SO?!
HFF!
WELL, WHATEVER THY WISHES MAY BE 'TWAS A STROKE OF GOOD LUCK FOR ME TO COME ACROSS THEE. MMM, A WENCH IN THE INNER CHAMBERS!
WHEN WAS THE LAST TIME I HAD A WENCH...? STRUGGLE NOT, AND STAY QUIET, AND I'LL GIVE THEE A RIGHT GOOD SCREWING.

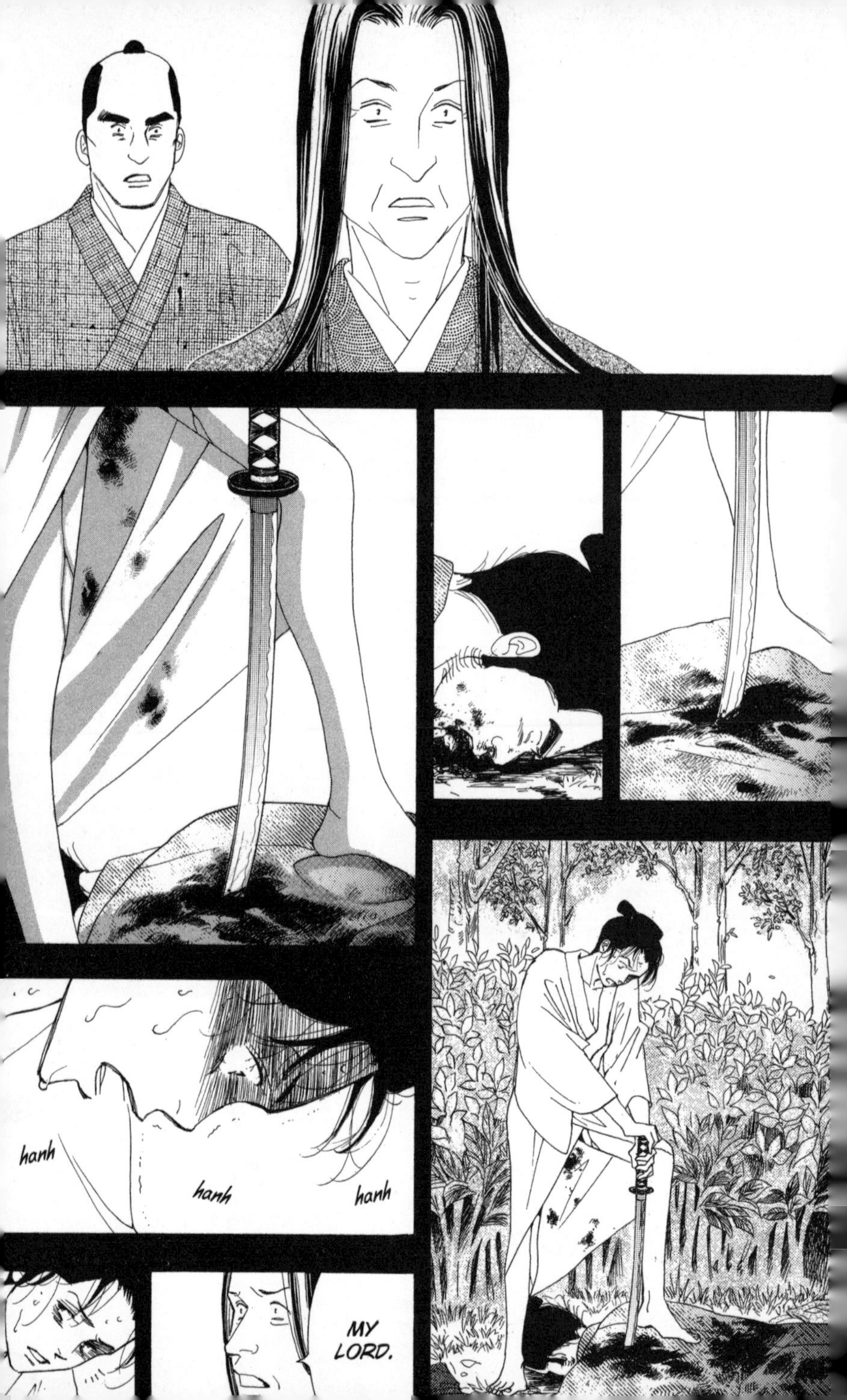
hanh
hanh
hanh
MY LORD.

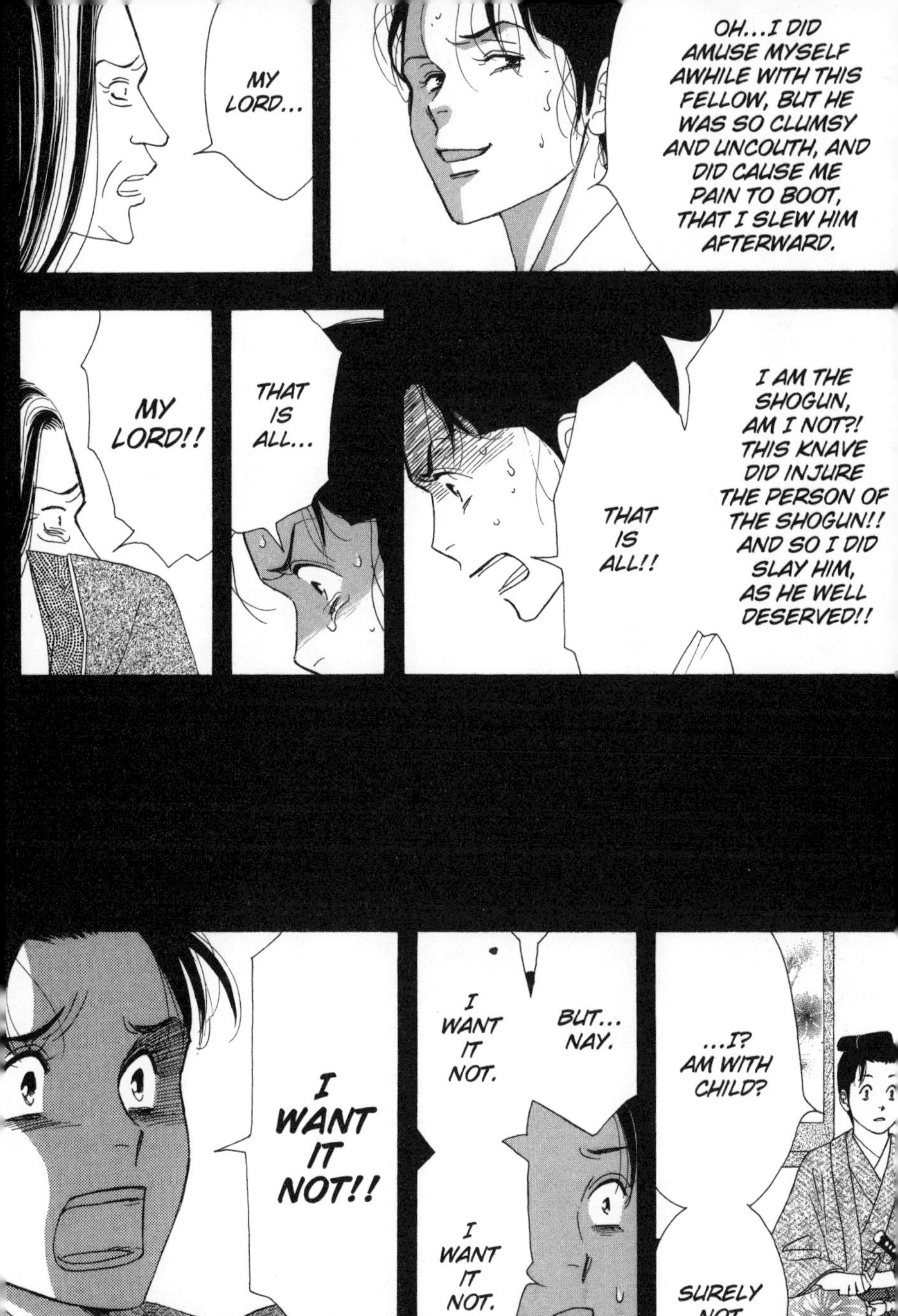

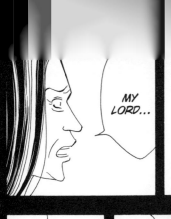

OH...I DID AMUSE MYSELF AWHILE WITH THIS FELLOW, BUT HE WAS SO CLUMSY AND UNCOUTH, AND DID CAUSE ME PAIN TO BOOT, THAT I SLEW HIM AFTERWARD.
MY LORD...
I AM THE SHOGUN, AM I NOT?! THIS KNAVE DID INJURE THE PERSON OF THE SHOGUN!! AND SO I DID SLAY HIM, AS HE WELL DESERVED!!
THAT IS ALL!!
THAT IS ALL...
MY LORD!!
...I? AM WITH CHILD?
SURELY NOT.
BUT... NAY.
I WANT IT NOT.
I WANT IT NOT.
I WANT IT NOT!!

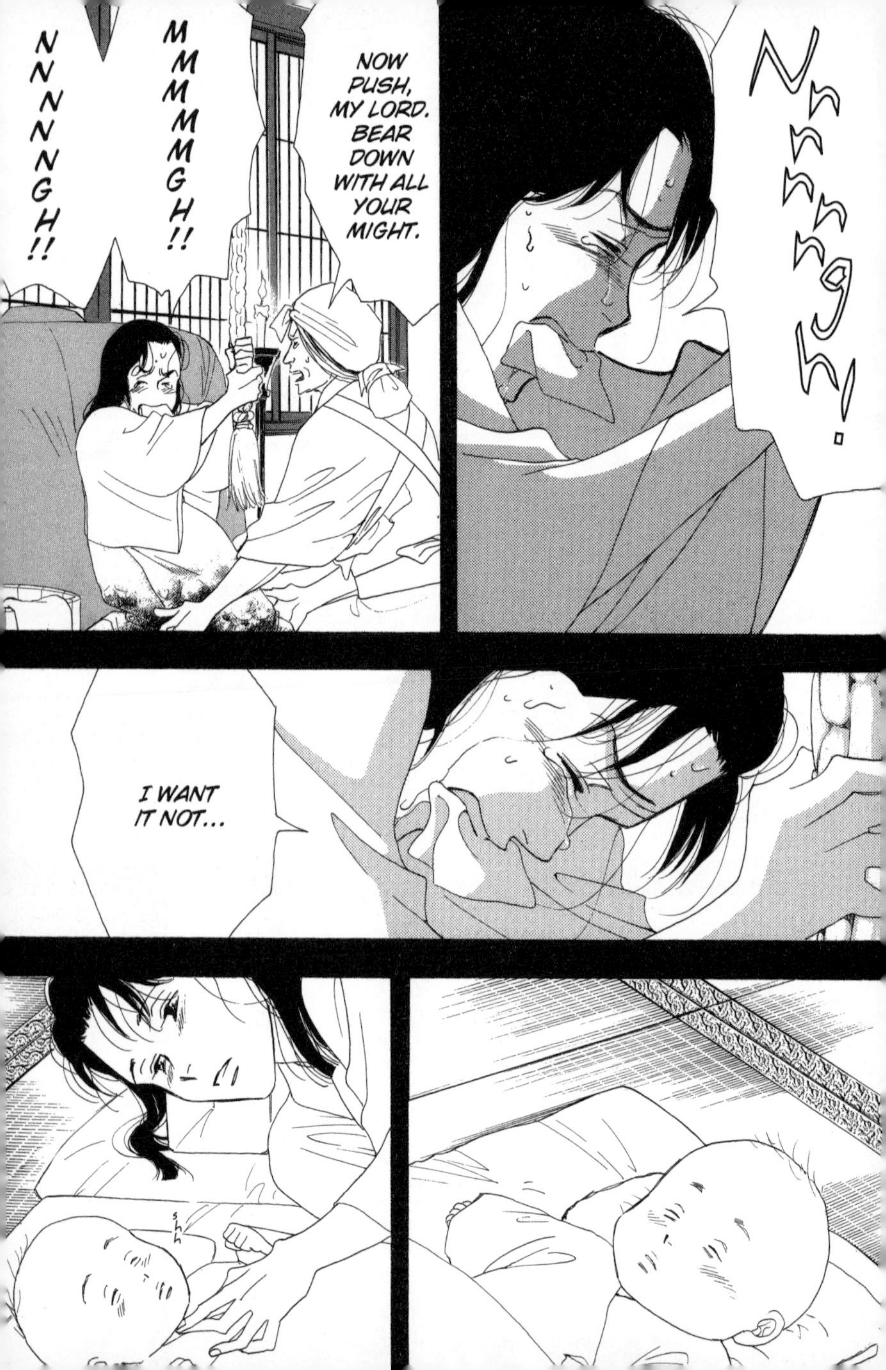
Nnnrrngh!
NOW PUSH, MY LORD. BEAR DOWN WITH ALL YOUR MIGHT.
MMMMMGH!!
NNNNNGH!!
I WANT IT NOT...
shh

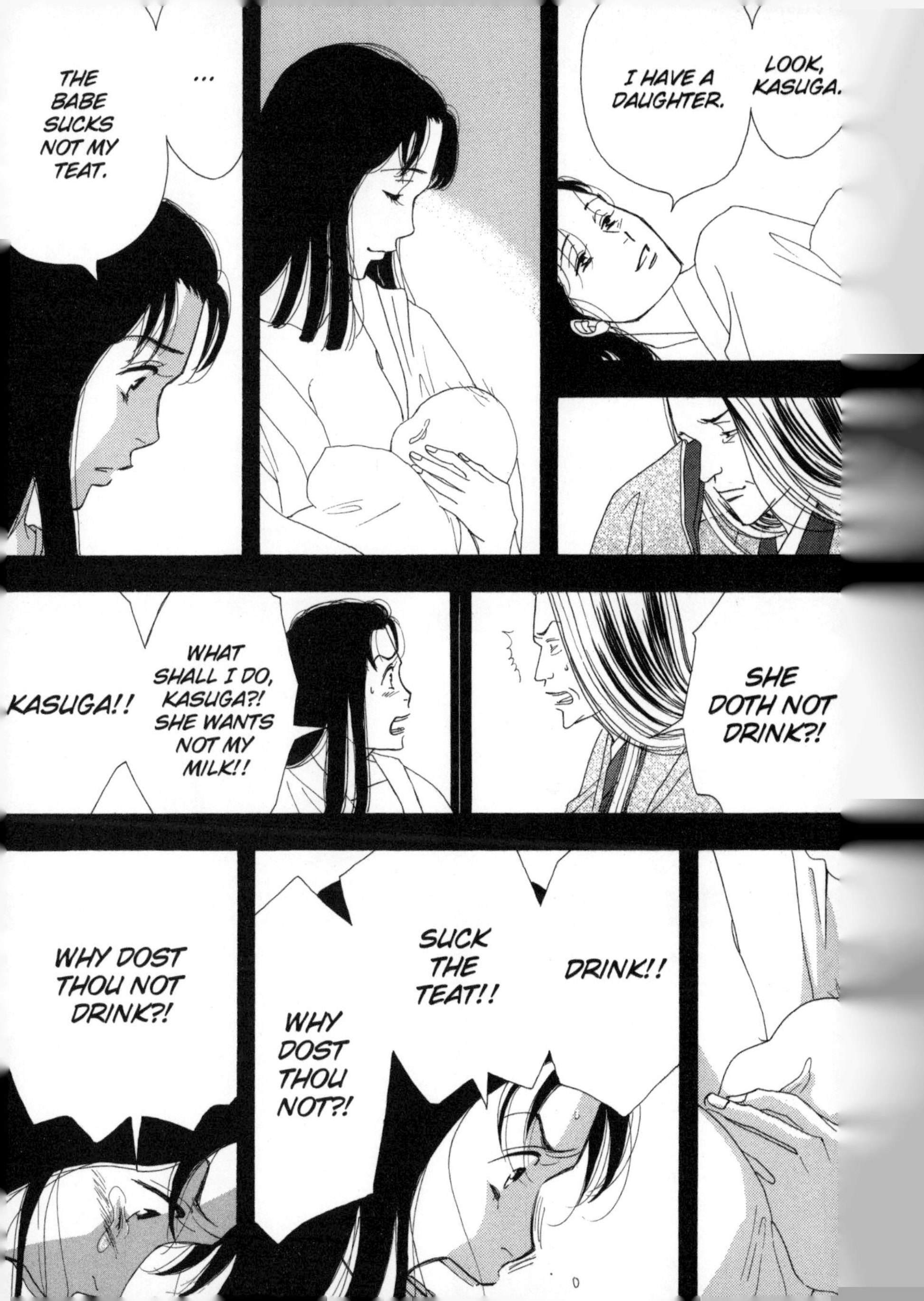

LOOK, KASUGA.
I HAVE A DAUGHTER.
...
THE BABE SUCKS NOT MY TEAT.
SHE DOTH NOT DRINK?!
WHAT SHALL I DO, KASUGA?! SHE WANTS NOT MY MILK!!
KASUGA!!
DRINK!!
SUCK THE TEAT!!
WHY DOST THOU NOT?!
WHY DOST THOU NOT DRINK?!

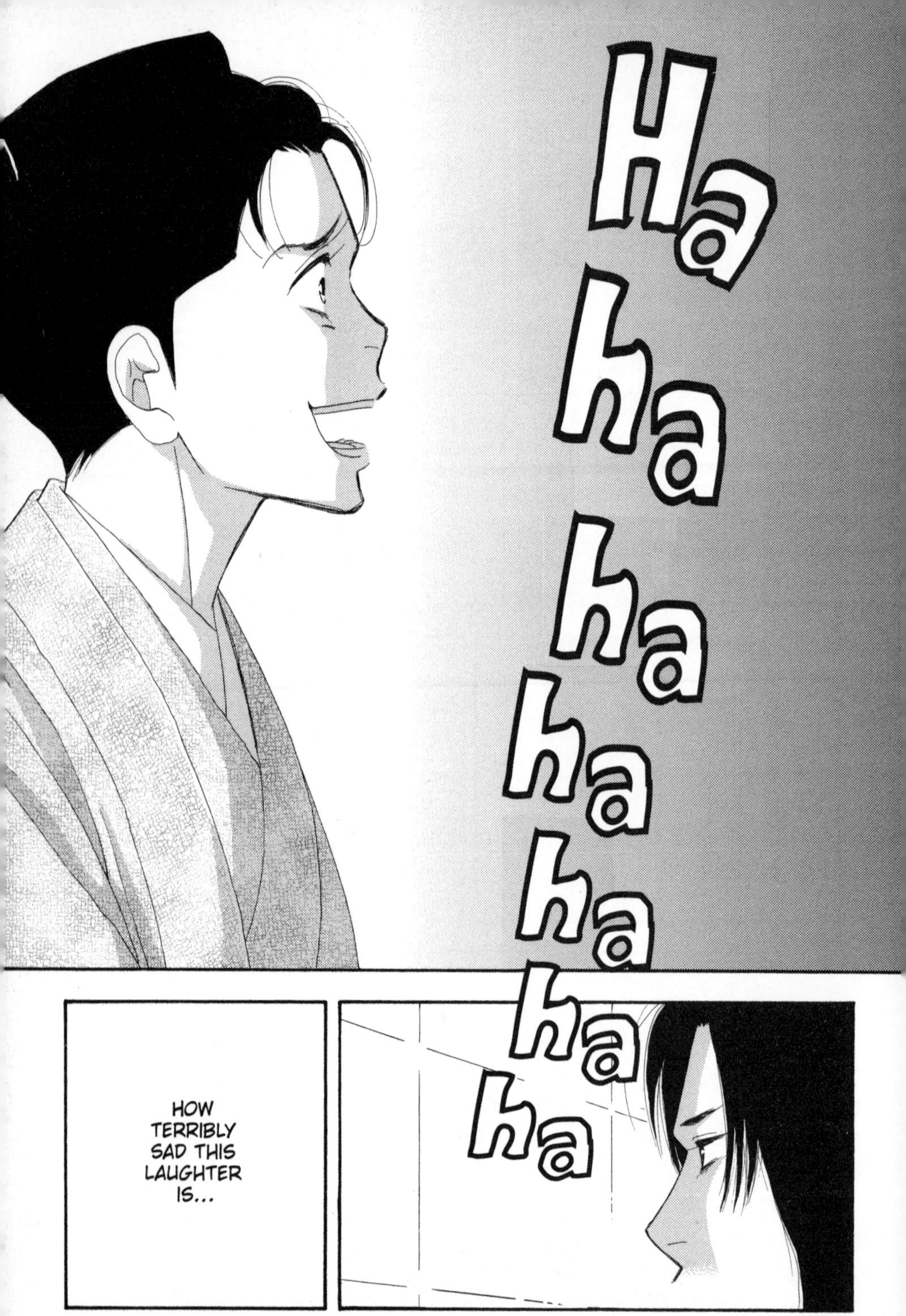
Hahahahahahaha
HOW TERRIBLY SAD THIS LAUGHTER IS...

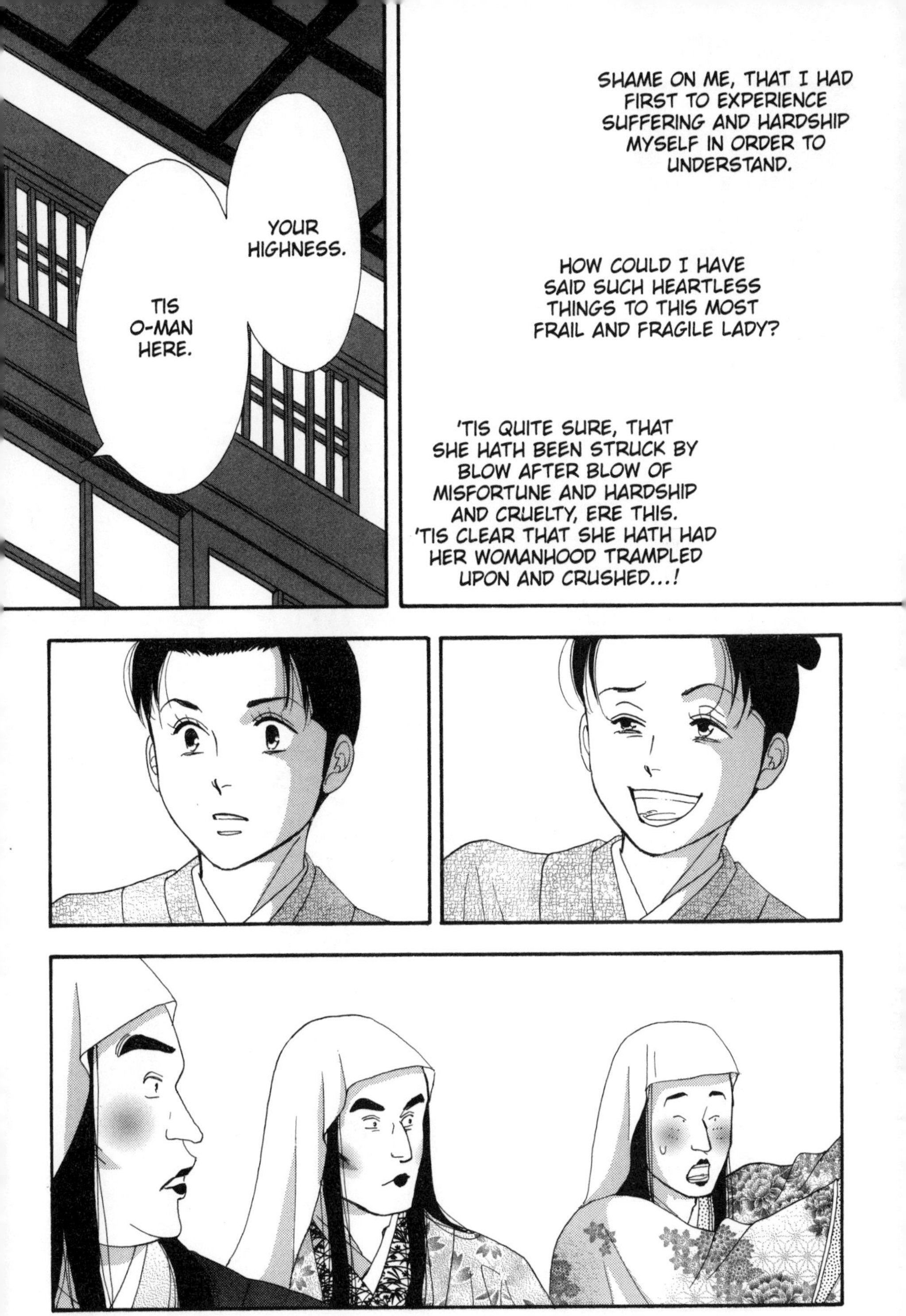
SHAME ON ME, THAT I HAD FIRST TO EXPERIENCE SUFFERING AND HARDSHIP MYSELF IN ORDER TO UNDERSTAND.
HOW COULD I HAVE SAID SUCH HEARTLESS THINGS TO THIS MOST FRAIL AND FRAGILE LADY?
'TIS QUITE SURE, THAT SHE HATH BEEN STRUCK BY BLOW AFTER BLOW OF MISFORTUNE AND HARDSHIP AND CRUELTY, ERE THIS. 'TIS CLEAR THAT SHE HATH HAD HER WOMANHOOD TRAMPLED UPON AND CRUSHED...!
YOUR HIGHNESS.
TIS O-MAN HERE.

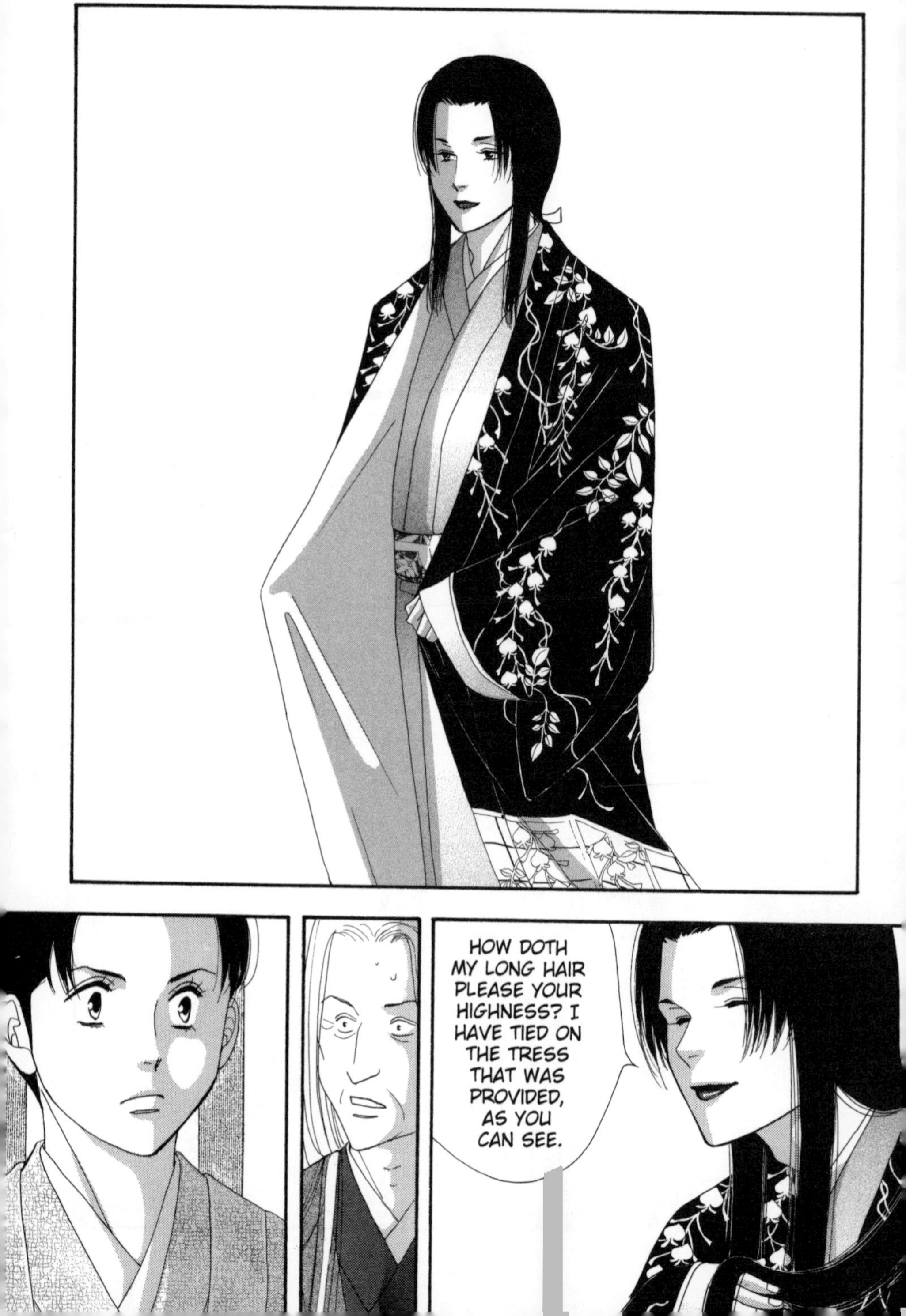
HOW DOTH MY LONG HAIR PLEASE YOUR HIGHNESS? I HAVE TIED ON THE TRESS THAT WAS PROVIDED, AS YOU CAN SEE.

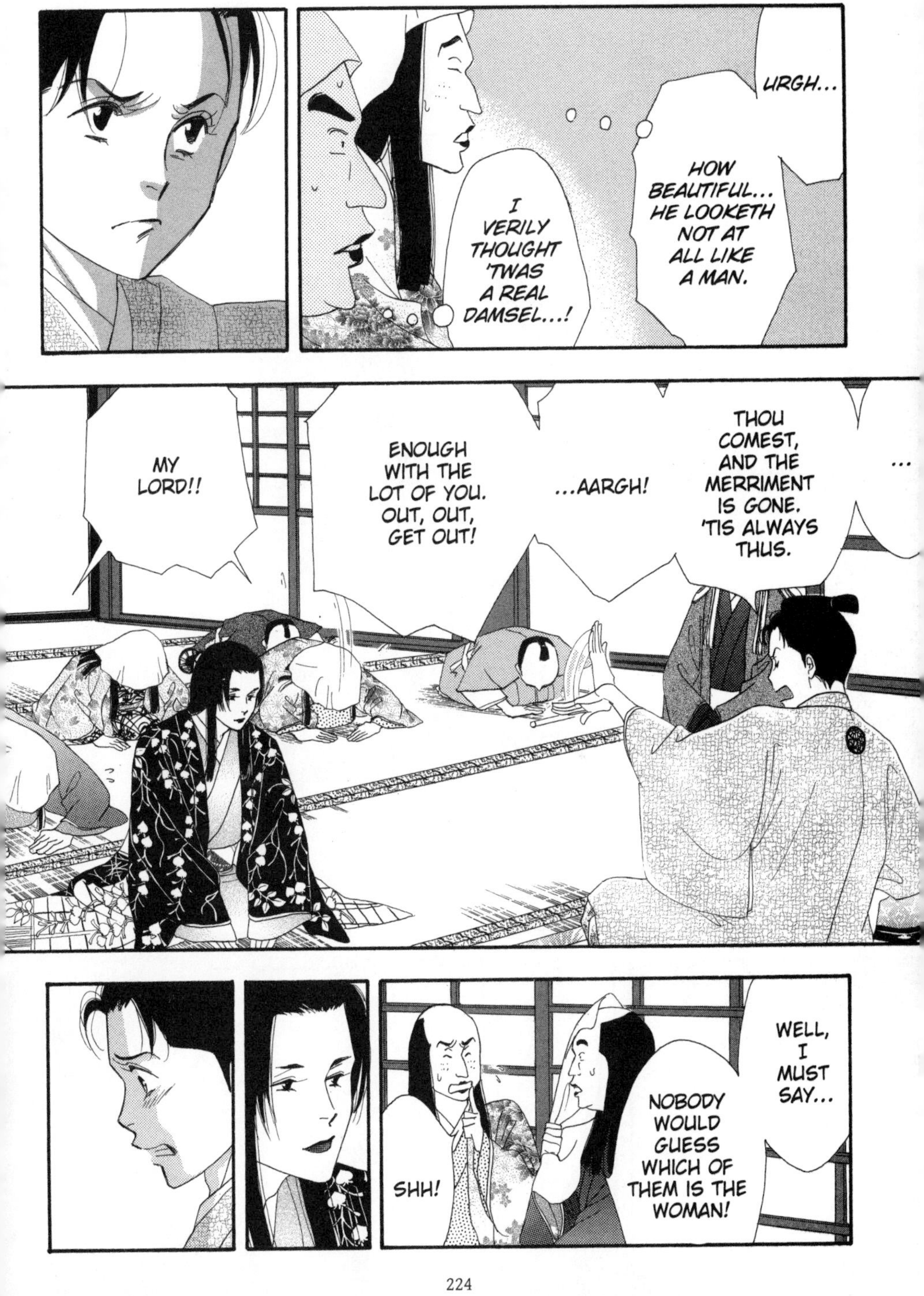
URGH...
HOW BEAUTIFUL... HE LOOKETH NOT AT ALL LIKE A MAN.
I VERILY THOUGHT 'TWAS A REAL DAMSEL...!
...
THOU COMEST, AND THE MERRIMENT IS GONE. 'TIS ALWAYS THUS.
...AARGH!
ENOUGH WITH THE LOT OF YOU. OUT, OUT, GET OUT!
MY LORD!!
WELL, I MUST SAY...
NOBODY WOULD GUESS WHICH OF THEM IS THE WOMAN!
SHH!

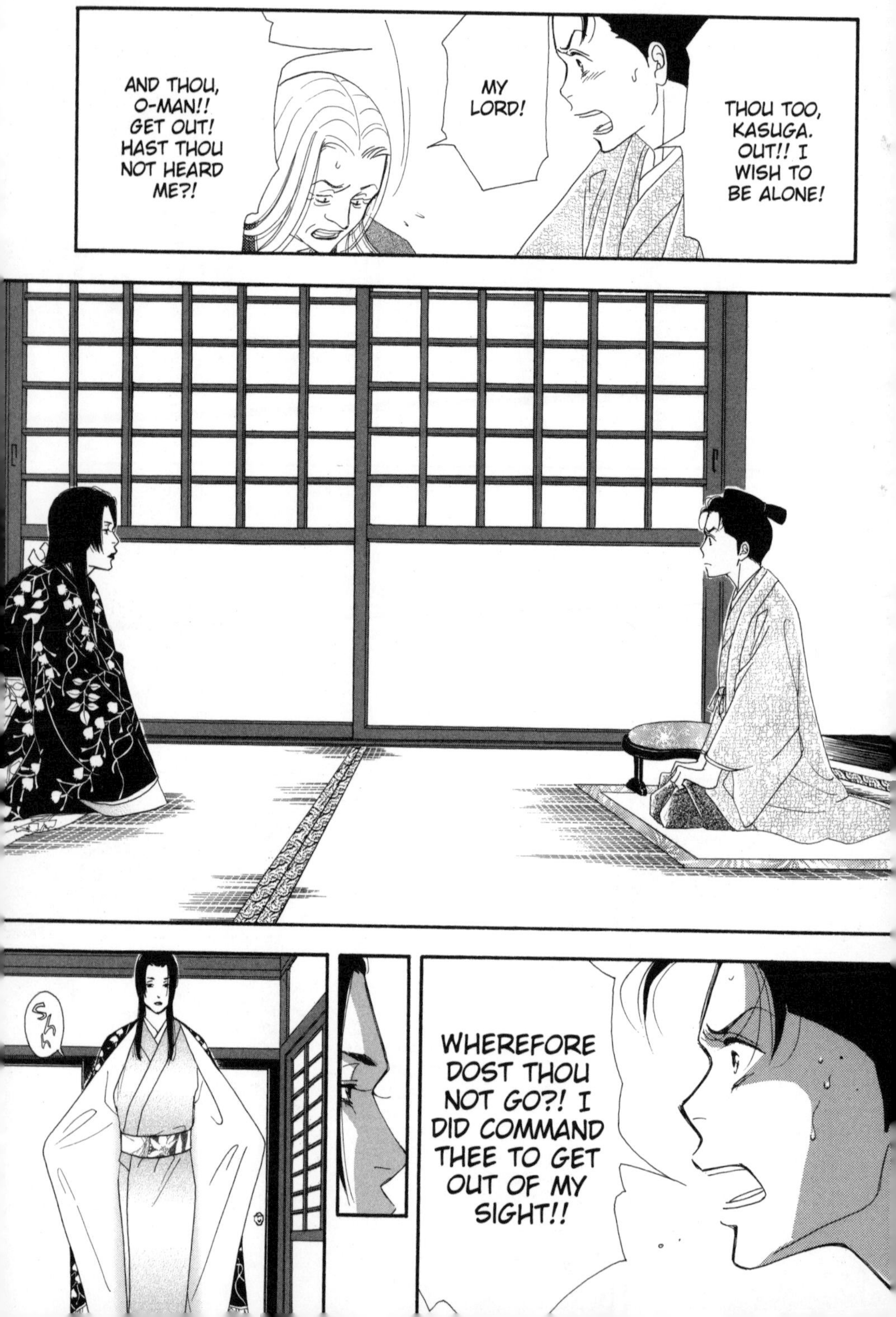
THOU TOO, KASUGA. OUT!! I WISH TO BE ALONE!
MY LORD!
AND THOU, O-MAN!! GET OUT! HAST THOU NOT HEARD ME?!
WHEREFORE DOST THOU NOT GO?! I DID COMMAND THEE TO GET OUT OF MY SIGHT!!
Shh

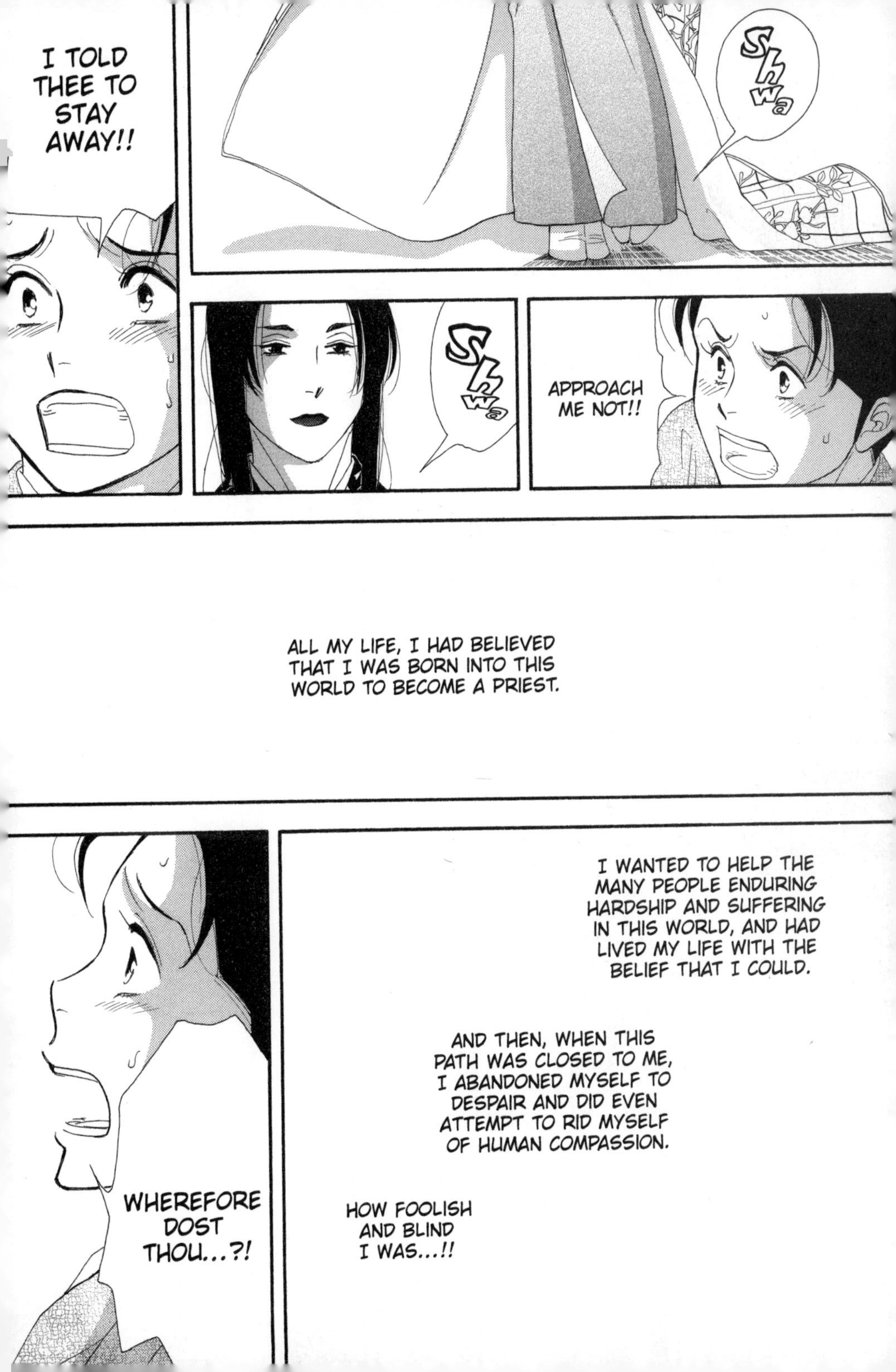
Shwa
APPROACH ME NOT!!
Shwa
I TOLD THEE TO STAY AWAY!!
ALL MY LIFE, I HAD BELIEVED THAT I WAS BORN INTO THIS WORLD TO BECOME A PRIEST.
I WANTED TO HELP THE MANY PEOPLE ENDURING HARDSHIP AND SUFFERING IN THIS WORLD, AND HAD LIVED MY LIFE WITH THE BELIEF THAT I COULD.
AND THEN, WHEN THIS PATH WAS CLOSED TO ME, I ABANDONED MYSELF TO DESPAIR AND DID EVEN ATTEMPT TO RID MYSELF OF HUMAN COMPASSION.
HOW FOOLISH AND BLIND I WAS...!!
WHEREFORE DOST THOU...?!

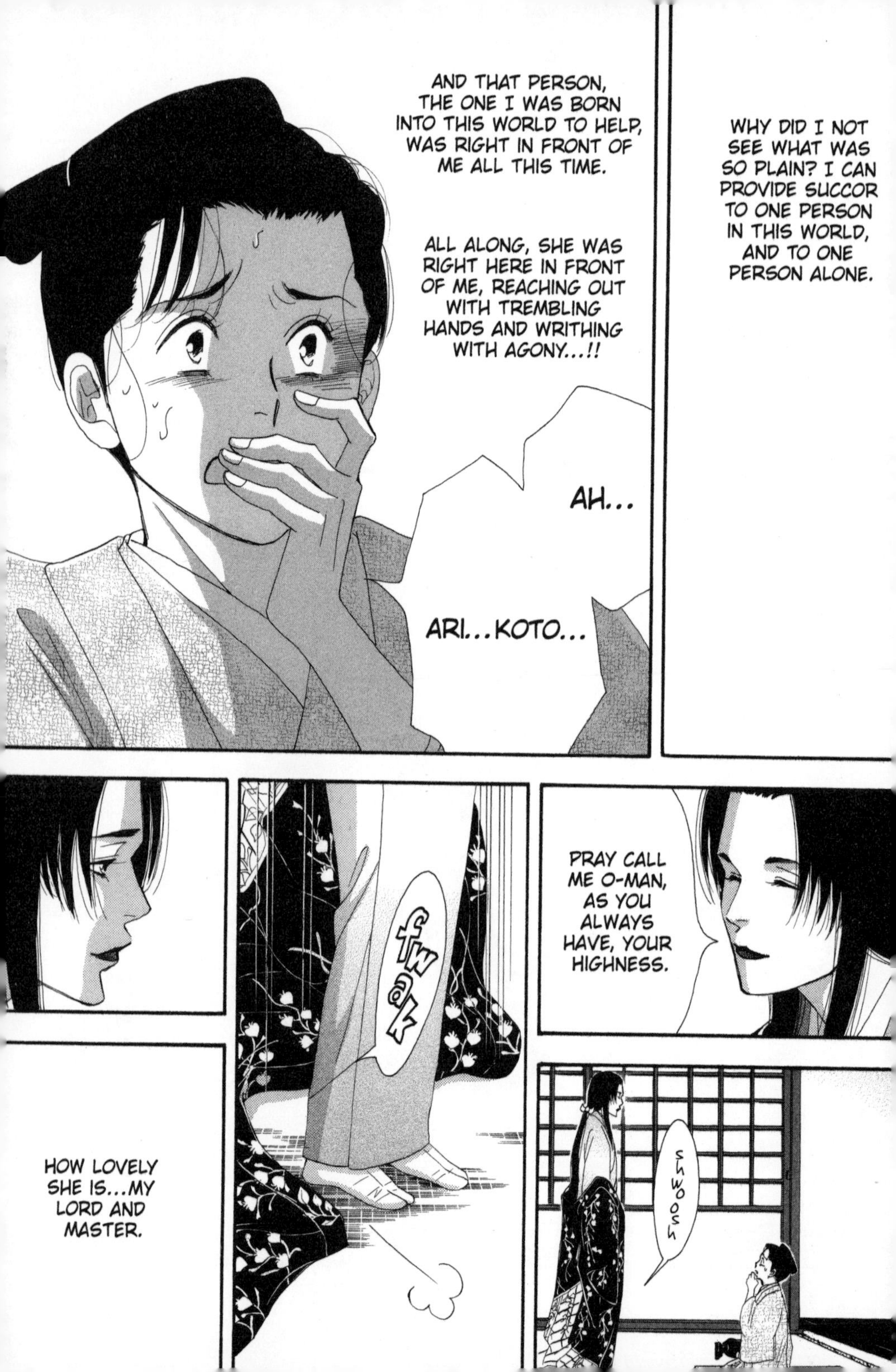
WHY DID I NOT SEE WHAT WAS SO PLAIN? I CAN PROVIDE SUCCOR TO ONE PERSON IN THIS WORLD, AND TO ONE PERSON ALONE.
AND THAT PERSON, THE ONE I WAS BORN INTO THIS WORLD TO HELP, WAS RIGHT IN FRONT OF ME ALL THIS TIME.
ALL ALONG, SHE WAS RIGHT HERE IN FRONT OF ME, REACHING OUT WITH TREMBLING HANDS AND WRITHING WITH AGONY...!!
AH...
ARI...KOTO...
PRAY CALL ME O-MAN, AS YOU ALWAYS HAVE, YOUR HIGHNESS.
shwoosh
fwak
HOW LOVELY SHE IS...MY LORD AND MASTER.

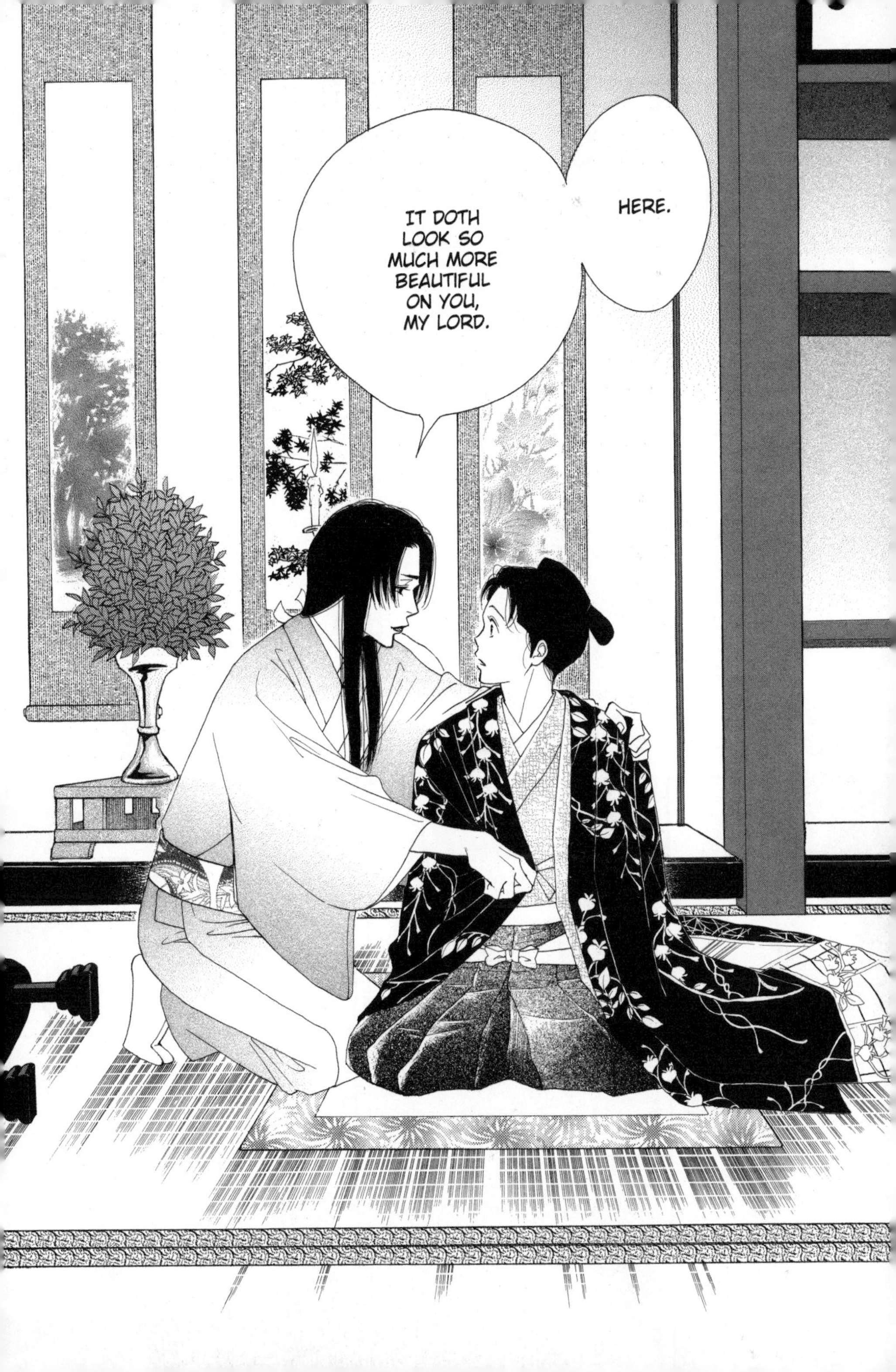
HERE.
IT DOTH LOOK SO MUCH MORE BEAUTIFUL ON YOU, MY LORD.

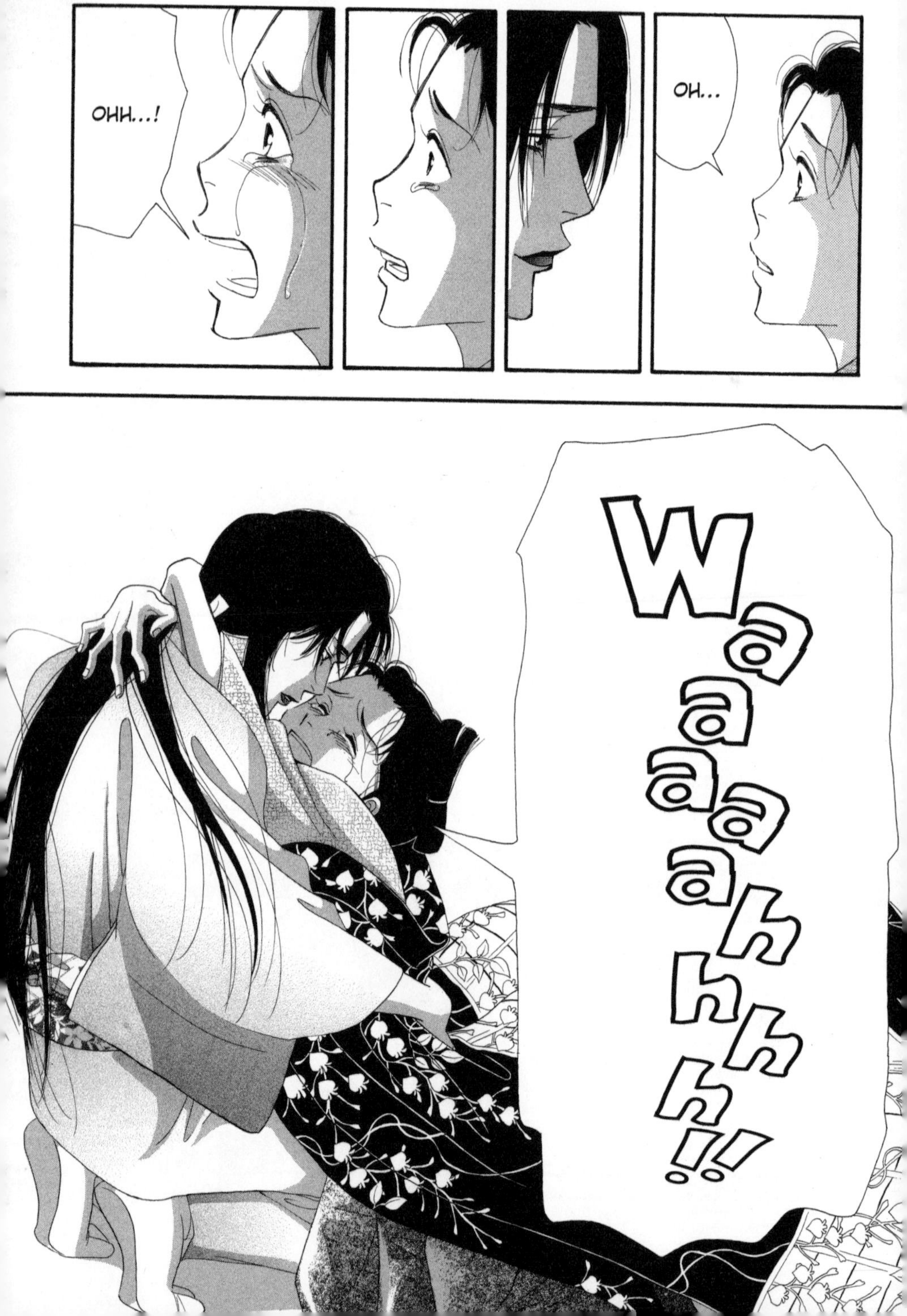
OH...
OHH...!
Waaaaahhhh!!

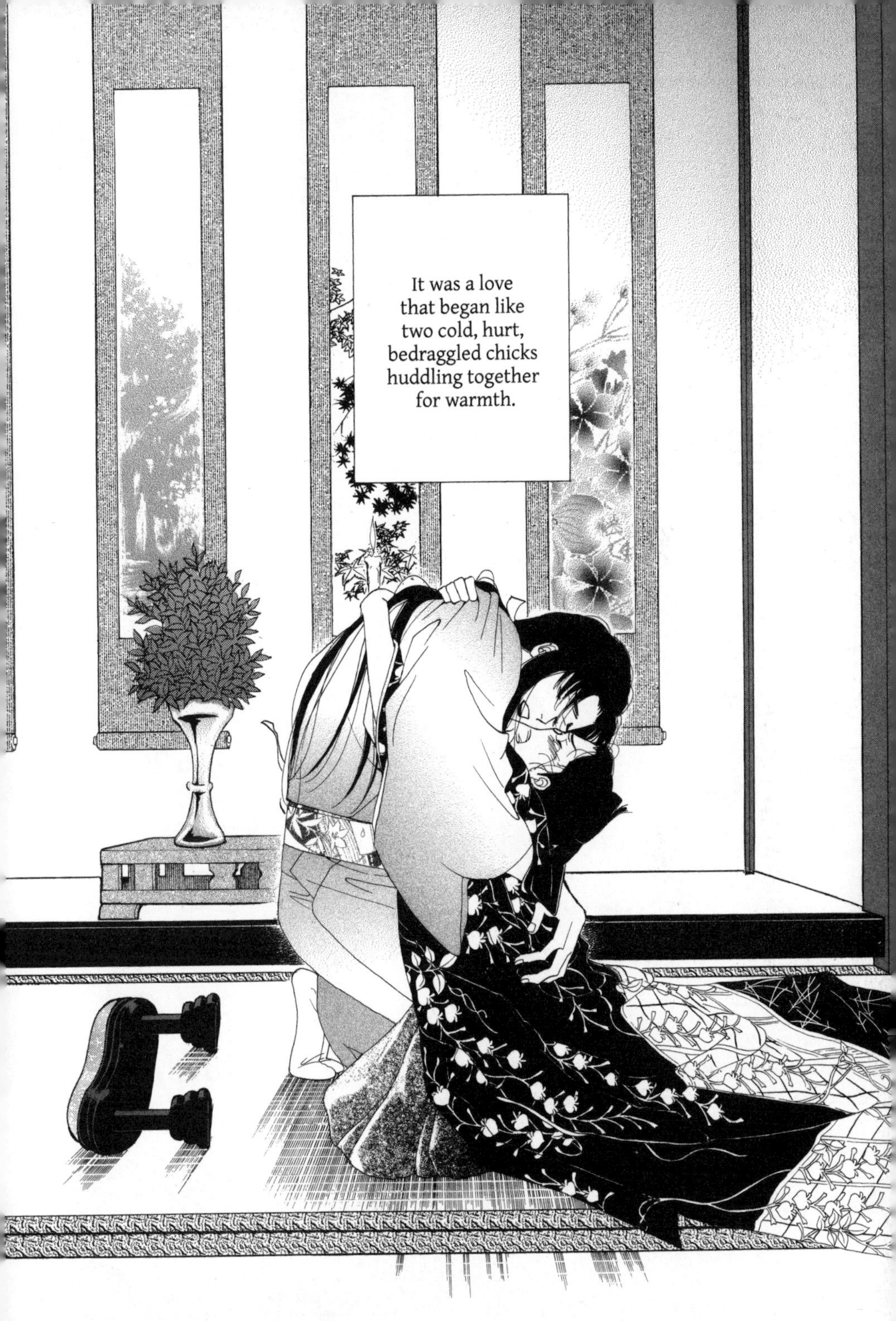
It was a love that began like two cold, hurt, bedraggled chicks huddling together for warmth.

Ōoku
THE INNER CHAMBERS

Ōoku: The Inner Chambers

VOLUME 2 · END NOTES

by Akemi Wegmüller

Page 7, panel 1 · EDO PERIOD

Also known as the Tokugawa period, from 1603 to 1868. It ended when the Meiji Restoration brought an end to the shogunate style of government and reinstated imperial rule.

Page 8, panel 2 · TENGU, USHIWAKA-MARU

Tengu are creatures from Japanese folklore that are sometimes depicted with red faces and long noses. Ushiwaka-maru is the boyhood name of Minamoto-no-Yoshitsune, a legendary warrior who was exiled as a youth to Mt. Kurama, where a tengu taught him martial arts.

Page 17, panel 3 · ARIKOTO

The character Arikoto is based on a real-life concubine of the shogun Iemitsu. She was the abbess of Keiko-in, a Buddhist nunnery in Ise, before she caught the eye of Iemitsu during an audience in Edo and was inducted into the Ōoku by Lady Kasuga. Prior to her induction, she was housed in a government mansion in Tayasudai until her hair grew out. She was of noble heritage, and her father was the aristocrat Rokujo Arizumi. After Kasuga's death, she took over the governance of the Ōoku at Iemitsu's behest and is credited with introducing many courtly refinements to the place.

Page 19, panel 3 · KEIKO-IN

A Buddhist nunnery that was once located in Ise city in Mie Prefecture. It closed in 1869 and is now the residence of the head priest of the Ise shrine.

Page 19, panel 3 · MIKADO

Another term for the emperor of Japan, though now obsolete.

Page 19, panel 3 · SUMMONED TO EDO

In the original Japanese, Myokei uses the verb "to descend" when describing travel to Edo because you "ascend" to the imperial capital Kyoto and descend when you leave it in any direction.

Page 29, panel 3 · BARBARIC EASTERN PROVINCES

Kyoto was the imperial capital and home of the aristocracy for centuries. Its culture was a highly refined court culture, and people there often looked down on what they saw as the "barbarians" of eastern Japan.

Page 31, panel 3 · FOUR BOOKS

Also called the Confucian cannon, these are classical Chinese texts used as an introduction to Confucianism. They include *The Great Learning, The Doctrine of the Mean, The Analects of Confucius* and *The Mencius.*

Page 35, panel 3 · ZOJO-JI, UENO TOSHO-GU

Zojo-ji is a Buddhist temple that was the Tokugawa family temple and burial ground. In the Japanese, Arikoto says he wants to pay his respects at the mausoleum there. Ueno Tosho-gu is a Shinto shrine that is likewise closely associated with the Tokugawa family. The first shogun, Ieyasu, was deified there.

Page 40, panel 1 · CATAMITE
The Japanese word is *o-koshō* (お小姓), which is a position as page or attendant that can also include a sexual relationship with their liege.

Page 42, panel 2 · TAYASUDAI
A rural area a short distance from Edo Castle.

Page 49, panel 1 · YOSHIWARA
The pleasure quarters, originally located near what is today Nihonbashi in central Tokyo and eventually moved to the outskirts of the city. The area was walled off from the rest of the city and the courtesans were restricted to its confines.

Page 54, panel 3 · THE SQUIRE...
This is one variation of the popular *ken-asobi*, or "games of the hands." Another is *jan-ken*, also known as rock-paper-scissors or rochambeau.

Page 98, panel 1 · PHYSICIAN
In the Japanese, the shogun's personal physician is referred to as o-saji, or "the spoon."

Page 125, panel 5 · MURASAKI
The kitten is named after one of the characters in *The Tale of Genji*, a young girl with whom Genji is enchanted.

Page 142, panel 2 · MORI RANMARU
One of Oda Nobunaga's trusted attendants (o-koshō).

Page 142, panel 3 · NOBUNAGA
One of the major daimyo or domain lords of the Sengoku era in the 16th century.

Page 146, panel 5 · THE GENTLEMAN SAYS...
A classic poem of the Tang period, *Farewell* by Wang Wei. Chinese poetry is written in rows of characters that reflect Chinese word order, so even though Japanese readers can understand the kanji, there is still a level of translation required. Arikoto and Gyokuei are reciting the Japanese translation, with Arikoto offering further exposition.

Page 156, panel 3 · SUBURI
Practice swings, an integral part of kendo training.

CREATOR BIOGRAPHY

FUMI YOSHINAGA

Fumi Yoshinaga is a Tokyo-born manga creator who debuted in 1994 with *Tsuki to Sandaru* (*The Moon and the Sandals*). Yoshinaga has won numerous awards, including the 2009 Osamu Tezuka Cultural Prize for *Ôoku*, the 2002 Kodansha Manga Award for her series *Antique Bakery* and the 2006 Japan Media Arts Festival Excellence Award for *Ôoku*. She was also nominated for the 2008 Eisner Award for Best Writer/Artist.

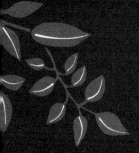

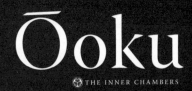

Ōoku

THE INNER CHAMBERS

Ōoku: The Inner Chambers
Vol. 2

VIZ Signature Edition

Story and Art by Fumi Yoshinaga

Translation & Adaptation/Akemi Wegmüller
Touch-up Art & Lettering/Monlisa De Asis
Design/Frances O. Liddell
Editor/Pancha Diaz

VP, Production/Alvin Lu
VP, Publishing Licensing/Rika Inouye
VP, Sales & Product Marketing/Gonzalo Ferreyra
VP, Creative/Linda Espinosa
Publisher/Hyoe Narita

Printed in the U.S.A.

Published by VIZ Media, LLC
P.O. Box 77010
San Francisco, CA 94107

10 9 8 7 6 5 4 3 2 1
First printing, December 2009

www.viz.com

www.vizsignature.com

Ōoku

THE INNER CHAMBERS

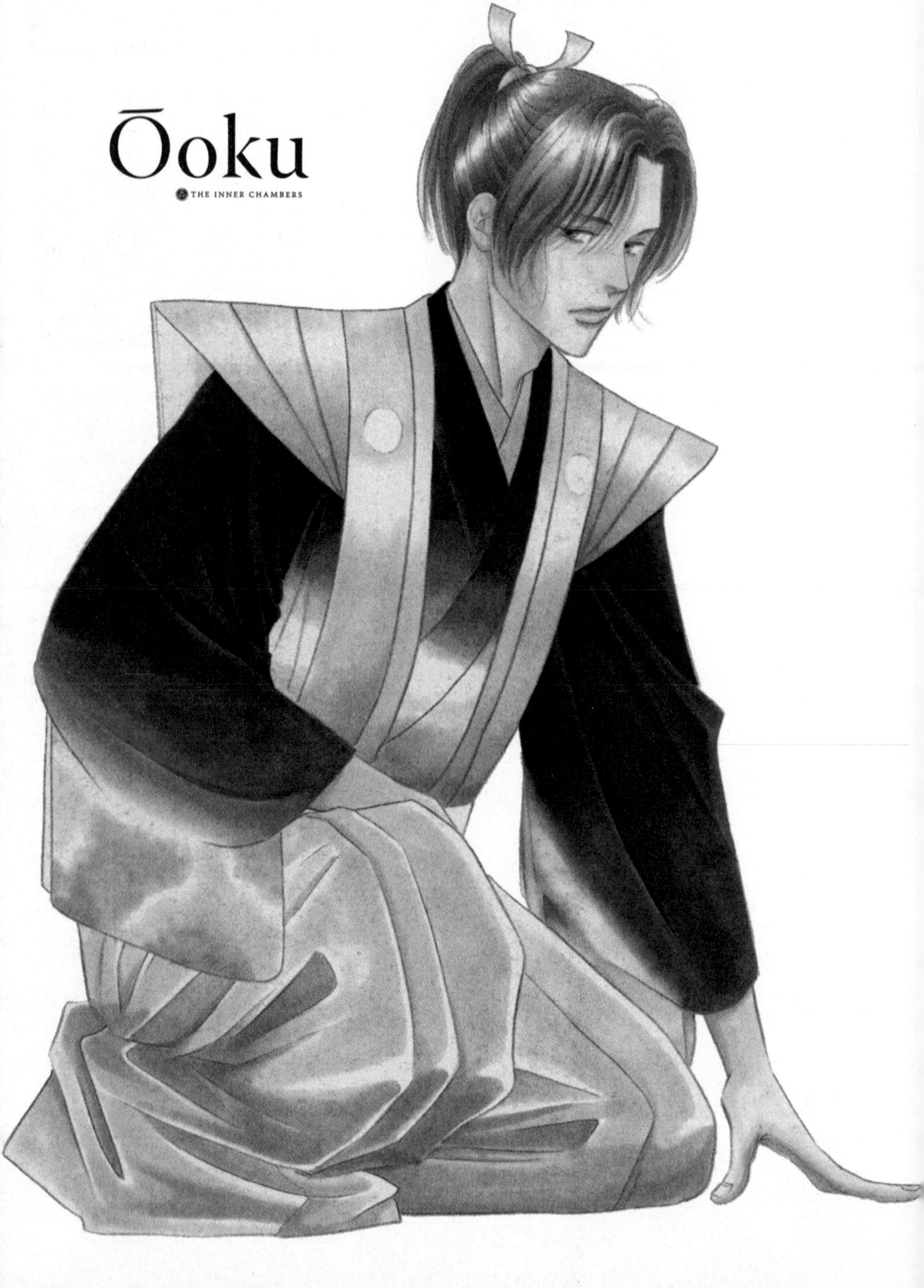

THIS IS THE LAST PAGE.

Ōoku: The In...

the original Ja...

the orien...